# MORE

□ □ □ □ □ □

# MATHEMATICAL

□ □ □ □ □ □

# PEOPLE

□ □ □ □ □ □

Contemporary

Conversations

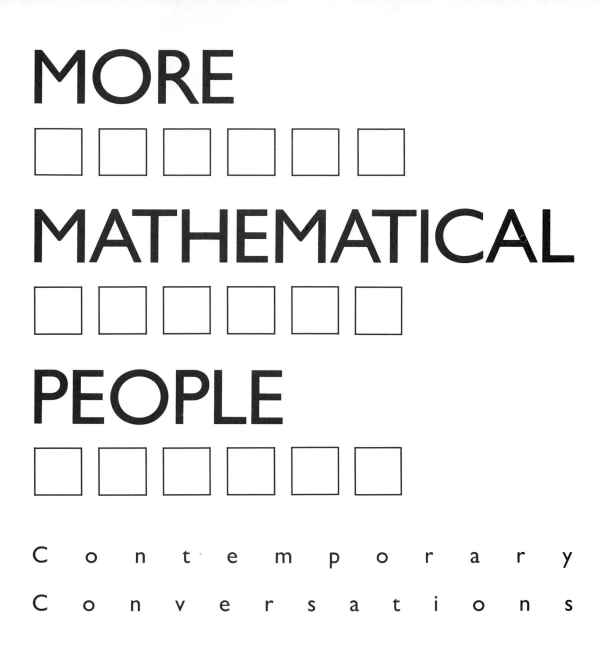

# MORE

# MATHEMATICAL

# PEOPLE

## Contemporary Conversations

Edited by

DONALD J. ALBERS
GERALD L. ALEXANDERSON
CONSTANCE REID

## HARCOURT BRACE JOVANOVICH, PUBLISHERS

Boston  San Diego  New York

This book is printed on acid-free paper. ♾

Designed by Amy Strong

Printed in the United States of America

**Library of Congress Cataloging-in-Publication Data**

More mathematical people: contemporary conversations / edited by
    Donald J. Albers. G.L. Alexanderson, Constance Reid. — 1st ed.
      p.  cm.
    Includes bibliographical references.
    ISBN 0-15-158175-4 (alk. paper)
    1.  Mathematicians — Interviews.   2.  Mathematicians — Biography.
I.  Albers, Donald J., 1941–    .  II.  Alexanderson, Gerald L.
III.  Reid, Constance.
QA28.M67   1990
510′.92′2—dc20                       90-4422
                                         CIP

First edition
A B C D E

# CONTENTS

# LIST OF PHOTO CREDITS

The many photographs and other memorabilia in this volume, unless otherwise credited, are from the collections of our subjects, who have generously shared them with us, even when they sometimes had to remove pictures from their family albums.

*Other illustrations:*

Gleason interview: Photograph of Hidehiko Yamabe, p. 92, reprinted with permission from the *Osaka Mathematical Journal* (now the *Osaka Journal of Mathematics*), 13, 1961, 1.

Gosper interview: Photographs on pp. 100, 103, 111, 112, 114, and 115 reprinted with permission from Sam Sargent.

Kaplansky interview: Photographs on pp. 134, 135, and 136 reprinted with permission from Tom Black.

Le Cam interview: Photograph of Georges Darmois, p. 166, reprinted with permission from the collection of Ingram Olkin.

Mosteller interview: Photograph of John Tukey, p. 252, reprinted with permission from AT&T Archives. Photographs on pp. 240, 242, 248, 251, 254, and 258 reprinted with permission from Jane Reed/Harvard University.

# ACKNOWLEDGMENTS

We are grateful to Mary Jackson, Rebecca Lasher, Kelly Shay, and Yvonne Sullivan for their assistance in the preparation of the manuscript of *More Mathematical People*, to Geri and Lisa Albers for their support and tolerance, and to Neil D. Reid for his many contributions along the way. We appreciate the advice, patience and good humor of the editorial and production staffs of Harcourt Brace Jovanovich, Inc., especially of Klaus Peters, Susan M. Gay, and Amy Strong.

The wide range of interviews and the extensive illustrations were made possible by the generous support of the Alfred P. Sloan Foundation. We are appreciative of their confidence in the project.

Donald J. Albers
Gerald L. Alexanderson
Constance Reid

# INTRODUCTION

By Martin Gardner

What are the properties of a mathematician? If a nonmathematician enters a social gathering of one hundred professional people, and is told that twenty are mathematicians, how would that person fare in picking out the twenty? We assume, of course, there would be no conversation about mathematics. I know of no such experiment, but I would wager that the probability of identifying a mathematician would be no higher than twenty percent.

It takes only a casual reading of this delightful, much-needed book to be impressed by the enormous variety among great mathematicians in their appearances, personalities, backgrounds and outside interests. Some came from poor families, others from well-to-do. Some had parents who loved mathematics, others did not. Some enjoy teaching, even administrative chores. Others do not. Some were and are political activists. Others have little interest in such issues. Some recognized their mathematical ability at an early age, others did not discover it until they were adults. Some think they did their best work before thirty. Others think it came much later.

Outside interests also vary. Perhaps mathematicians are more attracted than others to games such as chess, go and bridge than less intellectually demanding games, but hobbies mentioned in this book include hiking, gardening, skiing, swimming, mineral collecting, conjuring and stamp collecting. A surprising proportion of mathematicians are accomplished musicians. Is it because music and mathematics share patterns that are beautiful? "When you're sitting with a bit of paper creating mathematics," says Robin Wilson, "it is very like sitting with a sheet of paper and creating music. Both have rules you must follow.... A page of mathematics and a page of music are both meaningless unless you happen to know what the various symbols mean."

Nevertheless, there are some traits all mathematicians share. An obvious one is a sense of amazement over the infinite depth and the mysterious beauty and usefulness of mathematics. All testify to those moments, often when very young, when they were first smitten by mathematical elegance. Lipman Bers recalls his father showing how two straight lines on a cartesian graph solve a pair of linear equations. "This seemed to me the most beautiful thing in the world." For Fred Mosteller it was learning that a generating function would determine the probability that three tossed dice will show a sum of 10. No need to write down all the combinations and count! "It was the most marvelous thing I had ever seen in mathematics." Robin Wilson recalls being impressed as a child by simple proofs that the square root of 2 is irrational and that the number of primes is infinite.

Bill Gosper, one of our nation's foremost hackers, was early turned on by the power of computers. In recent years he has become entranced by continued fractions. Is there not something ugly, he thinks, about the decimal form of irrationals, with their disheveled digits that go on and on forever without repeating a pattern? Written as continued fractions, their patterns pop out in lovely ways, as cyclic as the digits of a rational decimal fraction. Moreover, Gosper discovered, you can do arithmetic with them. "It's completely astounding. It looks like you're cheating God."

The sheer pleasure mathematicians get from solving problems and making discoveries comes through in every interview. "Fun" is a word often used. "If it isn't fun, why do it?" asks Ralph Boas. "As I look back," recalls Peter Lax, "I think I did things merely because they were fun." William Thurston speaks of his efforts to convince a *Wall Street Journal* reporter that "mathematics is fun."

Another trait that seems more characteristic of mathematicians than of some other professional groups is a robust sense of humor. Mathematicians are notoriously fond of word play, jokes and humorous verse. "Flattery will get you nowhere" is the epigraph of the chapter on planar networks in Wilson's *Introduction to Graph Theory*. In the same book's preface he thanks his students "but for whom this book would have been completed a year earlier." He recalls that when his father, Harold, was prime minister of England he once invited a member of Parliament to a party honoring three astronauts solely because the man's name was Eric Moonman.

Other jokes abound. Boas recalls a famous paper in which he described numerous mathematical ways to catch a lion. (Example: Build a circular cage, then perform an inversion of the plane that puts the lion inside.) Saunders Mac Lane quotes the first two lines of a song he likes to sing to the tune of "You can't get to heaven in a rocking chair, the Lord don't allow no rocking chairs there":

> You can't get to heaven in a Banach space.
> The Lord ain't heard of any such place.

Mac Lane recalls the first stanza of Tom Apostol's song about the still unsolved Riemann conjecture:

> Where are the zeros of zeta of *s*?
> G. Bernard Riemann has made a good guess.
> They're all on the critical line, said he,
> And their density's one over $2\pi \log t$.

Another well-known poem, this one by Mac Lane, is about simple groups. It opens:

> What are the orders of all simple groups?
> I speak of the honest ones, not of the loops.

Many ancient controversies in mathematics, as well as some new ones, turn up in the interviews. What is the best way to teach mathematics in elementary grades? On Mondays, Wednesdays and Fridays, Bers says, he thinks one can convey the beauty of mathematics to others, but on other days he thinks the reverse. He recalls giving a copy of *What Is Mathematics?*

to a book publisher who wanted some insight into the subject, only to have the book returned a week later because the publisher couldn't get beyond the second page. Many of those interviewed deplore the sorry state of math teaching in the United States. Some think the most urgent need is a way of introducing calculus in high school so it doesn't discourage students who might otherwise major in mathematics at college or take up a science that requires calculus. Another crying need, emphasized by Mosteller, is to teach elementary statistics in lower grades. The topic is not only essential in the social sciences, but now physics and even number theory are known to be saturated with chaos.

What about computers? For George Dantzig, who invented the famous simplex method of linear programming, computer mathematics is as interesting and challenging as noncomputer math, a view shared by Steve Smale, for whom the "Smale horseshoe" is named in chaos theory. Others, less impressed by computers, make little use of them in research.

Andrew Gleason finds the lengthy computer proof of the four-color theorem ugly and unsatisfying. It fails to tell you anything about the plane's topology, or why the theorem holds. Thurston has similar misgivings. "We don't have a humanly comprehensible explanation of why every map can be colored with four colors. Maybe there's no explanation. But we would like to know." Similar remarks could be made about the recent proof, by C. W. H. Lam and his associates, that finite projective planes of order 10 do not exist. The proof checked more than 1014 cases and used several thousand hours of computer time. Is such a proof really a proof, or is it more like an experiment in physics that gives only probable results?

No one of course doubts the usefulness of computers in applied mathematics. This points up the age-old division between those who, like G. H. Hardy and Paul Halmos, find applied math somehow less elegant than pure, and those who see little difference between the two. There are some differences, Peter Lax argues, but he thinks the similarities are stronger. Dantzig agrees: "Students are being brainwashed into thinking that pure mathematics is in some way purer than other forms of mathematics. I have never been able to tell the difference... and don't believe there is any. Just because my mathematics has its origin in a real problem doesn't make it less interesting to me—just the other way around. I find it makes the puzzle I am working on all the more exciting."

"It's one of the great sorrows of my life," says Paul Cohen, "that I haven't done anything in physics. I still think about it."

What Eugene Wigner, in a famous paper, called "the unreasonable effectiveness of mathematics" is directly related to the deepest of all mathematical questions. Is mathematical structure in some sense "out there," independent of human minds? If there are any anti-Platonists in this book, I failed to find them. "A working mathematician is always a Platonist," says Bers. "It doesn't matter what he says ... I think that in mathematics he always has that feeling of discovery.... Mathematics is, as Ron Graham has said, the ultimate reality...."

Paul Cohen speaks of struggling with the riddle of whether transfinite sets exist outside our skulls. Is there a final, absolute answer to Cantor's continuum problem? Kurt Gödel, an unabashed Platonist, was sure there is. Cohen has his doubts. No one, he believes, will ever come up with a better solution than his proof that the continuum problem is undecidable. Even if it cannot some day be decided in a more comprehensive formal system,

Platonism remains undamaged. All of mathematics may be "out there," and still contain forever undecidable questions.

To Andrew Gleason, Wigner's point of view "drives me up the wall." Wigner thinks the success of mathematics in physics results from inexplicable coincidences. "My view is just the opposite. Of course mathematics works in physics! It is designed to discuss exactly the situation that physics confronts; namely, that there seems to be some order out there—let's find out what it is." Like all Platonists, Gleason thinks the uncanny effectiveness of mathematics rests on the simple fact that the universe is patterned. As Paul Dirac and James Jeans liked to put it, God is a great mathematician.

Thurston remembers telling Alfred Tarski that he had developed an interest in intuitionism. "Forget it!" was Tarski's blunt advice. "I guess I believe in a sort of mathematical reality," Thurston goes on, "but it's a reality that we can't hope to understand completely. It's hard to justify mathematical reality solely on the basis of formal reasoning."

Why are there so few women mathematicians? Is there a slight genetic bias of some sort, or is it wholly a matter of environmental pressures that put hurdles in the way of young women who might otherwise take up mathematics? The book does not resolve this, but the chapters on Cathleen Synge Morawetz, Mary Ellen Rudin and Julia Robinson leave no doubt that women are increasingly entering the fray with minds as subtle and creative as those of their male colleagues—colleagues who often are their husbands. To me the book's highlight is the chapter about Mrs. Robinson, perhaps because it was not an interview (Julia died of leukemia in 1985), but an essay written by her sister Constance Reid, one of today's finest writers about mathematicians.

Among David Hilbert's influential 1900 list of twenty-three unsolved problems, three were solved or substantially solved by persons in this book: Cohen, the first; Gleason, the fifth; Julia, the tenth. Each year when Julia blew out her birthday candles she wished, not that she would solve the tenth problem, but that it would be solved. "I felt that I couldn't bear to die without knowing the answer."

The breakthrough came in 1970 when a 22-year-old lad in Leningrad proved a result about diophantine equations and Fibonacci numbers that had been a stumbling block to Mrs. Robinson's efforts to prove Hilbert's tenth. John McCarthy, Stanford's artificial intelligence expert, took notes on a lecture about the proof that he had heard in Russia. He thought he understood it, but when he looked over his notes he couldn't make sense of them. He offered to send them to Julia.

One look at the notes and Mrs. Robinson instantly realized that the Russian student had done what he claimed. "Now I know it is true," she wrote to him. "It is beautiful, it is wonderful. If you really are 22, I am especially pleased to think that when I first made the conjecture you were a baby and I just had to wait for you to grow up!" That year, when she puffed out her birthday candles, she stopped in midbreath, realizing her wish had come true.

What made the proof especially wonderful was the fact that it used only elementary number theory. In 1971, when Mrs. Robinson met the Russian youth, she learned she was the second most famous Robinson in the Soviet Union. If you can't guess the first, turn to Constance Reid's moving chapter.

Although social forces inhibiting the entrance of women into mathematics may be abating, they are still very much with us. When Julia was elected to the National Academy of Sciences, the public relations office (at the University of California, Berkeley, where Julia taught on occasion) called the math department to find out who she was. "Why," a math secretary exclaimed, "that's Professor Robinson's wife!" The university at once made her a full professor. Later she became president of the American Mathematical Society, Smith College gave her an honorary degree, and even *Vogue* and the *Village Voice* found it worthwhile to interview her.

I regret that I have had space to comment on only a fraction of the interviews in this volume, all as informative and fascinating as the few I have mentioned. Let us hope that young people will discover this book, read it, and be inspired. If present trends continue, our country may soon find itself far behind many other nations in both science and technology—nations where, if you inform strangers you are a mathematician, they respond with admiration and not (as Mary Ellen Rudin reminds us) by telling you how much they hated math in school, and how they sure could use you to balance their checkbooks.

# BECOMING A MATHEMATICIAN

By Constance Reid

Mathematicians are not like other people any more than lawyers, doctors, accountants or investment bankers are like everybody else. They, like men and women in other professions, have "a habit of mind" that arises out of the nature of their vocation. They look at things and think and laugh in a way that their science has developed in them, a way that is also undoubtedly an integral part of their nature, the reason that they have become mathematicians. Individually they are very different in their mathematical personalities, the kind of mathematics they like, and the way that they do mathematics, but they are alike in one respect. Almost without exception, they love their subject, are happy in their choice of a career, and consider that they are exceptionally lucky in being able to do for a living what they would do for fun.

The men and women in this volume are all outstanding mathematicians, but they were chosen almost randomly, because of opportunities of time and place, from the many outstanding mathematicians working in the United States. The reader may find it interesting to learn something about them as a group, both professionally and personally, before learning what they are like as individuals.

The institutions with which they have been affiliated for most of their academic careers, and with which they are generally identified, are in various parts of the country: six in the east, seven in the west, and five in the midwest (although one of these five spends most of the academic year in England). The majority have been active in their professional organizations and on national committees. They include one president of the American Association for the Advancement of Science, six presidents of the American Mathematical Society (research-oriented) and two presidents of the Mathematical Association of America (teaching-oriented). One, Saunders Mac Lane, has been president of both the latter organizations and one, Frederick Mosteller, has been president of both the Institute of Mathematical Statistics (theoretical) and the American Statistical Association (applied). The majority have headed the mathematics departments of their universities. One, Irving Kaplansky, is now the director of the Mathematical Sciences Research Institute in Berkeley. All of them, because of the nature of their profession, have contributed services to their science beyond their own research: writing books, editing, refereeing, being on committees. Most are concerned about and several are very active in the improvement of mathematical education below the university level, including in the elementary schools.

Almost all the mathematicians in this volume have been the recipients of the outstanding prizes and honors of their professional organizations. In addition, three have been awarded the nation's highest scientific honor, the National Medal of Science, and twelve have been elected to the National Academy of Sciences. Three have been the recipients of the Fields Medal, which is looked upon by mathematicians as the Nobel Prize of their subject—there being no Nobel Prize for mathematics, and two have received the Wolf Prize, the most lucrative in mathematics.

Of the eighteen mathematicians in the volume, seven were born in countries other than the United States. All but one are married, and have stayed married to their original mates. (This is not a finding that can be extrapolated to all mathematicians.) All but one of the married have had children, ranging from one to four, and among the children there are three mathematicians (Harold Boas, Mike Lewy and Nat Smale). Two of the three women in our book are married to men who are mathematicians, and the spouses of three of the men are also mathematicians. Four additional spouses are academics in other fields.

Only one of the mathematicians in this book could have been considered a prodigy, although almost all of them showed early mathematical ability. One, however, was flunking math in junior high school and another received a warning from his department head in graduate school. The choice of mathematics as a career was not always immediate. Chemistry especially seems to have exercised an early attraction; it was abandoned almost equally early. Fathers played more of a role than mothers in encouraging mathematical talent. Teachers were important, especially at the university level, and one is struck by the fact that almost all the teachers mentioned as influential are mathematicians who emigrated to the United States during the second World War. Only one of the native-born mathematicians went abroad for his degree, but five of the foreign-born took their degrees in this country. Two do not have Ph.D.'s, generally considered the sine qua non for a career in mathematics. Ph.D. degrees were awarded by Berkeley (four), Harvard (three), NYU (two), Göttingen (two), and Chicago, Michigan, Pennsylvania, Princeton and Texas (one each).

The striking differences that can exist between one mathematician and another can be seen most quickly by pairing a few who have something in common and then reading their interviews in succession. Lipman Bers and Ralph Boas, who open the volume, are both in complex analysis. Andrew Gleason and Bill Thurston both use topological methods in their work. Paul Cohen and Julia Robinson are both well known for their work on famous problems in logic. Hans Lewy and Saunders Mac Lane both took their degrees at the famous Mathematical Institute of Göttingen.

A reading of any of these suggested pairs of interviews should convince the reader that in spite of the habit of mind that all mathematicians share and the common joy that they take in their subject, there is no such person as the typical mathematician.

# LIPMAN BERS

Lipman Bers is well known in the mathematical community as an advocate for human rights. He sees himself as part of a tradition "where you take the defense of human rights as a duty," but he did not always have the status to be effective. In 1934, as a young radical, he had to flee his native Latvia following a fascist coup d'état. Four years later, having just received his Ph.D. at the University of Prague, he had to flee again, this time because he was a Jew. He arrived ultimately in the United States as the result of what he terms a few "miracles." He believes that his political activism helped him to survive in the Europe of the thirties. "In catastrophic times," he says, "it is the people who are not conformists who have a better chance of surviving."

□ □ □

**MP**  *We know that you were born in Riga in 1914, but Latvia was not yet an independent nation in 1914, so what nationality were you officially?*

**BERS**  I was born under Nicholas II, the last czar of Russia before the revolution. I then spent the first four years of my life in Petrograd, now known as Leningrad.

**MP**  *So you were born a Russian citizen?*

**BERS**  I was born a Russian *subject*. I actually have some recollection of the Russian revolution. I recall standing at the window of our apartment looking down into the street and seeing large numbers of people going by with red flags. I checked with my mother, and she told me that this was the first legal socialist May 1 celebration in Russia. It was very soon after the revolution, and everyone was very optimistic. Somehow, even as a child, I felt the festive mood. I asked my mother what is a socialist, and she told me that a socialist is someone who loves the color red. (Incidentally, my parents were both Social-Democrats.) Later on, when I came to understand things better, I was offended that she didn't give me a "grown-up" answer.

**MP**  *How long did you stay in Russia?*

**BERS**  My parents and I remained in Petrograd until about 1919. At that time there was famine as well as civil war in Russia. Both my mother and father were from Riga so it was natural for us to go back there. Also Latvia was in the process of becoming an independent country. In fact, my father became a member of the constituent assembly of Latvia. He was an engineer by training and had worked in Petrograd as an engineer, but in Riga he became the director of a gymnasium. The school of which he was director was one of the few public Yiddish gymnasiums in the world. In Latvia there was a law, which my father helped write, that guaranteed to each ethnic group public schools in its own language. It was all part of what was called the "personal cultural autonomy movement." At that time, in fact, both the Russians and the Latvians introduced "ethnic nationality" as an official part of one's passport. It was not intended as a repressive measure, as it now is. On my passport, for example, I answered the following questions: Nationality? Latvian. Ethnic nationality? Jewish. Religion? None.

**MP**  *What memories do you have of elementary school?*

**BERS**  I had no interest in mathematics in elementary school in Riga, but I was for one year in an elementary school in Berlin. This was a secular experimental school. It was super-progressive. There were no rules, there was no curriculum, but there was a magnificent teacher. His name was Jensen. He was the founder and leader of the school, and I had the good luck of being in his class.

**MP**  *Did your parents send you to Berlin because they were interested in education and knew about this man?*

**A Little Concentration Camp**

**BERS**  Oh, no, no. My mother, who later became a psychoanalyst, was studying at the Berlin Psychoanalytical Institute that year. My parents were separated by then, and I was with her. The first day I went to the public

A revolutionary group in Riga c. 1905 with Bers's mother second from left in middle row and his father second from left in back row. There was a suspected police informer in the group, but Bers cannot identify him.

*More Mathematical People*

(Top) Bertha Bers (later Tumarin), mother of Lipman Bers. (Bottom) Isaac Bers, father of Lipman Bers.

school in our middle-class neighborhood (it was Charlottenburg) and came back shocked by what I witnessed. It was like a little concentration camp! Kids were beaten, regularly. This one day I saw a boy being asked a question. He gave the wrong answer; the teacher pulled his ear and asked him again; the answer was still wrong. The teacher gave his ear a second twist and a third twist. And the horrible thing was that everybody laughed. Then a student whispered something. The teacher slapped him! My mother went the next day and said that I would not be coming anymore. When the principal asked the reason and my mother explained, he said, "But, madam, if you don't like it—you are foreigners—nobody will touch him." After that my mother made inquiries and learned about Jensen's school. It was located in a working class neighborhood (Neuköln), and it took an hour to get there by public transportation, but she sent me there. It was a very interesting experience in all respects. We did "mathematics" for a few weeks only. Herr Jensen had us cutting out various shapes from colored paper and putting them together—doing things like that. At the end of three weeks he told me, "I think you will be a mathematician." I was eleven.

MP   *So at eleven the seeds were there.*

BERS   But I didn't believe him then!

MP   *But you enjoyed him. A lot. Do you think it was the person as much as it was the cutting of the paper into shapes?*

BERS   I can't tell you. I loved him as a person. I don't think that he knew much about mathematics. At least I have no reason to believe that he did. But after that I enjoyed mathematics. The real inspiration, however, I got from my father. He showed me a few mathematical things when I came back from Berlin. He showed me mathematical induction, for instance.

MP   *At age eleven!*

BERS   Well, my impression is that mathematical induction is either understood at an early age, or never understood. Maybe I was twelve. I don't remember. And then he showed me a proof of the Pythagorean theorem. He also taught me about cartesian coordinates and showed me how to represent equations by lines and how to solve two linear equations by seeing where the lines intersect. And this seemed to me the most beautiful thing in the world.

MP   *So you attended the gymnasium of which your father was director?*

BERS   Yes. I also attended the elementary school of which my mother had been principal. (At a very young age she was president of an organization devoted to building up Yiddish elementary schools in Latvia.) In that elementary school I not only learned something, but I also met my future wife!

MP   *What great things those were that your father showed you!*

BERS   Yes, after that mathematics came easy to me, but there was no way of learning much, because there were almost no popular books on mathematics available. We had one book in the school library, a Russian translation of a German book by Weber and Wellstein. It was not a very good book. I tried to read it but failed. On the first page it said that the concepts of *set* and *element* are the basic concepts of mathematics. And then these concepts were never explained or mentioned again! Yet this sentence was eventually to be very important for my mathematical development. Because I was good in math, I decided to study engineering. Later, when I was in Prague visiting an aunt of mine, I saw in a bookstore a small book on set theory, *Mengenlehre* by Kamke. I bought it.

**Such a Silly Question**

Now it so happens that when I was in high school, I had constructed somehow a one-to-one correspondence between an infinite set and a subset. I *think* it was geometric and involved two segments, but strangely enough I have no certain recollection. I was very surprised that such a thing is possible. I showed it to my mathematics teacher and said, "Look—what's wrong, what's going on?" And he said, "You know, I have taught mathematics for fifteen years and have never heard such a silly question." He was a friendly man, he just didn't know any better. But I slunk away, properly chastized— and then I opened Kamke, and there it was!

**MP**  *In my opinion that was a pretty deep observation on your part. You can show that construction to children and they can see that each point on the short segment matches up with one on the longer segment and vice versa. But for you to come up with that on your own . . .*

**BERS**  I suppose I would have forgotten the whole thing if I didn't remember the shock of recognition when I saw the same thing in Kamke. I read the first third of Kamke very fast, and I understood it! I learned about countable and uncountable sets, about Cantor's proof of the existence of transcendental numbers, about transfinite numbers and about the continuum hypothesis. The theory of point sets was too hard for me. But I fell in love with the subject and decided to study mathematics. I immediately withdrew my application for engineering school. The school I had applied to happened to be the Zürich Polytechnikum. I had no idea that it was a famous mathematics school as well as an engineering school, and so instead I applied to the University of Zürich.

Well, they accepted me. The hardest course was calculus, because unlike the Swiss students I had never had any cookbook calculus at all. The professor (it was A. Speiser) began with the rigorous theory of real numbers. He told us, "It will be hard in the beginning. If you don't understand it for a week or two, don't worry. If you don't understand it in two months, maybe you should look for another profession. And if you have any questions, my assistant's office hours are then and then." So I went to the assistant. He gave me a key and charged me a five franc deposit. The key had a tag that said "Mathematical Reading Room." This was a big room, and the walls were covered by books. It was quite clear to me that I was expected to read *all* these books! Well, the summer before I had got hold of some popular book on calculus. I hadn't understood much, but I knew that you study functions before you do calculus. So I picked up a book, *Function Theory.* This was Hurwitz-Courant. No good. I repeated the experiment several times. Finally I found a book by H. von Mangoldt entitled *Foundations of Higher Mathematics.* It contained epsilons and deltas, very slowly and laboriously explained. I spent hours reading this book, trying to prove those theorems with epsilons and deltas. And then I made a discovery: such a proof need not end with an epsilon. It could be $5\varepsilon$ or $10\varepsilon$. Mangoldt always adjusted it so that it should come out one epsilon, but I found out you didn't have to do it that way. From then on, it was easy sailing.

With mother in Berlin, where he was told at school, "You will be a mathematician."

*More Mathematical People*

It was Bers's father, the director of a high school in Riga, who introduced him to "real mathematics."

**"Where is Bers?"**

**MP** *Now what year was this?*

**BERS** I came to Zürich in 1932 and stayed only a term, because at that time the shock from the Wall Street crash of 1929 reached Europe. There was a panic, and most countries introduced rules against sending out currency. I could get no money from home. So I went back to Riga and entered the university there. It was very weak in mathematics. There wasn't even a full mathematics department. The library had no book published after 1914. I knew that I would not learn much in such a place. I took a few courses and passed a few exams. But I mostly did politics.

**MP** *So, really, your mathematical education took place in Zürich?*

**BERS** No. I was at the university in Riga for only two years. And then—on May 15, 1934—the fascist coup d'état came. My parents were fired from their positions. I was involved in the socialist youth movement and various underground activities, and so the police came to get me. They did it in such an exceedingly inefficient way that I was able to escape to Estonia, which was only semi-fascist. There were still legal unions there so I could get some protection. I had to decide what to do. One idea I had in mind was to go to Russia.

**MP** *That was a choice at that time?*

**BERS** It *looked* like a choice. Not to do politics there, but mathematics. I knew that they had excellent mathematicians. I must say that an inspector of the Latvian political police was smarter than I. He arrested a friend of mine and asked him, "Where is Bers?" "I don't know." "You must know something." "Well, there is a rumor that he has gone to Russia." "No—he is not so stupid. We would give him five years. The Russians would shoot him."

But from Estonia I got a visa for Czechoslovakia, which was then a haven for all political refugees. The way I got there resembled a Peano curve. In Prague there was a German-speaking university. The student body was very uninteresting. Mostly people wanted a high school teaching certificate. But Rudolf Carnap was teaching there. At that time I thought that I was interested primarily in set theory and mathematical logic, so it was quite clear that I should enroll. Anyway I couldn't get a job because as a foreigner I was not permitted to work—all I could do was study. There I got my serious mathematical education.

I started to take some courses from Carnap. I even decided to write my thesis with him, but he left for Chicago—fortunately for me, because I was not cut out to be a logician. Then I asked Charles Loewner (then Karl Löwner) for a thesis topic. There were some other good teachers in Prague, including Philip Frank in physics. But it was not an important center like Göttingen or Paris. As a matter of fact, a Russian philosopher I knew advised me to go to Göttingen, but I thought, "A philosopher—what does he know about mathematics?"

**MP** *Loewner's interests certainly seem to parallel yours in large part— complex variables, partial differential equations, fluid dynamics.*

**BERS** Nobody told me that he was a great mathmetician, and if you are not told you don't know. I knew he was interested in geometric function theory. And when I went to him to ask for a thesis topic, I specifically asked him for a topic *not* on geometric function theory and not on matrix functions,

Charles Loewner, Bers's Ph.D. adviser in Prague: "I expected him to say, 'What makes you think you can write a thesis on mathematics?'"

on which he was working at that time. That was quite impertinent, but I didn't know any better. He said that in that case I should come back in a week because he wanted to think. Then he gave me a topic which turned out to be much too difficult for me; but while working on that topic, I had an idea and I wrote my thesis on potential theory.

**MP** *You said that you were not suited to be a logician. Do you feel that there is any field other than those in which you have worked where you could work happily?*

**BERS** Oh yes. I think that under different circumstances I could have been a topologist or a differential geometer. Logic and algebra, I think, are not for me. Then, too, I have always been emotionally attracted to applied mathematics.

**MP** *Because of your father?*

**BERS** I don't know why. It was so. I certainly did better work in pure mathematics than in applied mathematics, and I am quite happy with how things turned out. Of course, they turned out much better than I had any right to expect. I didn't think I would become a research mathematician at all. I didn't have this ambition. I thought, if I would get a job, it would be something like a high school teacher in mathematics. I remember somebody visiting me in Prague. He had been several times in America. And I had wanted to go to America, always. He told me, "You come to America. You will be a professor." I certainly didn't believe him.

**MP** *So then did you get a high school teaching credential?*

**BERS** No. I didn't even bother to pick one up. Because I was a political refugee, I knew that for a long time I wouldn't be able to go back to Latvia; but if I should go back, I wouldn't need a teaching credential. That was one good thing about the Latvian school law, which, as I told you, my father had participated in writing. There were no teaching credentials for high schools; you only had to know something about the subject. So a Ph.D. would be sufficient.

**MP** *What year did you get your Ph.D.?*

**BERS** I got it in '38.

**MP** *So you were really on the brink of World War II?*

**BERS** Oh, yes. I was always on the brink.

**MP** *But you had had this feeling, as so many people did in that part of Europe, that you wanted to go to America.*

**BERS** Yes. And I know how I learned about America and how it was that I more or less fell in love with America. It was reading the novels of Sinclair Lewis. I read him in German in Zürich.

**MP** *Did you start with* Main Street?

**BERS** No, I started with *Babbitt*.

**MP** Arrowsmith, *too?*

**BERS** *Arrowsmith* did it, of course. The hero gets a job for $100 a week! A country which pays a scientist $100 a week! And a country which honors

In Riga with his father, who had spent eight years in a Siberian gulag and additional years of "internal exile" teaching in a Siberian engineering school.

a writer who makes fun of that country! Also Europe was so hopelessly sick. I had to decide what to do. I couldn't stay in Czechoslovakia forever. I thought about going to Russia, but even before I came to Prague, Kirov (the party boss of Leningrad) was murdered and several hundred so-called hostages were executed—people who were in jail at the time and had absolutely nothing to do with the murder.

**MP** *You got the message.*

**BERS** I got the message. So where else? Already, before I had to leave Riga, I had wanted to go to America. It didn't seem difficult then, because the Latvian quota was never filled—the U.S. had this quota system, so many of each nationality. My mother wanted to go to America, too. When she decided to go, she just went to the consulate and got a visa and went to America.

**MP** *Now wait. Were you married yet?*

**BERS** Yes, Mary came to Prague and we were married there. Before I got my degree, I applied for a visa to go to Paris in order to do post-doctoral work. Then came the "crisis" over the German minority in Czechoslovakia, which led to the Munich agreement and the dismemberment of that country by Hitler. We knew that it would end very badly, and I understood how a mouse feels when trapped. But then, after Munich, we received a telegram: "Come to the French consulate and pick up your visas." It seemed like a real miracle, but I think the miracle was performed by French socialists who wanted to help a political refugee. So we went to Paris, where we thought it would be easier to get an American visa. The consulate in Prague was for some reason exceedingly unfriendly. Well, we went to the U.S. consulate in Paris and were told that we would have to wait fifteen years: "Register and come back in fifteen years."

**MP** *You're kidding!*

**BERS** No. That was it. The Latvian quota was filled!

**MP** *But your mother had been able to go.*

**BERS** Yes, because she had gone before the quota was filled. After Munich everybody wanted to go so it filled up in no time. Thus we were in Paris when the war started. Our child—our daughter—was born there. Already there were air raid alerts so my wife said, "Why should we sit in Paris? Let's go south." I applied for permission to go to the south of France and got it. We left Paris ten days before the fall of Paris while everyone else got out of Paris just one day before it fell!

**MP** *Your timing seems to be pretty good.*

**"I literally owe my life to Mrs. Roosevelt."**

**BERS** So there we were, sitting in a small hamlet in unoccupied France, not far from Lourdes, near the Spanish border, and again having this unpleasant feeling of being in a mousetrap. We couldn't go anywhere; we just sat and waited. We decided, though, that if the Germans occupied that part of France, too, we would hike across the Pyrenees—with the baby carriage.

**MP** *With the baby carriage? Seriously?*

**BERS** What else was there to do? The idea was not to be under the Germans under any conditions. At that time there were those rumors of how civilized the Germans behave in Paris, how they buy everything and don't haggle over prices, and so on. But we knew . . . Then again a miracle happened. I got a telegram. "Come to the U.S. Consulate in Marseilles: there is a visa for you." I literally owe my life to Mrs. Roosevelt. She convinced her husband to issue special emergency visas to political refugees and intellectuals caught in France after the defeat of the French and considered particularly endangered. (At that time nobody had any idea that millions of people would be killed just for being Jews!) Committees in New York and in Washington were making lists of people who ought to be given these visas. All we had to do was identify ourselves.

MP   *So you came across the waters.*

BERS   We came across the waters.

MP   *And then did you go directly to Brown University?*

BERS   Not yet. My mother had already started working as a psychoanalyst. At the time she still didn't know any English, but there were enough people speaking German who needed a psychoanalyst. We moved in with her, and I got a small fellowship in a Yiddish research organization, YIVO. They suggested I look into old arithmetic texts in Yiddish, and this turned out to be very interesting. In order to do the job I also had to read the German textbooks of the time so I got some idea about the history of teaching. I wrote a paper (in Yiddish) which was published.

MP   *You weren't able to speak English at this time, were you?*

BERS   I could speak a little. So then I saw Stefan Bergman, whom I had met in Paris. He told me that there was going to be a summer program in applied mathematics at Brown and I should apply. I was accepted, but without support. Abe Gelbart was Bergman's assistant, and Bergman said, "I have $100 for an assistant. I will divide it between the two of you." So I spent the summer in Brown. Also somebody told me I ought to register with Hermann Weyl, who was advising the Committee for Displaced Scholars. I wrote, saying I would like to see him, and I got a letter from his secretary about when I should come. I was so impressed that a professor can have a secretary! Weyl was very friendly. I told him about my thesis and also about the original problem that I couldn't solve. He said, "Yes. I know this problem. It's very hard." I was happy to hear that. (Incidentally, the problem is still unsolved.) Weyl didn't promise me anything. He just said, "I'll give your name to the Committee for Displaced Scholars." After that summer in Brown, I wasn't kept on. So I returned to New York and did another non-mathematical research job, for a Yiddish encyclopedia this time. Then after Pearl Harbor the applied mathematics program at Brown expanded. I wrote to R. G. D. Richardson, who was the Graduate Dean there, asking what could I do for the war effort. He wrote back that I should come down for an interview with Willy Prager, who had just come to Brown. I was hired on the spot at $800 a year.

MP   *This was not the $100 a week that you had read about in* Arrowsmith.

BERS   No. But I had no choice. I borrowed some money and went to Brown. Then, fortunately, I had an offer from Illinois College. An assistant professorship of mathematics, astronomy and physics. They got my name

Bers's mother was still a practicing psychoanalyst in her eighties.

*More Mathematical People*

from the Committee for Displaced Scholars. On the basis of this offer Richardson raised my salary.

So I spent the war years at Brown. Incidentally, Loewner joined me there. When I left Prague, he was trying to get to America but he was still there when the Germans invaded. He was actually taken in by the Gestapo and for a week had a very unpleasant time. His wife, who was a very energetic lady, managed to pull some strings and they were permitted to emigrate. At first he had a very poor job in America. At that time the job situation was bad for everybody. He taught elementary calculus many hours a week. When the students asked him to teach an advanced course, he agreed to do so without being paid any more. At first the administration wouldn't let him—they said he should concentrate on his undergraduate teaching! When they finally said he could do it, they didn't give him a classroom so he taught at a local brewery before the first shift came to work! Richardson knew about Loewner and managed to get him to Brown.

**Infusion or Invasion?**   **MP**   *Richardson certainly took advantage of the opportunity to get top people from Europe.*

**BERS**   Yes. Indeed, some other leaders of American mathematics worried about whether the American mathematical community would be able to absorb the sudden infusion of so much talent and expertise. Would this not condemn young American mathematicians to become "hewers of wood and carriers of water"? That was a question asked by the great G. D. Birkhoff in an address he made on the occasion of the fiftieth anniversary of the American Mathematical Society—in 1938, I think. But it seems to me that this fear was not shared by the upcoming young mathematicians he was worrying about. It was a time when academic jobs were very hard to get, yet they received the Europeans with touching collegiality and friendship. Not just the world famous ones but also beginners like myself—I was one of the youngest in that group. Well, for once virtue was rewarded. Those allegedly threatened young American mathematicians became the leaders of American mathematics during the period when it gained world leadership.

**Virtue and Rewards**   **MP**   *I think many people feel that American mathematics gained world leadership* because of *the influx of European mathematicians.*

**BERS**   But that's a misapprehension. The European migration strengthened American mathematics, but this happened, I believe, only because American mathematics was already so strong. There were G. D. Birkhoff and Veblen, of course, and Marston Morse, R. L. Moore, Dickson, Wedderburn, Ritt, Albert and Post, just to name a few. Mathematicians driven out by the Nazis did go to other countries—but what happened in America did not happen in other countries, like Turkey, where some outstanding mathematicians also went—von Mises and Prager, for example. Where the native scientific establishment was not prepared, the newcomers could accomplish nothing.

I was lucky to have lived through that period, and I hope the story of it will be written some day before it's too late. There were many heroes in this story. I just mentioned a whole class of heroes—the American-educated mathematicians who were, roughly speaking, my contemporaries. But there were others—like Veblen, who was very active in finding places for refugees.

And I and all the others who came to this country owe special thanks to the patience, sense of humor and tolerance of American undergraduates. What linguistic horrors many of us committed! I cannot think of another country where such would have been tolerated—and the forbearance which was extended to us is now being extended to other immigrants with other accents.

**Secrets of Promotion**

MP    *But now what happened to you personally* after *the war?*

BERS    After the war W. T. Martin went to Syracuse as chairman of the mathematics department. He offered me an instructorship there. I accepted it but said, "I think I deserve an assistant professorship." So he promoted me.

MP    *You were coming along!*

BERS    Loewner also came to Syracuse. So we were colleagues at Brown, then we were colleagues in Syracuse and then, since I was one summer a visiting professor at Stanford, we were colleagues there too. We became very close friends.

MP    *How did you get from Syracuse to NYU and then to Columbia?*

BERS    Syracuse—the whole thing collapsed. We had there, at one time, Loewner, A. Milgram, Selberg, Erdős, Mostow, Rosenbloom, Samelson, Protter and myself and, for a shorter time, Halmos. It was too good for the level of the university. Within a year or two all those people left. I was very glad to get the job at NYU. Later, for personal reasons, I left NYU for Columbia.

Among Bers's many female Ph.D. students are Lesley Sibner, Linda Keen and Tillie Milnor: "It never occurred to me that women can be intellectually inferior to men."

*More Mathematical People*

**MP**  *Something that interests me is the fact that your mother, your wife and so many other women, European women, of your intellectual class were all active career women even at that time.*

**BERS**  You're right. My mother more than my wife, although my wife is a teacher of special education. It never occurred to me that women can be intellectually inferior to men! My mother was a professional woman from a very early age. My daughter is a professional (a clinical psychologist and a professor). And now I have been praised and honored for encouraging women to be mathematicians. A year or so ago the Association for Women in Mathematics even held a symposium on me as a teacher.

**MP**  *Mina Rees has said that it is hard to think of a woman mathematician who isn't married to a man mathematician. I've always wondered about male mathematicians and their non-mathematical wives and families. How is it with you? You have a subject that it is almost impossible to communicate. How do you feel about that problem?*

**BERS**  Well, it gives one a certain feeling of loneliness.

**The Village of Mathematics**

**MP**  *You once said that mathematicians are like a small isolated village.*

**BERS**  I think it is a correct observation. Of course, the "small village" is getting a little bigger now.

**MP**  *Yes. And the next part of the statement from which I am quoting is— this is Bers speaking: "There are too many nowadays, really, but they are a small village, partly because they are all alone." Do you really believe that there are too many mathematicians nowadays?*

**BERS**  Not too many, objectively. I meant too many to be described as a small village. In a small village you know everybody. Now you don't any-more. I talked to a very good mathematician recently and I said, "Thurston reminds me of Mozart." And he said, "Who is Thurston?" He is an older mathematician. But still!

**MP**  *Hans Lewy feels that even though the number of mathematicians has increased, the number of good mathematicians has stayed about the same. Basic mathematical talent has not increased. What do you think?*

**BERS**  I don't think he is right—with all due respect—although it is not respect, it is awe which I feel for Hans Lewy. I don't think he is right, because I think that now more people get a chance to become mathematicians and the talent is probably distributed more or less at random. If people don't have a chance to become mathematicians, they won't. My impression is that mathematics today is more exciting than it was when I got my degree.

**Mathematics Today Is More Exciting**

**MP**  *What do you think makes it more exciting now?*

**BERS**  The very good mathematics which is being done. All sorts of talented young people. And at this moment we are in a period of convergence. In other words, the different fields have become much more inter-mingled.

**MP**  *You think so?*

**BERS**  Right now, yes. Twenty or thirty years ago there was a tendency toward more and more specialization. But I know that I talk now to more people not in my specialty than I used to.

MP *Do you think that's your age—that maybe now you're not quite so committed to your specialty?*

BERS  I think it is really something objective, because my interests are not becoming more catholic. I wish they would, but they aren't. Partly it may be because I was very lucky about twenty years ago. I got attached to a sub-discipline—quasi-conformal mapping and Teichmüller spaces—which is now rather popular. So it may be just my individual luck.

MP *I'm trying to think of some recent things that I've seen that perhaps support your statement. Differential geometry—the old classical stuff—and computer science intersect very, very strongly with graphics.*

BERS  Computers, now, really begin to be used as a tool for mathematics.

MP *Do you think that, in a sense, computer science spreads over almost all mathematics?*

**An Exceedingly Cruel Profession**

BERS  In some sense it does. And I think it will have an unexpected good side effect. Mathematics is an exceedingly cruel profession. You notice that if somebody has a bachelor's degree in chemistry, he describes himself as a chemist. But if somebody has been a professor of mathematics for ten years and you ask him, "Are you a mathematician?" he may say, "I'm trying to be one!" With the computer, people can do useful things during their not most creative period. I may be wrong, of course. I may have unintentionally offended computer scientists. I have never worked on a computer, except on Mark I during World War II.

MP *When you say that mathematics is a very cruel profession, do you mean because the standard is so high?*

BERS  The standard is high, and you never know whether you will be able to hack it. First you are afraid that you won't be able to understand your professors. Then you are afraid that you won't be able to write a thesis. When I went to Loewner to ask him for a thesis topic, I expected him to grab me by the neck and say, "What makes you think you can write a thesis on mathematics? OUT!!!" Well, logically, of course, I knew that this was not inevitable—it was only likely.

MP *You have doubts when you're doing it, but don't you know when you've succeeded?*

BERS  If you have done something, yes. Nothing can compare with this pleasure! But then you start worrying—will you be able to do it again?

MP *Do you think that mathematicians as a group are very much inclined to make judgments on the basis of "Well, yes, that was good work, Bers, but what have you done lately?"*

BERS  No, I wouldn't say that it is as crass as that. You ask yourself. Others don't ask you.

MP *It seems to me that if you have done something really good in mathematics, you can sit on it for a while.*

A brilliant lecturer, Bers claims he learned his skills on a soapbox.

**BERS**  Ask somebody who has!

**MP**  *You've said elsewhere that thus far our attempts to communicate the beauty of our art to a wide audience have failed miserably.*

**BERS**  We haven't done it, and I'm really not sure that it can be done. I alternate between two attitudes. Mondays, Wednesdays and Fridays I believe it can be done if we do it properly; Tuesdays, Thursdays and Saturdays I believe it cannot.

**MP**  *On the days you believe it can be done if it is done properly, how do you think about doing it?*

**BERS**  Well, you see, the difficulty is I would like to try to do it. I have thought about what I can explain that I know really well. Suppose I'm to give, say, a twenty-minute talk before the American Philosophical Society. I have listened to these talks, and they are such good talks. The speakers communicate what their field is about. But for them it's relatively easy. Somebody shows pictures of a fly from which he has removed all parts of the brain except that which controls the appetite. Then the fly eats so much that it explodes. It is all very interesting. But he has these pictures to show.

**MP**  *Why don't you do as Poincaré did and say, "You don't have to understand this"?*

**BERS**  No. He was talking about mathematical discovery—not trying to explain mathematics.

**MP**  *Yes, but couldn't it be done, somehow, with mathematics? Couldn't you get on top of the subject, as it were, instead of into it?*

**BERS**  I don't know. I once met an exceedingly intelligent publisher, and he said to me, "I know nothing about mathematics. I would like to understand what it is about. Isn't there some book for laymen which I could read?" I said, "Of course! Here it is." And I gave him Courant-Robbins, *What Is*

*Mathematics?* What could be better? The next week we had another meeting. When he came in, he gave the book back to me and started to talk about something else. The whole time I was thinking, "My God! I couldn't have read that book in a week!" So I asked him, "Tell me, did you finish the book?" He said, "No. I got stuck on page two."

**Canned Thought**      What is the strength of mathematics? What makes mathematics possible? It is symbolic reasoning. It is like "canned thought." You have understood something once. You encode it, and then you go on using it without each time having to think about it. Now there may be people who are totally unable to follow symbolic reasoning—just as I am unable to carry a tune (and yet I do say to myself that I enjoy music). So you must try to explain mathematics without using any symbols. But this may be impossible. Without symbolic reasoning you cannot make a mathematical argument.

MP   *You can do a lot of gorgeous geometry, which is less dependent on symbolic reasoning.*

BERS   None of which will be art in the way that the Mona Lisa or a painting by Picasso is. So who the hell needs our works of art? We feel that they are beautiful because we know the mathematics behind them.

MP   *But maybe if you could give a sense of just how much mathematics is behind something, the person who looks at it might be able to get a sense of it.*

**Mathematics and Poetry**   BERS   Maybe. But I think that mathematics is very much like poetry. I think that what makes a good poem—a great poem—is that there is a large amount of thought expressed in very few words. In this sense formulas like

$$e^{\pi i} + 1 = 0$$

or

$$\int_{-\infty}^{+\infty} e^{-x^2}\, dx = \sqrt{\pi}$$

are poems. Now you can tell somebody what poetry is. Then you want to give him an example. If he doesn't know English, you can't give him a poem in English. That won't work. My son, who is a classicist, told me once that Pindar was one of the greatest poets ever. I said, "What is a good translation?" He said, "There is no good translation. Either you read it in Greek, or you just forget it!" As far as mathematics is concerned, something similar may be true. Either you can use symbols, or just forget it!

MP   *But you do take your son's word for Pindar.*

BERS   I take his word for it. People take our word for it, too. I mean, they pay our salaries, give us grants, endow our institutes; and we don't do anything useful like curing disease or helping to kill people.

MP   *G. H. Hardy, in* A Mathematician's Apology, *does a pretty good job of giving a non-mathematician a sense of mathematics.*

BERS   Well, I taught a class at Columbia which was called "Math for Poets." It had no prerequisites, and it was not a prerequisite for anything. People took it only because they never understood math and wanted to get some idea of it. I spent a term explaining the irrationality of the square root of 2 to that class. I think they understood it. The next term I tried to do a little calculus. In the most primitive way, you know. Drawing a curve and measuring the slope of the tangent—$x^2$, $2x^2$, $5x^2$—were the only things we did. And then I wanted to show thcm how to take the anti-derivative. So I asked a student, "What is the derivative of $x^2$?" "$2x$." Fine. "Now which function has the derivative $2x$?" "Uh. Uh. Uh." And yet this kid was certifiably smart in other subjects!

There is something very funny here. We can teach a computer to decide whether a mathematical formula is well formed or not. That's very easy. But we cannot teach a computer to talk, to form sentences. It is obviously a million times as hard. But take any kid who learns how to speak. If, as a kid, he hears two languages, he learns two languages. If he is mentally retarded, he still becomes bilingual. He will know fewer words, but he will know those words in both languages. He will form sentences. Now try to explain to him what is a well formed algebraic formula!

Sometimes I think we shouldn't even try to explain mathematics.

MP   *I think we have to. We are respected by people. "Oh, you are a teacher of mathematics. That's good!"*

BERS   And then the hostility comes.

MP   *Why?*

BERS   Suppose you are a teacher of English. People ask, "What do you teach?" "English." "English! I could never master the alphabet. A, B, C was okay, but then the next one . . ." Nobody will tell it to you like this.

MP   *As a former English teacher, I think I can say that they sometimes say such things. There is something about a teacher of any subject that you took in high school—whether it's history or mathematics or English. I think they would say something similar to a history teacher. Perhaps they say it more often to a mathematics teacher.*

BERS   Definitely more often. There is a certain aggression. People say, "I never could understand it!" Then they look at you and expect congratulations.

**A Phony Filter**   MP   *Part of it is, I think, that students perceive mathematics as a fraud. And in many cases the truth of the matter is that it is. It's a filter. A phony filter. It's just something that medical schools, for instance, can use as a way of keeping out those of lesser gifts.*

BERS   Once I needed minor emergency surgery. There I was, strapped to the table, and the surgeon started a conversation. "You know, I never wanted to be a surgeon, I wanted to be an engineer." I stupidly asked, "Why didn't you become one?" "I couldn't pass the calculus." But I was not scared at all. Because deep in my heart I knew that it didn't matter whether he had had calculus or not!

MP   *To go back to explaining mathematics, I think a mathematician has to remember that when he, or she, is explaining something, like why the number of primes is infinite, that is about the extent of the attention span of a non-mathematical person. But then the mathematician immediately throws in something else and begins to go faster.*

BERS   But, you know, many mathematicians don't have any longer attention span than non-mathematical people. We artificially prolong ours by

"A working mathematician is always a Platonist. It doesn't matter what he says."

using symbolic reasoning. Once we say prime number, we don't think, each time, prime number means one that cannot be divided. We just think P and take it for granted.

**MP** *But this is one of the the problems when you are explaining something to a non-mathematician. Because every time you say P, he still has to think, "prime number, a number that is not divisible." So he is working a lot harder than you are as he goes along.*

**BERS** Very likely his kindergarten teacher was scared of math. But what to do about it? I don't know.

**MP** *One of the people we interviewed in* Mathematical People *made the comment that elementary teachers are basically non-mathematically, non-scientifically oriented. That's why they are elementary school teachers. Perhaps the elementary schools should have special mathematics instructors just as they have special music and art instructors.*

**BERS** It would be harder to get special math teachers.

**MP** *But we could pay them.*

**BERS** We couldn't pay them more than the computer companies.

**MP** *Do you think mathematicians know how to teach children mathematics?*

**BERS** Some mathematicians are very good teachers. Some are not.

**MP** *What do you think of as your style of teaching?*

**BERS** I probably imitate Loewner a little. I ham it up more than he did. I tell stories. He never did, but he was an excellent teacher. He emphasized the important things. I was once at a symposium on partial differential equations in Nancy, and the three best presentations, in my opinion and I think the opinion of others, were those by Laurent Schwartz, Malgrange, and myself. Question: what do we three have in common?

**MP** *None of you wrote on the board?*

**Soapboxes and Teaching**

**BERS** No. We were all soapbox speakers before we became mathematics professors. I certainly acquired my speaking style while addressing from the soapbox and also by watching my father. When I gave my first colloquium talk in Prague, Loewner was very surprised how well I did. I didn't tell him then that I had learned on a soapbox.

**MP** *You really enjoy teaching?*

**BERS** Very much. Now I have no regular teaching duties. But I like to give seminar talks and colloquiums.

**MP** *I liked what you said in the interview in* Mathematics Today—*that when you teach you are communicating beautiful ideas. In that same interview I remember that you were very interested in getting an answer from Dennis Sullivan to the following question—what gives him more pleasure, inventing or discovering? I don't think Sullivan ever really answered the* *question. Now I'd like to turn the tables. What gives you more pleasure, inventing or discovering?*

**BERS**   That wasn't a real question. I was just curious about what Dennis would say. A working mathematician is always a platonist. It doesn't matter what he says. He may not be a platonist at other times. But I think that in mathematics he always has that feeling of discovery. There is no doubt in my mind that Dennis discovers—with the feeling that he discovers.

**MP**   *I think that what you just said is something that people who are not mathematicians can understand. That mathematics is, as Ron Graham has said, the ultimate reality: the sense that mathematics exists and you can find these things out.*

**BERS**   Actually, what exists may be our brain. Maybe we have really discovered something about the brain. A religious man can say that mathematics exists in God's mind. And Gödel himself simply believed in the platonic ideas.

**MP**   *You once said, as I recall, "I still say that the man or woman who does not know how Newton derived universal gravitation from Kepler's laws is not mathematically educated." Do you still think that?*

**BERS**   Cut out the word "mathematically," and then I will agree completely. Absolutely. You don't find that among mathematicians anymore. The whole attitude of mathematicians to physics and applications has changed, I think. Now everybody practices mathematical physics. It's "in." And every young person knows how to operate a computer. I think things happen by themselves. The specialization and super-specialization of mathematics were probably parts of the development, and now we are going through a period of convergence of fields. Maybe they will again separate but—I think—independent of the will or the desire of people. Mathematics develops, somehow, by its own inner laws.

The Bers family: Mary Kagan and Lipman Bers
with Saki, Victor and Ruth.

**An Atypical Mathematician**

MP   *You have described yourself as an atypical mathematician. What makes you atypical?*

BERS   Usually people do their best work when they are young. And this is probably true of very good mathematicians. But in my case—and I think that most people who know my work will agree—what I did after forty was more interesting and more important than what I did before forty.

MP   *Was that because you were in a more settled situation? Up to the age of thirty it sounds as if you were just very intent on surviving.*

BERS   Yes. But then I was here. I worked very intensively during the war years. I don't know. Maybe an accident.

MP   *You said that there were two things that make you atypical. That was the first thing. What was the other thing?*

BERS   I had very few expectations of mathematics. I am very lucky. I think I did better than I expected. I'm not talking now about recognition, which I got more than I deserved, but about being satisfied with the work. Another thing. People usually develop from pure to applied mathematics, and I went from applied to pure. But this could be accidental. I was applied because the war was on and I wanted to do something useful.

MP   *You're seventy years old now, a very young seventy, and you've given us a very nice account of your life, certainly not all of it—you have got to write your autobiography, you must do that—but when we read it—in a few years—I want to know what things will be in there that in some sense you feel especially good about.*

BERS   First comes a wife and children and grandchildren. I was very lucky in those. The fact that I could do any mathematics is really a very unusual thing. Very few people can do it and have the opportunity to do it. I disagree with Adler, who wrote (in the *New Yorker*) that there is no point in being a mathematician unless you can be a great mathematician. That's nonsense. Mathematics is like a gothic cathedral. If you can build a little part of it, it is there—forever—in some sense. At least I have the illusion that it is so. I feel good about a few things I have done in mathematics. They are not great discoveries, but I experienced great joy when I made them, and other people use them occasionally—it is very pleasant.

And another thing I feel good about. I was a good teacher and a good Ph.D. adviser.

As to my human rights work—well, of course, the pleasant thing is always if you can really help somebody. There are a few cases where I feel that the intervention which I and other people organized really helped. I don't think Plyushch would be out of Russia and out of the insane asylum if mathematicians all over the world had not campaigned for him. I am not sure about Massera. Many people put in a lot of work on his case. How much this contributed to his being liberated is hard to say because, after all, he spent eight or nine years in jail. Still he came out alive. Maybe, maybe we helped.

MP   *When did you first become active in human rights?*

**Nonconformity and Survival**

BERS   Well, I had a period of active politics in my early youth. This was not specifically concerned with human rights. Yet I belonged to a certain tradition which always put a great value on human rights. This is—it will sound funny when I say it in English—it is the Martov tradition. Martov was the leader of the Mensheviks. He was a left-wing Menshevik, and some people may consider him close to Lenin, but he was uncompromising about human rights—he protested vigorously when the Bolsheviks reintroduced the death penalty. And I had the pleasure and the honor of being very close to his sister, Lydia Dan. She was an old lady, and I was a young man. She was of his tradition, where you take the defense of human rights as an obvious duty. Later in my life I could do something, and I did, not because I was more interested than before, but because I now had a certain position, a status, which is important.

**MP** *As a political activist you could have lost it all when you were a student. It wasn't like being a radical over here, where you can be a radical and live.*

**BERS** I think that I actually survived because I was a political activist. In catastrophic times it is the people who are not conformists who have a better chance of surviving.

*April 1985 in Berkeley, California (DA, CR).†*

*LIPMAN BERS*    Riga, Latvia, May 22, 1914. Dr. Rer. Nat. 1938, Prague. Field: complex analysis. Davies Professor of Mathematics, Columbia. President AMS,* 1975–76. Colloquium Lecturer (AMS) 1971. Steele Prize (AMS) 1975. American Academy of Arts and Sciences, Finnish Academy of Sciences and Letters, National Academy of Sciences. Books: *Contributions to the Theory of Partial Differential Equations,* 1954; *Mathematical Aspects of Subsonic and Transonic Gas Dynamics,* 1958; *Partial Differential Equations,* 1964; *Calculus,* 1969; *Contributions to Analysis,* 1974; (with I. Kra) *A Crash Course in Kleinian Groups,* 1974.

†The interviews included in this volume took place on the dates and in the locations given after the interview. In some cases there were also follow-up sessions. Interviewers present are identified by initials in parentheses (DA = Donald J. Albers, GA = Gerald L. Alexanderson, CR = Constance Reid).
* Names of principal organizations are abbreviated as follows: AAAS = American Association for the Advancement of Science; AMS = American Mathematical Society; ASA = American Statistical Association; AWM = Association for Women in Mathematics; ICM = International Congress of Mathematicians; IMS = Institute of Mathematical Statistics; IMU = International Mathematical Union; MAA = Mathematical Association of America; NSF = National Science Foundation; ORSA–TIMS = Operations Research Society of America–The Institute of Management Sciences; SIAM = Society for Industrial and Applied Mathematics.

# RALPH P. BOAS, JR.

Ralph Boas calls himself a "quasi" mathematician because, although he has been a mathematician throughout his professional career, he has done many things besides mathematical research. He has been an editor (*Mathematical Reviews* and the *American Mathematical Monthly*), a translator of Russian mathematics, a longtime department chairman at Northwestern as well as a mathematical versifier and humorist. (See, for example, his work under the pseudonym H. Pétard on mathematical methods of catching lions.) He is married to a theoretical physicist, with whom he has had three children, and has always been dedicated to a two-career marriage. "Real mathematicians," he says, "do only mathematics." He prides himself also on "felling a tree so that it falls where I want it to." Following is his "self-profile of a quasi-mathematician."

□ □ □

I was once having dinner with a group of scientists who were reminiscing about how they had come to take up their professions. One (and only one) of the mathematicians had become a mathematician for a logical reason: he had taken an aptitude test at the age of eleven, had been told that he was best suited to being a mathematician, and so a mathematician he had become. I myself drifted into the field for no better reason than that I was too clumsy to be a chemist and happened to be farther along in mathematics than in anything else.

My parents had both graduated from Brown University (with Phi Beta Kappa keys) and gone on to master's degrees. They were married in 1911, and my father took a job in the English department of Whitman College in Walla Walla, Washington, where I was born in 1912. We moved around quite a bit in the next few years, and my sister, now Marie Boas Hall, who was to become a well-known historian of science, was born in Springfield, Massachusetts, where my father was teaching English at Central High School.

Sometime after my eighth birthday, my parents decided that it was high time I had some formal schooling. My mother escorted me to a nearby grade school and explained to the principal that I could read. The principal sent her home, saying that as soon as he had time he would see where I should be placed. When I got home, my mother asked, "What grade did they put you in?" I didn't know, but I said we had had to turn in some written work and we had put "6A" on it. My mother was quite alarmed, but I stayed in the sixth grade. School life was rather difficult, because I was not only two years younger than my classmates but also small for my age.

Both of my parents were gifted teachers. My father also had a talent that I wish I had inherited: he could sit through a committee meeting, never open his mouth, and at the end of the meeting say, in effect, "This is what you want to do," and have everybody agree. In his thirties he published some articles in the *Atlantic Monthly*, but by the time I was old enough to understand what he was doing, he refused to write any more articles, although he was always suggesting fascinating ideas for articles. He did write, alone or in collaboration, a number of textbooks. He and my mother collaborated on a biography of Cotton Mather, and my mother wrote several other biographies. Consequently I learned at an early age to read and correct proofs; this is a skill that I have had many occasions to use.

**Technique before Theory**

I got a good deal of my education from browsing in my parents' extensive library, in particular from the readings for college students that are the English professor's analogue of the algebra and calculus books that arrive in the mathematician's mail. I cannot recall that either parent made any effort to teach me how to write effectively. Any skill that I now have was learned by practice.

I have only vague memories of junior high school, but I remember learning some Latin and a good deal of formal algebra. In particular, we had worksheets with long lists of equations like $2xy^2 = x^3/y$, to be solved mentally for $y$, and fast. I developed a proficiency in simple algebra that lasted for a long time and has been very useful. My mother gave me her college algebra book. I learned from it how to solve word problems, although I remember distinctly that I never really understood them. I could do only the problems that followed the pattern of the examples in the book. Somewhat later my father gave me a table of logarithms, and I rapidly learned the techniques of using it; but, again, I didn't understand why logarithms worked. I still find that understanding tends to come after learning formal procedures, although according to conventional wisdom it should be the other way around. My view is that if you have a firm grasp of technique, you can then concentrate on theory without having to stop and think about the technical details. Perhaps that is why I have always liked languages, where practice generally precedes theory.

When I was twelve, my father became a professor of English composition at Mount Holyoke College. There was a kind of informality at Mount Holyoke and later at Wheaton that I believe still persists at small liberal arts colleges. Students were always dropping in on my parents (who lived close to the campus) to discuss their work or their personal problems. The students were, of course, all women and they tended to treat me like a younger brother or nephew until I was in college myself. Perhaps that is why I have never felt intimidated by women.

The principal of my high school was an enthusiast for mathematics and gave a course in solid geometry after school for me and another student. It is interesting that when I graduated in 1928, I knew about as much

In 1933 as a student at Harvard, where things were done in style: "A style long since vanished."

mathematics (I have been told) as had been required for a mathematics major at Brown twenty years earlier.

In high school I was probably more interested in languages than in mathematics. In my senior year my father asked Mount Holyoke to let me audit a class in first-year Greek. It was understood that I would eventually study the same languages that my parents had studied: French, German, Latin and Greek. After that, they said, I could go on to more exotic languages.

I did not find high school very demanding, and I expect that it was my parents who encouraged me to do various extracurricular things. For several years I helped Miss Hooker, a retired biologist, raise Buff Orpingtons (a rather specialized variety of chicken). I also worked as an assistant to the librarian of the South Hadley Library and learned how to catalogue and mend books. Miss Gault, who worked in the reference department of the Mount Holyoke Library, took me in hand one year and taught me how to use reference materials.

I graduated from high school two months before my sixteenth birthday. My parents thought (correctly) that I was too immature to go away to college, so my father obtained permission for me to audit classes at Mount Holyoke in Greek, German and calculus during the next academic year. Our calculus text was a combination of analytic geometry and calculus; this arrangement has come and gone several times since then.

When it was time to decide on a college, I first thought of Reed; but my uncle, George Boas, who taught philosophy at Johns Hopkins, pointed out to me (as I have subsequently done myself in similar situations) the advantages of a large university where there is more choice of subjects. Consequently I decided to go to Harvard. I say "decided to go" deliberately, because at that time Harvard was accepting, without examination, all students who had high enough rank in their high school classes.

My mother had done some substitute teaching, but up to the time when I started college she had never held a full-time job. In 1929 she decided, for reasons that were never explained to me, to get one, and she became an associate professor in the English department at Wheaton College in Norton, Massachusetts. A year later my father joined her as head of the same department.

I had had classes in both chemistry and physics in high school. I had enjoyed chemistry but had not cared much for physics. In the late 1920's there was beginning to be popular writing about the new physics, and people like my parents tried to understand in a general way what was going on. Of course my high school course was of no assistance, and even the Harvard physics course (which was rather boring) gave me no more understanding of either relativity or quantum mechanics than I had picked up from cocktail party conversation. What I know about these fields I learned much later, from my wife.

## Broken Glassware and Mathematics

At Harvard, since I had some idea of majoring in chemistry and eventually going to medical school, I talked my way into Qualitative Analysis, but my preparation turned out to be inadequate, and that, combined with my record bill for broken glassware, made me give up that idea. That is how I became a mathematics major.

Since I had had a year of analytic geometry and calculus, I thought I ought to be able to handle the next Harvard course, Mathematics 2. My freshman adviser, W. C. Graustein, asked me some questions, including the derivative of the sine funtion (which I didn't know). Since I did know some material that was not in Mathematics 1, he decided that I could learn what I had missed while the rest of the class was learning what I already knew. It worked out all right.

My teacher in Mathematics 2 was E. V. Huntington, who was an early enthusiast for axiomatized mathematics and wrote many articles on axioms for various systems. I knew nothing of that activity, of course, nor of his work on systems for proportional representation. (His system was subsequently adopted by the United States for apportioning representatives to the states.) He also gave a course on Mathematical Methods of Statistics, which I took to replace the second semester of Qualitative Analysis. This course did not pretend to teach any statistics (which was just as well, considering the state of statistics at the time); it was just mathematics. At midterm I had only a C. I said to myself that that would never do if I was to be a mathematics major, so I worked very hard and ended up with an A. Huntington had a number of unconventional ideas—for example, that weight was more fundamental a concept than mass—and he wrote Newton's second law as $F = (W/g)a$.

In my sophomore year I entered the Harvard tutorial system. Each major had a tutor, either a member of the faculty or an advanced graduate student, who was mainly your adviser but also directed your reading. In effect, it was an extra course in the major field, but you did more or less work according to your temperament. In my last two years, my tutor was D. V. Widder, who began by setting me to collect proofs of the fundamental theorem of algebra. This project got me into reading French and German textbooks and then into the periodical literature. (I ended up with a collection of more than thirty proofs; some years later I managed to devise a new one on my own.)

My mathematics course in my sophomore year was called Advanced Calculus, but actually it was more like what we would now call Methods of Mathematical Physics. One semester was taught (from W. F. Osgood's *Advanced Calculus*) by Osgood himself, who used to tell us German jokes. The pace of the mathematics program was leisurely by modern standards; we spent three years on what we now try to cover in two.

**A Vanished Style**

Harvard did things in style, a style long since vanished. In my sophomore year the first of the new Harvard "houses" were opened, and I was assigned to Dunster House. The dining room had printed menus and waitresses to take orders from them. Harvard examinations were printed from movable type by the University Press, which also produced for each department a brochure containing not only course descriptions but also a list of all the Ph.D.'s produced by the department with the titles of their theses. The course descriptions could be tantalizing. The one for Real Variables culminated in "the Riesz-Fischer theorem." We students wondered what that might be. When I took the course from J. L. Walsh, it happened one day that he finished a proof just as the bell rang. "That," he said, as he scooted out of the room, "was the Riesz-Fischer theorem."

In my junior year I took the first course in complex analysis; it was the first course based on rigorous proofs and was supposed to separate the mathematical sheep from the goats. I loved it. There were no textbooks for either real or complex analysis. The instructor lectured; the students took notes. I never thought much about this method of instruction—it was just the way things were—but later it came to seem pointless as long as a textbook could be had. The advent of copying machines has made it even more pointless. However, the escalating cost of printed books may lead to the return of the lecture system. At that point we will be where we were before the invention of printing, when the only way to learn a subject was to listen to someone expound it.

It was about this time that I began to watch the current journals as they came into the library. One day I noticed that Harvard was no longer subscribing to the *Recueil Mathématique* (now *Matematicheskii Sbornik*). Since that journal was mostly in French, I could read it, so I was disturbed enough to ask the then chairman of the department why the subscription had been allowed to lapse. (Perhaps fortunately, I have forgotten who the chairman was.) He replied, "Oh, are the Russians doing anything interesting?"

**A Possible Indic Philologist**

In my junior year I was taking three mathematics courses and wanted something as a distraction. More or less by accident I settled on Sanskrit. The Sanskritist, Walter E. Clark, provided us with a grammar, a dictionary and a text. After a week spent learning the alphabet (forty-eight letters, which combine with one another in elaborate ways), we started reading, learning the grammar as we went. Some people dislike learning a language this way, but I found it congenial. I kept up Sanskrit for two more years and with encouragement might have ended up as an Indic philologist.

During the summer of 1932 I tried to reproduce the proof of a theorem on Taylor series that I had seen in an old paper by Pringsheim. I couldn't do it, and when I went to Cambridge and looked it up, I found out why: the proof was wrong. This eventually led to my first research paper, the story of which I have written up for the *Mathematical Intelligencer*.

There was a senior comprehensive examination in mathematics at Harvard, about which I remember only that we were asked to prove that the distance to the horizon in miles is approximately the square root of $3/2$ of one's elevation in feet. I struggled with this for a long time but could only prove it with $8/5$ instead of $3/2$. It was only when I was walking away from the examination that it struck me that $8/5$ *is* approximately $3/2$.

When I graduated in 1933, I was high enough in my class to be awarded a Sheldon Fellowship, which was not for study but for travel. During 1933–34 I wandered around Europe, visiting places I had read about. In the course of my travels I found a proof of Pringsheim's theorem.

In the fall of 1934 I returned to Harvard and began to get into serious mathematics. I had a semester of modern algebra with Saunders Mac Lane and found it thrilling. I thought of specializing in it, but the second semester (with a different instructor) was so dull that I gave up that idea.

I took a course in potential theory with Oliver D. Kellogg when I was an undergraduate, and would have gone into that field except that Kellogg died. There was, however, a legacy from the course. In Kellogg's book there is a rather complicated derivation of the normalization constant for Legendre polynomials. I found a short proof by using recursion relations, which impressed Kellogg. This is now the standard proof but probably only because the time was ripe for it to be found. However, just at that time Pauling and Wilson were writing their book on quantum mechanics at MIT, and I like to think that Kellogg may have told them about my proof; it is given in an appendix to the book.

On a Sheldon Fellowship (awarded specifically for travel), Boas and a group of friends stumbled upon a skeleton during the course of a ramble in Greece.

Eventually I wrote my thesis with Widder, whose kind of mathematics appealed to me. Before I wrote my thesis, I had written, at Widder's suggestion, a paper on the Hausdorff moment problem. After I had presented my results at a Harvard colloquium, Marshall Stone asked me what I was planning to do next. I told him, adding diffidently that I didn't suppose it was really very interesting. He snapped, "Then why do it?" I took this comment very much to heart. As far as I can remember, I have never since written, "It may be interesting that ...." I say firmly, "It is interesting that ...," on the grounds that if it interests both me and the referee, then it *is* interesting. In fact, I rather pride myself on never having worked on anything that wasn't interesting, at least at the time.

## Uniformity by the Tail

Boas's thesis adviser, D. V. Widder, lecturing at a symposium in his honor.

My thesis was something that Widder wanted someone to work out; it was part of the evidence that led Widder and Hirschman to their theory of convolution transforms. Widder (whose ninetieth birthday was celebrated recently) is a rather formal person; it was only many years after I had left Harvard that he came to address me by my first name. It is always startling when he lapses into a colloquialism. During my senior year I once went to him with something I had worked out, and he said, "This shows that you have uniformity by the tail."

I also had to write a minor thesis. This, as far as I know, is a peculiarly Harvard institution. You are given a topic outside your own field and have to produce an essay on it in three weeks (if in the summer) and four (in term time). I drew dimension theory, about which there was at the time only Menger's book besides the periodical literature. There were two rules: you mustn't do research on your topic, and you mustn't repeat any mistakes that were in the literature. (Menger's book was notoriously full of mistakes.) People, even some now eminent people, have failed the minor thesis by getting carried away and doing research on the assigned topic. I think I have never worked so intensely, before or since, but I was left with the comforting feeling that I could learn anything in mathematics with three weeks' warning. In fact, in my first teaching job I suddenly had to prepare a course in probability, which I had never studied before. Years later I looked at my lecture notes and decided that I had done a pretty good job.

For 1937–38 I got a National Research Fellowship and went to Princeton to work with Salomon Bochner. It was a stimulating place because some of the basic theorems in functional analysis (a term that had not yet been invented) were being worked on there.

Bochner had a number of standard responses to any problem you asked him about. They ranged from "I think this is not very interesting" to "I think this cannot be." Once I got "I think this is difficult" and then solved the problem. When I took the result to Bochner, he said, "I think this is trivial." As Widder used to say, "Everything is trivial when you know the proof."

## Catching Lions with Mathematics

In Princeton I usually had dinner with a group of (mostly) mathematicians. One of the things we talked about was mathematical methods for catching lions. There were many jokes in this vein circulating at Princeton at that time. Below are a few examples:

*The method of inversive geometry.* We place a spherical cage in the desert, enter it, and lock it. We perform an inversion with respect to the cage. The lion is then in the interior of the cage, and we are outside.

*The Peano method.* Construct by standard methods a continuous curve passing through every point of the desert. It has been remarked [by Hilbert] that it is possible to traverse such a curve in an arbitrarily short time. Armed with a spear, we traverse the curve in a time shorter than that in which a lion can move his own length.

*A topological method.* We observe that a lion has the connectivity of the torus. We transport the desert into four-space. It is then possible to carry out such a deformation that the lion can be returned to three-space in a knotted condition. He is then helpless.

Frank Smithies (who was visiting from Cambridge, England) and I undertook to write an article about this interesting field, inventing a few extra methods as we went along. We picked Pondicherry (one of the French enclaves in India) as a pseudonym, spelling it Pondiczery to make it look Slavic; we thought of Pondiczery as being Poldavian like Bourbaki. We submitted our article to the *American Mathematical Monthly* with a cover letter saying that the author, afraid of repercussions, wanted to use the pen name H. Pétard. In an endeavor to establish a reputation for Pondiczery, we imitated Bourbaki by publishing short notes under his name. Later, when I was teaching at the Pre-Flight School during World War II and wasn't supposed to publish anything, Pondiczery wrote a substantial number of reviews for *Mathematical Reviews.*

At Smithies's suggestion I spent the second year of my fellowship in Cambridge, England, to which he was returning. The fellowship was not supposed to allow foreign travel, but I persuaded the authorities to let me go if I paid my own way, which I could do because I had saved enough from my $1600 stipend. In Cambridge I learned quite a lot about England and quite a lot of mathematics. I attended lectures by Hardy, Littlewood and Besicovitch and also Hardy and Littlewood's conversation class (American: seminar), which met in Littlewood's rooms but always without Littlewood.

One day I went into the mathematical library, glanced at the shelf of new journals, but saw nothing of interest. Smithies came in and asked, "Anything interesting today?" "No," I replied in a disgusted tone of voice, "only the *Proceedings of the Lund Physiographical Society.*" Frank went over and picked it up. It turned out to contain Thorin's famous paper on the Riesz convexity theorem and caused a sensation in Cambridge. I now distrust people who want to disregard minor journals.

## Hardy's Three Questions

At that time Hardy was an editor of the *Journal of the London Mathematical Society*. He used to tell referees to ask three questions: Is it new? Is it true? Is it interesting? The third was the most important. I would now add: Is it decently written? I think Hardy took that as a given. If he got a paper that was interesting but badly written, he would ask a graduate student to rewrite it. I know, because I did a couple of such rewrites for Hardy, for authors who subsequently became very well known.

I do not remember having thought very much in England about what I was going to do next. Before I had started to worry, I was offered an instructorship at Duke University. J. J. Gergen, who was chairman at Duke, had had me in his course in Fourier series while he was a Benjamin Peirce Instructor at Harvard. He must have been impressed, because somebody told me later that Gergen had worried that Leonard Carlitz and I might form a "Jewish clique"; however, I can't complain about the way Gergen treated me. Actually, Carlitz and I had very different interests and hardly ever spoke to each other.

## Evening Office Hours

In my first two years at Duke, I slept in a dormitory room but really lived in my office in the physics building. I kept evening office hours, which was popular with the students because, of course, evenings were when they tried to do their homework. Once a student came to see me because he couldn't understand why one problem on his final exam had been marked wrong. It turned out that it had been graded incorrectly; in fact, everybody's paper was incorrectly graded on that problem. We had to re-grade some two hundred bluebooks. The interesting thing was that, at least in my class, only one final grade had to be changed; it was the grade of the student who had complained.

While I was in Cambridge, *Mathematical Reviews* had been founded; when I got home, I found an invitation to be a reviewer. I would have been insulted if I had not been asked, but I couldn't help thinking that reviewing might be a lot of work. In fact, some members of the mathematical Establishment were worried at the time that reviewing might take people away from important research. This has hardly been the case for me. I not only found MR very helpful in my research, but some of my ideas were suggested by papers I reviewed.

## Reviewing and Real Mathematics

Since I had few demands on my time at Duke, I reviewed papers rather fast; consequently I got a lot to review. I eventually decided that I needed to be able to read Russian. My method of learning was to notify MR that I was willing to review Russian papers. I promptly received a four-page Russian paper. All that I had was a dictionary and the knowledge (acquired from a Russian-reading acquaintance) that *-ogo* is a genitive ending and is pronounced "ovo." It took me a week to puzzle out that paper. Ultimately I reviewed quite a number of Russian papers, many of which were useful in my fields of research.

My interest in reviewing was probably the first sign that I was not going to be a real mathematician. Real mathematicians, except for a small number of geniuses, don't do anything *except* mathematics. (My classmate Angus

Taylor claims that this is what his adviser told him was required for a successful career in mathematics.) I was already getting tired of doing almost nothing except mathematics, and over the years I have drifted into peripheral activities. Although I am fond of classical music, I never learned to play an instrument, and I am hopelessly unathletic. However, I grew up in the country and summered on Cape Cod, so I console myself by being able to do some things that my more cultivated colleagues probably can't. I do, for example, know how to sail a boat, shingle a roof, cut grass with a scythe, and fell a tree so that it will fall where I want it to.

**Miss Layne—Glowing Recommendations**

One day in the spring of 1940, when I was in Gergen's office, he mentioned that he had hired a woman to teach on the East Campus (the women's campus, although some of the women had classes with the men on the West Campus). For no particular reason that I could see, he gave me her (very glowing) letters of recommendation to look at. It was time to reserve seats for the next year's campus concert series, and it occurred to me that if Miss Layne liked symphonic music, it would be a friendly gesture to get tickets for her.

There was a complication, because Miss Layne was going to be a half-time student as well as a half-time instructor. I had grown up around college campuses, and I knew perfectly well that faculty don't date students. However, I chose to identify Miss Layne as a colleague rather than a student. I took her to the concerts, and we went on from there. By the next spring we were engaged, and everybody was surprised. We told our news to Gergen with considerable trepidation, but he raised no difficulties about Mary's keeping her job after we were married.

I had heard, in my parents' home, about engaged couples neglecting their work, but nothing like that happened to us. I did some of my best mathematics that spring; and in the multi-section course, of which we each had a section, where the examinations were graded collectively with results tallied by sections, we were very pleased to find that our two classes came out at the top. Mary actually had more teaching experience than I, and I learned a lot from her.

**Ahlfors Shocked**

We were married in June 1941. The United States entered World War II in December 1941. In 1942 the Navy Pre-Flight School was established in Chapel Hill, five miles away, and several of us local mathematicians applied for jobs there in the hope of not being drafted. We taught three classes a day, made up tests and graded papers. The classes included elementary physics as well as mathematics and went very fast. We were allowed fifteen minutes to teach interpolation, which was rather important in those pre-calculator days. The course included enough spherical trigonometry so that we could explain celestial navigation. I had never studied any kind of trigonometry beyond right triangles until I had to teach trigonometry at Duke. Incidentally, when Ahlfors arrived at Harvard in the 1930's, he professed to be shocked that no spherical trigonometry was taught there.

The day at the Pre-Flight School was divided into three segments: Academic, Military and Physical, which rotated through the day on a two-week cycle. On those days when the cadets had been on a twenty-mile hike in the Carolina sun, followed by lessons on how to kill each other with their bare hands, they were not very alert in mathematics class. Some of them were not very sophisticated in mathematics. One cadet, who had a private airplane

# Boas' (Almost) Secret Cambridge Album

At Cambridge young Boas, armed with an unobtrusive and quiet secondhand camera, managed to catch a number of mathematicians unaware before he was "apprehended" by Dame Mary Cartwright.

R. P. B. in 1938 in Cambridge, England.

J. E. Littlewood.

André Weil.

G. H. Hardy.

W. W. Rogosinski.

Dame Mary Cartwright.

A. S. Besicovitch.

pilot's license, was failing mathematics. When he was asked how much gas he would need to carry if he were going to fly two hundred miles at so many miles per gallon, he didn't know whether to multiply or divide. How, the officers asked, was he able to get the right answer? He replied that he did it both ways and took the reasonable answer. They felt that anybody who knew what was a reasonable answer had promise, so they gave him a second chance.

In the spring of 1942 the Navy decided that it wanted no more civilians in the program. Los Alamos was starting, and I interviewed for a job there. Although Hans Bethe, who interviewed me, was very closemouthed, I knew enough to see that they were intending to make what we then called an atom bomb. I didn't get the job, and I have since been very thankful that I didn't. At the same time Harvard was starting a couple of military training programs and recruited me.

It had been understood between Mary and me from the beginning that we were to have two careers, but it hasn't been altogether easy. In the first place, although my parents had both been teaching at the same college for years, there were more antinepotism rules in the 1940's than there are now. (It took twenty years to get Northwestern's abrogated, even though it was not written down anywhere.) Second, there was a general feeling (except at women's colleges) against employing women at all. Of course, under stringent circumstances like a war, the prejudice tended to be forgotten—temporarily. Almost as soon as we arrived in Cambridge, the telephone rang. The Widders were putting us up temporarily, and Tufts wanted to know if Widder knew any candidates for instructorships in mathematics. Widder replied that he had one right there, "if you can use a woman." They could, and Mary taught at Tufts for several years. A few years later, when they needed another mathematics instructor, someone said, "Of course, we don't want a woman." The point is that they no longer thought of Mary as "a woman" but as "Mrs. Boas," a respected member of the department. That didn't stop them from firing her when our first child was born, even though by that time she had her Ph.D. in physics from MIT.

At Harvard I taught primarily in the Navy program (as Mary did at Tufts), but I also taught some regular classes. One of these was a Radcliffe class (Harvard was not yet coeducational), which was better than any other calculus class I have ever seen. The Navy classes were very well disciplined, because if the students stepped out of line, they got sent back to the fleet. I had the satisfaction of seeing some sailors who had started with practically no background learn fast enough so that they came out in the end as commissioned officers.

**Grasping**

By early 1945 it was clear that the war was coming to an end and that the regular faculty would be returning to Harvard. Fortunately for me, just at that time Willy Feller had decided to leave the part-time editorship of *Mathematical Reviews*. The work had increased to the point that a full-time editor was needed. The American Mathematical Society offered me $4,000 a year. I had been getting $4,800 at Harvard, and I held out for that. The AMS thought that I was very "grasping," but since they had no other candidate, they gave in.

By that time Mary was working for her Ph.D. at MIT. We had a nice apartment in Cambridge, and apartments were scarce, so I commuted: fifty minutes on the train to Providence plus a walk up the hill; I did this for five years. The editorship made me temporarily well known in mathematical circles.

Part of my job at MR was to translate the titles of papers that were not in one of the four canonical languages (English, French, German and Italian). Of course I made some mistakes, but usually the reviewers corrected me. The worst problem, which occurred in 1947 when the Soviets started publishing exclusively in Russian or regional Soviet languages, was translating Russian titles, since even the papers in the other languages usually had Russian summaries. At one time there was an organization that issued a list of translated Russian titles, but they weren't always accurate. In some cases I could figure out the correct translation only by mentally putting the alleged translation back into Russian and then translating it.

In one case when I translated the Russian summary of a paper in Georgian, I found that it merely said, "A Russian translation of this paper will appear elsewhere." That, and similar experiences, induced me to learn a little (but only a little) Georgian, which is difficult because it belongs to a language family completely unrelated to the Indo-European languages. I have always been charmed by the fact that the Georgian word for "father" is "mama." This controverts psychologists who have convincing reasons why a child calls its mother "mama." (In case you are wondering, the Georgian for "mother" is "dedi.") The Georgian alphabet seems to have many unexploited possibilities for mathematicians who need new symbols.

MR once received a paper in Gaelic. I looked in the file where reviewers had listed the languages they could read. It included only one person, R. A. Rankin (whom I had met in Cambridge), who claimed to read Gaelic, so I sent the paper to him. The review came back with the note, "I suppose you know who wrote this paper." The author, Rob Alasdair MacFhraing, was Rankin himself in Gaelic disguise.

When I had to cope with a Chinese journal that was wholly in Chinese, I thought that I ought at least to find out who the authors were. I took it to C. C. Lin, and he transliterated the names for me. I asked him what would happen if a name contained a character that he didn't know. He gave me a funny look and said, "I'm supposed to know them all."

**Russians Publish Junk, Too.** When George Mackey told me that he had been learning Russian and was willing to review Russian papers, I sent him the first one that came along in his field. A few days later he said to me, "Did you know that the Russians publish junk, too?" Up to that time, of course, he had seen in translation only the most interesting Russian papers.

Willy Prager, a leading expert on, among other things, the theory of shells, also read Russian. One of his reviews merely said in effect, "This is a paper on shell theory." I complained because a review ought to say what was in a paper. Prager then told me that he himself knew that much deeper results were known in the United States, but they were classified. He hadn't wanted to give the impression that the Russian results were new, but he couldn't say why they weren't. What occurred to me was that if the Russians were publishing material that we classified, what must their classified material be like?

**"What other kind of derivative is there?"** In the early days at MR we had time to edit reviews. I remember when Feller and I went over Abraham Wald's review of von Neumann and Morgenstern's book, *The Theory of Games and Economic Behavior.* The review

R. P. B. relaxing.

had been long delayed. Feller had asked Wald why he had published a paper on game theory before sending in his review. He replied that he had to read only one chapter before writing his paper, whereas he had to read the whole book before he wrote the review. The review was twelve pages long; Feller and I managed to compress it to six pages. For example, Feller deleted "partial" from "partial derivative," saying, "What other kind of derivative is there?"

I became editor in 1945, when MR published 280 pages a year, or about two thousand reviews. The staff consisted of one secretary (Janet Sachs) and me. Between the two of us, we did everything outside of actually setting the type and mailing the issues. On Mondays, Janet gave me the journals that had come in during the past week. I assigned the papers to reviewers (there were about three hundred of them, and I very soon knew them, their fields, their idiosyncracies, and even their typewriters), and the papers went downstairs to be microfilmed. On Fridays they went into the mail.

I had been told that if there wasn't much to do, I needn't come in every day, but that never seemed to happen. One Monday there were only three papers to distribute, but then the mailman came in with a big load of Romanian journals from the war years. After that the work got heavier very rapidly. We had kept up with the German journals quite well, because Otto Neugebauer had been able to arrange for a friend in Switzerland to get them for us, but we hadn't received any Japanese or Italian material. There were few surprises from the war years. The biggest that I recall was Cesari's work on surface area.

We needed more reviewers for Russian papers after the Soviets went all-Russian, and for a while the ones we had were rather overworked. In the late 1940's the American Mathematical Society started translating Russian papers, and for a time that project was run from the MR office.

It was fascinating to have the world's mathematics flowing across my desk, but it got more and more tiring. In 1949 I applied for a Guggenheim Fellowship. At that time (although I didn't know it) Northwestern University was in the process of building a research-oriented department. They wanted a chairman, and I was asked to go for an interview. I remember that I asked the Dean what restrictions there were on the kinds of people I might hire. He replied, approximately, "None now, but two years ago I wouldn't have been allowed to hire you."

In the end I decided that I didn't really want to be a chairman, but Northwestern asked me to join the faculty anyway. Thus I jumped from having been nothing higher than an instructor to being a full professor. The administration worried that since I had been out of teaching for five years, I might no longer be able to teach, so they started me off with a five-year contract. (It was made permanent after the first year.)

With the move Mary needed a job too. It is hard, even now, for a couple to find jobs in the same area, even if not in the same institution. She was eventually hired at DePaul University and rose to a full professorship there. We would have moved to a more congenial location later, but we never found a place where there were two jobs and where we wanted to go.

At that time (1950) the normal course load of a professor was twelve hours a week, although I was given only nine to start with. There was no regular sabbatical system at Northwestern and still isn't, but the University has always supplemented Guggenheim and Fulbright awards and has been generous with leaves of absence. In my case they asked the Guggenheim Foundation to let me postpone my fellowship for a year so that I could start in my new position.

It turned out that it had been a good thing that I had not accepted the chairmanship. I rapidly made myself unpopular with the higher administration by asking them to be more idealistic, in small ways, than they wanted to be. A few years later, after H. T. Davis had retired as chairman, the Dean polled the department about whom they wanted as chairman. Some wanted Walter Scott, who had been acting chairman for a year; some wanted Jean Dieudonné; some wanted me. Although I was still considered unacceptable as chairman, the Dean found a solution. He discovered that the statutes of the University provided that a department could be governed by an administrative committee, which could choose its own front man (to have lunch with the Dean and do everything except make decisions). He called the three of

Dad Boas reading to Anne and Ralph L.

The Boas family in 1962: Mary, Anne, Harold, Ralph L. and Ralph P.

us into his office, gave us our mandate, and walked out. We looked at each other for a while. I knew that Dieudonné wouldn't do anything administrative, so finally I suggested that since Walter had been doing all the work during the past year, maybe it would be a good idea if I took a turn. That was that.

The arrangement had several advantages. In the first place, it allowed me to fit my own teaching schedule around Mary's. It was also ideal in another way: whatever I wanted to do, I had only to convince one of the other two; they were so different from each other that I was sure to get what I wanted from one of them. Things went so smoothly that I was asked to continue for another year. After that year the administration decided that I wasn't so bad after all, and I was appointed chairman for five years. I served two more five-year terms, after which I quit.

One of a chairman's duties is to keep peace in the department. This is not always easy. The chairman can do a certain amount by giving people what they want, but even this has its dangers. H. C. Wang once told me, "The trouble with you is that when I ask you to do something, you do it before I have time to change my mind." Sometimes people have conflicting wants. One day two professors both asked for private conferences, in which each complained bitterly about the other. On another occasion I received a deputation of students who complained about their instructor. They were followed by another group of students who admitted that they were doing something unusual: they wanted me to know what a wonderful teacher they had. Same class, same teacher.

**Keep away from the Office**

I found that as chairman it was best to keep away from my office as much as possible. If I was there too much, I found myself looking for things to make me appear busy.

Mary and I eventually had three children, and we made it a principle that there should always be a parent at home if any of the children were there. As I recall, only once in seventeen years was there a complete jam when I had to engage a sitter. In the early days Mary and I shared a study behind French

*More Mathematical People*

doors. It was an inviolable rule that if either parent was in the study with the doors closed, a child was not under any circumstances to enter the study but was to find the other parent. Mostly, however, we did our work in the study at night.

## A Position Secretly Coveted

As time went on, I came to do less research and more of other things. My involvement with the Mathematical Association of America began when I was invited to a conference of CUPM (the Committee on the Undergraduate Program in Mathematics). I do not have my father's ability to keep my mouth shut. What I said, however, must have seemed relevant, because I was invited to more conferences. I became a member of CUPM, then its chairman, and finally the president of the MAA. After that I became editor of the *American Mathematical Monthly* (a position I had secretly coveted).

As editor of the *Monthly* I inherited a year's backlog of articles. After I had worked these off, I tried to keep most of the main articles at a level appropriate for the majority of the readers, who are typically college teachers, but I did accept occasional articles at a higher level on the grounds that the more sophisticated readers of the MAA deserved to have something now and then.

I was able to maintain some control over the style of the articles by editing them, sometimes rather extensively. The ones that needed the most editing, I regret to say, were articles on teaching mathematics, written by educators. The amount of poor grammar and bad spelling in many articles (in whatever field) was quite distressing. One would hope that one's colleagues would write clearer and more accurate prose than reporters for a daily newspaper, but they don't always.

It has been only recently that editors of the *Monthly* have tried to modify it. Although some MAA members resist any change, the editor can change the format to some extent; modifying the content is more difficult, because the editor can do little more than select from what comes in. In my experience inviting people to write articles does not produce very much usable material. One modification that I made has persisted: changing the color of the cover from year to year.

With his son, Harold, also a mathematician.

At various times I have served on a fellowship panel for the National Science Foundation and on the Committee on the Advanced Mathematics Examination for the Educational Testing Service. Activities like these give me a feeling, perhaps factitious, that I am doing something socially useful. That is one reason why I am not a real mathematician. The best mathematicians either don't get on boards and panels or don't do any work if they are appointed. Real mathematicians (with a few exceptions) do nothing but research and only enough teaching to justify their professorships. I am more likely to think of myself as primarily a teacher. I was, in fact, reasonably successful as a classroom teacher and as a director of Ph.D. candidates. I spent most of my working time for two years editing two volumes of George Pólya's collected papers. Some of my activities have not turned out too well; in particular, CUPM did not live up to its promise, perhaps because we did

This is a mathematician who has just proved a theorem

These are mathematicians who would like to prove theorems, but can't.

Boas has a finely tuned sense of humor.

*More Mathematical People*

not foresee the changes that the computer would bring about and because we expected too much from the teachers.

After I retired, I expected to supplement my retirement stipend by doing things, like translating, that would keep me from being bored. The first year after my retirement, I was asked to teach the first quarter of advanced calculus. At the end of the quarter the department had no more money, but nobody wanted to take the course over, so I taught it without pay for two quarters. There was some static from the administration, but I contended that as Professor Emeritus I was officially entitled to "the privileges of the University," one of which is obviously the right to teach. In the end Northwestern hired me from time to time to do part-time teaching until I no longer had the physical stamina to meet classes.

**"If it isn't fun, why do it?"**   I believe very deeply in the importance of mathematics in general. I am not happy about the dichotomy between "pure" and "applied" mathematics, nor about that between teaching and research. I cannot agree with a past president of my own university, who claimed that only a successful research mathematician can be a successful teacher of mathematics. For many years I tried to be both as well as to carry on with other activities, some of which stemmed from my commitment to a two-career family. I believe that I did an approximately equal share in bringing up our three children and in the essential housework. Naturally enough, as I got older, I no longer kept up with mathematics as carefully as I used to, but I have never completely stopped thinking about mathematical problems, although my ideas tend to turn out to have been anticipated. I have put a good deal of effort into didactic and expository writing. I was nearly seventy when I rescued *Selecta Mathematica Sovietica* from early collapse. I was over seventy when I was invited to become one of the principal editors of the *Journal of Mathematical Analysis and Applications*. At seventy-five I undertook the lexicographical part of the American Mathematical Society's revision of the *Russian-English Dictionary of the Mathematical Sciences*, mainly because nobody else seemed willing to do it.

Some years ago, after I had given a talk, somebody said, "You seem to make mathematics sound like so much fun." I was inspired to reply, "If it isn't fun, why do it?" I am proud of the sentiment, even if it is overstated.

*RALPH PHILIP BOAS, JR.*   Walla Walla, Washington, August 8, 1912. A.B. 1933, Ph.D. 1937, Harvard. Field: complex analysis, Fourier analysis. Henry S. Noyes Professor, Northwestern. President MAA, 1973–74. Lester R. Ford Award (MAA) 1978, Distinguished Service Award (MAA) 1981. Books: *Entire Functions*, 1954; *A Primer of Real Functions*, 1960; (with R. C. Buck) *Polynomial Expansions of Analytic Functions*, 1964; *Integrability Theorems for Trigonometric Transforms*, 1967; *Invitation to Complex Analysis*, 1987.

# PAUL COHEN

Paul Cohen has won two of the most prestigious awards in mathematics (the Fields Medal and the Bôcher Prize), but this is not so surprising as the fact that in an age of increasing mathematical specialization he has won them in two completely different fields: analysis and logic. Switching fields is a risky business for a mathematician, and Cohen was warned by colleagues that he should stick to one thing. "But I've always been too restless," he says, explaining that in taking on David Hilbert's famous first problem, he wanted "[to rip] the universe of sets apart and [put] it back together like no one had done before." What he likes most, he says, is "to take a problem which looks very complicated and find a simple solution. That is the ideal."

□ □ □

**MP** *Since you grew up in Brooklyn, is it safe to assume that you were a Dodgers fan?*

**COHEN** Every kid in Brooklyn was a baseball fan. I was, in fact, a Giants fan, but I've tried to tell people what the atmosphere was like in Brooklyn in the forties and fifties. Brooklyn was like a village inside New York. I remember walking to Ebbets Field. I couldn't afford to buy a ticket to get into the games, but sometimes they would let kids in free. And I remember that October day in 1951 or '52 when Bobby Thompson of the New York Giants hit his famous home run off Ralph Branca of the Dodgers. I was on the Brooklyn College campus by that time, and a moan came up from the entire campus. There was a baseball game called "Brooklyn Against the World" that was sponsored by the *Brooklyn Eagle*. Brooklyn against the world—that was sort of the feeling in Brooklyn, a strange kind of combativeness that we were going to take on everybody.

**MP** *Were your parents born in the United States too?*

**COHEN** My parents were both immigrants. They came over to the U.S. in their teens. They were very typical of the Jewish immigrants of that

Cohen's father, Abraham Cohen.

period. The men had some religious education but almost no secular education. The women had little, if any, of either. My mother's parents hired a tutor one summer to teach her to read Polish, Russian and Yiddish. She always felt somewhat bitter that she had not had more education. In this country she often went to night school, as did many other immigrants at that time. I don't know much about my earlier ancestors. They lived in Poland, or rather Russia, since at that time Poland was just a part of Russia.

**MP**  *What did your father do?*

**COHEN**  My father had several different jobs. I gather there were years in the twenties when he was a fairly successful grocery jobber, but by the time I came along in 1934—I was the youngest of four—life was harder. That was right in the middle of the Depression. During the Depression he did various things. He worked in a factory that manufactured leather goods, for instance, and at the end of his life he drove a taxi.

**MP**  *When did you first get interested in mathematics?*

**COHEN**  At a fairly young age. When my sister Sylvia was doing her school work, I just started looking at the problems in her algebra book. I was about nine at the time. I don't really remember too well, but I was intrigued by them. By seeing how some problems were done, I would try to do others. Somehow I obtained some popular books on mathematics, and about a year later I was helping my brother and sisters with their math homework. When Sylvia started college and was taking trigonometry (they actually taught trigonometry in some colleges then), she would ask me for help. I would read the section and then figure out how to do the problems. At that time I had never met anybody who could give me mathematical advice. I would go to the Brooklyn Public Library, a very good library in those days, and I would try to read whatever math books were available. I picked up some strange and confused ideas which I think really affected my mathematical development. It's very hard for me to explain. Mostly at first I was just doing formal things like solving equations. Then I learned calculus, but it was still rather formal. I just read everything, whatever I could get my hands on. My mathematical education was not at all organized.

Sylvia, who was the first member of our family to go to college, was interested in me. She bought me a book on geometry, sort of a self-study book, at the local five and dime. It was a great eye-opener. Suddenly I saw rigorous proofs. I was able to understand what a proof was, but like many young children I was most interested in computational things. I was interested in solving equations. I knew formulas for the quadratic and the cubic, but then I looked at various books on the theory of equations and they said there was a subject called Galois theory, which was a general theory giving conditions under which an equation could be solved. That there could be such a thing was beyond my wildest comprehension!

**MP**  *I am astonished that you had interests like those at age ten or thereabouts.*

**A Period of Tremendous Intellectual Curiosity**

**COHEN**  In general, my childhood was a period of tremendous intellectual curiosity. I was interested in the biological sciences, the physical sciences—even chemistry appealed to me. I enjoyed reading books about mechanical inventions, electricity—anything. I really didn't distinguish.

Cohen's mother, Minnie Kaplan Cohen, with her father, Samuel Kaplan.

However, math especially appealed to me. If you read something about electricity, for instance, you find out that you need a lab to do anything yourself, but with math you can do problems right away. So I just naturally went further in math. There was one curious obstacle to my education. The main public library didn't want kids browsing through the adult books, but I would just sneak into the math section.

My sister Sylvia played a big role at this time. She had no interest in math herself, but after she started at Brooklyn College she would often get books for me out of the college library. One day I mentioned equations to her and she said, "I'll look in the catalogue for you." She brought back Klein's book on the icosahedron and the solution of the quintic equation. The frontispiece was a diagram of the icosahedral group. I got very depressed when I saw that. I thought that I was really trying to do something very difficult. I just felt that there was a world that was permanently beyond me. That was when I was eleven or twelve.

**MP** *You were discouraged even though you knew that these were very advanced ideas that were ordinarily studied by people considerably older than you?*

**COHEN** Well, I felt that if I could get some help I might be able to handle them, but I had no entree. I couldn't turn to anyone in my family for that kind of help. They didn't discourage me, but they didn't know what to make of me. There were a few people in the neighborhood studying engineering or science who gave me some books after they heard that I was reading math

Paul, the youngest, with his siblings: Sylvia, Tobel and Rubyn.

on my own. And Sylvia continued to get me books from the college library.

Another thing that I remember—she took a survey math course at Brooklyn College from Professor Moses Richardson. He had written a book called *A Survey of Mathematics*. I learned a lot from that book. He had one little section on this, another on that—one chapter contained a bit of calculus and one had some set theory. I particularly remember saying to myself that I didn't think that set theory had much content. I didn't really understand what that chapter was about. It seemed too "verbal." For example, it would say if one circle represents the set of red-haired people and another circle represents the set of left-handed people, then the intersection of the two circles represents red-haired and left-handed people. I particularly remember that it had all this *aleph* stuff. I felt I should understand it but I didn't.

To summarize, by the time I was in the sixth grade I understood algebra and geometry fairly well. I knew the rudiments of calculus and a smattering of number theory, which I liked very much. I felt rather isolated. A lot of teachers are very threatened when they find a child is studying advanced things. And I was reluctant at that time to talk to other children because I felt they found my interest in math somewhat strange.

MP   *You felt that some of your teachers were threatened by your advanced knowledge, but you yourself felt overwhelmed by mathematics. Yet I often see kids who are smart, who are two or three grades ahead of their supposed grade level, and that fact always seems to instill in them a certain confidence.*

**Confidence and Understanding**

COHEN   I had confidence—at one level, you know, a confidence level that said I would do well on school exams, but I was concerned more about really understanding very advanced mathematics. I would have felt differently if I'd had some people to help me over the rough spots. For example, I'll tell you a small thing that bothered me. I learned Cardano's formula for solving a cubic equation, but by trial I found out that it did not give the answers in real terms if all the roots were real. The answer is always in terms of cube roots of complex numbers. This was frustrating to me. Now when I teach algebra, I often ask the students if they have ever encountered the phenomenon and almost none of them has, although it's in books, of course. But that's the kind of rough spot that bothered me as a kid.

I liked calculation very much then. Not so much now. I would send off for catalogues of slide rules. I remember once working out for myself the algorithm for doing cube roots. I didn't particularly want to do cube roots; I just wondered how the binomial theorem could help with things like that.

MP   *Do you think that your mathematical development was different from that of other prodigies?*

COHEN   I wouldn't describe myself as a prodigy. I have occasionally met mathematical prodigies. A few years ago I talked to a boy from Australia. He was just phenomenal, but in a way I felt a little sorry for him. He was being taken to universities to have special tutors and personal direction, so there was not too much left for him to discover completely by himself.

I remember one of the first serious mathematical thoughts I had. I was about nine years old at the time. I read that the Egyptians had the 3-4-5 triangle. At first I thought, "That's the Pythagorean theorem," and then I thought, "No, it's not. That's the converse of the Pythagorean theorem." I don't know if I used those words, but I did understand that it was not the

Pythagorean theorem. Now most people would say, "Yes, I guess that's true, but of course the proof of the converse is immediate." But no, I said to myself, it isn't really proved—I want to see it proved. So I invented a kind of funny proof of the converse of the Pythagorean theorem. I was very proud of it. This kid I just mentioned will never discover little things like that for himself.

**The First Big Adventure**

MP  *It is amazing that all we have been talking about occurred in your elementary school years. What was high school like for you?*

COHEN  Everything really changed when I went to Stuyvesant High School. That was the biggest adventure of my life up to that time. I suddenly met people who have since become well known—Elias Stein, who is at Princeton now; Harold Widom of U.C. Santa Cruz; and Don Newman of Temple University. They introduced me to books beyond the calculus texts and steered me toward serious mathematics.

MP  *Stuyvesant was quite a specialized high school, wasn't it?*

COHEN  Stuyvesant High School and Bronx High School of Science were the two math-science schools. Bronx High School was in the Bronx, obviously, and Stuyvesant was in lower Manhattan and served Brooklyn and Manhattan. There was a third school, Brooklyn Tech, I think it was called, but it was not quite so well known.

There was a remarkable spirit at Stuyvesant. It had nothing to do with the teachers or the facilities or the amount of money that was spent or anything like that. It was great fun just to talk to the other students about a year or two older than myself.

MP  *When did the spirit of Stuyvesant first hit you?*

COHEN  Probably at my first "Math Team" meeting. That was when I met Elias Stein. He was about two years older, and he was reading measure theory and complex function theory. Oh yes, Stuyvesant really seemed quite advanced, but I think that starting mathematics early had given me a certain self-reliance. I felt you didn't learn anything in class, you just figured it out yourself. My mathematical personality has been strongly affected by that feeling. Sometimes I had wrong ideas. I remember, for example, one question that came up when I was talking with Harold Widom. It seems almost humorous now. I was about fourteen, and I was finding out about rigor. I knew calculus in the sense that I could probably easily pass a first-year calculus course, but I asked Harold about a problem about the logarithm in some book I had seen. I thought it was done by some special tricky property of log, but he said, "No, that just states the fact that log is continuous." I thought, "Boy, I really don't understand this continuity concept very well!" But that changed very quickly.

I was also very interested in physics. In fact, I probably would have considered going into physics except for the fact that I didn't know what current research in physics was. I was problem-oriented, and although physics problems seemed cute, they didn't seem to be that deep. They seemed like more or less straightforward applications of mathematics. I think it is harder for a young person to understand what physics is. One has to have some experience and physical intuition to know what the problems mean. I think mathematics is more accessible, but I did like physics a great deal—and still do. It's one of the great sorrows of my life that I haven't done anything in

Going to Stuyvesant High School was the biggest adventure up to that time.

Stuyvesant High School graduation picture: "The best high school in the greatest city in the world."

physics. I still think about it. I have some quasi-crackpot ideas that I have talked to people about now and then.

**MP**  *Did you already have the idea that being a mathematician could be a profession?*

**COHEN**  Oh yes, by high school I knew. You see, Stuyvesant was in the middle of Manhattan—a very sophisticated environment. I didn't meet any prominent mathematicians, but I certainly knew the names of prominent mathematicians.

I must say though, in spite of how great Stuyvesant was for me, I do have some regrets about my high school days. Stuyvesant is very close to NYU, and although once or twice I went over there, I didn't make any contact with people. I really should have. Peter Lax, whom later I got to know quite well, had also gone to Stuyvesant and he would have helped me greatly. But I didn't know about him at the time. I had very poor advice, even in high school.

**MP**  *When did you graduate from high school?*

**COHEN**  I had skipped a few grades and so I finished Stuyvesant at sixteen, but by the time I finished I had read Birkhoff and Mac Lane's algebra and Titchmarsh's book on the theory of functions—again there were some parts in the latter that I didn't understand well. I had also looked at Landau's book on number theory quite a bit but, again, I don't know how well I understood it because my reading of it was a bit dilettantish.

All in all, I had done quite well at Stuyvesant. The spirit there was very competitive. We were ranked according to our overall grade average, and I was proud of the fact that I was ranked sixth "in the best high school in the greatest city in the world." That's how we thought of ourselves. We were quite elitist. I had also been one of forty national winners in the Westinghouse Science Talent Search—that year Stuyvesant produced four of the forty—so I got various scholarship offers.

**MP**  *What was your project for the Talent Search?*

**The Second Big Adventure**  **COHEN**  I wrote an essay on relativity which contained a proof of the addition formula for velocities. Later someone told me that what I had done was well known. The prize didn't amount to much. For being one of the forty top winners I got one hundred dollars! Times were tough. That was 1950. I felt it would be a big strain on my family even to have to pay my living expenses away from home so I ended up going to Brooklyn College.

I studied seriously there, but I felt bored. Strangely enough—I don't know why—again I didn't travel up to NYU or Columbia. I did go once to City College and heard Martin Davis lecture on logic—I didn't know anything about the subject in those days. I wasn't aware of whatever research was going on at Brooklyn. Also I didn't enjoy the routine of all the required courses. I really wanted to do math. It happened that some of my friends had gone off to the University of Chicago. It was a very exciting and innovative place at that time and would take people for graduate study who had had just two years of college. One of the professors, Adrian Albert, had heard about me from my friend Ed Posner, and he wrote to me, "If you apply, I think we can give you something." So I applied and at nineteen went off to Chicago. That was the second great adventure of my early life.

*More Mathematical People*

The other day I bumped into Irving Kaplansky, who was at Chicago when I was there. I told him that one of my first memories of Chicago was walking down the corridor in Eckhart Hall and hearing him say that he had just proved that every B* algebra is a C* algebra—he was handing out mimeographed sheets in the hall. I thought, "Boy, you know this is where mathematics is being made—a B* algebra is a C* algebra!" Then I thought, "What is a B* algebra?" I knew then that I was at a topflight school!

Chicago was truly exciting. Marshall Stone had come around 1947 or 1948, and he had revived the department. I came in 1953 and, according to Kaplansky, that was the heyday of Chicago. The atmosphere, the faculty, and the students were all really good. The students were left alone in just the right way. Of course there was the pressure of having to pass certain exams. I had some anxieties, but on the other hand I felt that other students had done well and so I probably would do well too.

**Drifting into Analysis**     MP     *How soon did you come in contact with Antoni Zygmund after you came to Chicago?*

COHEN     Not right away. The first couple of years I floundered a bit. I found it very difficult to settle on one subject. I was interested in number theory—it seemed closest in spirit to problem-solving—but there was actually very little number theory at Chicago at that time. The mathematics there was more abstract. I felt that number theory was my first interest, but I wasn't making progress in it. To some extent I drifted into analysis, which of course was Zygmund's field. I didn't really decide. Analysis wasn't my first choice, I just saw what was available. There was a very good group around Zygmund. He himself was a little bit more classical than I wanted to be. I worked in the area he suggested, but I wanted to do—slightly more modern things. Well, I was sort of torn, but I became an analyst although I didn't really have that field in mind at the start.

MP     *What kind of teacher was Zygmund?*

COHEN     He was wonderful with students. He had one trait which I wish I could emulate. He made everybody feel extremely comfortable. He and his students talked to each other a great deal and had very good relationships. In some ways he was not really interested in the more abstract modern things, but he had a knack for finding the interesting problems in his own field. He got absolutely the most out of his students. He was—and is—a very modest man, but he has been very influential. Have you ever seen the genealogical chart of Zygmund students and students of Zygmund students? It's quite impressive.

MP     *He sounds as if he must have been perfect for you, given the developmental pattern you've described.*

COHEN     That's true. I was also very inspired when I met Raphael Salem at a conference at Chicago organized by Zygmund and Salem. They had both worked on the problems in trigonometric series that I was working on, but at the moment Salem seemed more interested in them.

The only thing I would object to about my Chicago training was that in some sense Zygmund had to hold classical analysis all by himself, and it was a heavy load for one man. I liked the modern approach, but I wanted to know the classical as well. There really wasn't enough analysis at Chicago.

I should mention also that when I first came to Chicago I had a mild interest in logic, which arose in an unusual way. It came through my interest in number theory. I had never studied logic. Although I had heard of Gödel's theorem, I hadn't paid much attention to it. Still I had been rather intrigued by it. I remember looking at Martin Davis's notes of a course given by Post at City College. I only looked at them cursorily, but it seemed to me that the subject of logic was more philosophical than mathematical. Because of my interest in number theory, however, I did become spontaneously interested in the idea of finding a decision procedure for certain identities, such as the famous Rogers-Ramanujan identity. I thought that a procedure might exist analogous to, let's say, checking an identity in algebra between polynomials. There are various famous identities involving formal power series. Of course, most of them, as I've understood later, are really connected with a certain branch of modular functions, but at that time they appeared to me to be of purely combinatorial interest. I saw that the first problem would be to develop some kind of formal system and then make an inductive analysis of the complexity of statements. In a remarkable twist this crude idea was to resurface in the method of "forcing" that I invented in my proof of the independence of the continuum hypothesis.

At the time these ideas were not clearly formulated in my mind, but they grew and grew and I thought, well, let's see—if you actually wrote down the rules of deduction—why couldn't you in principle get a decision procedure? I had in mind a kind of procedure which would gradually reduce statements to simpler and simpler statements. I met a few logicians at Chicago and told

David Hilbert (1862–1943), who in 1900 proposed a list of twenty-three important problems, the solutions of which he felt would result in progress in mathematics during the coming century.

them about my ideas. One of them, a graduate student too, said, "You certainly can't get a decision procedure for even such a limited class of problems, because that would contradict Gödel's theorem." He wasn't too sure of the details, so he wasn't able to convince me by his arguments, but he said, "Why don't you read Kleene's book, *Metamathematics*?" So I looked at Kleene's book. It is a massive book, and I was really concerned only with the one rather small section, which was the proof of Gödel's theorem. I read the proof over, but I was a little mistrustful and thought there was something circular about it. Then one day Kleene came down from Wisconsin and gave a talk at Chicago. I remember that day well. Afterwards someone introduced me, and I asked him point-blank: "Does Gödel's proof cover this class of problems?" He asked me some questions, thought for a while, and then said, "Definitely!" "Well," I thought, "this man obviously knows." So I decided to read Gödel's proof more carefully and, of course, was then convinced. But I still had no serious interest in it.

One other recollection connected with logic—I have this memory of myself standing in the library at Chicago and looking at a list of famous problems—perhaps it was even Hilbert's list. It included the problem of the continuum hypothesis, and I said to myself, "That's one problem that I really don't understand." I wondered what would it actually mean to solve it. I had a feeling that it really wasn't a problem in the same sense as other mathematical problems, but I definitely thought that it was something which I wasn't interested in.

MP   *So how did it happen that you finally did get involved in working on the problem of the continuum hypothesis? That was a real challenge—to try to get a satisfactory answer to Cantor's question of whether the transfinite cardinal number of the continuum of real numbers is the next largest after the transfinite cardinal of the integers!*

COHEN   Well, in Chicago I worked on the Littlewood problem, which was of course a problem in harmonic analysis, and in the end I was very happy with my partial solution of it. Then I went to MIT and started working on other branches of analysis. I really saw myself as an analyst, and I thought analysis was where I belonged. Then I came to Stanford in 1961.

During my first year I was at a departmental lunch one day with Sol Feferman and Halsey Royden. They were talking about a "consistency proof" for mathematics. I was a little bit distrustful of the idea of a consistency proof but I said, "If you really want an informal consistency proof, you could get one for all of set theory if in some sense you would suitably define your objectives and what you mean by a consistency proof." Sol was distrustful of such a philosophical approach, but I began to think about it. I had in mind a kind of vague induction scheme to show how all concepts could be more solidly based on previous concepts until you hit rock bottom and were satisfied. In this way you could in a sense convince yourself philosophically that set theory is based on some kind of truth. I tried to give a couple of lectures on the idea but I felt that Gödel's theorem, which says you can't prove the consistency of a system within itself, was always lurking in the background. If you tried to get around it by proving something philosophically appealing, you'd always run into some objection. You couldn't get around Gödel's theorem. However, because I had thought about the subject informally for several years, I thought I had developed some intuition about set theory, to which I was somewhat attached. I felt that I understood matters, but I also felt that I couldn't convince anyone, so to speak. Still the whole question seemed a side issue to me, not having any purely mathematical interest but being rather more philosophical—something to talk to students about in casual conversation. But I wondered whether there was any problem to which one actually could apply one's intuition.

**"Why not investigate the continuum hypothesis?"**

I don't know who said it to me, perhaps it was Sol Feferman, but somebody eventually said something like, "Well, if you think you understand set theory and you think it's consistent, why not investigate the problem of the continuum hypothesis?"

Not being a specialist in the field at that time, I did not know precisely how the problem was regarded. What I do remember is that the independence of the continuum hypothesis did not seem to be regarded as a really well posed problem. People said, "Well, what would it mean 'to solve it'?"

Gödel had published a famous article in the *American Mathematical Monthly* entitled "What Is Cantor's Continuum Problem?" I don't think I had read it, or at least not carefully. In general, I had the feeling that people thought the problem was hopeless since there was no new way of constructing models of set theory—indeed they thought you had to be slightly crazy even to think about the problem. It wasn't that it was considered such an impossible problem, but it seemed to be tied up with the philosophy of mathematics rather than with mathematics itself. No one specifically said so, but there was a feeling that something radically new would have to be done to solve it. Also, actually, I didn't get the impression that mathematicians not in logic were all that interested. That may sound strange, but it seemed true at the time. All in all, the problem seemed to be in a kind of limbo.

I was probably more interested in the problem of the axiom of choice at that time, because for many mathematicians the axiom of choice is used more frequently and plays a more important role than the continuum hypothesis. Philosophically people may feel that the problem of the continuum hypothesis is more interesting, but I was thinking more from the

Paul and Christina Karls Cohen, who met in her native Sweden, celebrating their fifth wedding anniversary.

Cohen in 1966, the year he was awarded the Fields Medal for solving (or, as some say, "unsolving") the problem of the continuum hypothesis.

**A New Notion of Truth**

point of view of what mathematicians use. For a few months I worked intensively on proving the independence of the axiom of choice. Then, for various reasons, I thought that some of my ideas were approaching those used by Gödel in his consistency proof of the axiom of choice, but my knowledge of his work was mostly hearsay because I still hadn't actually read his book. When I finally read it, I saw that I was really rediscovering known work. But—and this may be a controversial thing to say—I didn't really feel that Gödel's proof was understood very well by mathematicians. People evidently thought it was much more arcane than it was, possibly because of the rather formalistic exposition. It was after my work, I think, that people saw that the basic ideas were simpler than they were sometimes thought to be.

At that time I actually had ideas which were very close to the final solution of the problem of the continuum hypothesis. I had, intuitively, a very strong philosophical feeling about the direction the proof should go; nevertheless, I felt totally frustrated. I was so low at one point that I stopped thinking about the problem for four or five months. Then, during the winter holidays at the end of 1962, I went on a long trip with my wife-to-be, touring the Southwest, taking in the Grand Canyon and all that. I spent many hours in the car driving, and I began to get a strong feeling of confidence that the thing could be done. I didn't feel that the difficulties were entirely technical. I still felt, however, that there was a kind of philosophical conspiracy which was preventing me from pushing through, so I was still discouraged, and I let the problem lie fallow for some time even after I came back here.

It was about April 1963 that I started getting closer and closer. I suddenly felt that I had the general idea of what this new notion of "truth" was that I was looking for. It was still quasi-philosophical, and I really couldn't prove anything yet. But then I suddenly saw that the whole thing was beginning to fit together. I remember there was a period of about a week when I had a notion which was very close to my final notion. I was talking to a logician in the philosophy department about it in a general sort of way, and at one point he said to me, "Well, you know, you have some interesting ideas, but this idea you have is—I'm sure—wrong." I wasn't discouraged when he said that because I took it for exactly what I think it was; namely, things were becoming so specific that it was hard for someone to believe that there was a whole system of set theory that could be constructed with such ease—that you could have such control over it. I said to him, "Boy, once you can do this you can do just about anything!" In other words, you could handle almost all the famous set theory problems in a similar manner. And this seemed very hard for him to swallow. The reason he thought I was wrong was precisely because I was so close to the truth.

By the middle of April I thought I had solved the problem. What made it so exciting to me was how ideas which at first seemed merely philosophical could actually be made into precise mathematics. I went up to Berkeley to see Dana Scott and run the proof past him. I was very, very excited. At a coffee shop I bumped into an old Chicago friend who asked, "What brings you up to Berkeley?" And I said, "Well, have you heard of this problem of the continuum hypothesis?" From his reaction it began to dawn on me that my solution of the problem was going to excite people. Two months later Gödel gave the proof his stamp of approval.

MP *That's quite a story. Yet even after your work somebody like Donald Martin has described the continuum hypothesis as being "in the curious position that there is serious disagreement as to whether it has been solved and there is related disagreement as to whether the problem, in the natural way of understanding it, is a mathematical problem at all."*

**The Only Possible Solution**

COHEN   Would I myself say it's a mathematical problem? Well, philosophically, if you really believe sets exist—I mean, if you adopt the extreme platonic position—you can ask, what is the answer? Certainly Gödel himself had the platonic view that the question demanded an absolute answer and that, therefore, neither his proof of the consistency of the continuum hypothesis with the axioms of set theory nor mine of its independence from them was a final answer. My personal view is that I regard the present solution of the problem as very satisfactory. I think that it is the only possible solution. It gives one a feeling for what's possible and what's impossible, and in that sense I feel that one should be very satisfied. There are further problems, but they are fairly technical ones. If I were a betting man, I'd bet no one is going to come up with any other kind of solution. There will be philosophical papers, but I don't think any mathematical paper will say that there is any answer other than the answer that it's undecidable.

MP   *It must have required a lot of courage to take up a problem of that nature, and in a completely new field, at that point in your career. You had started out as an analyst. You'd already done your work on the Littlewood problem and were about to be awarded the Bôcher Prize for that. You were just an assistant professor at Stanford, so you must have been very concerned with promotion, and yet there you were driving through the desert and thinking about logic. Most people would have stuck to the field in which they had already had successes.*

**Always Too Restless**

COHEN   As a matter of fact, I was told by many people that I should stick to one thing, but I have always been too restless.

MP   *I still think you were fairly courageous.*

COHEN   I don't know that I would say that. There wasn't that much choice. You're stuck with whatever personality you've got. You just have to be what you are. So it wasn't a decision that I felt I had much to do with. I understand what you're saying but, no, I didn't think of it that way. I felt that it was what I had to do. I needed a change from analysis. I just couldn't work on more analysis at that time.

MP   *You feel then that you weren't consciously changing your direction but were simply following your interest? Do you think this came out of the fact that you started your education, as you have said, by moving around?*

COHEN   That may be a partial explanation. I think in a way it's very bad to start moving around that young because you tend to develop bad work habits. It becomes hard to work on subjects that require systematic work. But I think that to a large extent with me it's more a case of personality. I'm just a restless person. However, I certainly wouldn't say that I was unaware of the career pressures you mentioned, and I did feel a little foolish spending so much time thinking about consistency questions and not getting anywhere. I just felt I had invested too much to turn back. People say that for better or for worse you will probably do your best work by the time you're thirty, and I was approaching twenty-nine.

**MP**  *Do you agree with that idea?*

**COHEN**   I tend to think that you are at your peak around thirty. I'm not saying you won't equal it. I would like to think you could. But I don't think you will ever do better. That's my gut feeling. I haven't checked it out statistically.

**The Big Problems**   **MP**   *At the time when you were working on the continuum hypothesis what did you consider to be the really big problem or problems in mathematics?*

**COHEN**   The big problems? Well, probably things that I wasn't going to work on.

At the time I started being interested in the continuum hypothesis, I was working hard on a certain problem in differential equations. Again it was one of those problems that involve lots of machinery, and I am always trying to do things a little bit more primitively. I also wanted to do things completely independently, and that was bad. I later realized that the problem

With his youngest son, Charles, after receiving an honorary doctorate from USC.

couldn't be done that way. I would like to have solved it, but I didn't. Ehrenpreis solved it using sophisticated cohomology machinery, and Malgrange gave a somewhat similar proof. I never did find a simple method, and I doubt if any exists. I was also attracted to certain problems in harmonic analysis. From my early days I remember problems that I thought were very romantic. One of those, the famous Mordell conjecture, which gives an almost complete solution for Fermat's last theorem, was proved just a couple of years ago by Faltings. I always had it in the back of my mind as one of the great problems.

I worked on one very famous problem when I was a graduate student at Chicago. It's a funny story. I had learned about the problem through Landau's book. I admire that book. It's this big three-volume work, and it contains a theorem of Siegel's that I thought was one of the most beautiful theorems I'd ever seen. I started thinking about the ultimate conjecture of which Siegel's theorem was a step along the way. An English number theorist from Cambridge, Swinnerton-Dyer, was visiting Chicago, and I told him about my interest in the problem. He replied, "That problem will not be solved in our lifetime." Then one day he knocked at my door and said, "I have received a letter from Cambridge. It appears I was wrong. The problem has just been solved by Klaus Roth." In fact, Roth got the Fields Medal for his theorem on approximation of algebraic numbers, which solved the problem. Actually I had been thinking along the same general lines, but I didn't take the key step that Roth did. I didn't have completely wrong ideas; however, there was a main idea in Roth's proof that I wasn't at all close to. That was one of the first problems that I really thought I was going to give a whirl.

Off and on I have thought about various well-known problems, but I have never really thought that there was a single big problem in mathematics. Now if you'd ask me about physics—I have always thought that clearly there is one central problem in physics; namely, to get a unified field theory. That is one reason, I think, that physics appeals to me so much. But in mathematics I have never had the feeling that there was one problem that was dominant. I think the Riemann hypothesis does play a very important role. A

The Cohen boys: Steven, Charles and Eric. Is there a mathematician among them?

*More Mathematical People*

Cohen remembers conversing as a small boy in Yiddish with his maternal grandfather.

Since Jewish tradition decrees a child cannot be named for a living person, Cohen was named after his mother's paternal grandfather, Pesach (Paul) Kaplan.

well-known mathematician who just came through Stanford was saying that he still thinks that there is no other problem like it in mathematics: when it's done it will be the death knell in a certain sense for a whole era. There is no other problem which appears to tie so many things together and which appears to be sort of simple. It doesn't seem to be a technical problem. Sometimes, you know, you feel that mathematicians raise a tricky question and then spend a long long time trying to answer the question which they themselves have raised. On the other hand, the Riemann hypothesis seems to be a completely natural problem.

**MP**   *Have you thought some about it yourself?*

**COHEN**   Yes [with an embarrassed laugh], I have to admit that I have. At various times I've thought I have had good ideas. In fact, I had a rather intense period of working on it. It's still one of my great hopes but not one very likely to be realized.

**MP**   *You feel that basically you're a problem solver?*

**COHEN**   Yes, I would say that. I'm not particularly proud of it though. I don't think it's a good thing to be, but I don't think I've had much choice.

**MP**   *Why don't you think it's a good thing to be?*

**COHEN**   I mean it's a somewhat, well, egotistical way of being. You know—you want to do one problem. There are other people who have a larger view of mathematics. I would regard it as a higher activity for someone to have a wider perspective from which many new ideas and interactions emerge.

**MP**   *You really feel that?*

**COHEN**   Yes, I do. Take a man like Poincaré—the classic example. He had many interacting ideas from dynamics and topology and other fields. Another example, someone whom I've always admired, is Hermann Weyl. But I don't think I had much choice about the kind of mathematician I am.

**MP**   *What was the personal effect on you of solving such a famous problem as the continuum hypthesis—Hilbert's first problem—at such an early age?*

**COHEN**   I wasn't so young. I was twenty-nine.

**MP**   *Twenty-nine seems pretty young for a mathematician when you consider the amount of mathematics that one has to know before getting into a subject today.*

**COHEN**   Well, in the case of that particular problem I certainly had a different point of view from the conventional one. I would say it was a kind of impudence that I was going to rip apart the universe of sets and put it together in a way that no one had ever attempted.

**MP**   *What about the method of "forcing" that you developed for your proof? You haven't really carried on with that, have you?*

**COHEN**   No, I haven't. So many people jumped in so quickly I felt a little bit swamped, and I didn't really see any radically new application. It was clear that some routine results could be gotten. But it really surprised me how people used it more than I thought they would—even in things not related to set theory.

You know, once a problem is solved, I get a little bit bored. I guess that's the price you pay for being a problem solver. I am not really interested in problems that don't seem to stand out. The one problem related to the continuum hypothesis which I wanted to solve was one which Robert Solovay solved. It involved really new ideas. That was the problem of Lebesgue measurability. I thought it was a natural question, and he gave a very pretty solution. I have always wanted to find a simpler proof but I never could, and now it's clear why I couldn't. His proof involves another axiom—the axiom of inaccessible cardinals. I thought that was a defect. It has turned out it is not a defect—it's an essential element, as was shown by the Israeli mathematician Shelah.

**Every Mathematician's Ideal**

MP *So in certain cases you would enjoy proving something in a simpler and more direct way?*

COHEN   Yes, in some cases; however, I think rather that I have a mentality of enjoying the challenge of a difficult problem and going directly for it. That's primary, but it's somewhat curious that in a certain sense the continuum hypothesis and the axiom of choice are not really difficult problems—they don't involve technical complexity; nevertheless, at the time they were considered difficult. One might say in a humorous way that the attitude toward my proof was as follows. When it was first presented, some people thought it was wrong. Then it was thought to be extremely complicated. Then it was thought to be easy. But of course it *is* easy in the sense that there is a clear philosophical idea. There were technical points, you know, which bothered me, but basically it was not really an enormously involved combinatorial problem; it was a philosophical idea.

I think to some extent that what I would like to do most is to take a problem that looks very complicated and find a solution that is ideal. I think that's what almost every mathematician really wants to do. And I would like to think that the solutions of the great problems in mathematics have that character. Hopefully the Riemann hypothesis, if it's solved, will have that character.

*July 1985 in Stanford, California (DA, CR).*

*PAUL JOSEPH COHEN*   Long Branch, New Jersey, April 2, 1934. M.S. 1954, Ph.D. 1958, Chicago. Fields: analysis, logic. Professor of Mathematics, Stanford. Research Corporation Award 1964, Bôcher Prize (AMS) 1964, Fields Medal (IMU) 1966, National Medal of Science 1967. American Academy of Arts and Sciences, National Academy of Sciences. Book: *Set Theory and the Continuum Hypothesis*, 1966.

# GEORGE B. DANTZIG

Early in his career George Dantzig, the "father of linear programming," invented the powerful simplex method, which has applications in innumerable fields — an achievement for which some think he should have received the Nobel Prize in Economics. His mathematical accomplishments are especially noteworthy in view of the trouble he had with algebra in junior high school: "To be precise, I was flunking." As a graduate student, he arrived late to Jerzy Neyman's class one day, copied down what he thought was a homework assignment, and solved a famous, up to that time unsolved problem in statistics. Although his work is generally thought of as applied mathematics, he says he has never been able to tell the difference between applied and pure mathematics — and doesn't believe that there is any.

□ □ □

**MP**   *Professor Dantzig, thanks for taking time to talk about yourself today.*

**DANTZIG**   What's this "Professor Dantzig" stuff?

**MP**   *Okay, what should I call you?*

**DANTZIG**   Your name is Don, right? Do you remember my first name?

**MP**   *It's George.*

**DANTZIG**   Do you remember my middle name?

**MP**   *It's Bernard.*

**DANTZIG**   What does George Bernard suggest?

**MP**   *The well-known writer named George Bernard Shaw?*

**DANTZIG**   That's right. My father, Tobias Dantzig, was both a writer and a mathematician. He hoped that I would be a writer, and so he named me after George Bernard Shaw. He named my younger brother Henri Poincaré Dantzig after the great mathematician Henri Poincaré. My brother did, in fact, become a mathematician. He worked as an applied mathematician for

Henri Poincaré (1854–1912) was Tobias Dantzig's mathematical hero.

the Bendix Corporation until he died in 1972 at age 54.

**MP**  *I know your father's books, especially the wonderful* Number: The Language of Science, *but nothing much about him personally—except that he was born in Russia and studied in Paris with Poincaré.*

**DANTZIG**  Paris is a place where professors don't pay much attention to students so I can't say precisely what my father's relationship to Poincaré was. I do know that he attended his lectures, studied his works, and admired him greatly. One of his books is entitled *Henri Poincaré.*

**MP**  *How did your father get to the United States?*

**DANTZIG**  He came to this country twice, once before he married my mother. On that first trip he visited his aunt in South Carolina whose family owned a general apparel business. He worked for them for a while as a peddler. He must have decided it had no future, for he returned to Paris. My mother, Anja Ourisson, had grown up in Poland and was studying mathematics at the Sorbonne at the time she met my father. After their marriage they emigrated to Oregon, where my father worked as a lumberjack. In those days gangs of young men were hired to fell trees and nearly worked to death. Later he had a job as a road worker. On my birth certificate he is listed as a painter, probably a house painter. As a result of all that hard manual work, he developed huge arm muscles.

**MP**  *How did he manage to get back into mathematics?*

**DANTZIG**  My father believed that he could never get a job in a university because of his heavy Russian accent, but one day at the public library he ran into Frank Griffin, the head of the mathematics department at Reed College, who told him he was crazy to be working as a lumberjack and road builder. Griffin assured him that with his academic credentials he could get a job in any university. That was a turning point in my father's career. He applied to Indiana University and was hired. He didn't have a formal Ph.D. at the time, but he soon acquired one while a professor there.

**MP**  *Did he quit worrying about his accent after that?*

(Left) Tobias Dantzig (1884–1956), father of George and author of such mathematical classics as *Number: The Language of Science.* (Right) Anja Ourisson Dantzig, mother of George, was a student of mathematics at the Sorbonne but later specialized in languages at Johns Hopkins.

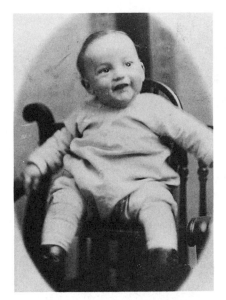

"The father of linear programming" at the age of one year.

With his younger brother, Henry, now deceased, who became an applied mathematician.

**DANTZIG** I don't think he ever worried much about his accent. His spoken English was otherwise fluent, and he was known for his marvelous English writing style.

**MP** *He obviously was very important in your life. Can you tell me a little bit more about him?*

**DANTZIG** He was a dynamic person with a very strong personality. He knew the classics and could quote them in Greek, Latin, and a dozen other languages. He was an excellent teacher and quite a raconteur. In the 1920's many of his friends were very interested in the philosophy of science. He used to hold salons in our home. From age eight until I was sixteen, I used to sit in the corner and listen to the smart-alec intellectuals of the 1920's expounding. I learned a lot but said little. After a while I began to suspect that they really didn't know what they were talking about. Perhaps this explains why to this day I can never get very excited about philosophical ideas.

**MP** *You mentioned to me earlier that there wasn't much money when you were growing up.*

**DANTZIG** We were always very poor. When my father taught at Johns Hopkins in 1919–20, we wore secondhand shoes. In the 1920's my mother obtained a master's degree in French from Johns Hopkins in order to qualify for a job at the Library of Congress. She was a linguist and a specialist in Slavic languages. Even with the income from two salaries, we were still poor. I don't remember ever having pocket money. There were hardly any jobs for kids. I did have a paper route once. My father never earned very much. When he retired as head of the math department at Maryland shortly after World War II, his pension was only $2,250 a year, which was half his yearly salary. This happened just before the post-war inflation. He moved to Los Angeles where he tried to pick up extra money teaching, consulting, doing that sort of thing. Although his health was failing, he managed somehow. He never asked us, his children, for money. I don't know how he ever managed. Although he had been in Los Angeles only a short time, when he died in 1957 hundreds of people came to his funeral. Nobody who ever met him forgot him. There was something magical about the way people were attracted to him.

**MP** *Can you remember when your own interest in mathematics was aroused?*

**Flunking Algebra**

**DANTZIG** Yes. I was in the ninth grade of Powell Junior High School in Washington D.C. My father was teaching nearby at the University of Maryland. I was doing very poorly in my first course in algebra. To be precise, I was flunking. I remember walking home one day, furious with myself. How is it, I asked myself, that I, a son of a mathematician, do poorly while all the other kids in the class do so much better? I was very angry with myself. After that I sailed through algebra.

**MP** *It sounds as if you had a lot of self-confidence by grade nine.*

**DANTZIG** Confidence came slowly. My interest in school work up to the seventh grade had been zero. I then began to blossom in science courses. Later on, after recovering from my poor start in algebra, I began to get top

Dantzig's parents couldn't afford to buy him (rear row center) a copy of his second grade picture, but he was awarded one for winning the long division contest.

marks in mathematics. I was good in math and science in high school. I was on the chess team. I can't remember being interested in any other subjects. I was certainly not good in spelling or grammar.

**MP**  *Do you remember any influential teachers?*

**DANTZIG**  Yes, especially Mr. Gilbert, my mathematics teacher at Central High School. I took geometry from him. Geometry really turned me on. Another important influence was Abe Seidenberg, who entered high school one year after I did. We did our math together and became good friends.

**MP**  *Abraham Seidenberg, the projective geometer?*

**DANTZIG**  Yes. He went on eventually to study with Oscar Zariski at Harvard. Later he was a professor at Berkeley.

**MP**  *I studied from his book,* Lectures on Projective Geometry.

**Thousands of Geometry Problems**

**DANTZIG**  Projective geometry was like mother's milk to me, to quote Eliza in Shaw's *Pygmalion*. I was brought up on it. My father taught me by giving me problems to solve. He gave me thousands of geometry problems while I was still in high school.

**MP**  *Thousands?*

**DANTZIG**  I would say over ten thousand. But it was I who asked for problems. After he gave me one and I came back with a solution, he would say, "Well, I'll give you another one." It seemed as if he had an infinite storehouse of them. At first he would check my solutions, but after a while he would accept them as correct and just give me another, and another, and another problem. The mental exercise required to solve them was the great gift from my father. The solving of thousands of problems during my high school days—at the time when my brain was growing—did more than anything else to develop my analytical power.

**MP**  *Just working those problems?*

Tobias Dantzig gave his son George a "great gift"—literally thousands of geometry problems to solve.

**DANTZIG**    Yes, it was brain exercise. Problems on any other subject probably would have done as well.

**MP**    *Did you give problems to your children?*

**DANTZIG**    No. They didn't take to mathematics in the same way.

**MP**    *Did you ever feel that your father was pushing you into mathematics?*

**DANTZIG**    Never! I believe he gave me the problems just to get rid of me. It was almost as if he were saying, "Here's another problem. Now go away and don't bother me." He was always busy with whatever Toby was busy with—taking care of his students, writing, doing research, and so on. Eventually, of course, he did run out of problems and had to go to the Library of Congress to dig up additional ones.

**MP**    *So you literally exhausted his supply of problems?*

**DANTZIG**    Eventually, yes. It seems that he didn't have an infinite supply after all. Later he brought home books containing collections of difficult problems, like the famous book *Geometric Constructions* by Julius Petersen.

**MP**    *By the time you finished high school was it clear to you that you would major in mathematics in college?*

**DANTZIG**    Yes.

**MP**    *You said your father was teaching at Maryland. So Maryland was a convenient place to go. Was that it?*

**DANTZIG**    Yes, of course. Those were depression days. It wasn't a time for high aspirations. I certainly had no dreams of going off to a fancy school which would require my family to support me away from home.

**MP**    *You have said that Maryland was sort of a third-rate cow college in those days and yet you were happy taking mathematics there. Did your mathematics study have a strongly applied flavor at that time?*

**DANTZIG**    No, absolutely not. I don't recall a single application in any of the mathematics courses I took at Maryland. What math there was in physics and chemistry was pretty primitive. I did, however, encounter an interesting application of mathematics in a freshman chemistry course given by a Professor White. I wrote a little applied mathematics paper on how to efficiently extract iodine from a water solution using carbon tetrachloride as an extractor. He looked at it and said that it was a very interesting idea to subdivide the carbon-tet, but that he was sure someone must have already published the idea. Two years later, when I was a junior, he came around, very shamefaced, and showed me a paper just published on the same idea. That was the only thing I ever did at Maryland in the way of an application. I wasn't opposed to doing applied mathematics. It just never sought me out, and I didn't seek it out.

**MP**    *After getting your bachelor's at Maryland in 1936, you went to Michigan for graduate study. What was Michigan like?*

**DANTZIG**    I studied under G. Y. Rainich, took courses from R. L. Wilder and T. H. Hildebrandt, and received a master's.

**MP**    *Did you take any statistics?*

**DANTZIG**   I did take a statistics course with H. C. Carver. In the summer of 1936 I married Anne Shmuner, and she came to Ann Arbor with me. We earned money working for Carver. He did some consulting on the side for a flour company. The company wanted to buy large quantities of wheat in the commodity market during the year at prices that would average out to the average annual price. Carver worked out a system of hedging which was supposed to be sensational. He swore me to secrecy; just the same, he was careful to camouflage the work sheets so that I would not discover his secret regression formula.

As for the field known as statistics as taught to me by Carver, it seemed to be just a bag of tricks—it didn't have any rationale that I could discern. Except for statistics, everything else I took at Michigan was terribly abstract—so abstract that I had but one desire: to quit my graduate studies and get a job, which I did.

**MP**   *So that's when you went to Washington D.C.?*

**DANTZIG**   Yes. By luck—that was 1937, still the Depression—I got a job as a statistical clerk with the Bureau of Labor Statistics. The job I took, at a lower grade, was one that had recently been vacated by Milton Friedman, who had left for the University of Chicago. I was assigned to a project called "Urban Study of Consumer Purchases" and asked to review a paper on double sampling by the famous statistician Jerzy Neyman, who was then at University College in London. It was my first encounter with statistical theory based on a logical rationale. I was very excited by the paper. Later I discovered it was the least representative of Neyman's contributions. I am sure that if I had seen anything more representative, I would have become even more excited.

**MP**   *Did you like your work at the Bureau of Labor Statistics?*

**DANTZIG**   Yes. I learned a lot about practical applications. Our group was very good. My co-worker was Duane Evans. He and I became good friends. Later Evans's work in World War II on Wassily Leontief's input-output model of the U.S. economy changed the course of my career.

**MP**   *So then how did you get from the Bureau to Berkeley? Like your father, you really moved around!*

**DANTZIG**   In retrospect I don't think I moved around too much. While at the Bureau, I wrote to Neyman, who was by then at Berkeley, and told him that I would like to finish my Ph.D. under him. He replied that he didn't think he would be able to get me a teaching assistantship, but in the end he did. I don't know why he thought I would make a good candidate. Perhaps it was my review of his paper. At Berkeley in 1939 statistics was still part of the mathematics department, and so the focus was on pure mathematics and not on statistics. The total number of courses in theoretical statistics that I was ever exposed to was two given by Neyman.

**MP**   *What was Neyman like as a person?*

**DANTZIG**   Neyman had a dominating personality which he was able to assert long after he had been officially retired. In his seventies and eighties he continued to run the statistical laboratory at Berkeley. No one dared to contradict him. He was top dog in every sense. I don't want to give the impression that he was a tyrant. He wasn't. He was very likable—everyone

As a graduate student at the University of Michigan.

Jerzy Neyman, who founded the Statistical Laboratory at Berkeley—"top dog in every sense."

respected him as the leading mathematical statistician in the world, quite correctly, I think.

**MP**  *How did it happen that you did your Ph.D. on a statistical topic when you took so few courses in statistics?*

**DANTZIG**  It happened because during my first year at Berkeley I arrived late one day to one of Neyman's classes. On the blackboard there were two problems which I assumed had been assigned for homework. I copied them down. A few days later I apologized to Neyman for taking so long to do the homework—the problems seemed to be a little harder to do than usual. I asked him if he still wanted the work. He told me to throw it on his desk. I did so reluctantly because his desk was covered with such a heap of papers that I feared my homework would be lost there forever. About six weeks later, one Sunday morning about eight o'clock, Anne and I were awakened by someone banging on our front door. It was Neyman. He rushed in with papers in hand, all excited: "I've just written an introduction to one of your papers. Read it so I can send it out right away for publication." For a minute I had no idea what he was talking about. To make a long story short, the problems on the blackboard which I had solved thinking they were homework were in fact two famous unsolved problems in statistics. That was the first inkling I had that there was anything special about them.

**MP**  *But you had apologized to Neyman for taking so long to do them.*

**DANTZIG**  Well, there was no particular deadline, and you know how graduate students take their time. A year later, when I began to worry about a thesis topic, Neyman just shrugged and told me to wrap the two problems in a binder and he would accept them as my thesis.

The second of the two problems, however, was not published until after World War II. It happened this way. Around 1950 I received a letter from Abraham Wald enclosing the final galley proofs of a paper of his about to go to press in the *Annals of Mathematical Statistics*. Someone had just pointed out to him that the main result in his paper was the same as the second "homework" problem solved in my thesis. I wrote back suggesting that we publish jointly, so he simply inserted my name as co-author into the galley proof.

**Subject for a Sermon**

**MP**  *Is it true, as I have heard, that the story of your "homework problems" has been used by ministers in sermons?*

**DANTZIG**  Apparently so. The other day as I was taking an early morning walk, I was hailed by Don Knuth as he rode by on his bicycle. He is a colleague at Stanford. He stopped and said, "Hey, George—I was visiting in Indiana recently and heard a sermon about you in church. Do you know that you are an influence on Christians of middle America?" I looked at him, amazed. "After the sermon," he went on, "the minister came over and asked me if I knew a George Dantzig at Stanford, because that was the name of the person his sermon was about."

**MP**  *How in the world did that happen?*

**DANTZIG**  The origin of that minister's sermon can be traced to another Lutheran minister, the Reverend Schuler of the Crystal Cathedral in Los Angeles. Several years ago he and I happened to have adjacent seats on an airplane. He told me his ideas about thinking positively, and I told him my story about the homework problems and my thesis. A few months later I received a letter from him asking permission to include my story in a book he was writing on the power of positive thinking. Schuler's published version was a bit garbled and exaggerated but essentially correct. The moral of his sermon was this: If I had known that the problems were not homework but were in fact two famous unsolved problems in statistics, I probably would not have thought positively, would have become discouraged, and would never have solved them.

**MP** *So then did you finish at Berkeley?*

**A Man Who Was Going Places**

**DANTZIG**  I didn't exactly finish then. I had completed my course work, and my thesis was settled in June 1941. But I had not defended my thesis or my minor thesis on dimension theory. This was six months before Pearl Harbor. Many of us wanted to contribute to World War II, which we believed the U. S. was about to enter. I went back to Washington during summer vacation and had an interview with Charles Bates ("Tex") Thornton, who had been selected by Secretary Lovett to set up Air Force Statistical Control. The Air Force at the time did not have a good system for reporting the status of their aircraft. They didn't even know their total number of planes, which at the time was less than a hundred. The interview took place on the corner of 20th Street and Constitution Avenue, across from the old Munitions Building. He said he couldn't wait: he wanted me to join him right away. My wife, Anne, was with me at the interview. She is very good at spotting talent. She told me Thornton was a man who was going places and I should take the job. She was right. As you know, after the war Tex founded Litton Industries.

**MP** *So it was your work with the Air Force that got you into this now famous subject, linear programming?*

**DANTZIG**  Not exactly right away. I stopped my graduate studies and joined the Air Force as a civilian. I was put in charge of the Combat Analysis Branch of Statistical Control. I set up a reporting system for combat units on the number of sorties flown, aircraft lost and damaged, bombs dropped, and targets attacked. I became quite expert at programming planning methods using the only "computing machines" we had then—people using hand-operated desk calculators.

My colleagues in the Pentagon included Brandon Barringer (a well-known Philadelphia banker), Robert McNamara (of World Bank fame), Edward Learned (of the Harvard Business School), and Warren Hirsch (the probabilist at New York University), who was my deputy.

In spring 1946 I returned to Berkeley and finished my Ph.D. I turned down an offer from Berkeley because it paid too little and returned to the Pentagon, where I became the mathematical adviser to the U.S. Air Force Comptroller. But I was really marking time while looking for an academic position. To entice me into remaining with the Air Force, two of my colleagues, Dal Hitchcock and Marshall Wood, challenged me to see what could be done to mechanize the planning process; that is, to find a more rapid way to compute a time-staged deployment, training and logistical supply program. Mechanization in those days meant using analog devices or punch-card equipment.

Consistent with my training as a mathematician, I set out to formulate a model. I was fascinated by the work being done at the Bureau of Labor Statistics by Duane Evans, Jerome Cornfield and Marvin Hoffenberg on the Input-Output Model of Wassily Leontief. I had learned about it during the war in telephone conversations at night with Duane Evans—we were much too busy during the day to talk.

**"In my book he is a hero."** In my *Linear Programming and Extensions* you will notice that I pay great tribute to Leontief. It was Leontief who around 1932 first formulated the Inter-industry Model of the American Economy, organized the collection of data during the Great Depression, and finally tried to convince policy makers to use the output from the analysis. All of these things are necessary steps for successful applications, and Leontief took them all. That is why in my book he is a hero.

Leontief's model had a matrix structure which was simple enough in concept with sufficient detail that it could be useful for practical planning. I soon saw that it had to be generalized. Leontief's was a steady-state model and what was needed was a highly dynamic model, one that could change over time. In his model there was a one-to-one correspondence between the production processes and the items produced by these processes. What was needed was a model with many alternative activities. Moreover, the application had to be large scale—with hundreds, perhaps thousands of activities and items. Finally, it had to be computable. In other words, once the model was formulated, there had to be a practical way to compute what quantities of these activities to engage in so as to be compatible with their input-output characteristics and given resources. The model I formulated would be described today as a time-staged dynamic linear program with a staircase matrix structure. Initially there was no objective function; in other words, no explicit goal. Such goals did not exist in any practical sense because planners simply had no way to implement them.

**An Earth Filled with Computers** A simple example illustrates the fundamental difficulty of formulating a planning program using such an activity-analysis approach. Consider the problem of assigning 70 men to 70 jobs. An "activity" consists of assigning the $i$-th man to the $j$-th job. The restrictions are (a) that there are 70 men, each of whom must be assigned, and (b) that all of the jobs, also 70, must be filled. The level of an activity is either 1, meaning it will be used, or 0, meaning it will not. Thus there are 2 x 70, or 140, restrictions and 70 x 70, or 4900, activities with 4900 corresponding zero-one decision variables. Unfortunately there are also 70 factorial permutations, or ways to make the assignments. The problem is to compare 70 factorial ways and to select the one which is optimal, or "best" by some criterion.

Now in this example 70 factorial is a very big number. To get some idea of how big, suppose we had had an IBM main-frame computer available at the time of the Big Bang fifteen million years ago. Would it—between then and now—have been able to examine all the possible solutions? No! But suppose that an even more powerful computer had been available, one that could have examined one billion assignments per second. The answer would still be no. Even if the Earth were filled with nanosecond-speed computers, all working in parallel, the answer would still be no. If, however, there were ten Earths, all filled with nanosecond-speed computers, all programmed in parallel from the time of the Big Bang until the sun grows cold, then perhaps

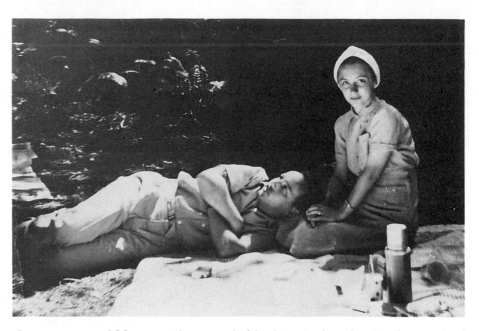

Newlyweds Anne Shmuner and George Dantzig enjoying a picnic in Michigan in 1937.

the answer would be yes. The remarkable thing is that the simplex method with the aid of a modern computer can solve this problem in a split second.

**A Gulf between Aspirations and Actions**

This example illustrates why, up to 1947 and for the most part up to this day, a great gulf exists between man's aspirations and his actions. Man may wish to state his wants in terms of an objective to be extremized, but there are so many ways to go about doing the job, each with its advantages and disadvantages, that it has been impossible to compare them and to choose among them that one which is best. So, invariably, man has always had to turn to a leader whose "experience" and "mature judgment" would guide the way. The leader's guidance usually consisted in the issuance of a series of edicts or ground rules to those developing the programs. Although such methods are still widely used, the world today is far too complex for such simplistic methods to work, and they don't.

In late 1946, before we knew that high-speed electronic computers were soon going to exist, I had formulated a mathematical model that satisfactorily represented the technological relations usually encountered in practice. However, in place of any explicitly stated goal, or function to be extremized, there were a large number of ad hoc ground rules issued by those in authority to aid in the selection of the solution. Without these it would have been impossible to choose from the astronomical number of feasible solutions.

**MP**   *That certainly has to be classed as a very messy real-world problem. Most mathematicians prefer problems which are cleanly formulated.*

**DANTZIG**   It is almost impossible for someone coming from a purely mathematical background with little exposure to applications to understand how to go about formulating a real-world problem in mathematical terms. There is a certain softness—a lack of precision—in the definition of many "dirty" real-world problems which permits them to have many equivalent mathematical formulations. When I say "equivalent," I don't mean equivalent in the mathematical sense of one-to-one correspondence, but equivalent for the purpose of the application. From the point of view of the person looking for an answer, one definition of the problem may be just as satisfactory as another. But one definition may turn out to be completely amenable to mathematical analysis and solution while another may be mathematically hopeless. Only through detailed knowledge of the problem can one decide whether the more tractable formulation is just as acceptable. Linear programming models have been successful because with them many large problems can be formulated so that they are acceptable to planners and solvable on a computer.

**The Young Father of Linear Programming**

**MP** *You are often called the Father of Linear Programming. Is that a title you're comfortable with?*

**DANTZIG** I have to tell you a story. Twenty-five years ago I visited Japan for the first time. When I got off the plane, the Japanese who met me were very surprised at how young I was. Since I had been billed as the Father of Linear Programming, they apparently expected to see an old man with white hair and a cane being helped down the ramp. I was forty-five at the time.

**MP** *The preface to your book* Linear Programming and Extensions *opens with a provocative statement: "The final test of a theory is its capacity to solve the problems which originated it."*

**DANTZIG** Did I say that? It's a great quote. Show me where.

**MP** *Your second paragraph isn't bad either: "This book is concerned with the theory and solution of linear inequality systems. On the surface, this field should be just as interesting to mathematicians as its special case, linear equation systems. Curiously enough, until 1947 linear inequality theory generated only a handful of isolated papers, while linear equations and the related subjects of linear algebra and approximation theory had developed a vast literature. Perhaps this disproportionate interest in linear equation theory was motivated more than mathematicians care to admit by its use as an important tool in theories concerned with the understanding of the physical universe."*

**Modern Mathematicians— A Distinct Race**

**DANTZIG** I think of modern mathematicians as a distinct race characterized by their non-interest in applications. From a historical point of view,

理計画シンポジウム

Audiences in Japan were amazed that "the father of linear programming" was not an old man.

mathematicians before let us say 1820 were very closely tied to physics — or, in the case of probability theory, to gambling. For the past 150 years, however, mathematicians have created their own abstractions and follow the mathematical fads that happen to be in fashion. The fact that there is a whole world of exciting new mathematics out there in such fields as Operations Research, Computer Science, Optimization Theory has not excited their interest. I for one have no interest in trying to re-educate them — it would be a hopeless task. The most we can hope for is that they can be educated to the point that they don't prejudice gifted students too much against that wonderful world of mathematics that goes by different names.

MP   *How do they bias students against applications?*

DANTZIG   By showing their contempt for anything which is not pure mathematics as they define it. Students are being brainwashed into thinking that pure mathematics is in some way purer than other forms of mathematics. I have never been able to tell the difference between the so-called pure and the non-pure and don't believe that there is any. Just because my mathematics has its origin in a real problem doesn't make it less interesting to me — just the other way around, I find it makes the puzzle I am working on all the more exciting. I get satisfaction out of knowing that I'm working on a relevant problem. I find that just as much mathematical ingenuity has to go into solving problems from a new developing area as from some old so-called pure math area.

**Mathematics outside
Mathematics Departments**

May I say a few words about these new mathematical areas? Computers are now being applied to almost every aspect of human activity. Every field of science, of medicine, engineering, business — you name it — is being computerized in some way. However, before you can put a problem into a computer and efficiently find a solution, you must abstract it. To abstract it, you have to build a model. Before you start to do anything with a model, you have to mathematize it. It is this process of abstracting applications from every aspect of life that has given rise to a vast new world of mathematics that is being developed outside mathematics departments. This mathematics is just as interesting and just as exciting and just as challenging as any mathematics that is taught in the regular courses. Most mathematicians remain completely unaware of it.

MP   *One scenario I've heard a few times of late goes like this. Given the innate nature of mathematicians and given that there are all kinds of mathematics outside mathematics departments — important stuff, where the applications value is often very apparent to students — we may see mathematics departments eventually take on a role similar to that of philosophy departments.*

DANTZIG   Possibly. However there will always be a few core courses that need to be taught: algebra, matrix theory, calculus, analysis, and some topology, so there will always be something for mathematics departments to do even if they continue to be indifferent to the developing new areas of mathematics.

MP   *Do you feel that mathematicians are biased against the people who do operations research?*

**DANTZIG**   I myself have never experienced any bias. I believe I am well accepted as a mathematician. In addition, I've got the right "union card," a Ph.D. in mathematics from Berkeley.

**MP**   *Can you remember your feelings when you first proposed the linear programming model and discovered the simplex algorithm for solving linear programming problems and found it to be efficient?*

**DANTZIG**   To tell the truth, it was a very gradual awakening. When the planning problem was first formulated for the Air Force, the very notion of an objective function, the idea of a sharply defined goal, was non-existent. Of course we paid lip service to the concept of a goal. In the military setting I often heard it said, "Our goal is to win the war." In a business setting one would hear, "Our goal is to make a profit." But you could never find any direct relationship between the stated goal and the actions to achieve the goal. If you looked closely at the next step, you would find that some leader in his conceit had promulgated a bunch of ground rules to guide the way to the goal. This is a far cry from honestly looking at all alternative combinations of actions across the board and picking the best combination. Those in charge often do a hand-wave and say, "I've considered all the alternatives," but this is so much garbage. They couldn't possibly look at all possible combinations. Before 1947 the possibility that there could be a tool like linear programming that would enable one to examine millions of combinations was inconceivable. There was no algorithm or computational tools for doing so.

I didn't discover the linear programming model all in a flash. It evolved. About a whole year was spent deciding whether my model could be used to formulate practical scheduling problems. Planning and scheduling, as you know, were carried out on a vast scale during the war. Running the Air Force was the equivalent of running the economy of a whole nation. Hundreds of thousands of people were involved in the process. The logistics were on a scale that it is impossible to convey to an outsider. My colleague Marshall Wood and I reviewed thousands of situations drawn from our wartime experience.

The ground rules used in planning were expressed in a completely different format from the way we now formulate a linear program. What we did was review these rules one by one and demonstrate that almost all could be reformulated acceptably in linear programming format. Not all. In some cases discreteness and non-convexity also had to be taken into account.

When I first formulated my linear programming model, I did so without an objective function or goal. I struggled for a while with adding ground rules for selecting from the feasible solutions one which was in some sense "optimal." But I soon abandoned this approach and replaced it with an objective function to be maximized. The model I formulated was not specialized to the military. It could be applied to all kinds of planning problems—all one had to do was change the names of the columns and the rows, and it was applicable to an economic planning problem or to an industrial planning problem.

The general model was one which I assumed economists had looked at and for which they had developed solution techniques. Albert Kahn of the National Bureau of Standards suggested I visit T. J. Koopmans at the Cowles

Foundation in Chicago. I did so in June 1947. Koopmans at first seemed indifferent to my presentation, but then he became very excited—it was as if, in a lightning flash, he suddenly saw its significance to economic theory. One reason why linear programming caught on so quickly outside the military can be traced back to the realization by Koopmans, in 1947, that a good part of economics could also be translated into the linear programming format. Incidentally, Koopmans became the leader of a brilliant group of economists who developed the theory of allocation of resources and its relation to linear programming. This culminated in 1975 when he received the Nobel Prize.

**MP**  *Do you think that economists other than Koopmans would have spotted the significance of linear programming?*

**DANTZIG**  Hard to say. Economists had been developing economic models for over two hundred years without realizing their importance in spite of the fact that their field began with a linear model proposed by the Technocrats back at the time of the French Revolution. It was a rather poorly formulated input-output model of the Leontief type with various economic sectors consisting of the peasant, the artisan and the nobility. But instead of developing the approach, economists over the next hundred years created more and more sophisticated nonlinear models. Walras's model, for example, was a very general nonlinear programming model. From the historical point of view, linear programming is an anachronism. It should have been the model that played a central role in economic thought from the beginning rather than emerging at a late date as a throwback. The anachronism came about because until very recently mathematical models were not being used

With Tjalling Koopmans and Leonid Kantorovich, who were awarded the Nobel Prize for Economics in 1975—Koopmans expressed regret that Dantzig was not sharing the honor.

*More Mathematical People*

by economists to obtain quantitative answers. They were used instead as a convenient substitute for long-winded logical verbal argument. Leontief was the first economist to break away from this classical use by constructing and solving a large scale quantitative model based on real data.

## The Simplex Algorithm

**MP**  *How did the discovery of the simplex algorithm come about?*

**DANTZIG**  I am coming to that. I learned from Koopmans in early 1947 that the economists didn't have an algorithm, and that was bad news. The generals in the Air Force were paying us to solve real planning problems. By hook or crook, we were expected to find a practical way to solve them.

I set out in the summer of 1947 to invent one. I began by observing that the feasible region is a convex body—a polyhedral set. Therefore, we could improve by moving along edges from one extreme point to the next. But this procedure seemed hopelessly inefficient. In three dimensions, the region could be visualized as a diamond with faces, edges and corner points. In the case of many edges, the procedure might wander along improving edges for a long time before reaching the optimal corner point of the diamond.

**MP**  *So that was your geometrical representation?*

**DANTZIG**  Yes. There was nothing novel in the procedure. Any mathematician with any background at all would consider it as a possibility but would immediately discard it. So obviously I initially rejected the idea. I next looked at the problem using the geometry of the columns instead of the rows. Curiously, in the column geometry the algorithm I just described looked efficient. I found it extremely difficult to create a problem in $m$ equations and $n$ non-negative variables which I couldn't solve in $m$ pivot steps, that is, in $m$ moves along edges.

At first I thought that the method might be efficient but not necessarily practical. For a big problem there could be many combinations (corner points)—perhaps as many as the stars in the heavens. It might require a million steps to solve it. That might be considered efficient, since this number is small relative to the number of combinations involved, but hardly practical. So I continued to look for a better alternative algorithm.

## Climbing the Beanpole

That summer Koopmans sent one of his students, Leonid Hurwitz, to see me. Leo and I kicked around an idea we called "climbing up the beanpole," which was a precursor of the simplex method. It assumed the variables summed to unity. Later I generalized the procedure by getting rid of the convexity constraint. My branch at the Pentagon experimented with it. We looked around for some small examples to solve. One of them was a nutrition problem of George Stigler's. This problem became famous because it was the first practical problem to be solved by the simplex method.

That fall, while my group at the Bureau of Standards was experimenting with the simplex algorithm, I decided to consult with the "great" Johnny von Neumann and see what he could suggest in the way of solution techniques. He was considered by many to be the leading mathematician in the world. On October 3, 1947, I visited him for the first time at the Institute for Advanced Study. I began by explaining to him the formulation of the linear programming model in terms of activities and items and so forth. I described it to him as I would describe it to an ordinary mortal. He responded in a way which I believe was uncharacteristic of him. "Get to the point," he snapped.

I said to myself, "Okay, if this man wants a quickie, then that's what he'll get." In less than a minute I slapped the geometric and the algebraic versions of my problem on the blackboard. He stood up and said, "Oh, that."

For the next hour and a half he proceeded to give me a lecture on the mathematical theory of linear programs. At one point, seeing me sitting there with my eyes popping and my mouth open (after all, I had searched the literature and found absolutely nothing), he said, "I don't want you to think that I am pulling all this out of my sleeve on the spur of the moment—like a magician. I have just recently completed a book with Oskar Morgenstern on the theory of games. What I am doing is conjecturing that the two problems are equivalent. The theory that I am outlining for your problem is an analogue to the one we have developed for games."

That was the way I learned for the first time about Farkas's lemma and the duality theorem.

On another visit to Princeton in June 1948 I met Albert Tucker. Soon Tucker and his students, Harold Kuhn and David Gale, began their historic work on game theory, nonlinear programming, and duality theory. Twelve years later Al Tucker, who had been reading the manuscript of my book *Linear Programming and Extensions*, asked me, "Why do you ascribe duality to von Neumann and not to my group?" I replied, "Because he was the first to show it to me." "That is strange," he said, "for we have found nothing in writing about what von Neumann has done." "True," I said, "but let me send you the paper I wrote as a result of my first meeting with von Neumann." I sent him the report I wrote for my Air Force branch, "A Theorem on Linear Inequalities," dated 5 January 1948, which contains (as far as I know) the first formal proof of duality. Later Tucker asked me, "Why didn't you publish it?" I replied, "Because it was not my result—it was von Neumann's. All I did was to write up, for internal circulation, my own proof of what von Neumann had outlined to me. It was my way of educating the people in my office in the Pentagon." Today everyone cites von Neumann as the originator of the duality theorem and credits Tucker, Kuhn and Gale as the publishers of the first rigorous proof.

**MP**  *Von Neumann apparently made a strong impression on anyone he came in contact with.*

**DANTZIG**  Yes, people would come to him because of his great insight. In the initial stages of the development of a new field like linear programming, atomic physics, computers or whatever, his advice proved invaluable. After these fields were developed in greater depth, however, it became increasingly more difficult for him to make the same spectacular contributions. I guess everyone has a finite capacity, and Johnny was no exception.

**MP**  *So while you were off seeing von Neumann and trying to come up with a better algorithm, your group at the Air Force was experimenting with the simplex algorithm that you had given them? You weren't very optimistic about its usefulness?*

**DANTZIG**  That's right. As I said, I thought the method might be efficient but not practical so I continued to look for a better algorithm. About a year later, in June 1948, my group asked me why I continued to look elsewhere when the simplex algorithm was working out so well on the test problems.

**MP**  *So it was completely unexpected?*

**DANTZIG** Yes. Most of the time it solved problems with $m$ equations in $2m$ or $3m$ steps—that was truly amazing. I certainly did not anticipate that it would turn out to be so terrific. I had had no experience at the time with problems in higher dimensions, and I didn't trust my geometrical intuition. For example, my intuition told me that the procedure would require too many steps wandering from one adjacent vertex to the next. In practice it takes few steps. In brief, one's intuition in higher dimensional space is not worth a damn! Only now, almost forty years from the time when the simplex method was first proposed, are people beginning to get some insight into why it works as well as it does.

**MP** *A fellow at Bell Labs, Narendra Karmarkar, has been reported to have done something new with linear programming.*

**DANTZIG** It is an important improvement on the theoretical result of Kachian that a linear program can be solved in polynomial time. Kachian's theorem states that the computational effort is guaranteed to be less than a polynomial expression in the dimensions of the problem and the number of digits of input data. The bound is extremely high, hence not a practical result. We will just have to wait and see if interior algorithms, such as Karmarkar's, will prove competitive in practice to the simplex method for general linear programs. I would not be surprised if it turns out to be an efficient way to solve problems with special structure, such as multi-stage problems.

**MP** *I notice that John D. Williams is one of the people whom you include in the dedication of your book on linear programming. How did he figure in your career?*

**DANTZIG** In 1952 I left the Air Force to work for Rand. John was my boss. After I had worked for several months without receiving any direction, I went to see him. I said, "John, what is it that I'm supposed to do?" He didn't say a word, not one—he just sat looking at me from across his desk. Five minutes passed, and I began to get uneasy. Still not a word. Ten minutes passed. Finally he said, "George, you know better than to ask that question." I understood what he meant and got out of his office fast. John's policy was to let his researchers do their thing. For example, he tolerated me for nine years while I wrote my book. Of course, I also wrote a lot of papers during the same period.

**Anarchistic or Dictatorial?** Williams's organization chart for the Mathematics Division at Rand was horizontal. Nobody reported to anyone. The research output was remarkable and gave the Rand Corporation a worldwide reputation. My impression, however, is that its top administration never knew from whence the reputation came. Ray Fulkerson, Lloyd Shapley, Richard Bellman, Ted Harris, Selmer Johnson, Olaf Helmer, George Dantzig, to name but a few, were all producing papers like mad and doing so without any direction whatsoever. During that time, network flow theory was developed by Fulkerson, game theory by Shapley, dynamic programming by Bellman, and linear programming by Dantzig. It was a complete contrast to the group I had worked with in the Air Force. In the Pentagon everything was organized vertically. Orders came down from the top in military fashion. Even so we were highly motivated and remarkably effective. I find it amusing that there could be these two very different ways to organize research—one anarchistic, the

Receiving the Medal of Science from President Ford in 1975.

other dictatorial, and yet both highly efficient. Apparently any form of government can be made to work if the people are motivated enough.

**MP**  *What caused you to leave Rand and return to the academic world?*

**DANTZIG**  My leaving had to do with the way we teamed up to do our research. In the beginning I was part of a team with Ray Fulkerson and Selmer Johnson. For a time we did great things together. Then after a while, although we remained good friends, each of us got busy doing his own thing. Rand at that time had about thirty in the Mathematics Division, which is a big group for doing just mathematical research. There were no new people being hired to work with us as disciples.

**MP**  *So you need young minds up against the experience and expertise of the senior people?*

**DANTZIG**  Yes, there must be change, dynamics. My stimulus comes from students and working closely with researchers elsewhere.

**MP**  *Let's turn to another topic. In an article about you in the* Stanford Campus Report, *you say that policy makers often ignore powerful analytical tools. Are you optimistic about modeling playing a larger role in the future?*

**Haphazard Decisions**  **DANTZIG**  I keep hoping it will. I have been involved since 1975 in the development of a macroeconomic energy model called PILOT, which stands for Planning Investment Level Over Time. It contains a lot of detail bearing on energy, such as energy conservation, energy supply, industrial use, energy-saving devices in households, and so on. Recently we expanded the detail in the economy part of the model in order to estimate the impact of innovation, modernization and foreign competition. It is a long-term model useful for analyzing trends forty years into the future, a tool that provides a tremendous insight into complex dynamic issues which face the nation.

In spite of the fact that the PILOT model is the real McCoy—a powerful tool for making policy decisions—decision makers do not line up to use

PILOT or, for that matter, any other model. Decision making in a complex society is a haphazard, unstructured and undisciplined process that doesn't lend itself to effective use of models. Policy makers, instead, look for quick answers to very complex questions—as a result the decisions they make are bad. Even when a decision maker is in a position to use the numbers produced by planning models as guidelines for action, he is reluctant to do so because the policies produced by models are never the whole answer. A model may help one to decide the best place to put a new airport, but then something unexpected always happens—like farmers or some other group, who have not been considered or even thought of when the model was formulated, coming forth with objections.

Politicians know the unexpected always happens so they tend to ignore the models and engage in an ad hoc, haphazard decision process instead.

**MP**  *Why then have linear programming models been so successful for refinery scheduling?*

**DANTZIG**  A refinery is typically headed up by one person so he can use a model to determine what crude oil to buy and what to produce with it.

**MP**  *But you are not optimistic about more complex applications?*

**DANTZIG**  No. Not at all. Many enterprises such as a nation are so complex that no one is really in charge. It is here that our models have the greatest potential for coming to grips with complexity and making a real contribution to the national well being. But this potential is frustrated by the lack of structure and discipline in the decision-making process itself.

The approach I favor for addressing this fundamental bottleneck to the effectiveness of models for national planning is to develop a disciplined structure for dialogue between all the special interest groups involved—one that will make use of a coordinating group whose job is to facilitate the bargaining process by supplying data from models on the feasibility and optimality of proposed compromises and trade-offs.

**MP**  *Thank you very much, George. That's a good note to end on!*

*November 1984 in Stanford, California (DA).*

*GEORGE BERNARD DANTZIG*  Portland, Oregon, November 8, 1914. A.B. 1936, Maryland; M.A. 1937, Michigan; Ph.D. 1946, UC Berkeley. Field: mathematical programming. Professor of Operations Research and Computer Science, Stanford. Gibbs Lecturer (AMS) 1990. Von Neumann Prize (ORSA–TIMS) 1975, National Medal of Science 1975, Harvey Prize 1985. American Academy of Arts and Sciences, National Academy of Engineering, National Academy of Sciences. Books: *Linear Programming and Extensions*, 1963; (with T. L. Saaty) *Compact City*, 1973.

# ANDREW M. GLEASON

Andrew Gleason is something of a rarity at Harvard, having no Ph.D. He made a mark very early in his career by contributing substantially to the solution of Hilbert's fifth problem. He says mathematics is harder to explain to nonmathematicians because it is "easier" than the other sciences—most of the easy problems have been solved so it is the hard ones, which are also harder to explain, that are being tackled today. Unlike the physicist Eugene Wigner, he sees nothing "unreasonable" about the effectiveness of mathematics in physics—"It is designed to discuss exactly the situation that physics confronts; namely, that there seems to be some order out there . . ."

□ □ □

**MP**  *You have been so connected with Harvard during your career, both as a graduate student and as a faculty member, that we were wondering if you were born in the Boston area.*

**GLEASON**  No. I was born in Fresno, California, where my mother's family was located. In fact, my maternal grandfather—his name was Mattei, the "M" in my name stands for Mattei—came from the south of Switzerland, where the family had been in the wine business for many generations, and he ultimately started a wine business in Fresno. At the time of my birth my mother and older brother and sister were in Fresno with her family because my father, who was a botanist, was off on an exploring trip in British Guiana. He was with the New York Botanical Gardens, so essentially I grew up in Bronxville, New York.

**MP**  *You were the youngest in your family?*

**GLEASON**  Yes. In fact, my first, very vivid photographic memory is of looking out the dining room window of our house in Bronxville and watching for my older brother to come home from school. He was four and a half years older so, assuming that he was then six, I was presumably two. I

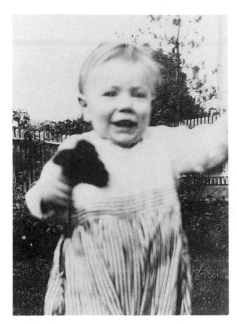

The mathematician at eighteen months.

couldn't see down to the street because my head wasn't high enough to see over the windowsill. It is a tremendously strong memory.

**MP**  *Then a few years later you were going to school yourself. How did you like it?*

**GLEASON**  I always got along well in school except at first. From kindergarten there is a lovely story. A little kid named David—I always remember his name—was making a nuisance of himself, at least as far as I was concerned, and so once when he was about to sit down I removed the chair and he fell on his behind. The kindergarten teacher was very upset. She sent some kids across the hall to get the first grade teacher, and the two of them began to lecture me. They leaned way down over me, whereupon I hauled off and hit one of them. I've forgotten which one.

**MP**  *Not the best beginning for an academic career.*

**GLEASON**  I was really rather fierce in my temper in those days. Since then I have not been so fierce.

**MP**  *Do you have any mathematical memories from your first years at school?*

**GLEASON**  Well, my father was not a mathematician, but he had a lot of natural mathematical talent. He had a real understanding of what the subject is about. Also he was very good at computing in his head. He came back from that trip to British Guiana which I mentioned earlier with a terrible case of malaria, and while he was ill—he told me that he was actually delirious at the time—he worked out a number of very curious arithmetic puzzles. I don't remember the details, but I do remember the style of one. It was called "How the World War Was Fought." That was, of course, the first World War. Each battle would consist of taking some numbers and multiplying them or dividing them, or whatever, and the result would be the outcome of the battle. What is important is that the numbers were all numbers that had very special properties. They weren't just made up. Now, a posteriori, I know why some of his things worked, but I don't know how he found out about them.

**MP**  *He definitely had mathematical leanings.*

**GLEASON**  No question.

**MP**  *What about your mother? Any mathematical leanings there?*

**GLEASON**  My mother was certainly not a mathematician, but she was a very good card player. She had what is called "card sense." She wasn't probabilistically oriented or anything like that, but she had a strong sense of what was going on in cards and an ability to read opponents. She played all kinds of card games very well. I often played games with my parents—cribbage, for example. Also we played a kind of dominoes that involved a lot of arithmetic. I learned to play bridge very early, but I never played so seriously that I worried about it. I don't play anymore because my wife doesn't play cards.

**MP**  *When did you really become seriously interested in mathematics? Was it in high school or before that?*

**GLEASON**  Well, I did a few other things at one time or another. Very early on, when I was nine or ten, I was quite interested in ancient Egypt. Then I was interested in astronomy. One year—it was in the spring of 1936—we lived for a semester in Berkeley, and I used to take the trolley car and go out to the Chabot Observatory. Someone out there had for sale—for $25, which was a vast sum of money in those days—a reflecting telescope. I bought it, and I used to take it up to the roof of the little apartment where we were living and try to look at the stars. (It wasn't so cold in Berkeley, but when I got back home I found that the only time I could significantly see stars in the vicinity of Bronxville was when it was real cold. I realized that looking at stars in the winter was not my métier.) However, in answer to your question, I think it was during that semester in Berkeley, when I was not quite fifteen, that I really switched into being serious about mathematics.

**MP**  *How did it happen?*

**GLEASON**  That semester I started taking the first half of the high school geometry course. I was very bored. The teacher didn't know anything about mathematics. I was not the kind of student that would say I didn't think the teacher knew anything, but she didn't. I know that now. Anyway I felt that I wasn't getting anywhere, so I started auditing the second half of the course. Finally I got signed up for it. I left Berkeley before the semester was actually over, so I had to bring some sort of record back to my home high school. I still remember the look on the face of the teacher of the first half when she discovered that I had also been taking the second half!

**MP**  *Was the teacher of the second half better?*

**GLEASON**  She was very different. I don't know if she really knew anything much about geometry, but what she said made sense to me. She was an absolute stickler for points and, looking back, I believe that her points were legitimate—if you were a stickler for points.

**MP**  *That was pretty gutsy of you to take on the second half of a course when you hadn't finished the first half.*

**GLEASON**  It was a cinch. As soon as I saw what geometry was about, it was immediately clear to me how the whole thing worked—I mean absolutely clear. I could visualize the figures rather well, and I didn't have any problem with understanding what proofs were supposed to be. Incidentally, the reason I started taking the second half of the course was that I had been helping the kids in that class with their homework in the cafeteria during lunch, so after about a month I just moved into the class.

**MP**  *Was it fun helping the other kids?*

**GLEASON**  Oh yes! I've always enjoyed helping other people with math.

**MP**  *It sounds as if you like teaching.*

**"I often frighten students . . ."**

**GLEASON**  I do. However, as a teacher I have a severe fault. I often frighten students by the way I answer questions. I answer very quickly, in purely mathematical terms, when I should be more concerned with what the questioner's problem is. I don't intend to put people down that way, but sometimes I do. It's very hard to understand what another person is having a problem with when you've never had a problem with it yourself. And, of course, even if you did, you've forgotten how it was.

Gleason's father, Henry Allan Gleason, a botanist with great mathematical intuition, and his granddaughter, Pam.

**MP** *I think that's a difficulty almost all mathematicians have in explaining mathematics.*

**GLEASON** Well, some seem to have more appreciation of other people's difficulties. Eventually I can usually figure out what the difficulties are, but not too easily when I'm at the board. I'm not good at that, I'm really not. It's too bad.

**MP** *Can we return a moment to your high school days? Where did you go to high school when you came back east?*

**GLEASON** Roosevelt High School in Yonkers.

**MP** *So you were not at one of the special schools of science?*

**GLEASON** No, but I don't think that made much difference as far as I was concerned. In New York we had what were called the State Regents Exams, and once I wound up taking four in one semester—I got 100's in the three math exams and 99 in the physics exam. I was always good at taking exams.

**MP** *From a man who cracked the Putnam [a mathematics competition for college students in the United States and Canada] three times, that's a master-piece of understatement. What sort of things other than math did you do in high school?*

**GLEASON** I was in the stamp club and the chess club. I was never a very good chess player, and I stopped playing seriously because it was just making me too nervous. I get just too wrapped up in it. I can do it, but . . . the bad time is the aftermath. So I don't play competitive board games much anymore. I very occasionally play Go, although I'm not very good at it. I really work at it when I do play, and I get very upset with myself if I don't play as well as I think I should.

**MP** *How did you happen to go to Yale as an undergraduate?*

**GLEASON** Well, the principal told me I should apply and so I did. I got a scholarship. After I'd been admitted, I went up to New Haven to see what courses I should take. I had studied a little calculus by myself—in those days a calculus course in high school was virtually unknown—and I had also learned a little from my brother, who graduated from Cornell the same year that I graduated from high school. I had been using a book I had borrowed from one of my teachers. It was Granville, Smith and Longley. So I went up to Yale and talked to somebody. He told me his name, but I didn't recognize it. When I got home I looked at the calculus book I had been using and, oh my god, it was Longley! I wrote him a letter and apologized for not recognizing his name. He wrote back that he thought it would be appropriate for me to take the course in mechanics that he was teaching that year. It was normally for juniors, but he thought I should try it. Now the fact of the matter is that I didn't really know anywhere near as much calculus as I should have known, but I wasn't in there for very long before it became obvious to me what I was going to have to know. So I learned first year calculus and second year calculus and became the consultant to one end of the whole Old Campus at Yale—that was the area then where all the freshmen lived.

**MP** *Same thing as your experience with high school geometry.*

**An Entirely Different Beast**

**GLEASON** Yes, but even more so. I used to do all the homework for all the sections in what was the equivalent of Math 1. I got plenty of practice in doing elementary calculus problems. I don't think that there exists a problem—the classical kind of pseudo reality problem which first and second year calculus students are given—that I haven't seen. At the same time I was working on this course with Longley. It was about balls on a string, you know. As I said, I didn't have any trouble figuring out what was going on and catching up on anything I didn't know. Then, about a month into the semester, I found that I had an hour between a couple of classes, and I noticed that at that time there was a differential equations course which was full of mostly seniors. I thought, what the hell, I might just as well see what's going on. So I started just sitting in, and then I started handing in the homework. In a few weeks the professor said, "Look, you're doing all the homework and doing better than anybody else in the class, why don't you sign up officially?" This turned out to be an important course for me, not so much for the course, but indirectly. For one thing I attracted the attention of the faculty. That's obvious. But it happened that the professor was taken ill in the middle of the semester. I should explain at this point that the two mathematics courses I was taking seemed like an extension of high school; they moved faster and the material was more sophisticated, but their basic style was the same, and I was aware that something was missing. Well, one day the professor was sick and in came Einar Hille. I don't think that he ever regularly taught undergraduates, but he just walked in and started doing his thing, and his style was so unbelievably different—well, I realized, I knew within five minutes, that this was an entirely different beast. He had a view of mathematics which was just vastly different from that of the regular professor. That was a very important experience for me. So after that I took a lot of courses from Hille, including a standard graduate course in real analysis the next year.

**MP** *Your sophomore year?*

**GLEASON** Yes. That was pretty unusual. I took as well a course from Nelson Dunford, who also gave me a lot of feeling for what he was trying to do. Those courses were very much over my head to start with, sometimes I really felt lost, but somehow or other I always managed ultimately to get a pretty good grip on what was going on. Starting with that course with Hille, I began to have some sense of what mathematics is about.

**MP** *What is mathematics about?*

**Why Proofs?** **GLEASON** Well, that's a good question. I don't know if I can say, but I do have a sense that I know what it's about. I think that it's really summed up in what I frequently tell my classes. That is that proofs really aren't there to convince you that something is true—they're there to show you why it is true. That's what it's all about—it's to try to figure out how it's all tied together. And that's what I think was missing from the other professors and what came through strongly from Hille.

Hille was a very interesting lecturer, a very polished lecturer, and he conveyed that sense of how things were hooked up. I've always prized my memory of Hille for that reason.

**MP** *Now you say that you took a graduate course from Hille in your sophomore year. That must also have been the first year that you entered the Putnam competition.*

**GLEASON** That's right. The first Putnam was in the spring of 1938 but the spring of 1940, my sophomore year in college, was the first I heard about it. Some professor wrote me a note saying that they wanted me to compete in this thing. Sure. So I and the others went to his office on the appropriate day. Well, I had no prior information about the Putnam, I had never seen an exam like it. When it was over, I was really absolutely disconsolate. There were fifteen problems, and I could only do thirteen of them. I thought, "I'm not even in it!"

**MP** *If you can do several of the Putnam problems, you're rather good in mathematics!*

Einar Hille, G. T. Whyburn and Marshall Stone at a meeting of the Mathematical Union in Rome.

Nine-year-old Gleason wrote on the back: "It is a picture of no one else than Andrew G. in one of his familiar attitudes."

GLEASON    I was always good at doing problems, and I'm still pretty good at it. I don't think I'm as good as I used to be. I was really very good once. I also took the Putnam in my junior year and in my senior year, and I was in the top five on all three of those occasions.

MP    *When did you graduate from Yale?*

GLEASON    I was a senior in December 1941 when the Japanese attacked Pearl Harbor. I hadn't been in the ROTC, so in the ordinary course of events I would have been drafted but I applied for, and got, a commission in the Navy. One of my professors had a commission in naval communications and he arranged for me to be attached to his office.

I stayed at Yale until June and got my degree. Then I found myself in a communications group which was involved in cryptanalysis. In the group there were a considerable number of people older than I, not much older but new Ph.D.'s in mathematics and junior faculty members. What we really had there was a strong mathematics department at a time when the mathematical faculties of all the universities in the country had been pretty much dispersed into various war projects. I got acquainted with a lot of mathematicians and found that my insight into mathematics was greater than that of most of them. A lot of problems in statistics and probability came up in our work, and frankly I just understood them better than they did, so I was very quickly right in the middle of all this mathematical statistics stuff. I got kind of interested in probability. Although I have never written a paper on it, there are several papers I probably ought to write.

MP    *So you spent four years or so on active duty solving puzzles in Washington D.C.*

GLEASON    Yes, that's right—that's what the subject (cryptanalysis) is, solving puzzles. In fact, in late 1945 and early 1946, the year before we were demobilized, when there was no longer any urgency, we did actually sit around and do puzzles and play games.

It was at that time that I got interested in the game of NIM and worked out a theory of the game. It turned out it was an old theory, worked out by somebody named Sprague in 1928, but—never mind—I didn't know that at the time. And actually the way I worked it out is, I think, more interesting in some ways than what he did.

MP    *What do you feel you gained from your war work?*

**Quick and Dirty Mathematics**

GLEASON    I certainly learned how to do something that a lot of pure mathematicians don't know how to do, and that is that I know how to do quick and dirty mathematics, at least in the area of statistics. It's an interesting knack just to be able to make a sort of quick appraisal as to whether there is sufficient statistical strength in a situation so that hopefully you will be able to get an answer out of it. I'm not the world's greatest applied mathematician, or anything like that, but it's something you learn when you work at it for four years.

MP    *How old were you when you were demobilized?*

GLEASON    I was just twenty when I was called up, and I got out when I was twenty-four.

Working in cryptography during World War II, Gleason learned to do "quick and dirty" mathematics.

**MP** *So you might look back and think that the Navy took some very good years out of your creative life.*

**GLEASON**  I can't complain. Look, many of my friends were out there getting shot at and some didn't come back. I was in a very good position for my mathematical health in the sense that I was with a number of people who were very well trained mathematicians from whom I could learn a great deal. I learned a lot about style and a lot of other things. I am still very good friends with some of the people. One of the guys in the section adjoining ours was Donald Menzel of the Harvard astronomy department. His real field was energy transport within the sun, but he was working on a problem called the anomalous propagation of radar. In those early days of radar there was a lot they didn't understand about it except that it worked. But there were occasions when airplanes that were visible did not appear on radar screens. This had people very upset. (The phenomenon was actually caused by temperature inversion in the atmosphere.) Menzel was a really profound applied mathematician. There is no question about that. The radar problem was a bootleg operation on his part. He wasn't supposed to be working on it, but he had found out about it and had turned a number of people in his section as well as himself onto working on it. I talked to him a fair amount about the problem. He liked my work, and he recommended me for the Society of Fellows here at Harvard. I came in 1946 as a Junior Fellow.

**MP** *Will you tell us how the Junior Fellows program worked?*

**GLEASON**  The program started in 1933 as the result of some conversations between then President Lowell and several other distinguished people on the Harvard faculty, including Alfred North Whitehead. The thought was originally that the Junior Fellows would be given complete operating freedom and would get into the academic world directly, circumventing the Ph.D. process, and for the first few years that was the way it indeed worked. President Lowell retired before it was actually founded, but he gave most of his personal fortune to found it. Some two million dollars. He really believed in it. He was a Senior Fellow, as I am now, for a time after he retired as president. The Senior Fellows select the Junior Fellows. Originally they would take bright people who were just beginning—or maybe just a year into—graduate school and thus get them out of the graduate school "vise," as they called it. There were eight new ones every year, and the appointment lasted for three years, so there were twenty-four at a time.

**Out of the Graduate School Vise**

Well, I got both the advantages and the disadvantages of the program. The good thing was that I could do what I wanted, and that worked out O.K. The bad thing was also that I could do what I wanted. Although I was acquainted with all the contemporary graduate students in math, I never got to know them well because I was living in one of the undergraduate houses and they were living in the graduate dorms or in apartments off campus. The people I did get to know were for the most part people in other areas of the academic world, very bright people who have become professors at significant institutions, but not mathematicians. It was also probably bad that I didn't really have anybody looking down my throat to see whether I really crossed all the i's and dotted all the t's, or whatever it is you do. There are a lot of technical things I might have learned and probably should have.

I have always felt that it's more crucial for me to come to grips on my

*More Mathematical People*

Taking a break in the early 1950's.

terms with the most elementary aspects of a subject. I haven't worried much about the advanced aspects. That is O.K. for certain things but not for others. Since I was a graduate student, mathematics has multiplied by a factor of eight. No one can keep up with it. I don't even try anymore. So I'm not well read.

I oftentimes get involved in working my way through what is really an elementary problem, somebody else's topic, just because I get interested. I am diverted far too easily.

You see, I was never formally involved in the graduate school. I never amassed a single credit in graduate school, and I never got a Ph.D. When I got out of the Society of Fellows, I was appointed an assistant professor here at Harvard.

MP   *How did they know you were ready to get out?*

GLEASON   Well, the Fellowship appointment was for three years, but then sometimes the relevant department here would say, "We'd like to make him an assistant professor, but we're not in a position to make an appointment now. If you will hang on to him for one more year, then we'll have a slot available." And that's in fact what happened to me. I stayed a fourth year in the Society of Fellows and then got an appointment as an assistant professor starting July 1, 1950.

Actually I think what had a lot to do with my coming to the attention of the faculty was that I gave a lecture to the math club on the theory of the game of NIM, which I was just telling you about. It went over very very well and attracted a lot of attention.

MP   *And you have stayed here at Harvard ever since.*

GLEASON   I suppose you could say that but, as it happens, the Korean War started on June 22, 1950, and on September 22, 1950, I got my marching orders to go back to Washington. I was a bit upset, since that was the day classes were beginning. But I went back and stayed for two years, doing more or less the same thing with almost all the same people. You see, at the beginning there was every reason to think that the war might go on for a long time, but it pretty well petered out after one year and then really petered out after two.

**MP** *Have you had visiting professorships at other universities from time to time?*

**GLEASON** I've stayed essentially here at Harvard. The first time that I had a sabbatical I got married. We went abroad for a semester and then spent a semester at the Institute in Princeton. The second time we had small children and didn't think it was a good idea to go out of town. I took half a year off and taught the other half at MIT. The third time—the children were still in school—we did actually move to Stanford, where I taught for two quarters. I have had still another sabbatical, but for one reason or another I felt it was impossible to leave. So my teaching experience outside Harvard has consisted of one semester at MIT and two quarters at Stanford.

**MP** *Can we go back to the Junior Fellows for a moment? That was a rather extraordinary kind of construct within the university. You clearly would have to be incredibly confident about the abilities of the individuals that you are singling out as Fellows because you're really saying that you don't think a Ph.D. is all that important and we know damned well that it is.*

**GLEASON** That's right. And we've changed the rules since then. For the most part we now take people who have just got their Ph.D.'s or are about to get them. We—when I say *we* I mean that the decision is made by the Senior Fellows; however, it was long enough ago that I had nothing to do with it personally—we get virtually no non-Ph.D.'s now. Occasionally there's somebody who does music or something like that, and we'll take him or her because we know that a Ph.D. isn't the only way to get ahead in the world. [Laughs.] You know, I'm in a funny position. I have no Ph.D., and there are lots of state universities whose rules would prevent them from hiring me. This place is not so hidebound.

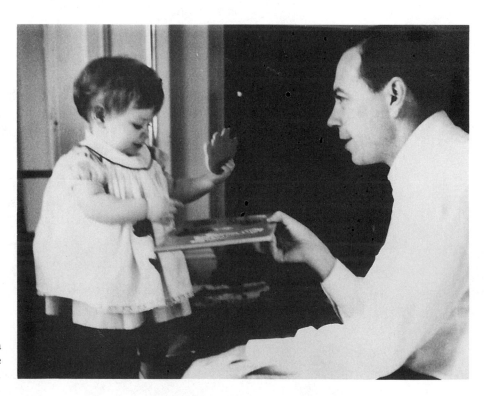

Gleason and his wife, Jean Berko Gleason, a professor at Boston University, have three daughters. Katherine was their firstborn.

**MP**  *Did you publish as a Junior Fellow?*

**GLEASON**  I was publishing a few papers by the end of my appointment. You see, I had started working on this problem in topological groups, which is known as Hilbert's fifth problem. That was as a result of a course that George Mackey gave in '47 or '48. He lectured on it, and I got quite interested. I don't think anybody at Harvard was really aware of how much I was doing with the Fifth Problem. Maybe Mackey was. I had really concentrated on it, and I had already made some pretty good progress while I was still a Junior Fellow. I got so interested in it that I think it would be perfectly honest to say that when I was back in Washington during the Korean war there wasn't a single day that I didn't think about it some of the time. There was also the fact that when I got my orders to go back to Washington, the Provost of the University said, "Well, the rules of the University say that you can have two years' leave, but if you don't come back by the end of two years your appointment will be automatically terminated and you will have to start again from scratch." I certainly was rather upset. I don't know whether it was the memory of that conversation, but at any rate I made a real breakthrough on the problem around February of 1952.

Anyway I was to be released in September 1952 in time to start classes again, but I fell ill and Mackey had to take over for me the first three or four weeks of the semester. I finally arrived in November and have been plugging along ever since. I have had an appointment from the Society of Fellows since '46, so this is my fortieth year of formal appointment at this institution—which is getting up in seniority, if I may say so.

**MP**  *What was it that caught your interest when you first heard about the Fifth Problem?*

**GLEASON**  Gee, I don't know how to comment from that point of view. It just attracted me. I've always had this tremendous fascination with problems which go from what might be called the qualitative way of looking at things to the quantitative way of looking at things. An example of that, which I'm very fond of, is the switch from classical geometry, which is qualitative description, to analytic geometry, which uses the techniques of numbers and algebra and so on. That switch-over is somehow a very important thing in my head. The fact that something like that happens is one of the really deep fundamental connections in mathematics. It happens, and it happens more than once. So in the Fifth Problem you have this notion of the topological group, which is a notion that doesn't have a word to say about the real numbers or any of those things, and then suddenly you grind out this fantastic property about real numbers and convergent power series and all the rest. That's really pretty surprising, and that's one of the things that I just found fascinating.

**Taking on Hilbert's Fifth**  **MP**  *In some of your popular lectures you have mentioned the fact that problems are often best attacked by first attacking a simpler problem. Did you start out that way with the Fifth Problem?*

**GLEASON**  No, because the kind of simpler aspects of the problem had been brought a long way. The compact case was done. The abelian case was done. The solvable case was done, although I am not sure it had really been cleaned up to the last detail. The question, therefore, was just pretty much up to the last place.

Deane Montgomery.

Hidehiko Yamabe.

Leo Zippin.

**MP** *Is there some "human" story you can tell us about the breakthrough when it came?*

**GLEASON** Yes, there's a really remarkable story about that. Sometime— I can't tell you the exact date but let's say around 1949—I was doing other things too, and one of the things that I found very interesting and very curious and which I really felt I should try to understand better was a very famous theorem to the effect that a monotonic function is almost everywhere differentiable. It's a rather remarkable and very difficult theorem—it's not easy to prove. A very very hard theorem of analysis and a really surprising theorem. Well, at the time I was sort of speculating about this theorem, but it wasn't for at least two years that I suddenly realized that *that* would solve the problem I was dealing with! Knowing that, in connection with some other stuff I had been working on, really put the whole thing together. It was a realization that although this theorem had been on my mind for maybe two years, I had never recognized that it was crucial to the arguments that I was trying to work through in the Hilbert problem. I hadn't realized it. Then suddenly it just came to me.

**MP** *It just came to you?*

**GLEASON** That's right. It just came to me that I could use this technique, this theorem, in connection with these curves in Hilbert space that I was dealing with—and get the answer! And that really surprised me. It just came to me out of the blue one day. I suddenly realized that, well, the answer to the question just sits in the fact that there is this almost everywhere differentiability theorem. It has always struck me as so amazing. One half of me had been bouncing around with this theorem a lot and the other half had been doing this problem, and [laughing] they had never gotten together.

What I remember very well is that I drove up to Princeton with a friend one weekend to lecture on it at the Institute. It was snowing, and we almost got hit when he went through a light after it had turned red. Anyway we got to Princeton all right, and I lectured all day long about how one would go about getting my results.

Usually I'm pretty dilatory about writing things up, but in this case I took a week's leave and came up here to Harvard. I holed up in one of the college's guestrooms and didn't come out until a week later when I was finished. The paper was rushed through the *Annals*—that was about March and it came out about July, very fast—along with a paper by Deane Montgomery and Leo Zippin that had a complementary result. They were published as consecutive papers in the *Annals*. Between them, those two papers sort of solved the Fifth Problem. Not quite. Of course, it all depends on a lot of other people's work, too. It is ridiculous to assume that any one person can solve a serious problem. That almost never happens.

**MP** *Now you talked about how you holed up and really worked on writing the paper. Did you know that Montgomery and Zippin had gotten a result too?*

**GLEASON** Yes.

**MP** *And they knew that you had gotten a result?*

**GLEASON** Yes.

**MP**  *So you weren't exactly racing against each other, but you both wanted to be in print at the same time.*

**GLEASON**  Well, the *Annals* editors were the ones that did that. You see, Montgomery and Zippin had been working on a different line of argument which had a great deal more to do with the local euclidean structure of these groups. The approach I was using, while it was a powerful new idea about how to get at the question, didn't even take account of the local euclideanness. That's why it didn't finish the problem by itself. A year later Hidehiko Yamabe showed that you can circumvent most of the finite dimensional topology using an extension of my method. The arguments of Montgomery and Zippin are almost gone in the final result, so most of the proof was eventually given using my method, but not by me.

Of course, many mathematicians are not aware that the problem as stated by Hilbert is not the problem that has been ultimately called the Fifth Problem. It was shown very, very early that what he was asking people to consider was actually false. He asked to show that the action of a locally-euclidean group on a manifold was always analytic, and that's false. It's only the group itself that's analytic, the action on a manifold need not be. So you had to change things considerably before you could make the statement he was concerned with true. That's sort of interesting, I think. It's also part of the way a mathematical theory develops. People have ideas about what ought to be so and they propose this as a good question to work on, and then it turns out that part of it isn't so.

**MP**  *Now your paper on the problem was published just before you started back at Harvard as an assistant professor?*

**GLEASON**  That's right. Then that December I was invited to lecture on the work at the math meeting in St. Louis. At that time the AAAS gave a prize for the best lecture given at the meeting by a young researcher, and they gave it to me, a nice little medal, gold, real gold, I think. So there I was, in the middle of my first actual year of appointment, coming back to Harvard with this medal. The next thing I knew I had a permanent appointment beginning the following July. I was in.

**MP**  *Solving one of Hilbert's problems gets you in very fast.*

**GLEASON**  It's good, yes.

**MP**  *You seem to be an inveterate problem solver.*

**Gripped by Explicit Things**  **GLEASON**  I'm very much given to being gripped by explicit things. Sometimes little things, sometimes big things. Most of my work has been in response to very explicit, easily stated things. I'm very fond of problems in which somehow an at least very simple sounding hypothesis is sufficient to really pinch something together and make something out of it.

**MP**  *That is a very interesting characteristic that you see in yourself.*

**GLEASON**  Well, that's the way I am. That's one of the great attractions of topological groups.

About the Fifth Problem. The original statement is about the analytic structure of the action of groups on manifolds. It was interpreted—well, reinterpreted, after the first statement was seen to be false—to be about local euclidean groups, but it turns out that you can solve it in a more general context of locally compact, locally connected groups of finite dimension. So that's a bit of a change, too. You see, that's part of what I said before. Montgomery and Zippin's arguments to a large extent made effective use immediately of the hypothesis that the group was locally euclidean. And it turns out that you can solve the problem without using that kind of information right away but using only the fact that it's locally compact, locally connected, and finite dimensional. And that's sort of a surprise. I don't think people expected that. At least not in the beginning. You see, the Fifth Problem is a statement about locally compact, locally connected topological groups, etc. It's a pretty remarkable fact that from it you can get a conclusion that a finite dimensional topological group has all this marvelous structure. It's really remarkable that that is possible. But, you know, in the end it's nothing more than a sort of vast generalization of the Cauchy functional equation. That's what it really is.

**MP**  *You apparently have quite a bit of personal feeling about your subject. Can you expand a little on that?*

### The Reasonable Effectiveness of Mathematics

**GLEASON**  Well, about four years ago I gave a talk at Los Alamos. I had read that paper by Eugene Wigner on "The Unreasonable Effectiveness of Mathematics in the Natural Sciences." There were a lot of things that I liked about it, but I did not like the point of view. Wigner had adopted a certain point of view toward mathematics which physicists are in the habit of taking and which, quite frankly, drives me up the wall. I felt I simply had to make an answer. You see, my idea of why mathematics is so effective in the natural sciences is quite different from his.

At one time I rewrote the description of what mathematics is for Harvard's student handbook on what we call Fields of Concentration. It contains a little description of every way of "concentrating" here at the University.

**MP**  *What would be called "majoring" at most places?*

**GLEASON**  Right. So I asked Shlomo Sternberg to help me.

**MP**  *I think we have a copy here. It begins: "Mathematics is the science of order and mathematicians seek to identify instances of order and to formulate and understand concepts that enable us to perceive order in complicated situations."*

**GLEASON**  That's it. And I think the formulation that "mathematics is the science of order" is Shlomo's actual phrase. We expanded on it, but that phrase really belongs to him. I'm very fond of it. I think that it's a very good description of what mathematics is about—figuring out why things are as orderly as they are. That sentence is really the background for why I felt as I did about Wigner's talk. He regards it as an extraordinary coincidence that mathematics works in physics, where my view is just the opposite. Of course mathematics should work in physics! It is designed to discuss exactly the situation that physics confronts; namely, that there seems to be some order out there—let's find out what it is. Incidentally, Wigner was in the audience when I gave my talk at Los Alamos.

**MP**  *Did he come up afterwards and discuss the idea with you?*

**GLEASON**  No, he didn't. He didn't say anything. It was interesting that he said not a word.

Gleason says that he too easily becomes interested in other people's problems.

What is he looking at?

**MP** *It helps, I think, for mathematicians to tell other people what they believe their subject is about as well as what it means to them to do the subject. I also have a copy here of an article by you which appeared in* Science. *It starts with the sentence: "It is notoriously difficult to convey a proper impression of the frontiers of mathematics to non-specialists." You go on to say, "Ultimately the difficulty stems from the fact that mathematics is an easier subject than the other sciences." That must have floored a good many readers! Then you go on and explain: "Consequently, many of the important primary problems of the subject—that is, problems which can be understood by an intelligent outsider—have either been solved or carried to a point where an indirect approach is clearly required. The great bulk of pure mathematical research is concerned with secondary, tertiary or higher-order problems, the very statement of which can hardly be understood until one has mastered a great deal of technical mathematics."*

*Now the readers of* Science *are very well-educated people and most of them, being scientists, have at least some background in mathematics, but there is a much bigger and less scientifically educated audience out there who probably would also like to know something about what modern mathematics is. What do you say to them?*

**GLEASON**   Well, I've given a lot of lectures of that type at one time or another. I work hard at them, and they generally go over pretty well with reasonably well-educated people.

**MP** *So you really do think that it is possible to convey some idea of modern mathematics to a general educated audience?*

**GLEASON**   Well, a certain amount. You have to work at it and you have to compromise to some extent. That's very difficult—to compromise. You don't want to say something that's too patently false, especially if you have all your professional colleagues looking down your throat. It's a little nerve-racking if they all turn up to hear what you have to say. You have to be pretty careful.

Now when I gave my closing address as president of the American Mathematical Society, I talked on the prime numbers. The first part of the lecture, almost two-thirds probably, was expository and the last part was a report on a new result, not yet published, on the prime number theorem. Of course, that talk was more for professional mathematicians, but still you're talking to many who are not specialists in the field you're talking about. At least they all know what a complex number is!

**MP**  *Are you like G. H. Hardy, who said that he preferred lecturing to teaching?*

**GLEASON**  I love to lecture, but I also like to teach. I still enjoy teaching middle-level courses. Those are really great to teach. I work hard on them, and I always work out for myself what I am going to teach. I really learn a lot, and I think the students learn a lot. I have a great time. I'm teaching probability right now, for example, and when I teach probability I start thinking about probability again. I'm a popular lecturer for that sort of thing, pretty popular.

**"I bounce around too much."**

**MP**  *From your various research areas it seems that your mathematical interests are quite diverse. You have really bounced around — topological groups, Banach algebras, foundations of quantum mechanics, finite projective geometry — and now coding theory and combinatorics.*

**GLEASON**  Quite seriously I would say that I bounce around too much. I frequently get distracted from something that I am doing. Then it's very difficult to get back. I have dozens of unpublished papers, and in part that's because somebody has come in and asked me an interesting question. So I end up having a paper half done.

**MP**  *You are just interested in lots of things.*

**GLEASON**  That's right. I have the reputation around here that if I don't know the answer to something, at least I'll be willing to talk to you about the question.

**MP**  *I understand that you even played around with the four-color problem for a while before Appel and Haken solved it by using a computer.*

**GLEASON**  I had two graduate students who worked their theses out on it, and I was perfectly willing to listen to them and argue with them when I didn't believe what they were saying. But I never got serious about the problem. I mean, I never saw the slightest chance of getting at it in a serious way. I have followed with some interest the work of Appel and Haken, but I haven't studied it in detail.

**MP**  *You haven't run it through your computer?*

**GLEASON**  No, I haven't run it through my computer. I understand the principle of what they were doing, but in my opinion their proof suffers from just one thing. When you're all done, you don't know anything more about the topology of the plane than you did before you started. That's an unfortunate fact but it's a fact. You don't get any real insight into the topology of the plane from their argument. The proof may very well be correct. I certainly don't know that it is correct, but I have to agree that more than one person has run the same kind of thing and come to the same conclusion. So

I suppose that it's likely that it's correct. You can give a probabilistic argument to suggest that it's just as likely as any other proof to be right. But, you see, this really crystallizes what I was saying when we started to talk. A proof isn't there to tell you what's true. It's there to tell you why it is true. And this proof of the four-color problem doesn't tell you much about that. So it doesn't do you much good.

I'm not trying to say don't do proofs. Often enough mathematicians have been caught off base with some pathological wrinkle in some funny function or something so, you know, you do have to do the proof, but still in the end the much more important function of a proof in my view is to figure out why it works. That's what is really the issue in regard to Appel and Haken's proof by computer.

**MP**  *You've done a lot of important research in many different fields, you've taught for many years, you've given general lectures to impressive audiences, you have served the American Mathematical Society in a number of capacities, including that of president—in fact, some people we have talked to have characterized you as a mathematical statesman.*

**GLEASON**  Statesman? I don't know. I've never been an activist, so I don't speak out a lot, but I do try to listen to everyone's point of view.

**MP**  *You were also involved very early in the School Mathematics Study Group.*

**GLEASON**  Yes. It was during that time that I first did classroom teaching of little kids. You know, that was the thing that everybody was doing in those days. When I first heard about them doing that, I thought, "Gee, these guys must be geniuses or something! How can I do that?" Then I found out it wasn't so hard. You just walk in, ask questions, and let the kids do the rest.

**MP**  *I think a lot of people are still absolutely scared out of their skins to go in and teach children.*

**GLEASON**  They're scared but they shouldn't be, that's what I'm saying. It's really easy. Much easier than I thought it would be.

**MP**  *Did you go in cold, without any material?*

**GLEASON**  Cold. I just walked in and did things.

**MP**  *What did you do, for example?*

**What's Wrong with American Education**

**GLEASON**  All kinds of things. I have a couple of marvelous stories out of that whole business. Do you know my story about multiplication? It's one of my favorite examples of what's wrong with the American educational system.

One summer I worked each morning with a group of five who had finished the first grade. One day I started by asking, "Do you know how to multiply?" Of course none of them did. In the first grade they don't teach multiplication. So I produced some squared paper and said, "Here's how you multiply." I drew a 3 × 4 rectangle and said, "This is 3 times 4; we count the squares and get 12. So 3 × 4 is 12." Then I did another, 4 × 5. Then I gave each kid some paper and said, "You do some." They were very soon doing two digit problems. The next day one of these kids comes up to me and says, "How much is 34 times 44?" I hadn't a clue why he asked that question, but I thought for a while and said, "It's 1496." He said, "Well, that's how many

squares there are on the whole piece of paper." It was an 8½ X 11 inch paper with quarter inch squares so there were 34 squares one way and 44 the other. I was tremendously impressed, because he had really grasped something. A few years later I was giving a talk to all of the math supervisors of a very large city, a huge room of them, and I told this story. At the end the chief supervisor—chief of all the math supervisors in this big city system—got up and said, "I can't understand why you would want a seven-year-old to know that 34 X 44 is 1496." And I feel that that really epitomizes what's wrong with American education in general as well as with mathematics education.

**MP**  *You have certainly participated at many levels of the mathematical community, from teaching first graders to heading the American Mathematical Society! Your schedule seems to be a very busy one at best.*

**GLEASON**  At worst! It's best when it's not so busy!

*November 1985 in Cambridge, Massachusetts (DA, CR).*

*ANDREW MATTEI GLEASON*  Fresno, California, November 4, 1921. B.S. 1942, Yale; M.A. (hon.) 1953, Harvard. Field: functional analysis. Hollis Professor of Mathematicks and Natural Philosophy, Harvard. President AMS, 1981–82. Hedrick Lecturer (MAA) 1962. Newcomb Cleveland Prize (AAAS) 1952. American Academy of Arts and Sciences, American Philosophical Society, National Academy of Sciences. Books: *Fundamentals of Abstract Analysis*, 1966; *Linear Algebra and Calculus*, 1972–73; (with R. E. Greenwood and L. M. Kelly) *The William Lowell Putnam Mathematical Competition: Problems and Solutions*, 1938–1964, 1980; *Elementary Course in Probability for the Cryptologist*.

(*Facing page*) Siamese cat with its master and good friend.

# BILL GOSPER

At the Symbolics Corporation in Mountain View, California, Bill Gosper works while other people sleep. Although his formal education ended with a bachelor's degree in mathematics from MIT in 1965, his research commands great respect among mathematicians and computer scientists both in and out of academia. He is one of the foremost scholars of the Game of Life, invented by John Horton Conway. He is also well known for his work with computer graphics, infinite series and continued fractions. (He doesn't like "unfinished numbers," and he has campaigned diligently for their representation by continued fractions.) Although he admits to having been "aced out" by Euler in high school, he considers Ramanujan his real nemesis.

We have just finished dinner at the Kabul, an Afghan restaurant in Mountain View. Bill loves Eastern food and as an MIT student even learned enough Chinese so that he could order the "real stuff" in Chinese restaurants. He was one of the early MIT hackers. *Hacker* is defined in the *Dictionary of Computer Terms* by Downing and Covington as follows:

> The word hacker means at least three things in relation to computer programming:
> 1) an exceptionally skilled computer programmer; 2) a person who programs computers for recreation or as a hobby; 3) a person who "breaks into" computers without authorization, either for malicious reasons or just to prove it can be done.

Gosper agrees that (1) and (2) characterize the original hackers, but argues that the original hackers did not maliciously break into computers. He says that they adhered to an unwritten Hacker Ethic as described in David Levy's *The Hackers: Heroes of the Computer Revolution*, a book in which Gosper plays a leading role.

THE HACKER ETHIC:
Access to computers—and anything that might teach you something about the way the world works—should be unlimited and total. Always yield to the Hands-On Imperative!

After dinner we go to Symbolics, a computer company, where his work-night is about to begin. It is eight p.m. He sits down in front of his computer, hits a few keys; quickly the screen fills with beautiful and intricate color images that recently were featured in *Omni* magazine. He says he created the images in order better to see the answer to a mathematics problem. Unlike those of most hackers, nearly all of Bill's "hacks" are inspired by mathematics. The reporting of these hacks, and most of his professional contacts, are via electronic mail.

"When I get a neat result, I mail it out to a list called MATH FUN. I occasionally just dump a bunch of formulas that I have found in the last few months into a letter and mail it off to a dozen or so interested people."

Bill is the only person working at Symbolics tonight.

□ □ □

**GOSPER**   The whole reason I'm here at night is so there are no other people around.

**MP**   *Do you work all night?*

**GOSPER**   I try to leave around four in the morning, and I almost never get out before six. Every night it's the same struggle. And then all of a sudden, after saying that it's time to start going home, two or three hours of frantic activity follow. I don't know how to explain it. There is smoke pouring out of my ears. It isn't anger. It is a funny kind of excitement but kind of a struggle. It is a pleasant kind of reason to stay awake, really, because, after all, if you aren't interested, you can just stop thinking about it. I can tell when I have stayed too long. The drive home is no longer pleasant because there are a whole bunch of people out going to work, and I start missing traffic lights.

**The Purest Activity**   **MP**   *Are you still a hacker in the style of your student days?*

**GOSPER**   I guess so. Back in my student days [1961–1965] we referred to ourselves as "hackers" and hacking was, in our opinion, the purest activity. It was completely unsupervised and a completely honest kind of pursuit— either to make something happen or to find a bug—that was hacking.

The thing that distinguishes hacking from other activities is that you're not just showing up at meetings discussing proposals and project reports. Our group of hackers trusted each other to spend their time wisely. Our only source of approval was the rest of the group.

The word *hacking* in those days was nothing like the pejorative that it has been turned into by the media. I don't know if the media got that negative impression from Levy's book or not. But somehow the image of a hacker being a punk who trespasses and vandalizes computers has been perpetuated.

If I'm talking to someone I know, and they ask what I'm doing, I normally say that I'm hacking—like finding a continued fraction in closed form for some physicist in Boston. Hacking is probably a hedonistic practice, but also one that is intellectually honest. I think I understand the origins of the idea of the kind of hacking that involves breaking into computer systems and damaging them. That is a different matter. That negative characterization of hacking may be due to some self-styled security experts who were around before the problem was severe and when a system's security was just breached by a non-malicious person who simply wanted to demonstrate that the system wasn't secure. These security experts, who were trying to create employment for themselves, would make sensations out of such events and

Gosper admires a favorite toy.

cry, "Look, *hackers*!" It was certainly the case that hackers had a kind of ethical code that was drastically opposed to computer security. The systems that we hackers designed were the antithesis of security and contained totally distributed authority. One had to be a little careful *not* to damage our systems. In some sense a machine's refusal to do what you tell it to is sort of like a bug and the antithesis of what a computer should be. It's very sad for those of us who call ourselves hackers that the word seems to be such a pejorative now.

**MP**  *Well, you certainly have some reputation as a hacker.*

**GOSPER**  Yes. Not only various relatives, but even waiters, ask me if I had something to do with the recent computer "virus" flap on the ARPAnet computer network. What was done in that case was completely benign and accidental. I even got called by the television program "Nightline", which, of course, was interested in the network's link to computers at Lawrence Livermore Labs—nuclear weapons, etc. In fact I worked at the Labs from 1982–1987.

**MP**  *I'm surprised that a free spirit like you would work there.*

**GOSPER**  An exciting thing was happening at Livermore. They were building a supercomputer, and I will certainly confess to being a cycle junkie. Computers are never big enough or fast enough. I have no patience at all with these damned PC's. What I didn't realize when I went over to Livermore was that as long as physicists are running the show you're never going to get any software. And if you don't get any software, you're never going to get anywhere.

**MP**  *Why won't physicists provide software?*

**GOSPER**  Physicists have the most abysmal taste in programming environments. It's the software equivalent of a junk-strewn lab with plug boards, bare wires and alligator clips. They also seem to think that computers (and programmers for that matter) are the sorts of things to which you submit punched card decks like you did in the mid-sixties.

**Witchcraft at MIT**  **MP**  *Let's get back to MIT for a minute. You graduated in 1965 with a bachelor's degree in mathematics.*

**GOSPER**  But just barely. In my last year I slacked off completely. It was on the basis of what I had done earlier that they decided to give me a diploma. I didn't realize that I was in academic difficulty until I got this strange notice that said the Committee on Academic Performance had decided to give me a diploma. It was the first time that I had heard from them.

I had been getting very good grades all along, but then I got fed up in my last year. First of all, the Mathematics Department was radically anti-computer. They would literally preach against it. They had essentially driven Marvin Minsky out of the Department, into the Electrical Engineering Department. But the Electrical Engineering Department had a bizarre attitude toward computers. The electrical engineers wanted as many of them as they could get, but they denied the existence of anything remotely like computer science. They used to ridicule the notion of computer science. They said that there is no computer science and that it is all witchcraft.

**MP**  *They actually used the term "witchcraft"?*

As an MIT freshman working with an early computer in the Technical Model Railroad Club.

**GOSPER** Absolutely! It was their slogan. They tried to keep computers in a strict engineering context. Of course, essentially all of the MIT computers were under the control of electrical engineering and this fact further alienated the Mathematics Department. I can remember the mathematician C. C. Lin saying to our class, "Whatever you do, don't go near computers. They will turn you into a clerk."

**MP** *How did you react to that?*

**GOSPER** I was probably the only hacker refugee from the Mathematics Department—I realized that he was wrong.

**MP** *You're shattering my image of MIT as a bastion of rationality.*

**GOSPER** There is ample evidence that the good guys at MIT triumphed, but only by subversion. For example, the TX-O was the machine that really led to the PDP-1 and, of course, the PDP-1 in some sense led to personal computing, Steve Jobs of Apple fame notwithstanding. The political opposition to the idea that you could build a computer out of transistors as opposed to vacuum tubes was so great that the designers of the TX-O actually had to pretend that they were building only a memory testing device. This was in 1959–60. MIT's reputation as what you call a bastion of rationality in some sense is well earned, but it certainly is not unblemished. Real accomplishments happen there, but not necessarily by the people who get the credit.

### The Technical Model Railroad Club

**MP** *Yet you had a good time at MIT.*

**GOSPER** Yes, but not so much in the classroom. MIT was a marvelous place that didn't know I existed, and that was just great. The independence was wonderful. The only thing people cared about was how I did on tests. That let me budget my time optimally. After my first semester at MIT, I was filled with rage over my twelve previous years of school for essentially having stolen my educational life. I felt that I had learned more in my first semester at MIT than in all my previous years.

What happened outside the classroom was vastly more important than what happened inside, particularly when I got to play with that PDP-1 computer near the end of my freshman year. That brought me into contact with students in the Technical Model Railroad Club (TMRC), who had either dropped out or were in academic trouble and who knew infinitely more than the professors about computers. The professors just knew the IBM "party line" at that time.

**MP** *But you're talking about some outstanding MIT professors, aren't you?*

**GOSPER** Claude Shannon had already punted. If he had been there, it would have been different. John McCarthy came later and got me started. He did a very elitist thing. He rescued a group of freshman (after one semester) just on the basis of grades and gave us an unbelievable computer course. We got to program everything, writing in FORTRAN and machine language for the 709 and physically getting our hands on the PDP-1. He taught us LISP—it was unbelievable! The other poor freshmen never got to touch a computer. They had to make do with a simulated computer called the Rochester machine. Shortly afterwards McCarthy left MIT for Stanford, where his analogous course was called "Uncle John's Mystery Hour." After he left there was nothing in the way of computer courses at MIT.

**MP**  *So in your sophomore year you were getting these "bad" computer courses, but at the same time you had discovered this exciting group of students at the TMRC.*

**GOSPER**  Yes, these guys had learned logic by wiring together telephone relays in order to control model railroad switches.

**MP**  *So the Tech Model Railroad Club really did come out of a railroad club! I thought it was simply a humorous name that you computer guys gave to your group.*

**GOSPER**  Oh no! Professor Dennis, a highly respected faculty member, built the original relay system. He really cut his teeth there. The club used to give mock courses—like 6901, "How to Build a Shunt-Down Pulse Divider." The club guys specified and programmed the PDP-6 a year before it existed—on a blackboard in a classroom that adjoined the club. We were totally excited by the prospect of the PDP-6 and its architecture. It completely contradicted the notion that machine language is grubby and low level. It's my second favorite language next to the high-level LISP that I now use.

**Nerdliness Was a Virtue**  **MP**  *How did you happen to go to MIT? You must have been doing pretty well in high school to get in.*

**GOSPER**  I think I got in by being a nerd and getting good grades. Furthermore, MIT did take mavericks. I don't know if I had any maverick qualities in those days. I don't think that I did. But in the old days MIT placed an incredible amount of stock in interviews conducted by MIT graduates. That's not the case today, and I'm distressed by the current admissions policy. I was amazed to find at MIT students who were genuine mavericks and had really kissed off their high schools. Many had been told by their high school counselors that they would never get into any college. MIT was really great at finding these people by having MIT grads identify them.

**MP**  *Are the mavericks you describe what were called nerds?*

**GOSPER**  Absolutely not! Nerdliness in those days [the early sixties] was a virtue. Nerdliness was spelled "Gnurdliness" at MIT! A "J. Random Gnurd" was someone who had committed a kind of nebbishness. The real grinds were called "Tools" and "Supertools." MIT's slogan for the Second Century Fund was "A University Polarized around Science," which we paraphrased as "A University Paralyzed around Science." The fact was that we liked it, we wanted it that way. There was a great camaraderie. There was a great pride in the absence of things like a football program. Then the sixties and seventies "new age" madness reset the place.

**MP**  *Did you really want to go to MIT?*

**GOSPER**  Sure. I think I was just turned on by all the computers that MIT had when my parents took me up for a visit in 1961, my senior year of high school. But I didn't really know what I was in for in college. I was equally interested in going to the Air Force Academy, but that would have been a disaster.

**MP**  *Had you played with computers before visiting MIT?*

Jim and Bill Gosper in 1954 with unidentified fish.

**GOSPER** Oh no! I had only looked at them through glass windows. I had heard about all the wonderful things that they could do. I used to go over to the Franklin Institute in Philadelphia and look at their computers through their windows too. Everything in those days was batch processing, and they never let anyone go near the computer.

The miracle at MIT was that they had this PDP-1 computer that they let students use without supervision. It was incredible. That's where it all started.

**MP** *The modifier "counter-intuitive" has come up several times in conversations about you.*

**GOSPER** I'm very happy to hear that accusation. I will confess to sometimes being deliberately unorthodox. I like surprises. I've often been traumatized by discovering something and then learning that Euler knew about it in his adolescence. You end up getting self-consciously weird after a while.

**MP** *But Euler was a pretty smart guy.*

**GOSPER** Yes. But at the same time that I never really felt I was going to ace him out of anything, I still felt rather inferior and inadequate that I had been aced out by him. That's a real contradiction! I can remember having such feelings back in high school.

I had such an amazingly deprived high school education. There wasn't a useful math book in the library.

**MP** *What did you study on your own in high school?*

**GOSPER** I was just fooling around with recreational math. I had one other friend who was interested in that sort of thing. We were just sitting there, probably reinventing seventeenth-century mathematics to some slight extent.

**MP** *What kinds of things were you inventing?*

**GOSPER** The thing that started it all was this silly newspaper puzzle that asked you to count up the total number of ways that you could spell the words "Pyramid of Values" from a triangular array of letters. This led my friend and me to discover Pascal's triangle. This happened in grade ten or eleven. We found all of these neat things that are part of the subject now called discrete mathematics. By the time I got to MIT, I was offered a freshman elective in discrete mathematics. I didn't take it because I didn't know what it was. And it sounded sort of like "effete" mathematics. It sounded like it was some useless abstract thing. That shows how much I knew about conventional terminology.

In high school Gosper felt that he was being "aced out" by Leonhard Euler (1707–1783).

**Gut Ripping**

In high school I figured out most of the obvious things and got into Bernoulli polynomials, not knowing that they were called Bernoulli polynomials. In retrospect, the best thing that I did back then was to discover what are now called Eulerian numbers. At the time, and even after four years of math at MIT, I thought that I had been so grotesque [in making that discovery] that I didn't tell anybody about them. Of course the Bernoulli numbers are so vastly complicated that it's hopeless to expect a high school student ever to figure out where they're coming from. Don Knuth calls Bernoulli numbers a full history of recurrence. We never did figure out a formula

Bill Gosper, 8, on the right with Jim, 10, and their father, William Gosper, Sr., a physician. Jim also became a doctor.

for the $n$th Bernoulli number and since we didn't know their name, we couldn't ask.

We just didn't have names for anything. It's really embarrassing, but the term that we had for telescoping series was "gut ripping." We ripped the guts out of the series, and we were so excited to see the series collapse. Up until now I think there's only one other person in the world who knows that, a guy who was my only mathematical confidante in those days. He eventually turned into a business major.

There was one pretty good guy on the faculty. He was a poor teacher, but he was a very knowledgeable mathematician. He showed me a book that had a formula for the $n$th Fibonacci number in terms of the square root of 5. And boy I wasn't ready for that! That was just so completely off the wall.

**MP**  *Did you read Martin Gardner's column in* Scientific American *in those days?*

**GOSPER**  Martin Gardner was something of a heroic figure to me. I would say that I was actually intimidated by him. I was pretty ignorant in those days. It wasn't until 1970, five years after I had graduated from MIT, that I wrote to Gardner about the Game of Life and our invention, the Glider Gun, which was something we knew he'd be interested in. Let me tell you, writing to Gardner was like approaching a demi-god. We felt that it was almost an effrontery to write him a letter. Then we finally had an excuse to send something to Martin Gardner. It was fantastic. It was something he would want to hear about.

**The End of Rocket Dreams**

**MP**  *It sounds as if high school was fun for you in spite of the classes.*

**GOSPER**  It was except for a very disastrous event, which sort of scarred my whole life. In high school I was intensely interested in what nowadays would be called the Space Program. If I had my choice of a book, it would be one of the science fact books that were being written in those days by Werner von Braun and Willy Ley—that gang of German rocket scientists and their converts who managed to get some futuristic pictures published in the

Gosper on the right with his mother, Maria Turini Gosper, and brother, Jim.

Even at three, Gosper was intrigued by flight.

*Saturday Evening Post* magazine. Those books really got me excited. I was extremely interested in them and I would read statements such as, "We know that our colleagues who went East are working like mad on a Russian space program." Here I was reading this stuff as a little kid. I told this to all the grownups, but nobody would listen. It was totally weird. They'd say, "What other comics have you read lately?" I completely understood what the moon program was going to be like.

I was also very interested in building model rockets. In those days there really wasn't a model rocket hobby. A friend of mine manufactured one out of steel and other goodies and gave it to me to launch. To launch the thing, we drove down to this two-mile uninhabited strip of the island where our summer home was. My father didn't want anyone else along, but two other guys who were cross-country runners knew that I was going to do the launch. They jogged on ahead, and we encountered them a mile down the beach. My father picked them up and took them on down with us. By golly, that rocket just blew up and hit one of those kids in the head. He appeared to be making a full recovery, but on one of his subsequent visits to the hospital he contracted a fatal staph infection in the brain. I was living with that for years. I just didn't feel that I had any right to be happy for ten years or even more. It was a pretty rough thing. It completely deflected me from my interest in rocketry and things like that. Rocketry is probably where I would have wound up had that not happened.

MP   *How did your classmates react? Did they blame you for his death?*

GOSPER   No, but the event was also a pretty big, deep dark secret. The lawyers cautioned us just never to say anything about it to anybody. It hung fire for the longest time. The day before the statute of limitations expired, that guy's family brought suit. Then the case was in litigation for five years, and so it was just really bad. I didn't want to bring dishonor on the family. Hardly any of my classmates knew what was going on except for the kid who had actually made the rocket. The lawyers went after him, too. That guy and I never exchanged a word on the subject, and that's just how uptight the situation was. In fact, I guess we never said another word to each other after that. It was really amazingly traumatic.

**Fighting with Minsky**   MP   *Why did you stop your education with a bachelor's degree and go to work at MIT's Artificial Intelligence Lab?*

GOSPER   I didn't feel that I was neglecting my education in the least by taking a job at the AI Lab. It's just that I was neglecting my formal education. I was absolutely at odds with the Math Department and with my advisor in the Math Department. I realized that, in a moment of panic on registration day, I had misread an inequality and had thought that, in order to get a bachelor's degree, I had to take a whole bunch of math courses I didn't want to take when, in fact, it was exactly the opposite. There was really just not much to look forward to there. There were a lot of weird things going on about the time I was to graduate in 1965, not the least of which was a new computer [the PDP-6] on the horizon, and this tremendously exciting environment was keeping me up all night every night. The PDP-1 and Model Railroad Club were essentially synonymous. The people who designed the programming environment for that machine were all Model Railroaders.

**MP**  *Marvin Minsky was already the big name in artificial intelligence when you were there at MIT's AI Lab. What was his influence on you?*

**GOSPER**  Minsky and I used to have raging, night-long arguments about the administration of the robot project at the AI Lab. We almost never had a cordial encounter. Yet the strange thing was that we both liked each other; we just had polar opinions on what a robot should look like and how it should be programmed. It was amazing and frustrating.

The greatest gratification I've ever experienced has not been mathematics at all but just the marginally successful operation of a robot in the sense of being able to honestly see the world through its own eyes and manipulate it with a hydraulic arm and TV camera. The gratification from that is an order of magnitude greater than the gratification in finding a mathematical theorem. But to have to fight constantly to do things that way ["real time" programming and debugging at the "interrupt level," which precludes multi-user timesharing] with Minsky and eventually to lose. . . . This is not to say that I was right and Minsky was wrong. He was subjected to other immense constraints that I didn't have to worry about—such as what everybody else was going to do while I was using the whole computer and he felt he needed to share it twenty-five ways. We never had any animosity toward each other. We just disagreed strenuously then and probably now on how you go about that sort of thing. If anybody's looking for a career and they want the maximum kick, I still claim that you wouldn't believe the difference between robotics and mathematics. After robotics, mathematics was almost like retreating. Unfortunately, even though robotics could have happened fifteen years ago, it's still not happening for all kinds of crazy reasons.

There's a real sense in which I feel contempt for all computers, including Symbolics, for the simple reason that the only thing they know are the lies people tell them from keyboards and that the prospect of the machine actually being able to see and affect the world is drastic. Unfortunately people just run off and build ever faster versions of the same old computer and then treat it as a god-given physical reality. They have to stick to whatever language gets the best use out of it. And the result is that we still have these god-awful programming environments, the C and UNIX kinds of programming environments—that the hackers abandoned (in favor of LISP) ten years ago.

**MP**  *What was the impact on the rest of the hackers at the AI lab when you decided to leave for California to work with Don Knuth in 1974?*

**GOSPER**  Actually, the hacker scene had broken up quite a bit by then, more or less coincident with Minsky's leaving the directorship at the AI Lab and Pat Winston taking over in a very, very strained situation. It put Pat in an extremely insecure position with a large faction of the faculty refusing to recognize him as Lab Director, because he wasn't tenured and weird things like that. So Winston felt it necessary to more or less clean the hackers out of there or at least to make it look very much like hacking wasn't going on. Hacking had an extremely bad reputation then—not because the hacking had the connotation it does nowadays of sort of vandalistic, anti-social behavior, but because it just sort of conveyed a kind of sandbox environment with which no funding agency wanted to be associated. More particularly, it caused a tremendous number of bright students to flunk out of MIT because it was more interesting than classwork. There were all of these very good people who were academically on the ropes because they couldn't bring themselves to listen to these IBM-oid professors spout off inanities about computers.

MIT was trying to discourage hacking, and the lab officers were trying to discourage it. I can remember that Mike Speciner decided that he would implement a fast multiplier and look for a new Mersenne prime. This was when $2^{11213} - 1$ was the record. So he wrote a program to do this, but he was told to stop because certain people were afraid he would be competing for computer resources on the project. He then made the program absolutely unobtrusive: if nothing was happening, it would run, looking for the next Mersenne prime. When the directors heard about this, they ordered him to remove that program because if it found another Mersenne prime, we would become a laughing stock. In the computer science community, finding new Mersenne primes was not regarded as remotely serious. It would also give people the impression that we had excess computational resources.

**MP**  *Don Knuth has described you as a modern-day Ramanujan.*

**GOSPER**  Wow! Ramanujan has always been my idol. I'm not even a worthy student of Ramanujan. When I look at his collected papers, let alone his "Lost Notebooks," I say, "I'm not going to live long enough to get to the last page." It's not just because of this habit I have of going a little bit nuts when I'm on page 1. I don't think I've ever rated one of my results above 750 milli-Ramanujans.

**MP**  *Yet one of your computer science friends says that you've rejuvenated parts of classical mathematics. In the case of accelerating series, he says that, depending on one's perspective, you've either run the subject into the ground or up into the skies.*

**GOSPER**  The world is still thinking about series, recurrences, and continued fractions as being different things. It has this unbelievable, haphazard assortment of different tricks for handling all these things when there is an amazingly simple unification of all of them that I've been attempting to trumpet. Admittedly I haven't done everything I can to get my idea published, but I certainly have it in a pipe in a couple of places. I have gotten up in front of groups of people and yelled it, and I have certainly put it in any number of letters—that there's a technique for doing all this stuff. I can sit down with Macsyma, the symbol manipulation program, and I can just manufacture Ramanujan-like identities from this automatic process. My gosh, that's how I can crank out these identities. But Ramamujan was much better at it, coming up with the real startling nugget.

At the 1987 Ramanujan conference, the title of my talk was "Ramanujan as Nemesis." I got up there and said, "How can we all pretend to love this guy [Ramanujan] when he's forever reaching out from the grave and snatching away our neatest results?" Then I showed my matrix technique of getting these neat identities, and George Andrews would point to a page of Ramanujan's collected papers, or "Lost Notebooks," where he'd have the son-of-a-gun.

**MP**  *It's clear that you think computers are important to mathematics.*

**GOSPER**  Yes. I think my computer is, not because it's mine, but because it does mathematics instead of arithmetic. My computer is a so-called symbolic computer. It's a computer whose operands are not necessarily numbers or even symbols. They are for the most part live objects that can answer

Srinivasa Ramanujan (1887–1920): "My nemesis."

**Cheating God with Continued Fractions**

*More Mathematical People*

questions about themselves and exchange messages with other objects. When I type even at the low level of the machine and get something back and point the mouse at it, it immediately offers to do things for me. A wonderful symbol-manipulating program called Macsyma lives inside my machine. Macsyma does algebra, calculus and other advanced mathematics. It is able to solve messy systems of equations. *It does mathematics!*

This is not to say that my symbolic computer can't do arithmetic; it is the computer with which I briefly captured the pi digit calculation record in 1985. But I couldn't have done the pi stunt without building in some special mathematical structures. I built a novel kind of computational structure called a matrix tower. For my pi-hack I applied this matrix tower idea to the Ramanujan series for pi. This took the machine absolutely to its limit because of a very counter-intuitive property of the algorithm (due to Schroeppel) that looks like a killer. You are evaluating the series *exactly*. In other words, if you evaluate a million terms of this series and that's worth say

Bikes are fun, too, especially when they are equipped with Aerobies.

Who else?

eight million digits of pi, what you actually have is the exact rational fraction which is the sum of those million terms, which is something massively larger than eight million digits. I must have a hundred million digits of stuff in there!

**MP**  *What motivated you to do that great pi-hack?*

**GOSPER**  I wanted to get a whole bunch of the continued fraction of pi. There also was this personal thing. The company [Symbolics] said that they'd give me my own machine if there was a good chance that we could take the digits record. So there was a considerable amount of motivation to get the digits because that way you could corroborate it against the other computations. But my chief goal and chief disappointment was to try to change the object of the game from decimal to continued fraction, since they're sort of the only mathematically meaningful representation of real numbers.

**MP**  *You are fairly passionate about continued fractions. How did you get interested in them?*

**GOSPER**  A hacker friend, Rich Schroeppel, and I both love numbers, and when we saw continued fractions, we realized that was really the way that numbers ought to be represented. After all, a decimal is not so much a representation as an encryption. In other words, if you write down a rational number, you can say, "Oh, you can see it's rational because the digits repeat." Well, you can't! If you write down, say, the ratio of two 30-digit numbers, the decimal representation will look as random as pi and not in your lifetime will you see the repetition. Or even if you do, so what? If you wrote down the square root of 69, you'd never see anything in the decimal expansion; however, you'd see a very simple pattern repeating in its continued fraction, and similarly in the case of *e*. Khinchin, in his book, talks about how wonderful continued fractions are but says, "Of course, there is no way to do arithmetic with them." When I sort of talked longingly of finding an algorithm to do arithmetic with continued fractions, Schroeppel just turned to me and said, "Good luck." I'm sure he feels a little bit guilty for that. When I showed him the algorithm that I found, his very first reaction was, "Oh, feedback." And then he said, "Oh, it won't work." It took me a while to realize that, in fact, it did work, that you really can write an algorithm [in this case, a Newton's method] and have the thing eat its own output as input and just take the square root of a continued fraction outright without any successive approximation at all. And that's true of anything amenable to Newton's method. It's completely astounding. It looks like you're cheating God somehow, and it really works.

**A Solution Looking for a Problem**

**MP**  *You put up a very convincing argument for continued fractions.*

**GOSPER**  They're just a canonical example of a solution looking for a problem. But it's so hard to figure out who really needs them. They're just so pretty, and if there were an application, well, then maybe you really would build the Large Scale Integration and you'd be able to do these insanely precise computations at insanely high speeds with no error. The original motivation for me was aesthetic. I couldn't stand it when I would have a problem and would have to type in 3.14 when I meant pi, because no matter where I stopped, there I was introducing an error at a place where there was no

*More Mathematical People*

error. I really wanted to have a box with pi in it from which I could pull out as much pi as I wanted, and that's essentially what a continued fraction thing is. It's just completely errorless, and this is where there might be an application. It's completely reversible because it's errorless. There's also a low cost factor there. Many computer languages and even mental constructs consider numbers as sort of accomplished. Who wants a number that hasn't finished describing itself? But people expect to be able to pick this number up and run off with it, and they're willing to tolerate an error in a number, just because of the convenience of not having a string of digits hanging off of it. Continued fractions aren't yet competitive in the marketplace of ideas because people aren't used to thinking of unfinished numbers that are really complete.

**Life—The Game**

MP   *How did you get interested in the Game of Life?*

GOSPER   When the article on the Game of Life by John Horton Conway first came out in 1970, other people were more enthused about the whole activity than I was. I got into it rather gradually. I was not motivated to write a Life program myself. I only hacked Life because somebody else [Mike Speciner] wrote the program. I really felt a little bit ashamed about doing it the whole time I was doing it. It just seemed kind of nugatory. I felt it had nothing to do with AI, and it was just the most idle kind of playing around. Conway called it a zero-person game, which I think is really great.

I have watched so much Life on computer screens that I can recall times when literally thumbtacks on a bulletin board would run three generations without even my trying to have it happen. I would not be even thinking about it, and it would happen—also with tiles on a bathroom floor. I had just seen so many generations go by that it was like my retina was expecting motions. But I definitely felt I was wasting my time on Life.

MP   *Do you feel you're still wasting your time?*

GOSPER   No. But I'm playing it a bit more scientifically now. It's partly because the world is coming to accept Life. People are beginning to realize that there actually might be something to some of this Life stuff. For example, to exhibit a simple configuration that grows like $n \log n$ might actually be a useful datum to somebody who is doing serious work with Life. I just believe that giving concrete examples of interesting behavior is useful to people. That is not an outrageous thing!

MP   *How long will Life live?*

GOSPER   A few years ago I would have said it was a fad that was going to die, or it was a fad that would just have resurgences at certain times when personal computing passes thresholds of performance and interactiveness. But now I'm convinced that Life is going to be a fact of life. It's going to be a fact of mathematical life. There's a definite future. I really believe that. It's so many existence theorems for behavior.

**A Soup of All Your Favorite Numbers**

MP   *Number recognition, like continued fraction, is another term associated with you. Can you explain what it means to you?*

GOSPER   This is one of these pipe dreams that I told Schroeppel about. It turned out that he had the same pipe dream, which was: wouldn't it be nice

Before the Aerobie: Billy Gosper in the sandbox at eighteen months.

to walk up to the computer and just start typing in this number which you got by summing some series or doing some integral, like the sum of the reciprocals of Fibonacci numbers, or the solution to cosine $x = x$, or just pulling up any one of these completely miscellaneous numbers and having the computer type out "stop-stop-stop, that's the square root of $e$ over pi plus 17." The idea was that maybe you could make a soup out of all your favorite numbers plus maybe numbers that have multiple definitions, or maybe not, and just let the soup boil for a long time, and then empirically discover a relationship among quantities like zeta of 3, which the analysts had overlooked and which, in fact, might not even be accessible to the analysts. This would be another interesting way in which computer science might stick it to traditional mathematics, which in fact was sort of our attitude in the old days at MIT—we were so pro-machine and the mathematical (curricular) stuff seemed so anti-machine. I guess that sort of formulated our maverick attitudes.

**MP**  *I understand that you enjoy word games.*

**GOSPER**  A friend of mine ran a program over a large word list and looked for every four-letter sequence that occurred only once. The problem is to reconstruct the word itself from just those four letters. The archetype of this is "h-i-p-e." What word has that sequence? Only "archipelago." It turns out to be marvelously hard sometimes to think of these. Like, you take "a-c-l-y" and you're constantly looking for an adverb, but almost all adverbs do "c-a-l-l-y," except for "publicly" but that's "i-c-l-y." So you just look forever, and eventually it turns out to be "cataclysm," a word you use almost every day. I'll almost guarantee it will take you a month to find "a-c-u-r".

Instructing youngsters in the fine art of the Aerobie is a regular part of Gosper's week.

*More Mathematical People*

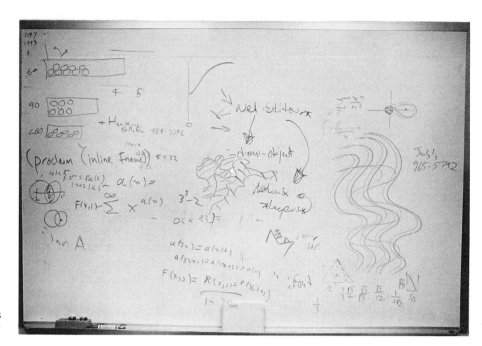

Doodles and inspiration on Gosper's "whiteboard."

**MP** *I noticed back at the restaurant that children you know from the playground came over to talk to you. You seem to enjoy children a lot. Have you ever thought about being a father?*

**GOSPER** I have a feeling that no matter how conscious an effort I made to give kids the attention that they deserve, they would sense that the computer was winning out. I get these computer fixations and just get so involved.

**MP** *Would this feeling pose the same kind of trouble in terms of just having a mate?*

**GOSPER** Yes. It would really be like all those jokes about being married to a machine. Probably it would look that way. It's really narcissistic, too, because when you really think about what you're doing with computers you realize that you're looking at yourself when you're looking at that machine, because it's doing what you told it. Often what you told it is not what you expect, but it doesn't seem like that. So this machine is surprising you, and in fact you're surprising yourself. The machine is necessary for it to happen.

*November 1988 in Mountain View, California (DA).*

# Continued Fractions and Chopsticks

Bill Gosper is a big fan of continued fractions, and he has used them to do some computer graphics and dazzling calculations. The first few paragraphs of the introduction to his "Continued Fraction Arithmetic" underscores his love for them:

> Continued fractions are hard to like. People who like continued fractions eat pickled okra and drive Citroens. Books on the subject are filled with dull proofs of dull properties, and recent papers relating continued fractions to computers have bordered on libel.
>
> But the literature is not the real problem. Let's face it; a continued fraction is a very awkward object for our intuitions to grasp. Just to estimate the size of a purely numerical continued fraction would seem, at first, to require discarding all but the first few terms, followed by converting to improper fractions in a bottom-to-top repetition. Since it isn't immediately clear how much error we committed by discarding the "tail," we have been penalized for asking even a simple question about size. Do continued fractions suffer from the "observer effect"? Why, if they are so intractable, are we about to attempt arithmetic with them? In fact, modern mathematical writers have denied the feasibility of the idea!
>
> Of course, chopsticks are, at first, very awkward objects for our fingers to grasp, and many Chinatown tourists have doubted the feasibility of eating with them. With practice and the proper technique, however, we eventually learn to pity those poor Europeans who must stab their salad greens with a sour-tasting, bent metal object with no moving parts.
>
> Such is the pity I feel for everyone who must crunch his numbers decimally, or cast his points to float among electronic registers.
>
> I will admit that continued fraction techniques are not the best way to handle everything, but then neither are chopsticks.

By now you've heard enough and are ready to see a continued fraction. Here goes. Just follow the manipulations.

$$\frac{13}{5} = 2 + \frac{3}{5}$$

$$= 2 + \cfrac{1}{\cfrac{5}{3}}$$

$$= 2 + \cfrac{1}{1 + \cfrac{2}{3}}$$

$$= 2 + \cfrac{1}{1 + \cfrac{1}{\cfrac{3}{2}}}$$

$$= 2 + \cfrac{1}{1 + \cfrac{1}{1 + \cfrac{1}{2}}},$$

a continued fraction representation of $\frac{13}{5}$.

In order to save space we write

$$\frac{13}{5} = [2, 1, 1, 2].$$

Following the same procedure, we obtain $\frac{67}{29} = [2, 3, 4, 2]$, a continued fraction representation of $\frac{67}{29}$.

By now you can see that any fraction [rational number] can be written as a continued fraction, but what about irrational numbers such as $\sqrt{2}$, $\sqrt{3}$, and $e$? With a bit of work one can show that:

$\sqrt{2} = [1, 2, 2, 2, \ldots] = [1, \overline{2}]$, where the bar over the 2 indicates that 2 is repeated over and over.

Similarly,

$\sqrt{3} = [1, 1, 2, 1, 2, 1, 2, \ldots] = [1, \overline{1, 2}]$.

These examples are illustrations of a theorem first proved by Lagrange in 1770:

The continued fraction expansion of any quadratic irrational is periodic after a certain stage.

Recall that the decimal expansion of any irrational number does *not* repeat. Thus we have a sharp difference between decimal and continued fraction representations of numbers.

With a bit more work, one can show that

$\pi = [3, 7, 15, 1, 292, 1, 1, 1, 2, 1, 3, 1, 14, 2, 1, 1, 2, 2, 2, 2, \ldots]$

and that $e = [2, 1, 2, 1, 1, 4, 1, 1, 6, \ldots]$.

The reader who wants to know more about continued fractions can get off to a nice start with *Continued Fractions* by C. D. Olds, Mathematical Association of America, Washington, D.C., 1963.

WILLIAM GOSPER    Camden, New Jersey, April 26, 1943. B.S. 1965, MIT. Field: computation, computer graphics. Symbolics Incorporated and Wolfram Research.

# IRVING KAPLANSKY

Irving "Kap" Kaplansky, long a distinguished professor at the University of Chicago, is now director of the Mathematical Sciences Research Institute in Berkeley. He says that as an administrator he has been guided by the advice of his teacher, Saunders Mac Lane: "Always behave as though you'll have to explain your actions to a Senate Investigating Committee . . ." He feels that mathematicians should understand important mathematics in areas other than their own, so he has studied and written up for a general mathematical audience the work of many of the Fields Medalists and the contributions that have been made to the solution of a number of the problems on David Hilbert's famous list of 1900. On the side he is "a perfect accompanist" and a lyricist as well as an enthusiastic swimmer.

□ □ □

**MP**  *Did you fall in love with mathematics at an early age?*

**KAPLANSKY**  There's something else I have to tell you at some point, so let's get that out of the way first. It happens that in the beginning my family thought that I was going to become a concert pianist.

**MP**  *Where did they get that idea?*

**KAPLANSKY**  I have a clear memory of the incident but I can't date it. My mother says I was four years old and that's approximately right. Anyway, I was taken to a Yiddish musical comedy. I remember the name of it. It was *Die Goldene Kala—The Golden Bride*. It was probably a low-grade piece of musical comedy, but it was a revelation to me that there could be this kind of entertainment with music. The family had acquired a piano so that my sister could take lessons, and when I came home I sat down and played the show's hit song. I can still play it for you. A dreadful little tune. So I was rushed off to piano lessons before I even started school. The lessons continued for approximately eleven years. Then I realized that there was no point in continuing. I was not going to be a pianist of any distinction.

**MP**  *Did you enjoy playing?*

**KAPLANSKY**  I didn't enjoy practicing. Nobody does. But I enjoy playing the piano to this day. I sometimes say that God intended me to be the perfect accompanist—the perfect rehearsal pianist might be a better way of saying it. I play loud, I play in time, but I don't play very well. However, music has remained a hobby for me. In high school I started playing in dance bands. I got a little income that way. During my graduate studies at Harvard I was in a small combo that played various nightclubs in the area. At that time Harvard had a big band—a big jazz band—and during my last year there I was invited to join. By then I was an instructor, perhaps the only faculty member in the band. I remember that I was teaching calculus at Radcliffe, and a lot of the girls from my class who were at a dance were amazed to see their teacher playing the piano.

**Kaplansky Kapers**

**MP**  *You were shattering the stereotype of a mathematician.*

**KAPLANSKY**  At Harvard I also made contact with kids running the radio station. I had a regular program. They called it "K²" (Kaplansky Kapers).

**MP**  *Did you make up little songs like Tom Lehrer?*

**KAPLANSKY**  Not quite. Tom Lehrer was actually a student of mine at Harvard, but I don't have his talents in that direction. I played imitations of the popular artists of the day and made comments on them. Frankie Carle, for instance. Hazel Scott was another whose style I imitated. After I went to the University of Chicago as an instructor, all that sort of thing stopped for a long time. It was the better part of twenty years before I wound up being what I would describe as the campus accompanist. Whatever crazy show needed to be done on campus, people knew I would be willing and presumably able to accompany it.

**MP**  *How do you explain the twenty-year hiatus? Raising children and things like that?*

**KAPLANSKY**  That was part of it. Mainly I just didn't know how to make contact. I finally did, accidentally, through Bob Ashenhurst, who was on the faculty of the Business School. Maybe we're spending too much time on this?

**MP**  *Oh no.*

**KAPLANSKY**  I was chairman of the mathematics department, and we were setting up an applied mathematics program. Bob had taken his degree at Harvard in applied mathematics, so he was invited to be on our committee. Then somehow or other in conversation it came up that he was very active in a Gilbert and Sullivan group on campus. I allowed that I had had a lot of experience accompanying Gilbert and Sullivan, at which he perked up and said, "Boy, do we need a rehearsal pianist!" The very next thing I knew I was at rehearsals of *Ruddigore*. After that, I got to know the people who were interested in having accompanist-type personnel. I even got to write little bits of music for shows. Then for several years, in an attempt to have some student spirit at Chicago—we had finally got a football team and played nearby teams like Knox College—they hired a calliope and ran it through the streets near the university, and I played the calliope. I have a scrapbook here that I can show you.

His parents wanted him to be a concert pianist, but he recognized that he was "the perfect accompanist."

MP   [*Taking the scrapbook.*] *Oh, this is great!*

**Sing a Song of Pi**   KAPLANSKY   That's a full blown song. The chorus takes the first fourteen decimals of pi and in the obvious fashion converts them into notes of the scale. Before we drop this entirely, I'd like to take a couple of minutes to explain how that came about.

MP   *O.K.*

KAPLANSKY   I'll be brief, although I can give a full hour lecture on the subject, and I've done that several times. Bob Ashenhurst figures in this too. I'm going to talk about songs from what I call the golden age of song, roughly speaking from 1920 to 1950. In 1950 rock and roll started and popular music changed. Most of the songs of the earlier era were in the form AABA and even the man in the street probably knows what that means. There's an A theme that's repeated, then a contrasting theme, then back to the A. But not all the songs were like that. And, according to my memory, it was back in my days of playing in dance bands that I first noticed there was a second form. Subsequently I called it Type 2. A schematic for Type 2 is:

$$AA'BAA'BA''.$$
$$2$$

Here A is a four-bar phrase, A′ and A″ are variants, and B is a contrasting eight-bar phrase. I used to feel that any jazz musician was well aware of the existence of that type. I mentioned this to Bob Ashenhurst once and he was taken aback, but then he agreed with me. So I then went through the literature, but I could find no reference in the literature to Type 2 — perhaps I didn't do a complete search. I wrote the song about pi when I gave my first lecture about Type 2 songs. It was to be the climax of the lecture, the idea being that you could take such an unpromising source of thematic material as the first fourteen decimals of pi and make a passable song out of it if you used Type 2. The point was that Type 2 is really a better form for songs. I'll wind up by remarking that when I saw Woody Allen's *Radio Days*, which uses some twenty-five songs of the golden age, I noticed that the majority of them were Type 2.

I once did a census. I examined one hundred songs and found that seventy were AABA, twenty were Type 2, and ten were irregular. So although only one-fifth in general are Type 2, more than one-half the songs Woody Allen selected are Type 2. I wonder if that was an accident. I offer the theory that his taste is instinctively good. For example, "Dancing in the Dark" is the first song that's played. The second one is "Chinatown, My Chinatown." They're both excellent Type 2 songs.

**MP**  *You should write to Woody Allen.*

**KAPLANSKY**  I'm not going to write to Woody Allen. He would dismiss me as a crackpot. I did write a letter to Alec Wilder, who is the author of the definitive book about these songs, but I never got an answer. That's enough about music. Let's get on with your questions.

**MP**  *O.K. Why don't you tell me a little bit about your Canadian origins?*

**KAPLANSKY**  The beginning was in Toronto. My parents came from Poland before World War I just in the nick of time. World War II was even worse for Poland, but World War I was bad enough. I was born in 1917, the youngest of four children. My father was a typical case of the learning of a curious kind which was revered by the Eastern European Jews, knowing the Talmud and being ready to dispute the fine points — that the sages really meant *y* when they said *x*. He was well prepared to be a rabbi, but when he arrived in Canada he was not well prepared to enter the world of earning a living. He worked as a tailor in Toronto's garment district. He did not really make a living adequate to feed four hungry children. So my mother had the gumption to open a grocery store to supplement the family income. It prospered fairly well, so she tried other businesses. Finally she opened a bakery which grew to be a chain of ten bakeries and became well known in Toronto. Everybody in the family worked in the bakery. I worked too, but then I ran away for graduate studies.

**MP**  *What was the name of the bakeries?*

**KAPLANSKY**  They were called Health Bread Bakeries. My mother baked a wholewheat bread that neighbors and friends praised greatly, so it was the basis of starting the bakery, but the bakery actually made its way selling

ON AN ASTEROID WITH YOU

Words and music by Irving Kaplansky

Written on a honeymoon in May, 1951 and dedicated to
Chellie Kaplansky

Verse

Where shall we go for a ho-ney-moon? The Taj Ma-hal? Peyton Place? They're fine but if you really want a great place to spoon, you ought to try out-er space. Now be-tween Mars and Ju-pi-ter it's not a void, there's real es-tate that you can buy, a cot-tage for two on an as-ter-oid is the best blue chip in the sky! So - When I first get a chance for an in-ter-stel-lar ro-mance on a rock-et ship that's built for two, I'll go

Chorus

cakes. That's where the money is. But the health bread from her own recipe continued until the bakeries were finally sold.

MP  *Your mother must have been quite a person to put that kind of venture together and expand it.*

KAPLANSKY  She had never been sent to school. Eastern European Jews, especially the more orthodox, did not educate their daughters. Nevertheless, she learned to read and write Yiddish adequately. Of course her knowledge of English was fragmentary. She just somehow or other did all these things.

**"If you're debating it, forget it!"**

MP  *When did you first get the idea that mathematics might be what you were going to do with your life?*

KAPLANSKY  At some reasonably early age I knew that mathematics was the one thing I wanted. Sometimes I say to someone who's debating graduate study in mathematics, "If you're debating it, forget it. Only enter mathematics if you know it is the one thing you want to do for the rest of your

At two with his father, Samuel Kaplansky, his siblings (Morris, Max, and Mary) and his mother.

life, because you won't be well rewarded financially and there will be lots of frustrations."

**MP** *But you knew?*

**KAPLANSKY** I knew. I certainly knew very firmly at the time I told the family to stop spending money on piano lessons for me. However, my earliest recollection of feeling that mathematics might some day be something special was perhaps in the fourth grade when I showed the arithmetic teacher that the squares always end in—well, whatever it is that they end in. I remember the teacher being surprised at this little squirt fooling around that way.

**MP** *That was empirical?*

**KAPLANSKY** Yes. I had written down a lot of squares in my notebook. I don't think I proved it. A second recollection several years later is of a teacher giving us one of those arithmetic questions where a hundred objects are to be divided between blue ones and green ones, or whatever. It was simply two linear equations in two variables. I had picked up some algebra from a book that belonged to my older brother—later I got his calculus book. So when the teacher asked for a solution, I put the algebraic solution on the board. She smiled politely and said, "We can't do that," and erased it.

**MP** *Did any of the popularizations of mathematics inspire you?*

**Hooked on Perfect Numbers**  **KAPLANSKY** I got from the public library one of those books on mathematical recreations, not a very good book as I remember. There were little squibs of an elementary kind, one of which was about perfect numbers. That was my introduction to perfect numbers. All the author did was to give the definition and the first few examples, but I was hooked for life. I guess that has happened to a lot of people, starting with Pythagoras. Since then I've enjoyed watching the developments on odd perfect numbers and Mersenne primes. The author didn't point out the obvious pattern which shows

*More Mathematical People*

up even in the first few perfect numbers. I observed it and then proved that every even perfect number must be of that form. That's probably the first thing I ever proved.

**MP**  *That was at what age?*

**KAPLANSKY**  Age thirteen. So I wrote the publishers, saying I wanted to contact the author. They gave me his real name and his address, which was in Athens. Greece being so far away, I gave up the idea of writing to him. The matter lay dormant until my last year in high school when I had a mathematics teacher who was very indulgent to me. He allowed me to pay no attention to what was going on in class and to work on anything I wanted.

**MP**  *Smart teacher.*

**KAPLANSKY**  I showed him this proof and he said he would check it. The next day he told me I was a little late—Euler had proved it two hundred years earlier. Of course my proof was essentially the same as Euler's. Everybody proves it the same way. I was a little disappointed, I guess.

**MP**  *Now we've got you to the point of entering college. You've said that by that time your commitment to mathematics was serious. You were doing these musical things too. Were there other interests in high school?*

**KAPLANSKY**  That was enough to keep me busy.

**MP**  *So you went off to the University of Toronto and declared yourself for mathematics immediately?*

**KAPLANSKY**  That's more or less right. Actually the first year was common to mathematics and physics; in the second year one declared for either mathematics or physics. In the British style we were packed full of classical mathematics. Perhaps that stood me in good stead for the rest of my career. On the other hand, it could have been too much of a good thing. It wasn't balanced with glimpses of modern mathematics—except in the case of Richard Brauer. He arrived when I was a sophomore, and in my third and fourth years I had courses from him. I knew the real thing the moment I saw it. I think, although it may not be so, that my preference for an algebraic way of looking at things owes a lot to Brauer.

**MP**  *Can you expand on that?*

A graduate of the University of Toronto in 1938.

**KAPLANSKY**  Take the case of C*-algebras, which I spent a good many years on. I wound up converting a large part of that theory into a pure piece of algebra because I thought that would delineate clearly some of the ideas. In hunting up the algebra, you don't do everything by any means, but you do clarify a good portion by generalizing. Have you heard Ralph Boas's excellent joke? His proposed motto for mathematicians in the 1940's was "Be wise, generalize." That was a play on an advertising slogan for Simonizing, a way of waxing a car. "Be wise, Simonize." "Be wise, generalize." I find that the generation of younger mathematicians has never heard of Simonizing, so the joke is lost. Are you of that generation?

**MP**  *I'm afraid so.*

**KAPLANSKY**  That brings us to the Putnam Competition, which I entered during my last undergraduate year at Toronto — the first year of the competition. When the announcement came, the faculty at Toronto paid close attention because they wisely figured that the kind of drilling we were given there would give Toronto an advantage. Among other things our classical courses had been accompanied with good stiff Tripos-type problems. At that time that probably was good training for the Putnam. Nowadays it's necessary to get some training in things with a more modern flavor as well. It was announced that there would be a team prize as well as individual prizes. Furthermore, one of the contestants was to get a scholarship to Harvard. Well, Toronto's team won and I got the scholarship without having to apply anywhere or having to wonder what was going to happen to me next.

Another thing happened in 1938 which also set the course for me to a certain extent. The University of Chicago announced a special summer program in algebra. Today our bright students take it for granted that they'll get financial help every step of the way, but those were do-it-yourself days and my going to Chicago was self-financed. There was a conference that kicked off the program, and Saunders Mac Lane gave one of the talks. I thought, there was a man who did my kind of mathematics!

**"I like infinite things."**    MP   *When you say that, what do you mean?*

KAPLANSKY   It was a lecture on valuation theory, which was his field at the time and which became my initial field. The precision, the elegance impressed me. It was so obvious that he was completely on top of it. I don't know if I can amplify that. I said earlier that I liked the algebraic way of looking at things. I'm additionally fascinated when the algebraic method is applied to infinite objects. Perhaps the difficulties and the subtleties are greater than with finite things. Oh, I like purely finite things too, but I like infinite things even more. That's exactly the kind of algebra his was. Infinite algebra, beautifully presented, elegant, fascinating. I have been fascinated by valuation rings ever since. I keep wandering back to them.

MP   *Did you know then that you were going to work under him at Harvard?*

KAPLANSKY   That was a possibility. The moment I arrived at Harvard I made contact and did begin to work with him. I was his first Ph.D. But let me jump ahead a moment to a non-mathematical piece of wisdom he imparted to me when I later took over the chairmanship at Chicago. He said, "Always behave as though you'll have to explain your actions to a Senate Investigating Committee the next day."

MP   *There are a lot of people these days who would have profited from that same advice!*

KAPLANSKY   So my path was laid out with a minimum of effort on my part, and I wound up with a Ph.D. in 1941. The country was crawling out of the Depression. It wasn't as bad as 1935, say, but it seemed to me that it might take a miracle for me to get a job. How different it has been since World War II! Even the more difficult years in the 1970's and early 1980's weren't that bad. I applied here and there, and in particular I applied to stay on at Harvard as a Benjamin Peirce Instructor. Maybe I should have been discouraged but I was allowed to do that, and it was very agreeable with me.

MP   *Why do you think you should have been discouraged?*

**KAPLANSKY**   I think that on the whole a fresh young Ph.D. should go somewhere else — see new faces and get new ideas. But of course I was very happy to be able to stay on at Harvard.

**MP**   *Were you in a very productive period then?*

**KAPLANSKY**   I don't like to answer questions like that. My mathematics should speak for itself — let other people scan my mathematics.

**MP**   *O.K. But you felt good about that time.*

**KAPLANSKY**   Then in 1944 — the war was still on, of course — Saunders went off to the Applied Mathematics Group at Columbia, and he suggested that I join that group. So there was one year spent largely on ordinary differential equations. I had a taste of real life and found that mathematics could actually be used for something.

**MP**   *When the war ended, were you glad to be done with applied mathematics?*

**KAPLANSKY**   Well, no. I liked it too. I think I could have been a mathematician in industry with some measure of happiness and perhaps also success.

**Miracle at Chicago**   **MP**   *It's hard for me to think of you in industry.*

**KAPLANSKY**   There were some mathematical challenges even though they were on a rather modest level. Anyway, at the conclusion of the war our group began to fold. My future was uncertain but then a miracle happened. The University of Chicago offered me an instructorship.

**MP**   *Was Mac Lane already there?*

**KAPLANSKY**   No. The sequence of events at Chicago is the following. In 1946 Marshall Stone was brought in to rebuild the department. John Kelley and I were the last two appointments before the beginning of the "Stone Age." That is an old joke at Chicago. Kelley promptly left, but I happily stayed on — for thirty-nine years. Stone made four colossal appointments — that's not counting Stone himself — which had an enormous effect on the Chicago department. They were Mac Lane, Zygmund, Weil and Chern. Not bad!

**MP**   *Not bad at all.*

**KAPLANSKY**   And he also brought in a crowd of topnotch younger people. The story is told very well in Paul Halmos's *Automathography*. Well, Saunders and I were together again and it was marvelous. Chicago fulfilled my dreams perfectly. It was all I had thought it would be. Now here I am, let's see, forty-one years later at MSRI, and I like to think that, though different in many ways, MSRI has something of that same spirit for the young people who come here. I sure hope so.

**MP**   *Certainly a lot of the people who have come have been enormously stimulated.*

**KAPLANSKY**   As a little side remark, I'd like to mention that Chicago's quarter system served me very well. The four quarters of the school year were equal in principle, so you could, for instance, teach in the summer and take a quarter off in the middle of the year. I did that year after year — for two reasons. In the middle of the year I could go someplace else where mathematics was flourishing, and in the summer I could stay in Chicago where, unlike most places, things were very active because of the quarter system. I also liked to teach in the summer at Chicago, even though Chicago's summer climate is not considered the greatest, because I love to swim in Lake Michigan.

**MP**  *It's kind of chilly, isn't it?*

**KAPLANSKY**  By the middle of the summer it warms up admirably. I recommend it.

**MP**  *How long were your swims?*

**KAPLANSKY**  Oh, several hours. I would have my classes in the mornings and swim in the afternoons. I would swim the length of the lake shore in that area.

**MP**  *Do you still swim?*

**KAPLANSKY**  Yes. After we split today, I'll go down to the pool. Swimming is another one of my hobbies.

**MP**  *Now we've got you to Chicago....*

**KAPLANSKY**  At this point this is simply going to become a mathematical autobiography, I guess. What did I work on? Why? I don't know how much of that I really want to talk about. Have somebody else talk about that. But let me pay tribute to my fifty-three Ph.D. students. I think of Alex Rosenberg, Donald Ornstein, Harold Widom, Hy Bass, Steve Chase, Steve McAdam, Graham Evans, Judy Sally and many, many others. Not my students but adding immeasurably were Dick Kadison, Iz Singer, John Thompson, Paul Cohen and many, many others. A good student is one who will teach you something and, boy, I learned a lot from my students!

**MP**  *Did you enjoy teaching?*

**KAPLANSKY**  Yes indeed. Not only did I enjoy my Ph.D. students, but I also enjoyed the classroom situation.

**MP**  *What makes the classroom side of teaching fun?*

**KAPLANSKY**  On the one hand, I like the challenge of organizing my thoughts and trying to present them in a clear and useful and interesting way. On the other hand, to see the faces light up, as they occasionally do, to even get them excited so that maybe they can do a little mathematical experimentation themselves—that's possible, on a limited scale, even in a calculus class.

**MP**  *Let's go back to the Stone Age for a moment.*

**KAPLANSKY**  There we were at Chicago, lucky enough to have André Weil, one of the greatest mathematicians in the world. There were several times in my life that I've, one way or another, got that feeling, my gosh, here is a tremendous mathematician; for instance, Weil, von Neumann, Serre, Milnor, Atiyah. Well, those are obvious names. But, above all, André Weil. We were colleagues for about ten years. I can even pinpoint mathematics I did that I wouldn't have done if he had not been there. It's not that he showed me how to do it or anything like that, but by just a casual remark he would

"But, above all, André Weil."

start me off on something. He was very impatient with what he regarded as incompetence. I don't think he'll mind my saying that. Then there is his extraordinary quickness. You may know about that. You can take an area of mathematics that he presumably never heard of before and just like that he'll have something to say about it. Serre, Milnor and Atiyah have a lot of that too, but I think of them more as transmitting a wonderful mastery—what's really going on in a subject. They say exactly the right thing at the right time so that listening to them is such a worthwhile experience. Other people who are expert in a field will often hide the kernel of the subject, maybe sometimes because they don't understand it properly themselves.

**A Question of Essence**   **MP**   *That's what I was going to ask. Do you think that this gift you speak of is related in large part to just a very full understanding of the subject?*

**KAPLANSKY**   It's a question of essence. When a great mathematician has mastered a subject to his satisfaction and is presenting it, that mastery comes through unmistakably, so you have an excellent chance of understanding quickly the main ideas.

**MP**   *Are there people you've read, whom you perhaps have never met—maybe they were long gone by the time you read their work—who have made a big difference to you, even though their actual mathematics is not exciting anymore?*

**KAPLANSKY**   I'll come to that in a second, but first I would like to pay tribute to the younger colleagues at Chicago—Irving Segal, Paul Halmos and Ed Spanier. In each case we had good and stimulating mathematical conversations again and again. I'll mention Segal especially. That was a period when he was so productive on $C^*$-algebras, representations of locally compact groups, and related topics. Subsequently he moved vigorously into the relation of these things to physics. I followed in his footsteps. To begin with I was like a student. After a while I did have the feeling that I was speaking to him as an equal, but initially he was way ahead of me. With Halmos and Spanier, I felt at once that we were colleagues—equal colleagues. I trust they felt the same way—I hope they don't mind my saying that. We constantly interchanged so many interesting ideas.

**Living on the Heritage of Gauss**   Now, as to your question about reading the classics. Every time I go back and read some classic, I find that it is hard work but I realize it's a good thing to do. It was rather late in life before I actually began to read any Gauss. (Do you realize that Gauss's *Disquisitiones* was made available in English translation only about ten years ago?) Once in a talk I remember that I said that Gauss's predecessors—Euler, Lagrange, Legendre—were extremely clever mathematicians and if they had only had a chance to go to a good graduate school they really would have gone to town. But with Gauss it was different—he was a good graduate school all by himself. I think André Weil said somewhere, "We're still living on the heritage of Gauss." Maybe that's a little bit exaggerated, but there's a lot of truth in it. Gauss inaugurated mathematics as we know it today.

One thing I've always enjoyed and go back to now and then is Dedekind's collected works as edited by Fricke, Noether and Ore. The three editors make discerning comments after most of the papers. Dedekind's papers are beautiful as they stand, but then to have those marvelous comments as well! Emmy Noether is supposed to have said, "Es steht schon alles bei Dedekind." (You find everything in Dedekind.)

**An Expository Urge**

**MP**  *I understand that you have also gone back to Hilbert and have been working on a book treating the twenty-three problems he proposed to mathematicians at the International Mathematical Congress in Paris in 1900.*

**KAPLANSKY**  Once I was browsing through Richard Bellman's book of mathematical classics, one of which is Hilbert's 1900 talk, when I realized that until that moment I had never actually looked at Hilbert's own words. I was ashamed and dismayed. Then, as I read, I realized that in several cases I didn't quite understand what Hilbert was driving at and that in most cases I wasn't quite sure what had happened subsequently. At that point there was no book in print on the progress which had been made since 1900 in solving the problems. I daydreamed—there ought to be a write-up on each problem just the way a reader would want it. Really tell why Hilbert was interested in the problem, what the background was, how each one fits into mathematics, and—of course—exactly what has happened with the problem since he gave his talk. An expository urge overcame me, and I just started doing it.

**MP**  *What is the current status of the project?*

Early in his chairmanship at the University of Chicago.

**KAPLANSKY**  It got a certain distance and then was put aside. I'll probably never finish it, although I have in fact written up twelve of the twenty-three problems in a set of Chicago notes. It's crazy, I guess, for one person to try to write up all of them. The normal thing is to get twenty-three people, each one an expert on one of the problems. That's what the Russians did, and that's what the American Mathematical Society did. Since I first started, they have both produced fine books on the current status of the Hilbert problems, although frankly there is some unevenness in both books. There is bound to be with a number of authors. So stubbornly I have persisted. I think that there may be some merit in having just one author: a more unified style and the fact that the threads which exist every now and then between different problems will be followed up because it's the same author. Also an expert may be so busy telling you what he proved last night that he quite fails to tell what the heck the problem is about in words that a bright graduate student can understand.

**MP**  *I like your expression, "an expository urge."*

**KAPLANSKY**  Something similar to the Hilbert thing came up in connection with the Fields Medalists. I was talking with Yitz Herstein and I said, "You know, it's a little scandalous the way we gossip about what this and that guy has done, saying that something is a nice piece of work without exactly knowing what we're talking about. For example, our heroes—the winners of the Fields Medals—what exactly have they done?" We started talking about that, and in several cases we knew exactly but in other cases we didn't know at all. So we said even if we can't prove their theorems, let's see if we can't at least state them accurately. I started with Jesse Douglas, who was one of the first two winners in 1936. I did master what he did to the point where I could write out his main theorem in plain, easily understood graduate school mathematical English.

This all connects with the thing that bedevils the mathematical profession—the difficulty we have in telling the world outside mathematics what it is that mathematicians do. And for shame, for shame, right within mathematics itself we don't tell each other properly.

MP  *What solution do you have to offer?*

KAPLANSKY  Work harder at it. Everybody's uncle says that we need more good expository writing, but nothing too much has happened, has it?

We shouldn't surrender so readily to only half understanding all kinds of things. Try harder to understand, and then when you have understood take a little time out maybe to explain to others.

MP  *The excuse is often made that mathematics is so big now that it's difficult for people even in different subfields of the same subject to understand one another.*

KAPLANSKY  I don't accept that. It reminds me of the defense people make when they repeat a piece of work, even reproducing something that is well known. It's shameful. I've scolded people for that. Mathematics literature has grown enormously, but in any well-defined field several afternoons spent with *Math Reviews* will get you ninety per cent of the literature. If you don't do that, you can waste months of time. Of course, there is another side to the coin. Sometimes by starting fresh you can come up with something new and interesting. Nevertheless, at some point you should check the literature. Mathematics has advanced to where it is—what's the phrase?—by standing on the shoulders of the giants that preceded us.

MP  *Could we turn to your own research style, if we may. How do you do mathematics?*

"Do a million examples."

KAPLANSKY  Let me go back to the advice for better or for worse that I have occasionally given to students. Certainly one thing is to look at the first case—the easiest case that you don't understand completely. That general theorem down the road—hopefully you'll get to it by and by. The second piece of advice: do examples. Do a million examples. I think there are shameful cases of people making (I'll even say) silly and reckless conjectures just because they didn't take the trouble to look at the first few examples. A well-chosen example can teach you so much.

MP  *"Well-chosen" is a heavily loaded phrase.*

KAPLANSKY  Well, let's say instead a "lucky" example. Sometimes when you work through an example, you suddenly get an insight which you wouldn't have got if you'd just been working abstractly with the hypothesis of your future theorem. I guess both of these are obvious pieces of advice, but they are ignored more often than they should be.

A third piece of advice: if the problem is worthwhile, give it a good try. Take months, maybe years if necessary, before you announce to the world, "This is as far as I can go. I'm quitting." It is disgraceful to give up before you have given it a good college try.

MP  *That's pretty tough advice.*

KAPLANSKY  Oh, and here's a fourth piece of advice that's especially hard to follow in the years before you have tenure. The advice of Gauss: publish little but make it good. I haven't followed that advice myself. To put it more

Groundbreaking for the Mathematical Sciences Research Institute at Berkeley: Martin Kruskal, an unidentified onlooker, Robert Osserman, Hyman Bass, Reese Harvey, S. S. Chern, Kaplansky, I. M. Singer, Daniel Quillen, and Al Thaler.

dramatically, if your problem is a little bit on the obvious side, it's very likely that someone on the planet will do it within the next five years anyway, so don't bother publishing it—turn your attention to other things. Try something that no one else is likely to do for at least twenty years. That's a high ideal but one to keep in mind. Don't feel the least bit bad when you see an abstract in the *Notices* and find out that somebody else has the theorem already. Fine, you don't have to work through the details. And somebody else is interested. That's always good because it does away with the disappointment of publishing a paper and finding in a few years that absolutely no one has paid any attention.

**MP** *There is another question I would like to ask.*

**KAPLANSKY** But first maybe we should mention my connection with physics. Herstein plays a role in this too and so does Peter Freund, a physicist at Chicago. As I understand, they played billiards at lunch and one day Peter, leaning over to take a shot, said, "You know, there's some kind of twisted Lie algebra that physicists are all excited about—a mathematician should take a look at it." Well, right after they finished their game, they came up to me. I paid close attention to what Peter was saying and got all excited. Ever since then I've been on the fringes of supersymmetry, which is what physicists call Lie superalgebras. I got invited to the Aspen Physics Center in 1981. I was the only mathematician there among sixty physicists—the token mathematician. I think I made a good impression. I was eager to talk to them and I listened carefully, sometimes to no avail, but sometimes I was able to say something. Mainly I tried to understand their language, which is not easily translated into mathematics.

I believe that to this day there has been no application of the subject of Lie superalgebras to physics. There's been no experimental verification for it, no sign it means anything. Nevertheless, a substantial number of physicists continue to believe that this may well be one of the keys to the grand unification they're seeking that will unite in a single mathematical theory all their four forces. In the meantime there are a lot of charming mathematical problems which, for better or for worse, could be worked on. And there is hope that one of these may be something that somebody out there needs.

I am going to Aspen again this summer. Since all summer long there's also a music festival in Aspen, I'm looking forward to it for two reasons. Now what was the question you had when I interrupted you with my physics?

**MP**  *In the article you wrote for the* Mathematical Intelligencer *about the founding of MSRI, you go back to an NSF meeting of scientists in various fields, which was held about twenty-five years prior to the founding. You wrote that the following question was posed by some unidentified NSF person: "What in your discipline could make for a quantum leap in achievement?" When your turn came (going around the table), you said that it would be the founding of two new mathematical institutes. Now a quantum leap in achievement—that's asking for a lot.*

**KAPLANSKY**  He was a physicist, and physicists like that phrase.

**MP**  *Well, certainly you've seen a lot of achievement as a result of the establishment of the two new institutes of mathematical sciences in Berkeley and in Minneapolis, but I am wondering if you can give some sort of a time frame in which that quantum leap will be made.*

**KAPLANSKY**  Five years have now gone by. Are you asking whether we see something like a large leap already, or at any rate hope for such a decisive step forward in the not too distant future?

**MP**  *Yes.*

**Ask Ten Years from Now**  **KAPLANSKY**  To answer, I am going to quote other people's opinions. I believe it is the generally perceived impression that MSRI has accomplished all that was hoped for it and maybe a little more. Five years is too short a time for a judgment on whether there's been something like a quantum leap or will be in the not too distant future. It seems to me that it takes a substantial period of time for a development of this kind to have its influence fairly clearly discernible. By way of comparison I think back to the time the Institute for Advanced Study opened its doors in 1932. Let's say it was at least fifteen years, perhaps closer to twenty, before there was a definite perception that this had been very important for the development of American mathematics. Ask me again ten years from now.

**MP**  *Another question regarding MSRI: how did you happen three years ago to come to the decision to make the switch from one kind of life in Chicago to a totally different one in Berkeley?*

**KAPLANSKY**  I was chairman at Chicago for five years, so the world of administration was not new to me. The directorship of MSRI has some elements in common with a chairmanship, but it's quite a bit different too. For one thing, here—as compared with the Minneapolis Institute, which is part of the University of Minnesota—we are entirely free standing. Everything needs to be done by us. The new tax law makes for certain changes that will need attention. The new immigration law is giving us a headache with the paperwork involved. Although I don't exactly do these things myself—we have a very able business manager—I am involved in them, knowing what needs to be done and trying to be sure that it's done right. However, the bulk of the job is arranging the annual programs and working with the stream of visitors. The number of visitors each year is approximately 180, although not all of them stay for the whole year. I've compared it with hiring a new faculty of 180 every year. Each case is a little different. It generates a new file, which can be sizeable, and requires innumerable letters and phone calls. So that can be a bit demanding but, on the other hand, there's frequently enough a feeling that something worthwhile is being accomplished. That is a feeling that is often missing in a good deal of a department chairman's work.

MP   *Can you elaborate a bit on that sense of accomplishment?*

KAPLANSKY   An example is when we decided to have a jumbo program in number theory. Of course, that was not my individual decision. I was not yet the director, although I was in on the decision as director-elect. We had to decide on the program some years in advance and then try to make sure that the right people came. Well, it was crowned with two very fine pieces of work coming out of it that year. I feel that I had a kind of direct hand in that, helping it along at every stage. Is that clear? A chairman could have something comparable but it's less likely. A department becomes so stable over a period of time that a chairman, who sometimes has a rather brief term of office, can't disturb it much.

MP   *What do you mean when you say "having a hand in it"?*

KAPLANSKY   We didn't have to have a jumbo year in number theory. The idea was explored while sitting around a table with our Scientific Advisory Council. Then there was a committee, of course. The Program Committee was all important. Executing their ideas was my job. It was vital to have certain special people take part. I came back again and again and again to make sure that they came. On a more humble level I try, with what measure of success I won't try to say, to make sure that the everyday things around here run tolerably smoothly so that these bright young people—I especially think of the young ones, the others are already established—will have a rewarding experience here.

MP   *You started to answer a question which I am not quite sure you have answered; that is, why did you take the job?*

KAPLANSKY   Well, here I had been running around for twenty years saying how desperately we needed two new institutes. Then the dream came true. For reasons that still mystify me the people out here decided that they wanted me as director. It was inconceivable to say no. Cal Moore had done a spectacular job of getting the place going. I had been out here and had been very favorably impressed. It was the right offer at the right time. Let's say, it was a nice way of capping my career. On the whole, I'm glad I did it, although I haven't been able to do much mathematics.

MP   *It looks as if you have taken more than a passing interest in this recent microprogram on commutative algebra.*

KAPLANSKY   I joked once to Cal Moore that we had better have some algebra here or people would think that I am just a figurehead. Earlier there was a program on infinite-dimensional Lie algebras which I chaired, but it had such heavy overtones of topology and analysis that it can't count as hard core algebra. The microprogram you just mentioned was our first bona fide algebra program.

The Director at the entrance of the Mathematical Sciences Research Institute (commonly referred to as MSRI or "Misery").

*More Mathematical People*

Taking a break at MSRI with Don Albers and S. S. Chern.

**MP**  *One last question. Of all the things you've done in mathematics is there any one thing—you can mention even a couple of things—about which you have a special sense of pride?*

**KAPLANSKY**  I actually already have an answer to that in writing. I'm not sure where it appears, but I remember giving it once. I am proudest of the paper "Any orthocomplemented complete modular lattice is a continuous geometry." It's not that it is especially important, but nevertheless I am proudest of it. It required a sustained effort of about six months, an effort of a kind that I don't think I could ever put out again. I did it in 1955—thirty-three years ago—but, in part because no one else really much cares, I don't think it would have been done otherwise, even by now in 1988. I think there is an unexpectedness about it—I don't want to use a word like ingenuity—and a high level of infinite algebra—the kind that I'm especially fond of, as I mentioned to you in the earlier part of this conversation.

A companion nomination—I think that the one of my papers that has been most quoted, most influential, is "Rings with a polynomial identity." It is an exercise for a graduate student today, but it nevertheless opened up a whole new field. I think that if one were to test that paper with a citation index, it would be verified that it has had a substantial number of quotations—more than any other of my papers.

I also like the way some of my expository efforts have apparently inspired people. Quite a few people seem to have discovered the beauties of infinite abelian groups through my "little red book," as some students fondly refer to it. And even though I had nothing to do with the basic ideas of differential algebra, the little pamphlet I wrote on the subject may have brought people's attention to that beautiful field.

**MP**  *It was a little more than a pamphlet, as I recall.*

**KAPLANSKY**  It's very short—only sixty-odd pages. In fact, anything I write is short. I run out of ideas, I guess, or energy—or both.

**MP**  *Is there a question you wanted to answer that I haven't asked?*

**KAPLANSKY**  I think not. At one point I did think, goodness, we haven't mentioned physics. Not mentioning it would have left a ten-year gap, but I did remember to bring it in. I think we have covered almost everything. But you must be getting exhausted. Are your other conversations similar to this one?

**MP**  *Each one is different. I think that more than most people you have thought in advance about what you wanted to say.*

**KAPLANSKY**  Yes. I wondered in advance how much we would talk about music. Then you gave me a chance and I got carried away.

**Addendum by I. K.**  Reading over the transcript of my interview, I realized that I had completely omitted my Presidency of the American Mathematical Society:

When nominated for the presidency of the AMS, my first thought was that I did not deserve the honor. After all, the holder of the post might be regarded as the titular head of American mathematics for two years. But if others felt that I was the appropriate choice, I was not going to refuse. So during 1985 and 1986 there were lots of meetings and lots of work between

Kaplansky and Chern discussing a problem.

the meetings. The AMS is an impressive organization. A large number of capable, hardworking people in Providence and Ann Arbor tend an enterprise that, among other things, is the largest publisher of mathematics in the world. Maybe other presidents have left a big imprint; I didn't. The one thing I can point to as something that I personally pushed through is the offering of life memberships.

*July 1988 in Berkeley, California (DA).*

*IRVING KAPLANSKY*   Toronto, Ontario, Canada, March 22, 1917. B.A. 1938, M.A. 1939, Toronto; Ph.D. 1941, Harvard. Field: algebra. George Herbert Mead Distinguished Service Professor, Chicago; Director, Mathematical Sciences Research Institute, Berkeley. President AMS, 1985–86. Steele Prize 1989. American Academy of Arts and Sciences, National Academy of Sciences. Books: *Infinite Abelian Groups*, 1954; *An Introduction to Differential Algebra*, 1957; *Functional Analysis*, 1958; *Commutative Rings*, 1968; *Rings of Operators*, 1968; *Fields and Rings*, 1969; *Linear Algebra and Geometry: A Second Course*, 1970; *Lie Algebras and Locally Compact Groups*, 1971; *Set Theory and Metric Spaces*, 1972; (with I. N. Herstein) *Matters Mathematical*, 1974.

# PETER D. LAX

The quantity and quality of Hungarian mathematicians who emigrated to the U.S. before World War II is especially impressive given the size and population of that country. The youngest and the last to arrive was Peter Lax, age 15. Fellow Hungarians, including von Neumann, directed him to Richard Courant. Today he is a professor at NYU's Courant Institute and its former director. In the tradition of the Institute's founder, he proselytizes tirelessly for the unity of mathematics. A powerful mathematician who has contributed to both pure and applied mathematics, he has no patience with theorists who disdain applications. His wife, Anneli, is also a mathematics professor at NYU, the long-time technical editor of the Mathematical Association of America's *New Mathematical Library*, and an active worker for the improvement of mathematics education.

□ □ □

**MP**  *Were both of you born in Hungary?*

**ANNELI LAX**  No. Only Peter. I was born in Upper Silesia, which was then German and is now Polish.

**MP**  *Somebody has said—in fact, maybe it was you, Peter—that you don't have to be Hungarian to be a mathematician, but it helps. Why do you think Hungary has produced so many more mathematicians than one would expect for its size?*

**LAX**  In Hungary, mathematics was very much an honorable profession. I think that was on account of János Bolyai, who with Lobachevsky and Gauss showed that consistent geometries other than Euclid's could exist. The Nobel Prize was founded about the same time that the Hungarian government founded the Bolyai Prize. It was awarded in 1908 and 1912, first to Poincaré and then to Hilbert. Then the First World War came along, and it had to be abandoned. Bolyai was a singularity; the actual founder of Hungarian mathematics was a man named Julius König, who had studied with Kronecker in Germany. He was a very good organizer, and that's also very important for the development of a mathematical tradition. Incidentally, his son, Dénes König, became a very distinguished mathematician. He is the father of graph theory; he wrote the first book on the subject.

**MP**  *Can you tell us something about your youth in Hungary?*

**LAX**  Both my parents were medical doctors in Budapest. However, I have an uncle, a younger brother of my mother's—he's still alive—who was a terrific mathematician. His name is Albert Korodi, Kornfeld originally. He was an engineer by profession, but he was very, very talented in mathematics. At eighteen he won the mathematics prize in the Eötvös competition. It was the same year Leó Szilárd won the physics prize. They met and became very good friends. I learned a lot from my uncle.

My mother was quite good at mathematics, but I remember very distinctly her describing what a shock it was for her to realize when her brother came along on what a higher level the subject can be understood. She remained quite interested in mathematics; my father respected it but from afar.

**MP**  *You say you learned a lot from your uncle. Can you tell us something you remember that you learned specifically from him?*

**LAX**  I remember that when I was about twelve I learned from him that by the distributive law −1 times −1 equals +1. I thought that was great.

**Better Than Ballet**

**MP**  *Before the age of twelve, did you exhibit any special interest in mathematics?*

**LAX**  My mother told all kinds of stories I don't remember, but I know I became very interested in math when I got to the Gymnasium.

**MP**  *So it was O.K. in Hungary for a young person to like mathematics and to want to become a mathematician? That is not necessarily the way it is in this country.*

**LAX**  It's considered better than wanting to become a ballet dancer.

**MP**  *What was it about mathematics that attracted you?*

**LAX**  I liked to do problems.

**MP**  *K. O. Friedrichs said that as a youth you were looked upon as the new von Neumann.*

**LAX**  I am very happy to say that this is the first time I have heard that.

**MP**  *You didn't hear anything like that when you were growing up?*

**LAX**  No. When my parents saw that I was interested in mathematics and good at it, they had me tutored by a mathematician—Miss Péter, Rózsa Péter; she was wonderful.

**MP**  *What made her wonderful?*

**LAX**  The trouble with education is that if you ask what is the secret of such a wonderful paragon you never can quite pinpoint it—nor can you bottle it, unfortunately. She was immersed in mathematics. She was interested in how people think. The very first thing we did was to read *The Enjoyment of Mathematics* by Rademacher and Toeplitz. I was twelve or thirteen.

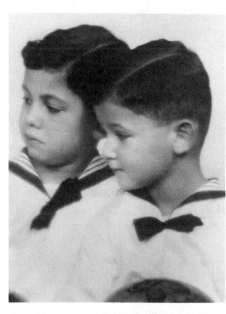

Young sailors, Peter (right) with his older brother, John, who became a theoretical physicist.

**MP**  *I am impressed that you could go through that book at that age. Would you simply discuss what you had read or would you do problems?*

**LAX**  She would sometimes ask me before we read a proof, "Can you do it yourself? Next week when you come try to do it." But she would also give me problems. I went to her house maybe twice a week for a period of a couple of years — until I left Hungary at fifteen and a half. She would also take me sometimes to the meetings of the Mathematical Society. I remember that at one meeting someone was presenting a proof of a theorem of Robbins on directing the edges of a graph so that you can get from any point to any other point. The theorem is that you can do that unless the graph can be disconnected by removing a single edge.

**MP**  *Were there other children your age at these meetings?*

**LAX**  No, I was the youngest. I was a little shy but I went anyway. The very last lecture I heard was Hajós presenting his solution of the Minkowski problem about paving space. I didn't really understand it.

**MP**  *Was it already clear to you that you were going to do mathematics as your life work?*

**LAX**  Oh, sure.

**MP**  *So how much time, roughly, were you spending on mathematics during those years — let's say per day or per week?*

"... always a problem in my head."

**LAX**  Oh, I don't know. There was always a problem in my head, but I didn't read a great deal. I never was a great reader; even now I have difficulty reading mathematics. Otherwise I like to read.

**ANNELI LAX**  When you ask how much time does Peter spend on mathematics, that's a very difficult question to answer. I know he spends a lot of subconscious time on it. He can think about a problem and still talk to you or read a book. There's always something going on.

**MP**  *You think he's doing that right now?*

**ANNELI LAX**  Probably.

**LAX**  Another thing Miss Péter did was to take me to the Eötvös competitions. I was able to sort of participate. You had to be a high school senior to enter officially. I did very well, and that's how I met Dénes König. When I went to America, he wrote to other Hungarian mathematicians — von Neumann and Szegő and Szász — saying that they should look out for me. Only two years later he killed himself to avoid arrest and deportation by the Nazis.

**MP**  *I understand that you were related to the Szegős?*

**LAX**  My mother and Mrs. Szegő were first cousins, and the two families had been friendly when the Szegős were in Hungary. When we came to America, the friendship was renewed. They were very nice to me.

**MP**  *What specifically prompted your parents to leave Hungary?*

**LAX**  It was quite obvious by 1941 that it was high time to go, but it was difficult for my parents to tear themselves away, especially for my father. He was a very successful doctor in Budapest. My mother, who practiced with him and ran his lab, was very anxious to go. The problem was really the other way around; it was not so easy to get permission to come to the United States.

MP  *How was it possible for your parents?*

LAX  I don't know for sure. There was an American who had visited Hungary a few years before; he had been involved in an accident and my father had saved his life. He sent an affidavit. Another thing was that the American consul in Budapest was a patient of my father's.

MP  *Can you remember how you felt about leaving Hungary for the United States?*

LAX  That was so long ago!

MP  *I'm trying to imagine my daughter, soon to be fourteen, being told that we were going to move to Hungary.*

**Skyscrapers, Hollywood, and the Electric Chair**

LAX  At that time America was a child's dream. It's certainly true, however, that I didn't know much about America. I really didn't know English, although I had studied it for two years. What did I know about America? Skyscrapers, tap dancing, Hollywood, chewing gum, and the electric chair. As children we were fascinated by the idea of an electric chair. I had read *The Last of the Mohicans*, *Tom Sawyer* and *Huckleberry Finn*, and a novel by Jack London about two dogs that could sing—you know, sort of howl. I had also read *Helen's Babies* and *The Diary of a Bad Boy*. All were in Hungarian translations.

MP  *When did you actually leave Hungary?*

LAX  November 15, 1941. We sailed from Lisbon on the fifth of December, two days before the Japanese attacked Pearl Harbor and brought the United States into the war. The war had been going on in Europe for two years; France had fallen. Today when people say to me, "Aren't you afraid to bring up a child in a world with the atomic bomb?" I say that for me that isn't nearly as scary as a world with Hitler in it.

MP  *Where did you go to school when you got to the United States?*

LAX  I spent a year at Stuyvesant, a very good high school. Everybody there was friendly. It was and still is, as you know, a very high level math and science school. I rated because I was on the math team and did very well. We won the City Championship that year. A child's ego has to be nurtured as much, if not more, than a grownup's. Coming to a new country I was at first a fish out of water. Somehow nothing but mathematics is the same everywhere. There were other students I could talk to about mathematics. Two of them, Marshall Rosenbluth and Rolf Landauer, became very successful physicists.

MP  *Were you sent to an American high school mainly so that you could build up your English skills?*

**"Courant got quite excited."**

LAX  Absolutely. Very shortly after we arrived in America, von Neumann, who had received König's letter and also one from Rózsa Péter, was in New York and came to see me and my father. He wanted to know what kind of problems I could solve, so I told him. He thought I should go to high school for a year. Then he recommended that I go to see F. J. Murray, who was at

With his father, Dr. Henry Lax, who now lives in the same apartment building as the Laxes on Central Park West.

Columbia, and also Richard Courant at NYU. Of course he knew Courant from Göttingen. I still have the letter von Neumann wrote to my father. Szegő also advised me to see Courant. Neither he nor von Neumann particularly liked Courant, but they recommended him as being very good with young people. So my father took me down to see him at NYU.

**MP** *Was this while you were still at Stuyvesant?*

**LAX** That's right. Courant got quite excited after he talked to me a little and called Friedrichs and told him to come over and meet this young boy. We—Courant, Friedrichs and I—discussed things that interested me at that time. I remember I told Friedrichs that I was interested in function theory and he said, "I wrote only one paper in function theory," and gave me a reprint. Now, more than forty years later, I wrote a commentary about that paper for Friedrichs's *Selecta*. It is Friedrichs's best written paper, although not his most important; it *flows*.

**MP** *Incidentally, I noticed that your first published paper was "On a conjecture of Erdős." Was he another Hungarian mathematician whom you knew when you came to the United States?*

**LAX** Sure. He was very friendly and helpful to me when I first arrived in the States. While I was still at Stuyvesant, he invited me a number of times to visit him in Princeton at the Institute for Advanced Study. Once he introduced me to Einstein as "a talented young Hungarian mathematician." Einstein was genuinely puzzled: "Why Hungarian?"

**MP** *Did you and Erdős talk mathematics?*

**LAX** Of course. He gave me lots of problems, some of which I managed to solve; two of them were worth publishing. But Erdős was a little disappointed that I eventually turned my back on mathematics in the Hungarian style and in the areas beloved by Hungarians. But that was of course much later. Courant always said that there was a tradition in Hungary to paint exquisite miniatures.

I graduated from Stuyvesant in 1943 and then went on to NYU. I was not yet seventeen.

**MP**  *So you were not of draft age?*

**LAX**  No, I had three semesters to do work, although there was a question about the spring of '44 since I became eighteen on May 1. I remember going to my draft board and asking if they could postpone drafting me until the semester was over. They said yes. That was only an additional four weeks, so they weren't being too generous.

At NYU I took a bunch of undergraduate courses, but in math I took only graduate courses. You know, the level of the math classes was much lower in this country than in Europe. I met Anneli in a graduate course on complex variables.

Peter first spotted Anneli in an NYU class on complex variables.

*More Mathematical People*

Drafted for World War II, Lax ended up at Los Alamos.

**MP**  *How did you happen to spot her?*

**LAX**  Anneli was extremely beautiful. Have you seen pictures of her then? She has not changed all that much because her beauty was in her bone structure. I had no problem picking her out.

**MP**  *So how did you get acquainted?*

**LAX**  By the time honored method of the male—showing off. The peacock has its tail and I had my mathematics. I already knew complex variables; I had read Knopp. The teacher was a leftover from before Courant came to NYU. He realized that I knew more of the subject than he, so he let me just sort of take over the class.

**MP [To Anneli]**  *What was your impression of this young showoff?*

**ANNELI LAX**  Well, he was clearly a mathematician. It wasn't clear whether he was socially awkward or just putting on an act. There was this rather charming mixture of mathematical know-how and shyness and quite a bit of wit.

**MP**  *Did you two start dating during the course?*

**ANNELI LAX**  No. I was married at the time. That marriage was very brief and was later annulled. I was no longer married by the time Peter had his first furlough from the Army.

**MP**  *Much to his relief?*

**ANNELI LAX**  I don't think so. The relationship didn't develop right away.

**Living Science Fiction**

**LAX**  I was first sent to a camp in Florida—an "Infantry Replacement Training Center," a very ominous sounding description; the Army didn't mince words. I did very well actually. I was thin but very strong, I could handle a rifle, and I had no trouble on the marches. I got along with the people in my barracks. They were a cross-section, including some hillbillies, who I am sure found me as strange as I found them. I missed "Village Fighting" because I was sent to ASTP—the Army Specialized Training Program. It was a program to take out of the ranks people who had had some college education or had scored high on the Army intelligence test. They were sent to school—mainly languages, engineering, navigation. I was sent to Texas A. & M. Today it is a very good school, but then it wasn't. It was deservedly the butt of a lot of "Aggie" jokes. It was all male, no blacks, a very antiquated faculty with some exceptions like Dr. Klipple, who conducted a Moore-type seminar for three of us. Everybody was in uniform. I had been there about six months when I got orders to go to Oak Ridge. Then one morning, about four weeks later, we were told to fall out and pile into a train. After a couple of days we arrived in Santa Fe. There we fell out again and piled into buses and went up into the hills to Los Alamos. The day after our arrival, we got a lecture about how they were building a bomb out of plutonium, an element that doesn't exist naturally—that they were making it in Hanford, Washington. It was partly because of that experience that I have never cared for science fiction; I've lived it.

**MP**  *What were they using soldiers for?*

**LAX**   We had all had some training in mathematics or physics or chemistry or engineering. They needed people who could do technical tasks. There was a tremendous shortage of qualified personnel at all levels. At first I was asked to do calculations with a Marchant, a hand-operated electric calculating machine, but very soon I graduated from that.

**MP**   *Did Courant have anything to do with your ending up at Los Alamos?*

**LAX**   I think so. He had written to Oswald Veblen to see what could be done about me. Because of his own experience in the trenches in the First World War, he was very concerned about the possible loss of talented young people.

**Los Alamos—A Dream**

**MP**   *At Los Alamos you must have had personal contact with a lot of famous scientists.*

**LAX**   That was another thing that made it seem so much like science fiction. Von Neumann was around a lot. He was a very important person already then and extremely busy; but whenever he came, he would give a lecture. At that time he talked about game theory and computers. He was very much convinced that the task at Los Alamos would turn toward computing, since they would be unable to fulfill their mission without it. Richard Feynman was also there. Although he was quite young, he was already legendary.

I had just turned nineteen, so my interaction was more with young mathematicians like Richard Bellman, John Kemény, Alex Heller and Paul Olum. I also saw a lot of Stan Ulam. I knew very little physics then; I still wish I knew more.

**MP**   *Yet you were using mathematics in a truly applied fashion.*

**LAX**   I worked on neutron transport problems, linear problems. The fanciest piece of work I did was a calculation of the criticality of an ellipsoid.

**MP**   *So your Los Alamos experience was enjoyable?*

**LAX**   Oh yes, it was like a dream. First of all, the Army didn't have much power over us, so it was the first time I was really on my own. Then there was the pleasure of being in a group working on a specific project. There was one goal really, and I realized where mathematics fit into it.

**MP**   *It sounds as if your nice mix of work in Los Alamos has really shaped your view of a proper mathematical education.*

**LAX**   That is right. The following September, after the bomb was dropped and the war was over, the physicists there, who had been kept from academic work, organized the Los Alamos branch of the University of New Mexico. All of a sudden there were courses being given, and I took some. I was assistant in the course on mechanics given by Chaim Richman; I wrote up the notes. I didn't know too much, but I was learning.

Even after the war the Army still needed us at Los Alamos, so they made a deal. They agreed to discharge us if we agreed to stay on as civilians until the following May. It was a very good deal. Afterwards I went right away to California and spent another summer semester at Stanford with the Szegős. This time I took some reading courses with George Pólya.

**MP**   *Another Hungarian. Did you have the kind of family relationship with Pólya that you had with Szegő?*

Dismissed by the Nazis from his position as director of the internationally famous Mathematics Institute in Göttingen, Richard Courant (1888–1972) emigrated to the United States and created another famous institute at New York University.

**Marriage between Mathematicians**

**LAX**  Pólya's older brother was a good friend of my father's. He was a very prominent surgeon, not only very skillful but also very innovative. In fact, George Pólya was known in Budapest as the talented kid brother of the famous surgeon.

**MP**  *So you were close to three Hungarian mathematicians—Szegő, Pólya and von Neumann—none of whom liked Courant but all of whom recommended that you study with him?*

**LAX**  Those who were close to Courant loved him dearly, and even those who were put off by his strong personality realized that he was a great teacher.

I went back to NYU in the fall of 1946. My problem was to get a bachelor's degree, which I managed by scrounging together credits from NYU, Stanford, Texas A. & M., and the University of New Mexico. I got my A.B. in February 1947 and my Ph.D. two years later.

**MP**  *Were you a Courant student?*

**LAX**  No. A Friedrichs student.

**MP**  *How did that happen?*

**LAX**  I don't know. Courant was running around an awful lot at that time. To Washington and to Germany. Probably that was the reason. My dissertation wasn't much actually.

**MP**  *Well, I've heard it said that you should do your dissertation on anything you can get away with—then get on to your real work.*

**LAX**  Yes, but Louis Nirenberg, in *his* dissertation half a year ahead of me, had just solved the Weyl problem in differential geometry. That was very impressive!

**MP**  *So you got your Ph.D. and then married Anneli, right?*

**LAX**  No. We were married in '48. I got my degree in '49.

**ANNELI LAX**  It had nothing to do with when he got his Ph.D.

**MP**  *Yours has been a real mathematical marriage. Are there any distinct advantages in a mathematician's being married to another mathematician?*

**LAX**  I've only been married to a mathematician.

**MP**  *Well, Anneli, can you talk from your experience?*

**ANNELI LAX**  I think it certainly is an advantage to have many common interests. Another advantage is that it's good to be able to supplement one another's talents. For instance, I occasionally edit something which Peter has written or suggest he should be more explicit about something, or I attend to some details—things like that which I like to do. He explains things to me when I get curious. Of course he enjoys explaining—that's why he likes to teach. So that's pure benefit from my point of view.

**MP**  *As a mathematician yourself you can understand those things.*

**ANNELI LAX**  Some. There are still many things that Peter works on that I absolutely do not understand.

**LAX**   You are unwilling to go through a state of half understanding.

**ANNELI LAX**   Yes, that's right. That's a big shortcoming of mine, and I'm not the only one. There are certain people who just have to understand every step. They can't say, "Oh, I'll leave this for the moment and just go on." And that's of course a terrible hindrance. That's why I never learned more mathematics than I did.

**MP**   *You've mentioned some of the pluses of a mathematical marriage. Are there minuses too?*

**ANNELI LAX**   Well, there could be. As I see it, it's a big advantage that I am not at all competitive. It doesn't bother me that Peter is much better than I am. I think with some people it would. I'm just totally noncompetitive. Another thing that helps is that both of us have many non-mathematical interests, many of which we share.

**MP**   *The two of you have also collaborated with Sam Burstein on at least one mathematical project—your* Calculus with Applications and Computing. *I know you have occasionally said that there is a great need for new textbooks in which the applied view is treated attractively and in depth. Was your calculus book a case of "put up or shut up"? It must have taken quite a bit of time from your other work. Calculus books aren't generated in a month or two.*

**"Abolish the calculus committees!"**

**LAX**   Well, this one was generated too fast! I wish we had spent more time on it. It's not apparently a good book to teach from. But let me tell you how I feel about the teaching of calculus. I think it has completely diverged from the way in which calculus is thought about and used by professionals. What is taught under the name of calculus has become a ritual, that's all. There is a long essay on education by Alfred North Whitehead which he starts by saying that the biggest problem is how to stop teaching inert matter. Most of what we teach in calculus is inert.

The solution is to sweep away the cobwebs but, as one publisher has explained to me, for economic reasons that cannot be done. All those fancy textbooks cost so much to produce that at least fifty thousand copies have to be sold to cover production costs. That means they have to include everybody's pet topic; the result is that you get monstrosities that have no point of view at all.

**MP**   *So how do you effect such a change?*

**LAX**   Abolish the calculus committees! And the annual ceremony of selecting a departmental text!

The trouble is that calculus is a big enterprise. It has to be taught to many people, so not everybody can be entrusted to teach his own version. Still each department should encourage those who have sound ideas to forget about the big text, write their own notes, and explain to the students their ideas of the subject and the problems that they can be applied to. Calculus shouldn't be taught as just one rote thing after another. If we taught music like we teach calculus, we'd just be teaching scales.

**MP**   *A big difference is that most music teachers have had some real experience playing their music but a great many calculus teachers have had next to no experience "playing" their calculus.*

Rózsa Péter.

**LAX**  That is true, and for that reason the person in charge of calculus—usually there is some one person in charge of the teaching assistants—should be a person who has had such experience. The reform has to come from people who have a good idea of what calculus is used for. Happily there is a groundswell for a change; the response to the reforms proposed at the Tulane Conference, sponsored by the Sloan Foundation, has been enthusiastic; the NSF [National Science Foundation] is getting into the act.

**MP**  *Not many people have the combination you two have of real knowledge and the ability to communicate, so it seems to me that—in spite of your second thoughts about your book—you should contemplate a revision or a continuation.*

**LAX**  I'm teaching calculus right now because I felt a little sheepish to talk about it and not do it. I have a class of thirty-five or forty, and I am enjoying it tremendously.

**MP**  *It's nice to hear you talk about the fun of teaching calculus to freshmen. What makes teaching fun for you?*

**LAX**  I like to let them see how I think.

**MP**  *Are you a good teacher?*

**LAX**  I think so. Anneli?

**ANNELI LAX**  I think he is an extremely good teacher for the right kind of kids. Not for everybody.

---

## ROZSA PETER

### 1905–1977

By the time Rózsa Péter was tutoring the young Peter Lax in mathematics, six years after obtaining her Ph.D., she had already presented papers at two International Mathematical Congresses and was serving on the editorial board of an international mathematical journal. In Budapest, however, she was still "a temporary teacher," something like a long-term substitute in "lower type secondary schools." In 1939, under fascist laws, even this employment was taken from her. She obtained a permanent and more appropriate position at the University only after the end of World War II.

Rózsa Péter's mathematical research was in the field of recursive functions, a type of function that is defined by its value at zero and a procedure that makes it possible to compute its value at any positive integer if the values assigned to previous integers are known. Although she pursued the subject without concern for its possible applications, it has turned out to play an important role in computer science. She summarized her results and those of others in her book, *Rekursive Funktionen in der Komputer-Theorie*, which appeared just months before her death in 1977.

As a teacher, she has been described as "an artist of pedagogy," her method being to engage her students in the joint discovery of mathematics. According to a memoir written by her adoptive son, B.

Andrásfai, to whom we are indebted for the information about her in this sketch, "She found that this joint discovery not only gives permanent experience and solid knowledge to the pupils, but also frequently presents the well-known subject from a new, unexpected and surprising aspect to the experienced teacher."

Her popular book, *Playing With Infinity*, which has been translated into twelve languages, grew out of letters to the writer Marcell Benedek, who felt that without some knowledge of mathematics he was less effective in literary expression. Happily for the reader who would like to experience firsthand the method and the charm of Peter Lax's "wonderful paragon" of a teacher, her book is still available from Dover.

With son Johnny, who was a graduate student in history at Columbia when he was killed in a collision with a drunk driver.

**LAX**  They have to be interested in the subject to begin with. I cannot easily convince them that they should become interested.

**MP**  *In a 1971 interview you said you would never have gotten into or stayed in applied mathematics if it had been the old-fashioned applied mathematics.*

**LAX**  In the old-fashioned applied mathematics you had to do the numerical calculation with patently inadequate methods and equipment. That made it an entirely different game then from what it is now.

**MP**  *Do you consider yourself an applied mathematician?*

**LAX**  I'm both pure and applied.

**MP**  *Some people say that you claim to be an applied mathematician on Mondays, Wednesdays and Fridays and a pure mathematician on the other days, but they think you're a pure mathematician every day. How do you yourself distinguish between pure and applied mathematics?*

**LAX**  There actually isn't that much difference. You know, for instance, that my native language, Hungarian, is not an Indo-European language and so it is supposed to be very different from English, which is. But when I speak the two and try to switch from one to the other, or to translate from one to the other, although I notice that they are different, mostly what I notice is that they are both languages. It's the same with pure and applied mathematics. They are different, but the similarities are much greater than the differences.

**MP**  *But if you were going to describe one person as a pure mathematician and someone else as an applied mathematician, where would you draw the line?*

**LAX**  In applied mathematics you are very much aware of where the question comes from and also where the answer is going. After all, when a

With son Jimmy, who now practices medicine in his grandfather's old office.

*More Mathematical People*

mathematician says he has solved a problem, that doesn't have a definite meaning—rather it means usually that he has understood something about the problem. So the kind of understanding that you need to be able to say you have solved the problem as an applied problem is different from the kind of understanding you need to be able to make the same statement about a problem in pure mathematics.

**MP**  *Can we fuss about this a bit longer? In that same 1971 interview the interviewer said to you, "You're a real applied mathematician then, aren't you?" and you said, "Well, not that. I think a real applied mathematician would dismiss me." Now my question is, why would a real applied mathematician dismiss you?*

**LAX**  I've done a certain amount of computing, but I've preferred working on methods and theory. I've never walked that last mile, actually participating in a large scale computation. I may yet do it. I probably couldn't go as far as Tony Jameson, who is interested in modeling whole airplanes.

**MP**  *Modeling whole airplanes?*

**LAX**  Yes, computing the airflow, not just over an airplane wing or fuselage but over everything put together. That's real. That's probably the reason for the adjective "real" in the quote you just read.

**MP**  *There is another quote of yours which is fairly striking. You say applied and pure mathematics are more closely bound together today than at any other time in the last seventy years.*

**LAX**  I said that in '71?

**MP**  *No. You said that in '84.*

**Shocked by the Fields Medalists**

**LAX**  O.K. then. There was quite a change in that decade. Today I think very few people would say publicly anything nasty about applied mathematics. Actually, though, I got a bit of a shock in the summer of '86 in Berkeley when the *New York Times* interviewed the Fields Medalists. They all came out very "pro" pure and "anti" applied. They said that mathematics trickles down from pure theory to applications. They didn't realize that it is a two-

The family that sleds together . . .

way street: theory and applications influence each other. I wrote a letter to the *Times*, which didn't get published.

**MP**  *You should have written a letter to the Medalists.*

**LAX**  You don't argue with Medalists. They earned their Medals, they should enjoy them. One shouldn't interfere with their pleasure.

**MP**  *You have pointed out that American mathematics, like American art, has developed a very pure and very abstract tradition. You have also said, however, that the political activists in American mathematics are usually the pure mathematicians, "[who] work on [mathematical] problems completely unmotivated by the problems of the real world." Why is that? Why don't we have applied mathematicians jumping up at the Council meetings of the American Mathematical Society and objecting to something on political grounds? Why do you think that the very pure people are more active on such things?*

**LAX**  I guess maybe their conscience bothers them about wasting their professional talents on matters so divorced from the real world.

**MP**  *Another reason may be that the kind of problems they work with in pure mathematics are more clearcut than the kind of problems one works with in applied mathematics, so they see the problems of real life as more clearcut.*

**LAX**  There is probably a great deal to that. I once asked Leó Szilárd, who had very original ideas about international cooperation and was the very opposite of a clearcut left or right winger, why a man as intelligent as Eugene Wigner would have such an apocalyptic view of the unavoidability of conflict with the Soviet Union. Szilárd said, "His own thinking is formal and legalistic and he sees no formal, legalistic solution; yet in human affairs other forms of solution are possible." There is such a thing as being too clearcut. Anyway I don't want to knock either pure mathematics or pure mathematicians.

**MP**  *You already have. In print.*

**LAX**  What I put in print I very carefully consider; it has to be a balanced statement. I am trying to do that in my centennial lecture for the American Mathematical Society on "The Flowering of Applied Mathematics in America."

**"It takes one to catch one."**  **MP**  *In a somewhat similar vein, you have said that mathematics has always attracted those who wish to escape from the real world. Now obviously you don't put yourself among those who are trying to escape the real world, do you?*

**LAX**  Sure I do. It takes one to catch one.

**MP**  *But certainly your mathematical involvement has been very worldly.*

**LAX**  That's true. I was thrust into the Army and sent to Los Alamos. I wasn't asked whether I wanted to go. But I consider myself enormously lucky; that experience has shaped my whole outlook.

**MP**  *Was it really a more decisive experience for you than the Courant-NYU experience?*

**LAX**  No. Both were important.

**MP**  *They combine?*

**LAX**  They combine, but Los Alamos did play a big role.

**MP**  *You have also been involved in another aspect of mathematics that some people regard as the real world. You have been an administrator since you were about thirty-eight.*

**LAX**  No, I didn't become Director of the Institute until—well, yes, I did take over the Department of Energy's Computing Laboratory at the Courant Institute in '64. But I have never regarded administration as my main job. My main job is doing mathematics. In Europe, you know, there's never been that great a distinction between a scientist and an administrator. Administration is just part of a professor's role. The professional administrator is an American invention.

**The Right Mixture of Concerns**   **MP**  *Do you enjoy administration?*

**LAX**  Well, no. I'm not that good an administrator.

**MP**  *You've been at it so long you must have some special skills.*

**LAX**  I suppose I have the right mixture of concerns. You know, I have never sought these jobs. In the case of the Computing Laboratory, Robert Richtmyer, who was running it, wanted to leave New York. At that time I was already heavily involved in computing, so Courant asked me to take over. I didn't feel I could say no, and I wanted to know what it was like. I had lots of help. The Courant Institute is not a very hierarchical place. People who have good ideas have a chance to have them examined. I directed people by letting them do as they wanted.

**MP**  *Is that fundamental to your "administrative style"?*

**LAX**  That's right. Every once in a while I have had to make a hard decision. For instance, in '66 we had acquired a supercomputer and ten years later we still had it. It was running, but it was by then obsolete and costing too much to run. There were lots of people involved with the machine, so it was complicated to get rid of it, but I did.

**MP**  *Earlier you said that you didn't think you were a good administrator, but listening to you makes me believe that you are.*

**LAX**  What does a good administrator do? Tries to bring in people who work on a novel range of problems. Gives people a chance to express their ideas and to carry them out.

**MP**  *So as an administrator you were never a builder in the sense that Courant was a builder?*

**LAX**  I could not have done such a thing as Courant. Besides, the need was not there.

**MP**  *You sound, from what you have said, almost as if you've done things out of a sense of obligation. You were asked to take over and you felt you should give administration a try so you did it.*

Reading to a group of children.

**LAX**  Actually, let me also say that as I look back I think I did things mainly because they were fun.

**ANNELI LAX**  So much for obligation.

**LAX**  Well, I have my own notion of what is fun. I think that if I hadn't done it I would have wondered ever after what administration is like. If you never do something others have done, you always wonder what it would have been like. I think that was the way I felt about administration. I don't really think of myself as an administrator but the records show, of course, that I have been one.

**ANNELI LAX**  I don't think of you as one either.

**MP**  *What do you think of him as?*

**Our Place**  **ANNELI LAX**  Well, not in terms of what he does. Mathematics pervades it all on some level. Sometimes subconsciously. But it's always present, and I guess when other things need to be done, especially if they affect mathematics or the manner in which it's done at our place, then administration becomes somewhat interesting to him.

**MP**  *You just used the words "our place." That must partially explain why you and so many others among your contemporaries have stayed at the Courant Institute. You have been students there, then faculty members there, and as faculty members you have stayed. That is pretty unusual in the academic world today.*

**LAX**  I can't imagine that we'll continue in that style in the future.

**MP**  *Why is that?*

**LAX**  In the old days our view of the role of applications in mathematics was so singular that someone with the Courant outlook would have felt out of place anywhere else. Today this is no longer the case. There are many reasons for this change: the variety of new applications, the obvious need for mathematics in science and technology, the availability of powerful computers, the structure of government support, and—last but not least—the example of the intellectual vigor and success of the Courant Institute.

**ANNELI LAX**   I think also it's a function of size. When you're building from scratch, as Courant, Friedrichs and Stoker were, there has to be a nucleus. Others somehow fit in. But then the whole thing gets much bigger and other forces enter.

**MP**   *Did you ever wish that you had gone—I guess you couldn't say that, but did you ever consider leaving NYU and going somewhere else? Of course you have spent a lot of time at Stanford over the years.*

**LAX**   That's right. I did a lot of work there with Ralph Phillips, which was very important to me. So I was for a long period exposed to a way that was different from ours here.

**MP**   *But you've been happy in New York?*

**LAX**   I've been very happy here.

**MP**   *Too happy to want to go?*

**LAX**   Yes. I've had offers but I have felt I belonged here. My parents lived here, and perhaps that played a role too. I don't know.

**MP**   *To go back to mathematics itself, can you tell us how you do mathematics?*

**LAX**   Well, you know, there's this interesting problem that you get hooked on . . . Eventually it is a person's taste in problems that decides what kind of mathematics he does.

**The Art of Formulating Problems**   **ANNELI LAX**   An applied mathematician is forced to formulate problems; they don't come already formulated. Most people usually begin with intrinsically interesting problems already formulated that they get hooked on. The art of formulating problems is terribly important. Some people like that and some don't.

**LAX**   I guess I never much cared to work on formulated problems. I like to choose my own.

**MP**   *How does such a problem develop?*

**LAX**   I like to start with some phenomenon, the more striking the better, and then use mathematics to try to understand it. The formation, propagation, interaction, decay of shock waves is an example of a striking phenomenon. So is the scattering of electromagnetic and acoustic waves. So is the stability and coherence of solitary waves governed by completely integrable equations. So is the weak but not strong convergence of oscillating solutions of dispersive systems. I find such problems both natural and central.

**ANNELI LAX**   There's an aesthetic quality.

**LAX**   There's an aesthetic quality, yes, but if you try to pin that down, you are just begging the question. What is beautiful is purely subjective. Saying something is beautiful may be no different from saying that you have a feeling that something is important. You know, one of the complaints that pure mathematicians have against applied mathematics is that it is ugly.

**MP**  *Yes, that was one of Paul Halmos's charges in the first volume of* Mathematical People.

**LAX**  Beauty is in the eye of the beholder. It's a poor guide, aesthetics is. You have to feel that what you are doing is beautiful but, after all, someone used to classical art regards modern art as horrible and ugly.

When I was younger I liked very general things; now I find I like more specific problems. I don't know why that is, but it is part of the aesthetic judgment one makes: "Oh, that thing is too general. Oh, this thing is too special." You want to work on things that are just right, but I find that my sense of what is just right is shifting toward the specific. That may be a general trend in mathematics, although the wave lengths of mathematics are long, longer than those of physics. I am a little disconcerted by the faddishness of physics. To the physics community there are at any one time only a few problems worth working on.

**MP**  *Do you think that the Nobel Prize has an effect there?*

**Fads in Mathematics**  **LAX**  I don't think so. And certainly there are fads in mathematics, too. Bourbaki was such a fad. For a while there was a fad to study linear topological vector spaces, motivated I think by the tremendous success of distribution theory, after Hilbert space and Banach space had proved their worth. People thought, "Aha, there must be gold in them thar hills," and there was just sand.

The number of mathematicians is much greater today, so fads have a much shorter run. In two, three, four years it's clear if something is not going anywhere.

**ANNELI LAX**  What do you think will happen to fractals?

**LAX**  Fractals have been known to exist for a long time, like Weierstrass's and Takagi's nowhere differentiable function, Peano's, Sierpiński's and Pólya's area filling curves, von Koch's snowflake. But they were regarded as freaks, to be put in museums. Mandelbrot's great observation was that, far from being freaks, they are the shapes of nature. Furthermore he observed that each natural object, such as a jagged mountain range, a shoreline, a cloud, the foliage of a tree, has its own characteristic Hausdorff dimension. There must be something in the differential equations describing the evolution that shapes nature that leads to such fractal objects. We are beginning to glimpse how such jagged objects as fractals emerge from solutions of analytic differential equations—strange attractors, singularity formation and all that—but it will take many decades before we get to the bottom of how fractals emerge, if ever. The problems studied today are mostly baby problems. There is so little information in them—you know, just one parameter—that all this complexity must be only apparent. Information content is very little, so the same thing must be repeated over and over again. It cannot be different, because you haven't put in anything different. Something like that must be understandable on that level.

**MP**  *Now we're touching on the future development of mathematics. You've lived through a lot of changes already. Do you want to prognosticate a bit, tell us what you see happening into, say, the year 2000?*

*(Facing page)* Ready for the serve.

*More Mathematical People*

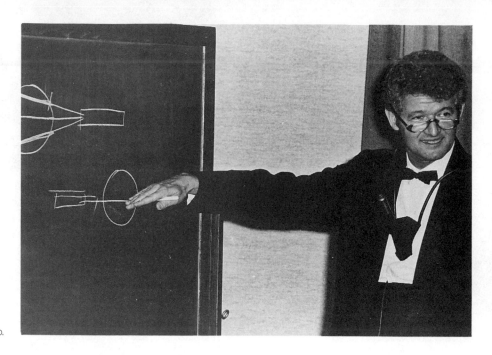

Lax does not always lecture in a tuxedo.

**LAX**   Certainly computer simulations will play a big role. After all, as great a mathematician as G. D. Birkhoff, believed all his life that the ergodic hypothesis was true and devoted most of his life to studying it, whereas if he had been able to take one look at a computer's simulation he would have seen that it ain't so.

**MP**   *That's a bit scary.*

**LAX**   Von Neumann, who was the central figure of the mid-century, firmly believed that computing was central not only to the numerical side of applied mathematics but also to progress in theory. That is why he invented computers and pushed for their development. He foresaw that computations are essential to discover basic phenomena in nonlinear systems.

I guess to my mind the most interesting problem about numerical simulations is that they work. If you think about it for a little bit, round-offs should destroy any relation. There are probably rather deep reasons, certain kinds of stabilities that make calculations a good guide to chaotic phenomena. You talk about iterating some quadratic transformation—but that's not all that you do. You are iterating an enormously complicated algorithm imbedded in your computer, coupled to the particular compiler, that produces some pattern which if you do the same calculation on another computer, or on another compiler, will give you an entirely different sequence of numbers, but the same pattern. So there is some kind of deep seated stability. A prediction, to come true, must have the same kind of stability. I'm far too cautious to make one.

*February 1987 in New York, New York (DA, CR).*

PETER DAVID LAX   Budapest, Hungary, May 1, 1926. B.A. 1947, Ph.D. 1949, NYU.
Fields: partial differential equations, numerical analysis. Professor
of Mathematics and former Director, Courant Institute of Mathe-
matical Sciences, NYU. President AMS, 1979–80. Von Neumann
Lecturer (SIAM) 1968, Hedrick Lecturer (MAA) 1972, Plenary
Lecturer (ICM Warsaw) 1983, Colloquium Lecturer (AMS) 1987.
Lester R. Ford Award (MAA) 1966, 1973, Chauvenet Prize
(MAA) 1974, Semmelweis Medal 1975, Wiener Prize (AMS–
SIAM) 1975, National Medal of Science 1986, Wolf Prize 1987.
Académie des Sciences (Paris), American Academy of Arts and
Sciences, National Academy of Sciences, U.S.S.R. Academy of
Sciences. Books: (with Ralph Phillips) *Scattering Theory*, 1967;
(with James Glimm) *Decay of Solutions of Systems of Nonlinear
Hyperbolic Conservation Laws*, 1970; *Hyperbolic Systems of
Conservation Laws and the Mathematical Theory of Waves*,
1973; (with Ralph Phillips) *Scattering Theory for Automorphic
Functions*, 1976; (with A. Lax and S. Z. Burstein) *Calculus with
Applications and Computing*, 1976; *Mathematical Aspects of
Production and Distribution of Energy*, 1976; *Wave Motion*,
1987.

# LUCIEN LE CAM

Although Lucien Le Cam started his career as a statistician for Electricité de France, he is now known and respected as a very deep and theoretical worker in mathematical statistics. When, however, his twelve-year-old daughter lost a leg and a lung to cancer, he effectively put his statistical expertise at the disposal of the medical team treating her. He says he finds all systems of statistics too "religious" for him: "One has to think—one can't just have a system that will guarantee all the answers." As a result of the vagaries of taxis in Berkeley, we arrived very late for our appointment with Le Cam. Fortunately, in preparation for the interview, he had already written the following account of his early, haphazard life and education in France.

□ □ □

Jerzy Neyman, who had a great fondness for people whom he considered "underdogs," used to describe me as a peasant's son, but this was not really accurate. I am a *fils de paysans*. The French word does not have to me the "uncouth clod" connotation of the American. My parents were hardworking people, not "clods." They were born in a poor part of Brittany and had to leave elementary school at ten or eleven because they had to work, but they were fine, strong, intelligent people.

My father spent a bit of his youth, four years, fighting in the First World War. After that he started from scratch in Brittany but in 1922 decided to move to the center of France, where he could be a *fermier*. That is someone who leases a farm owned by someone else. The American "farmer" has a different meaning. In the center of France my parents could be *fermiers*. In Brittany they would have had to be farmhands or, at best, sharecroppers.

I was born November 18, 1924, on a little farm called La Jasseix in Creuse, France. That is on the flanks of the Massif Central, blessed with an intemperate climate and a soil that has difficulties supporting any kind of crops. A year or so after my birth, my family moved to a bigger farm (seventy-five acres) with an eleven-year lease. That is where I spent my early years.

The place had no electricity, no plumbing at all, no heat except the kitchen stove. My family did not consider themselves poor, but they were not rich. My mattress was made of burlap bags filled with straw. It was a considerable improvement when the straw was replaced by oat chaff. I remember the first time my family had enough money to buy a mattress. I must have been close to five years old at the time.

The only book in the house was a small veterinary book that my father treasured. When I was about five, he borrowed a book to teach me to read. He also taught several farmhands.

My elementary school was uneventful. My elder brother had distinguished himself there, and I benefited from his shadow. A difficulty occurred when it was time for him to leave elementary school. He had done exceedingly well on the mandatory state examinations and on the optional competitive ones for scholarships. A committee of bureaucrats who came to investigate our farm decided that a scholarship was not needed: my father could pay for the expenses of continuing school for one of us by selling two cows a year. We may have had six or seven cows at the time! From that time on, I have looked with disfavor on officials who determine matters of need.

My brother and I wound up in a Catholic school called Notre Dame. It was a boarding school in Guéret, some thirty miles from our little town of Felletin. Notre Dame was a nice place where you got up at about 5 a.m., washed your face in a little individual basin, and then went to mass. After mass there was a one-hour study period, then breakfast, then a 15-minute break to use the outside toilets. Those were as dirty and stinky as any I have seen anywhere.

Le Cam's father, François Le Cam, returned from the First World War to become a farmer.

Actually, I was privileged. I served mass every morning for five years and had the opportunity to witness exactly how much the priests believed in their rituals. Also I could have an occasional glass of the excellent white wine they used.

My father died when I was thirteen, leaving three boys. I was the middle son. My mother just took over. It was not easy because, as the French laws were at that time, she could not do so legally. She had to get permission from my uncles to be in charge, which she did. My elder brother, who had done very well in school, had to quit to help on the farm. It took a long time and lots of hard work, especially from my mother, to get decent living conditions for us. My brothers both became *paysans* in the sense that they worked on the land, but they were not *fermiers*, like my father, since they owned their farms.

After my father's death the priests at Notre Dame decided to keep me on and pay for my room and board. They were a nice bunch in many ways, with a very relaxed attitude about certain matters of behavior or religion. (The director of the school was the one to teach us about human institutions, in particular the institution of marriage. He did that by reading us the memoirs of Fouché, Napoléon's chief of police, who kept track of who was sleeping with whom!) The only problem was that their horizon was very, very limited.

At that time I became interested in chemistry. My physics-chemistry teacher did not believe in such things as electrons. When I discovered that I could integrate things such as $(1+ax+bx^2)^{-1/2}$, a specialist, l'Abbé Mirguet, was brought in to check on what was going on. He recommended that I read some calculus books. However, books of all kinds were unavailable locally.

Some became available accidentally in the late spring 1940. Part of a warehouse from Les Presses Universitaires was shipped to Guéret to shield it from the Nazis' advance. I bought a book by Hilbert on quadratic fields and one by Planck on electromagnetism. These I still have. Another one, translated from English, was fascinating. The author (maybe Thomson) computed forces between atoms and energy released by chemical reactions from quantum mechanical models of the atom. The fourth book was a treatise on radio communication with a complete description of the properties of radar systems—that was 1939, before radar was developed in World War II! These last two books left for an undetermined fate in 1942.

I had full run of the physics and chemistry lab, having provided myself with a passkey. My teacher, Anatole Jamet, found me in there at odd times but never bothered to ask how I could get in. Occasionally he would say, "Since you are here, what about cleaning up the stocks of chemicals?" Or he would engage me in some of his projects, such as constructing a torsion balance, rewiring an electric motor, or patching up a radio set. I would also be asked to set up the apparatus for experiments to be performed by other students.

**Blackmail**

At the time of my graduation from high school, in 1942, some decision had to be made about future studies, if any. Because of the limited horizons of my school teachers and for other reasons, it was decided that I would go to the seminary in Limoges and become a priest. I did go but got out of it the next day by explaining to them that I could not stand "blackmail." The next step was to go to the university in Clermont-Ferrand. It was already two or three weeks past the start of the teaching year. Chemistry labs were full.

Since I could not be admitted in chemistry, I opted for math. That was O.K., but money was needed, not for fees—they were minimal—but for lodging and food. The university people advised me to go to the lycée, where I could get room and board.

The lycées are government-run high schools. Most of them terminate

La Jasseix, the farm where Le Cam was born.

A youthful *photo d'identité*.

The Le Cam family shortly before the father's death: François and Marie Jouanno Le Cam with Lucien, Joseph, and Jean.

with the *baccalauréat*, but some have programs that go beyond the high school curriculum. These prepare students for the competitive entrance examinations of the Grandes Ecoles. The Grandes Ecoles include Ecole Polytechnique, Ecole Normale Supérieure, many engineering schools, Ecole Nationale d'Agriculture and others. Mathématiques Supérieures (first year) and Mathématiques Spéciales (second year) are the training programs for examinations for Polytechnique, Normale and the various engineering schools.

So I went to the lycée. It was too late for me to get a bed, but I got my noon meal for two years.

I decided against applying for the engineering schools because I was not very good at drafting. I could not try for the Ecole Polytechnique exam because I could not get from Brittany a citizenship certificate for my paternal grandfather. This certificate was required because the Germans were trying to eliminate Jews from the Polytechnique. So I decided to try for Ecole Normale.

The lack of communication between the so-called "occupied zone" and the "non-occupied" one made a few things difficult, but sometimes things worked out. As an example, I should mention how I got my first Bourbaki book. I had seen, in a bookstore, the Bourbaki "Fascicule de Résultats" on set theory. It was strange and very different from anything we had studied in Math Sup-Spé. In it there was a statement of Zorn's lemma. I was unable to prove it and asked Professor Delange, at the Université, for help. He did not help the way I expected but told me that there were other books by Bourbaki. Of course, there was no possibility of ordering the books from Paris by letter. The only things that could cross the *ligne de démarcation* were preprinted postcards on which you simply checked the appropriate lines except for one line of text which you could write yourself. I sent one of these cards to the Hermann firm in Paris asking, "Give me news of Bourbaki." They sent back the first volume of Bourbaki's topology, at no charge. Several years later, in Paris, I went to their office and met Enrique Freymann, who said to forget about my overdue bill and buy a few books if I wanted to. He also took my address and sent me the next Bourbaki books as they appeared. Those I paid for.

The schedule in Math Spé was heavy: sixteen hours of lectures on math, seven on physics, six on chemistry, etc., per week. Oral exams in math every week and alternating exams in physics and chemistry. However, that still left me a bit of leeway to see a few things at the Université. At that time the faculty from Strasbourg had taken refuge in Clermont. Some courses were taught Bourbaki-style, but the exams were on old style (early nineteenth century) calculus and such. This system threw quite a few people off balance. It was hard to impossible to talk to any professors, but one could still get some feeling of what they were trying to convey.

(Incidentally, my asking Delange for a proof of Zorn's lemma was apparently an episode out of the ordinary. The next time I saw him, around 1961 in Paris, he advanced on me, pointing his finger, "Ha! Le Cam, have you found a proof of Zorn's lemma?" He repeated the performance when I saw him again at Orsay in 1975.)

The war years brought a certain amount of misery, part in the form of lack of food, part in the form of disruption due to the fact that it was often hard to figure out who was actively working with the Germans and who was

*More Mathematical People*

in the Underground. I escaped the German attempt to send people to labor camps, being at the same time a certified student and, on another set of papers, a certified farm laborer. The appropriate papers for the last classification were provided to me by Madame de Brinon, wife of the Vichy ambassador to Germany. She had a farm a few miles away from my mother's.

**Almost Court-Martialed**    In May 1944 I joined an underground group in the woods. That was a small group of about twenty people, led by someone I had known from my days at Notre Dame. At the time of the landing in Normandy the group swelled overnight to more than fifteen hundred people. Something had to be done. A group of fifteen people, including one of my favorite cousins, took over the military camp at La Courtine. It was "defended," if one can call it that, by some 150 French soldiers under the command of a dozen German officers. The next day the crowd of us went there. The French military, who had been invisible since 1940, came out of the woodwork and tried to teach us to march in step and the like. I got into a hassle with one of them and was about to be court-martialed when somebody spread the rumor that the Germans were coming back. The French officers disappeared again into the woodwork, and I escaped court-martial.

I went back to the farm and stayed there until late October. Returning to Clermont-Ferrand in November 1944, I found that I was a suspicious character. The story was that I had volunteered to battle the Russians in a German outfit and had been killed in action. The fact that I was there, very much alive, was not enough to kill the story.

I shortly left for Paris. It had been arranged (by my Clermont-Ferrand teachers) that I would join the Lycée Henri IV in the Math Spé class directed by Professor Perrichet. Unfortunately, Perrichet insisted on my being a boarder in his school. Having tasted some freedom, I refused.

In December 1944 I took the exam for Ecole Normale and flunked the oral part of the exam. The ordinary possibility was just to take the exam over again. That I could do the next June, which was not so far away. However, I would have to survive in the meantime; and if I supported myself, I probably wouldn't be able to study enough to take the exam again, so I decided to go to the Université and direct my attention towards getting a *licence*, which is approximately the equivalent of an A.B. or a B.S. in the United States.

Registration at the Université was something peculiar in those days, peculiar by American standards, but in a way a very good system. You went to the window and said, "I want to register at the Université." "Do you have your high school diploma?" "Yes, but I don't have a copy of it." "Well, that's all right. We can check. Which kind of courses are you going to take? Humanities or sciences?" "Well, I will take this and that course." So they wrote that down and said, "Go pay your fee." And that was it. No. Not quite. "Can you pay the fee?" "Well, I don't know. How much is it?" "Oh, five hundred francs." That was about one dollar at that time.

So I was registered, and that gave me the right to use the students' restaurants, which were quite cheap, and other nice privileges like that. I supported myself as a *pion* in a boarding school just out of Paris. It was a miserable job. I supervised the students, all boys, to make sure they got up in the morning and washed their ears and went to classes.

**"I know I can flunk you."**

Nobody ever asked me to attend any courses at the Université. That was not the purpose. You did what you pleased. When you thought that you had learned something about a subject, you registered for that examination. You took a written exam first. If you passed that, then you took an oral exam. You paid about a one dollar fee for each. If you wanted to get the *licence*, you had to take three examinations; and if the *licence* was to be any good, it had to involve a collection of subjects. There was a standard course, but for the *licence de mathématique* you also had to take physics and chemistry. I attended some of the lectures in chemistry, also some of the lectures in physics. For physics you had to go to the lab experiments, and since I was working outside Paris I did not have time. So I dropped that and took a course in theoretical physics, but that was mostly logic, so I didn't feel that I was prepared for a true examination in theoretical physics. I was looking around for another exam to take when I was told by somebody that the examination in probability would be quite feasible. I went to see Maurice Fréchet and explained my situation. That was about two weeks before the examination. And Fréchet told me, "I know I have not seen you in my courses, so I know I can flunk you at the exam. And if you manage to pass the written exam, I will flunk you at the oral exam. However, if Darmois allows you to take the statistics examination . . ."

So I went to see Georges Darmois, but before going I braced myself for statistics. He had published a little book, so I read it and went to see him with it under my arm. He laughed his head off. "Ho ho ho! That book was written in 1928. A few things have happened in the meantime. However," said he, "If you can get the notes for my course, why not try it?" So I worked hard—finding the notes—and I had all of three days to read the notes over, but I thought, "Why not?" Now one of the features of the French system which I should mention was this. In those days—no longer so—you registered for an examination and took it; but if you did not pass, although the professor who gave it might keep that in his own personal records, it was never recorded anywhere officially at the university. If you did pass, then that was recorded.

I got my *licence* in October 1945. It was a nice, but useless, certificate. After I got it, I wanted to take some more courses, but I needed a better job. So I went to talk to Gros Georges—that's what Darmois was called—and he said, "Well, I'm going to walk a little. Why don't you come with me?" We walked to the post office, and on the way he told me, "You have passed the statistics examination, so maybe you could be a statistician. I have a friend who needs somebody." The friend was Etienne Halphen at one of the branches of what was to become Electricité de France. Some people interviewed me. The interview did not take very long. They asked me how much money I wanted, and I just said a figure. Then they gave me a bunch of papers—typed papers about rainfall, stream flow, and the operation of dams—and told me to read them over—"and if you feel you can do something, come back in two weeks." So that's what I did. I did not really think that I could do anything, but I needed a job. As it happens, I did do something, eventually.

Electricité de France was then in the making. One of the leaders for nationalization of the electric system was Pierre Massé, a very intelligent, well educated person who at the time was director of seventeen different electric companies. I was later told by his wife that in 1940 when the German were invading France and everybody was fleeing toward the south, the

Georges Darmois, known to his students as ''Gros Georges'' because of his imposing size.

Massés also started fleeing, but when they were perhaps fifty miles out of Paris, he suddenly drove into a field and stopped the car: "My god! We are going to be short of electricity! Something has to be done." He started right then and there making plans on how to organize a national system, and he worked at it all during the war.

A few days after I was hired, Massé held a small meeting, attended by perhaps fifteen people. We were told that we needed to know many things about the availability and the fluctuations of hydroelectric power. He said, "I don't expect the answers tomorrow. You might not even have them in ten years, but I expect you to do your best."

Massé was later "Minister in charge of planning" for the whole of France. He was a powerhouse and an extremely nice person. I fondly remember going to a concert with him and his wife. "Look at him scribbling on the program," she whispered. "When he runs out of space, he will use his shirtcuffs." He did. Massé had developed a lot of mathematics about programming for the future. What became known in this country as "dynamic programming," invented by Richard Bellman, was very much alive in Massé's work, long before Bellman had a go at it. One superior who was close to me was André Nizery, an engineer, a very good one and a very understanding one.

**Pifometry**     What became Electricité de France was a nice place to work. My direct boss was Etienne Halphen, a descendant from an old French Jewish family who had had to hide from the Nazis in a monastery. He had become converted to Catholicism and had tried to become a priest, but had been rejected for health reasons. It was while he was hiding from the Nazis in the Pyrénées that he got in touch with Massé and began to work on the idea of Electricité de France with him. I learned a lot from Halphen. He had a very sharp intellect. He could deal with theoretical statistics easily, but he also had a nose for handling data. (I mean "nose." He used to joke about his nose, and the advantage it gave him in "pifometry"—"pif" is a slang term for nose.) He was a Bayesian and, long before Jimmy Savage propagandized that creed, he tried to convert me.

Our work at Electricité de France revolved around three main subjects: (1) where and how to construct new hydroelectric plants, (2) how to operate dams for the best results, and (3) how to evaluate the probabilities of drastic droughts or destructive floods.

During that time my relations with the Université were distant yet very strong. If there were lectures by somebody of interest, I would go and listen, even when they weren't directly on a topic connected with my work. Leray was giving courses at the Collège de France on fixed point theorems, and somehow I was interested because of some difficulties with the differential equations we encountered in the hydraulic problems, so I went to listen to him. There was no difficulty with my job. All my bosses assumed that what counted was the production, so they said, "If you want to go walk in the woods and think, that's your privilege."

But then we all knew—very well—that we did not know much statistics. So with Colette Rothschild, Edith Mourier, Jean Fourgeaud and a few other people, we formed a group that met once a week at the Institut Henri Poincaré to teach ourselves about statistics. We tried to report on what we had read about statistics and ask questions about it. Actually we mostly chattered about everything and nothing in particular.

I didn't really have any academic ambitions. Frankly, the question of degrees did not matter at that time. When I started working for Electricité de France they did not even bother to ask me whether I had a degree. I was not from Polytechnique. That was all that mattered.

Our university mentor was Darmois, who was in charge of too many things. However, he was very bright and could smell a new idea miles away. He spent about two hours a week at the Université. The rest of the time he helped run his wife's steel mills. At one time, feeling too busy, he asked me to provide speakers for his weekly seminar, so for several years I had relations with the speakers. That was how I happened to meet Jerzy Neyman. I already knew of him through the *Statistical Research Memoirs* that he and E. S. Pearson published in the late thirties. I had even seen him briefly in 1946 when he was returning from Greece. However, in 1946 I had been unable to attend his lectures because that same week Harald Cramér and R. A. Fisher had both given talks which I had attended. A third absence from work, although permissible, would have slowed down the computation I was carrying out at Electricité de France.

**High Tea with Neyman**

When Neyman came again in 1950, Edith Mourier, who had spent a year at Berkeley, told us that he would like a "high tea." So we prepared one for after his talk. There was tea, coffee, pastries and cookies, and a good supply of cognac. Neyman seemed to enjoy it a lot, even though the tea leaves had spread in the teapot and our cognac glasses were just plain water glasses and teacups.

Shortly after this episode, Fréchet told me that if I would like to spend a year in Berkeley, it could be arranged. That was around Easter 1950. After checking with Nizery, I said yes. Nothing happened. Knowing Fréchet, I assumed he had totally forgotten the entire thing. Then on August 18, 1950, I got a telegram from Neyman: "Where are you? We are waiting for you here."

My preferred young lady had by then decided that she could not stand the sight of me. My mother and my brothers were a fair distance from Paris, and I did not see them often anyway. So it seemed that a year at Berkeley was a good idea and not a very disruptive one. Nizery did the paperwork for my leave from Electricité de France and provided me with an airplane ticket (one way).

I arrived in New York on October 7, 1950, and missed my connecting flight to San Francisco. That first contact with the U.S. was not too good. I was used to the streets of Paris. At that time they were relatively clean. New York was filthy. The next day I made it to San Francisco. Somehow Neyman had prepaid my busfare to Berkeley, and that bit of travel ended well.

I should have known something about Berkeley. Charles Stein had just spent a year in Paris. Edith Mourier had just returned from a year in Berkeley. But neither of the two warned me about what to expect.

One difficulty was my English. I could read and write. I could hardly speak or understand. It took about three months to cure that to a reasonable extent.

The other difficulties were mathematical. My statistics was of the applied type. At Electricité de France one did not worry about proofs or such niceties. But at Berkeley everything was full of measure theory and other fanciful mathematics. I had had no formal training in such things, only a superficial knowledge gathered in odd ways. Whatever I knew of abstract mathematics

Le Cam just about to shake hands with Jerzy Neyman, who in 1950 brought him to Berkeley.

had been learned from the Bourbaki books. Those I read, carefully at times, having eventually a "subscription" to them.

To catch up with the rest of the crew, I read some books: Saks's *Theory of the Integral*, Banach's *Théorie des opérations linéaires*, and a few odd papers.

In the spring of 1951 things got complicated. There was some mixup about my leave. Electricité de France threatened to fire me if I did not return at once. At the same time Neyman told me that if I got a doctorate I could stay another year, or perhaps more. As I said, in France the degree had not mattered. The French doctoral degree in those days was not given that easily, and it was assumed that you would take your time about it and write something reasonable. I had registered for the doctor's degree there, because it was a possibility. I had some ideas, but they were a little bit vague, let's say.

I decided to register for a Ph.D. at Berkeley and take the qualifying exams. But then it turned out that the University, which had accepted me as a "lecturer," did not want me as a student. Poor grades. But Neyman insisted, and he could be very insistent. I was admitted to the Ph.D. program. Then I proceeded to fail my qualifying examination! That was April 1951. I tried again in October and barely passed.

One associate dean declared that too many exceptions had already been made in my case and put himself on my thesis committee to make sure that the rules were going to be followed. However, I ultimately received my Ph.D. with a total residency as a student of two and a half semesters although the book of rules specified a minimum of four semesters.

**A Very Insistent Man**
In the meantime, in February 1951, I had met a young lady by the name of Louise Romig. It happened this way. One Saturday Terry Jeeves, who was at Berkeley at that time, was moving from the south part of town to the north; and all of us in the Statistical Laboratory, including Neyman, were helping him. In the course of the move Neyman took me aside and said, "Look, I need your help. One of my colleagues has written to me that his daughter is arriving here. It would be nice if you would meet her." "Well, how old is she?" "Oh, I don't know. About thirteen." "O.K." Well, Louise arrived. She was twenty-three and quite able to take care of herself! But we became friendly. The next year, when I told Neyman I was going to Los Angeles to get married, he flew into a rage. He called my future father-in-law, Harry Romig, who was also a statistician, and told him it was "illegal" for me to get married because I had not finished my thesis. Actually it was finished except for a few pages still to be typed. I went ahead and got married anyway in April 1952. I was awarded my Ph.D. that June.

# Afterword with Le Cam

**MP**  *What do you think now, in retrospect, about the effect of Jerzy Neyman on your career as a statistician—other than the fact that he brought you here to Berkeley, where you have stayed ever since?*

**LE CAM**  Well, he did have influence, but it's hard [chuckles] to describe. I think it always bothered him that I never wrote a joint paper with him; yet it's clear that I follow his kind of philosophy, his theories of statistics, which were definitely not the Bayesian ideas of Halphen at Electricité de France. Also, he kept asking questions. Is that true? Is that better? He kept me moving, let's say. Otherwise I would have just sat down and not done much.

**MP**  *Come now!*

**LE CAM**  Well, certainly I would not have done as much mathematical stuff. When I was at Electricité de France, I needed to know, but not in a mathematical sense. I thought of theorems but sitting down, writing them out, trying to find the best possible assumptions—it would not have occurred to me.

**MP**  *Did you not have any interest, then, in the abstract side of statistics?*

**LE CAM**  I did not make the difference. Even now I have a bit of difficulty—what is abstract and what is practical? The abstract side has the virtue that you can simplify things, and when you simplify things, they appear more reasonable, clearer, and so forth. But if you want to apply statistics, you have to get down to the nitty-gritty and do things that may not be so simple.

The young Le Cams with Denis, their firstborn.

*More Mathematical People*

**Modeling Is Missing**    **MP**    *So actually this, your attitude toward applications and theory, although it isn't exactly Neyman's, is in the spirit of Neyman?*

**LE CAM**    Yes. One thing that Neyman was very good at was making models. For instance, when studying the distribution of insects in a field, he tried to find out the way in which they dispersed from a mass of eggs. When studying the effects of radiation on cells, he tried to visualize what happens when particles hit DNA, how DNA repairs itself, and so forth. That was also my way of thinking even before I came here, but of course I got a lot of it here, too. I think that modeling is one of the things that's missing from many people who call themselves applied statisticians—the idea that you have to look at a thing in detail and find out what's going on. And then you carry out some mathematics—in fact, explain things mathematically. The typical applied statistician says, "That's such and such kind of data. Let's use a linear regression." They don't care about the mechanism.

**MP**    *It's very well known that statisticians consult a lot, certainly by comparison with mathematicians, even with applied mathematicians. Do you think that consulting is just something that goes with the turf?*

**LE CAM**    There are people in statistics who don't consult at all, but it's probably more natural for statisticians. Problems come up, and the people involved come to see a statistician either because they cannot handle the statistics themselves or because the answer they get from their book or their program doesn't make sense to them. So they need advice on what to do. I've done very little consulting for many, many years. When I was working for Electricité de France, that was practical work; but after I came here, somehow it was just easier to prove theorems. So that's what I did until approximately 1974.

**Very Special Consulting**    **MP**    *That was when you became involved with the work of Vera Byers and Alan Levin as a result of your daughter's cancer?*

**LE CAM**    Yes.

**MP**    *So after your involvement in your daughter's treatment, you became really active in medical experimentation. Isn't that right?*

**LE CAM**    Well, it turned out that way. Vera is a very pleasant person, and she had this research laboratory, and from time to time she needed help with the statistics, so why not?

**MP**    *We understand from some of your colleagues that you became something of an authority on the subject of osteogenic sarcoma.*

**LE CAM**    Not really. In the case of the boy in Linda's group who later died, the doctors did call me when he developed a tumor on the lung. They said, "You've read all the literature. What should we do?" I said, "Well, you should operate." There was not much chance. Thirty percent. But that was all there was to do. They said they couldn't operate. Later, when it was too late, they said, "You were right. We should have operated." But even though the people at the Mayo Clinic, some of them but not all of them, say I know more

MP NOTE: Details of Le Cam's involvement as a statistician in the treatment that eventually cured his daughter, Linda, are contained in the remarks of Dr. Vera Byers under the heading "Statistics and Medicine."

about the disease than they do, it's not true. For the last four or five years I have not followed up on the work at all.

**MP**  *Why is that?*

**LE CAM**  Well, I found it very hard to get accurate information. There were well designed, well conducted clinical trials carried out in Europe; but when I tried to get that data, I could not get it. The data has never been published. And my statistical friends who were working on that data tell me that they can no longer put their hands on it.

**MP**  *There have been cases in the recent past where fraud has come to the surface in medical experimentation. Certainly you have egos involved to a much greater extent than in proving a theorem, although there's an ego involved there too.*

**LE CAM**  There are egos involved. There are also large amounts of money. The pharmaceutical industry is attuned to that. When Vera and Alan applied to NIH [National Institutes of Health] for money to carry out a proper clinical trial of their procedure, NIH denied their application on "ethical grounds." They said that chemicals had been proved effective, so nothing else—no other treatment—would be ethical. As far as I know, the chemicals have not proved themselves yet. The lady in charge of the office of that person who wrote the letter of disapproval went to work for a pharmaceutical company a couple of years later. It doesn't give you a good feeling.

**Learning, Doing, Thinking**  **MP**  *Do you like mixing a few applications with your theoretical work?*

**LE CAM**  Oh yes! For one thing, one has the feeling that one is more helpful. Prove a theorem, and so what? While if somebody has a problem and you help in some way to solve it, you feel that you have done something. For another thing, one learns a lot more by doing than by just thinking up theorems.

**MP**  *You've nevertheless proved more than your share of theorems. We've heard you described as a very, very deep theoretician. Do you see the theoretical things you have done and are doing as ultimately coming down to applications?*

**LE CAM**  Yes.

**MP**  *You definitely do?*

**LE CAM**  Well, maybe I should not say that so brutally, but roughly my work—my theoretical work—has been due to two kinds of things. One kind is simply that people come up and they have questions. So somebody with a problem wants to use maximum likelihood and asks, "Well, but the conditions of so and so's book are not quite satisfied—are the conclusions still true?" "Oh, sure!" I may say. But then I have to prove it. So that type of thing. The other type of thing is that I have had to teach, and somehow it's not pleasant when you teach something if you don't understand it a bit. So you try to understand, and so you get involved, trying to see what is it that makes it work.

**MP**  *So in fact trying to understand has been a motivation for you in both applications and theory. Have you always had a need to understand? Was it a characteristic of you as a young person?*

# STATISTICS AND MEDICINE

*In 1972 a malignant tumor developed on the left leg of Le Cam's daughter, Linda, who was not quite thirteen. Her leg had to be removed at the hip; the following year her left lung also had to be removed. Ultimately the Le Cams turned to Vera Byers and A. S. Levin of the University of California Medical School, who were pioneering an essentially untried immunological treatment. We asked Dr. Byers about the treatment and the statistical assistance provided by Le Cam:*

Osteogenic sarcoma is an extremely rare disease—four per million per year. It mainly hits teenagers, and it's absolutely devastating. The mortality rate is something like ninety percent.

The disease usually presents itself as a tumor on the leg or the arm. There has to be an amputation. There's no other treatment. And there's already been a seeding of tumor cells to the lung while the tumor's growing but not yet recognized. Patients generally die as a result of the pulmonary metastasis, which occurs about six months after the amputation.

Because of the predictable pattern of the disease, my colleagues and I thought that it would be an excellent model for prophylactic immunotherapy. Earlier we had done a study in which we had found that some, although not all, household contacts of patients develop immunity against the cancer as evidenced by their lymphocytes, a kind of white blood cell. So our protocol involved screening household contacts, taking the lymphocytes of those who had developed an immunity, making an extract (transfer factor) of the lymphocytes, assaying it to be sure that it was active, and injecting patients with the transfer factor in the so-called "disease free" period (between the amputation and the development of the pulmonary tumor) every two weeks for two years. Our goal was to arm the patients' own lymphocytes so that they could carry out a seek-and-destroy mission.

We had just started this protocol when Lucien contacted me and asked me to attend a meeting with him and his wife and a specialist in radiation and chemotherapy to decide on follow-up treatment for Linda. The chemotherapist came on very strong, and in the end the decision of the family was to use the then widely accepted approach of radiation and chemotherapy. I was dismayed. At that time, although I had a Ph.D. in immunology, I hadn't yet gone through medical school, so I didn't realize that people can't make up their minds on medical things—you have got to make up their minds for them. Now I would be more forceful.

The treatment decided upon, which has since been declared ineffective on the basis of nationwide trials, nearly killed Linda. Lucien called me. Would I take her? At that time, because we were an academic institution, we could pretty well do what we wanted. I said, "Sure." We checked the family for immunity. Lucien and the two boys were positive, so we made up a transfer factor from their white cells and started Linda on the protocol.

It was only somewhat later that I found out Lucien was a statistician. I was describing to him what we were doing, and he said, "Well, you know, maybe I can help you a bit." I said that would be very nice because I didn't know any statistics and when I'd gone to statisticians they had seemed unable to answer my questions—they would just say that I ought to have a whole lot more patients and so forth.

Lucien did all our statistical work—most important and difficult was analyzing and characterizing the transfer factor. In addition, he became an expert on the therapy of osteogenic sarcoma. You see, if you work in a particular disease, you're going to know personally all the medical people in the world who work on that same disease, but you never know the statisticians who work with them at their various institutions. There is a network of statisticians just like there is of medical people, and Lucien plugged into that network.

Now when Linda came into our protocol, she was in quite bad shape compared to all but one of our other patients. But things went really well for her, as they did for the others. In fact, we were having such success that sometimes I thought, "Gee, maybe these kids don't really have osteogenic sarcoma after all!" But then we lost one patient, our only one out of the eight. As a matter of fact, he gave me this piece of jade [indicating a disk on a thin gold chain around her neck] which I always wear kind of in memory of him.

I'll tell you that one of the best days of my life was when I went to Linda Le Cam's wedding last year. I was standing there with Linda's husband and Lucien, and somebody said, "Is this the doctor who cured Linda of osteogenic sarcoma?" and Lucien said in his French accent and his very modest way, "Well, we wrote a little paper that said that." It was very sweet the way he said it.*

*See Byers, V. S., Le Cam, L., Levin, A. S., Johnston, J. O., and Hackett, A. J. Immunotherapy of Osteogenic Sarcoma with Transfer Factor, Long-Term Follow-Up. *Cancer Immunology and Immunotherapy* 6, 243-253 (1979).

**LE CAM**  Well, when I was in high school, I guess it was not quite so. I needed to know, but not necessarily to understand. I think the need for understanding came quite a bit later.

**MP**  *So you're distinguishing between knowing and understanding in the sense that knowing is a little more on the surface and understanding means really getting down underneath the thing?*

**LE CAM**  Very true.

**Statistical Ideas Are Not Very Clean**

**MP**  *You are usually described as "a mathematical statistician." How do you distinguish between a mathematician and a statistician, or more generally between mathematics and statistics?*

**LE CAM**  Well, to me it's all the same, so it's hard for me to make a distinction. The distinction is more what people like to do. There are mathematicians who do mathematics simply because they like it—it's a work of art. Some people work very hard on problems that have no relation to anything else. But in statistics—well, you have the mathematical part of it, one has to be able to handle the concepts, but you also have the fact that the concepts are not very clean. The idea of probability, of randomness, is not a clean mathematical idea. You cannot produce random numbers mathematically. They can only be produced by things like tossing dice or spinning a roulette wheel. With a formula, any formula, the number you get would be predictable and therefore not random. So as a statistician you have to rely on some conception of a world where things happen in some way at random, a conception which mathematicians don't need to have.

Louise Romig Le Cam in 1961 with the three children: Denis, Linda and Steven.

*More Mathematical People*

**MP** *And the kind of problems you take up as a statistician—you expect—will come down to the practical some day? They will have a connection with problems that are faced in the applications, even though now they're still at this theoretical level and there's a long way to go?*

**LE CAM** Yes. A lot of my work has been theoretical so far but motivated by the idea that one should be able to justify certain procedures and that if I get a practical problem, I should be able to do something reasonable about it.

**The Difference between Mathematics and Statistics**

**MP** *I think that you would be the perfect individual to teach an elementary course in statistics. And of course at the first class meeting you would have to answer the big question: "Will you please tell me just what is statistics, Professor Le Cam? Why should I study it? I know I have to take it to graduate but, well, get me worked up."*

**LE CAM** [Chuckles.] Well, I think it comes back to what I was just saying. If you perceive the world as some place where things happen at random—random events over which you have sometimes very little control, sometimes fairly good control, but still random events—well, one has to be able to have some idea of how these things behave. Can one modify them, or is it impossible to modify them? If you try to do something like, let's say, testing a new drug, what can you expect? You cannot expect that the effects will be clean and visible at the first try. People who are not used to statistics tend to see things in data—there are random fluctuations which can sometimes delude them—so you have to understand what can happen randomly and try to control whatever can be controlled. You have to expect that you are not going to get a cleancut answer. So how do you interpret what you do get? You do it by statistics.

**MP** *So, in every aspect, statistics is really determined by this random quality of the world?*

**LE CAM** Yes.

**MP** *And that makes the difference between it and mathematics?*

**LE CAM** That's right.

**MP** *Do you think that the general public can be made more statistically sophisticated? There certainly is a need. I don't know how many times in the last few days I have read a result followed by the statement that the statistical error is plus or minus such and such!*

**LE CAM** Well, it *could* be done. What should be done is to introduce people, at least in high school, to the idea of random things, random events. Once you get that basic concept, the idea, then the rest is easy.

**MP** *But the big problem in establishing such a high school statistics course is that the high school curriculum is locked in concrete.*

**LE CAM** One of the difficulties also is that the teachers in high schools, the mathematics teachers, have the same attitude that is prevalent in the scientific community. They don't know what statistics is! We just had, a few months ago, a meeting with our dean. He wanted us to limit our admissions of foreign students. When we told him that we need many teaching assistants and that we don't have enough American applicants, he told us to hire some

The door to Le Cam's office is open even when he is not there.

of the mathematics students as T.A.'s. To me that's gross, absolutely gross! Here is a dean, somebody who is supposed to know something, telling us that we should take mathematics students who have never heard of statistics and have them teach statistics courses!

MP   *It is quite possible to get a Ph.D. in mathematics without ever studying statistics.*

LE CAM   There was another incident that is sort of funny also. I have worked quite a bit with Grace Yang, who is at the University of Maryland—she's a former student of mine—and she works with a physicist there. Recently, when he was here to visit his son, he came by to say hello. I had never met him before. So we had a little chat, and when he left, he said something about adding numbers, something like that, which sounded funny. Somebody who has worked with a statistician—that he would think that what I do is just add numbers! So I thought about it and realized that he had never referred to Grace as a statistician but always as a mathematician! Apparently statisticians to him are people who keep track of baseball scores and things like that.

MP   *It occurs to me that there are two big fields that have split off from mathematics in recent years, first statistics and now computer science. Would the dean have assumed that computer science could be taught by mathematics students? Certainly most mathematicians don't feel that they can teach computer science.*

LE CAM   But in many, many places you will find that the attitude of the mathematicians is that any damn fool can teach statistics—just take the book and do it!

MP   *How do you see computers as affecting statistics?*

*More Mathematical People*

**LE CAM**   The computer has made it so that the sort of things that in the past we could not do on our own are now feasible, so we are trying all sorts of procedures, but we don't really know at all what they do. I don't think that's going to last. Somehow, sometime, somebody will have to find out what are the properties of these procedures. It's not going to be easy to do, mathematically, but somebody will have to try because, even though computers are very efficient, it's impossible for them to try all procedures under all possible circumstances. We will have to decide on other grounds what's good and what's not good.

**MP**   *But these new methods, bootstraps and things like that, are working well.*

**LE CAM**   So they say.

**MP**   *In other words, you feel that we are rushing on with what can be done right now but the time will come when the hard work will have to be done?*

**LE CAM**   Yes. That's right.

*August 1986 in Berkeley, California (DA, CR).*

## *Postscript*
# Le Cam on His Work

*For the benefit of anyone who thinks that all a statistician like Le Cam does is "add up numbers," MP asked him to write a brief description of some of his work. A few days later he brought us the following:*

**Distance between Experiments**

A lot of my work has been on asymptotic methods in statistics. Around 1955 the available results used ad hoc assumptions and methods that actually can be traced back to Laplace. They applied mostly to independent identically distributed (i.i.d.) observations as $n$ tends to infinity. People were

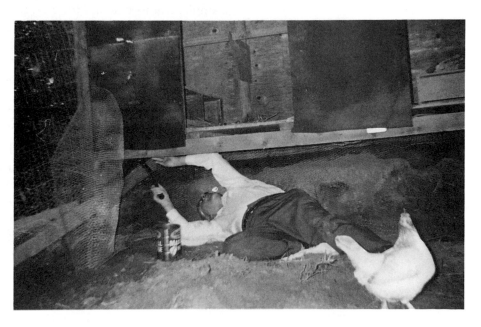

Working on his Russian River home in Northern California (with a little help from a chicken).

Visiting in China.

starting to use similar ad hoc assumptions for observations that are not independent, such as Markov chains and other dependent situations. I decided against such case-by-case extensions and somehow, with the help of a 1943 paper of Abraham Wald, developed a definition of distance between statistical experiments. If two experiments are very close to each other in the sense of their distance, any statistical problem with a good solution on one family has an almost equivalent solution on the other. At about the same time, I introduced the "locally asymptotically normal" (LAN) families. These families are described by local quadratic behavior of logarithms of likelihood ratios instead of independence or near independence of the observations. They are nice to use because various relations often proved separately are automatic for them. The distance allowed me to give necessary and sufficient conditions for i.i.d. variables to lead to LAN and a number of other results. For instance, Jaroslav Hájek and I obtained the now classic asymptotic minimax theorems and theorems on asymptotic admissibility. However, the main benefit for me is that as a result I had an organized system in which to think about asymptotic problems. It does not cover everything, by far, but it is organized. Some people will complain that it is too organized and thereby leaves out many interesting problems. That is true, but such is life!

### Concrete Problems

Most people think of me as some sort of mathematician dealing in abstract and abstruse problems. This is funny since I have essentially no formal mathematical training. However I did and still do get involved in concrete problems. In concrete problems the famous $n$ does not tend to infinity and I have psychological difficulties in relying upon pure limit theorems, even those that come with a rate of convergence. So one can look for bounds on approximations. I did some of that for deviations between estimates and the "true values," using definitions of metric dimension taken from the metric entropies of Kolmogorov. Also, in 1963, I was able to improve a theorem published in 1957 by Kolmogorov on approximation of distributions of sums of independent variables by infinitely divisible distributions. That was a change from an epsilon to the power $1/5$ to an epsilon to the power $1/3$. I did not know at the time that Kolmogorov had in the meantime obtained a similar improvement. However, there were enough differences between the problems we tackled and the approaches we used that I can claim independence. The epsilon to the power $1/3$ has now been cut to $\varepsilon|\log \varepsilon|$ by Zaitsev, using some of my results.

I did a few other things, such as theorems on random elements in Banach spaces. At first that was done for convenience in treating some statistical questions; however, it has developed a life of its own. Even though I contributed a few tricks and a few new items of terminology, my work there is now a drop in a sea of contributions by many famous mathematicians. Right now I am trying to understand the mechanisms by which radiation affects survivals of cells in culture. That takes more time than proving theorems but, in a way, it is more interesting. Incidentally, in such problems I don't bother with the niceties of finding optimal or asymptotically optimal estimation procedures. Anything that gives a reasonable result goes, but it has to be reasonable as checked against what is known of the biology or biophysics of the situation.

In Hong Kong with Grace Yang, a former student with whom he has continued to work.

*LUCIEN MARIE LE CAM* Croze, Creuse, France, November 18, 1924. Lic. es Scis. 1945, Paris; Ph.D. 1952, UC Berkeley. Field: mathematical statistics. Professor of Mathematics and Statistics, UC Berkeley. President IMS, 1972–73. American Academy of Arts and Sciences. Books: *On Some Asymptotic Properties of Maximum Likelihood Estimates and Related Bayes' Estimates*, 1953; *Convergence in Distribution of Stochastic Processes*, 1957; *Locally Asymptotically Normal Families of Distributions*, 1960; (with J. Neyman) *Bernoulli, 1713, Bayes, 1763, Laplace, 1813, Anniversary Volume*, 1965; (with J. Neyman) *Berkeley Symposium on Mathematical Statistics and Probability*, 1967; *(with others) Berkeley Symposium on Mathematical Statistics and Probability*, 1972; *Asymptotic Methods in Statistical Decision Theory*, 1986; (with Grace Lo Yang) *Asymptotics in Statistics: Some Basic Concepts*, 1990.

# HANS LEWY

At eighteen Hans Lewy chose a career in mathematics over one in music. At twenty-two he took his Ph.D. in Göttingen. He was still only twenty-four when the *Mathematische Annalen* published the classic Courant-Friedrichs-Lewy paper "On the partial differential equations of mathematical physics"—a paper that IBM reprinted in its entirety forty years later because "the ideas espoused still prevail." One of the first mathematicians to leave Germany when Hitler came to power, Lewy was always quick to recognize threats to freedom and was one of the "non-signers" who successfully challenged the University of California's notorious loyalty oath. He never liked to talk publicly about himself or his achievements and limited himself here mainly to observations on the great European mathematical centers and the development of mathematics in the United States.

□ □ □

**MP**  *So you came to Göttingen as a student during the 1920s?*

**LEWY**  Yes, 1922.

**MP**  *Almost sixty-five years ago!*

**LEWY**  Yes. Almost. I came from Breslau. The reputation of Göttingen was great, partly due to Klein and Hilbert, and a former teacher of mine, a high school teacher, went to see my father and told him I should not study in Breslau, where there was also a university, but I should go to Göttingen, because Breslau was too stuffy and old-fashioned.

**MP**  *It was rather unusual for a mathematics student to go to Göttingen so young, wasn't it? Obviously you had to go to some university when you got out of the Gymnasium, but I remember K. O. Friedrichs told me that he went to three or four universities before he felt he could say to himself, "Now I must go to the mecca of mathematics!"*

**LEWY**  Yes. When I arrived in Göttingen, I was quite overwhelmed by the atmosphere. Most of the people were a little older than myself. Among them was Friedrichs, and I greatly admired his knowledge. He knew much more than I did, as did many others that I met there. I remember that I went to the lectures of Edmund Landau on algebraic number theory during my first semester. They were somewhat over my head at the time, but they helped me to adjust my expectations of myself so they were a little higher than they would have been otherwise.

**MP**  *I know that there was no formal list of requirements at a German university, but did anyone advise you about what lectures you should hear?*

**Not Like Understanding a Novel**

**LEWY**  No, no. Complete freedom. Also the attendance was absolutely free. And there were no examinations. I think this was a crass case of malfunctioning in the German system. There is an obvious gap between the ability to master a subject and the listening to theorems and proofs. I know that there were many students who would believe that they understood what was going on in mathematics, and yet when they came to their first examination, which was only at the end of four years of study, they would find out that they really hadn't grasped what was going on because, to them, to understand mathematics meant the same as to understand a novel. They didn't realize that it meant an active mastery of the subject. When they went into their first examination, then of course they collapsed. I think that the system was bad, because it allowed a person to go on for so long without realizing that he was not actually understanding the subject. There were some cases where a person took his life—upon noticing. For the very good students, of course, the freedom that the system allowed was a great boon. It allowed them to go into subjects which, at first, were vastly over their heads, but it would speed up their becoming familiar with them. Of course, they had to make a very great effort, but for good students there is no subject that is so difficult that they cannot master it if they put their energy into it. For the good students the German system was excellent. For the average students and the poor students it was just a failure.

**MP**  *When you took a course like the one you mentioned as being so much over your head, the algebraic number theory course of Landau, how did you attack it?*

**LEWY**  Well, of course, I took notes and worked on them. What I mean is that I tried to fill in the gaps. Landau would mention certain things, and I hadn't heard of them. I didn't understand the drift of things, what was really in his mind, until later. I would struggle. I would go in the library from one book about the subject to another book about the same subject. Not finding what I wanted in one, I would find it in another. And that was a very good education in mathematics, I believe.

**MP**  *I know that the Lesezimmer, or reading room, in Göttingen is always spoken of as one of Klein's most important innovations.*

**LEWY**  Yes. Now here in Berkeley and other places in America we have this system in which we allow the books to be taken out of the library for an extended time, which means that others who would like to consult the books can't find them on the shelves. Our students—unfortunately, in my opinion—are one-book students. They learn a subject from one book when they should learn it from many books. Now in the library in Göttingen, the Lesezimmer, all the books were always there. They were never taken away unless they were stolen. I think this was a very good system, and I have

Sketched by his wife, Helen Crosby Lewy.

Hans with his sister, Edith.

always tried—but unsuccessfully—to have also our library here to be a "presence" library.

**MP** *It is an idea that is very alien to our American idea of a library where the goal is to have all the books in circulation! Yet today with the ability to copy material . . . .*

**LEWY** Yes. There are many books that are just to be consulted. In mathematics you don't want to read a whole book. You want to find out what a book says about some very restricted subject, then go to another book and see what it says. And thereby, by leafing through various books, you not only become better informed on the subject you are interested in, but you become familiar with other things. So this I consider a better education than what our students get. Ours are usually narrower in their knowledge of mathematics.

**MP** *I am interested from a pedagogical point of view in your motivation in working so hard in the course of Landau's that you mentioned. Were you motivated by the fact that in four years you would have to take an examination on the subject, or were you motivated simply by your interest in the subject?*

**LEWY** The subject interested me greatly.

**MP** *So you might attend other lectures and not work so hard?*

**LEWY** That's right. Of course, you realize that except for people like Landau, whose courses were very well organized, the level of explanation in the courses—the attention to detail—was much less than what is customary here. So the teacher would say, "Now one can easily find out such and such a thing," and then go on without doing the easy work—and that was often the most difficult part. But that was also a good education if you had enough conscience not to slip over it and abide by the word "easy" said by somebody else. Then, of course, it forced you thereby to find out if you really were mastering the subject. From that point of view it was a good education.

**MP** *Is it a method which you recommend to teachers?*

**LEWY** I am divided against myself in this. I am avoiding saying that it's easy in my own lectures, and I do everything for the students. But now, if I were sufficiently confident that the students would work out everything, every detail that I left out, then I probably would do it the same way as was usually done in Göttingen—which is of course much easier for the teacher. When you do work out all the details yourself, you often find that you should have arranged the material a little differently so that whatever it was would have come out more easily. So then you have to revise.

**MP** *Do you think that the fact that the German students had a better high school preparation made possible the kind of lectures you speak of?*

**A Certain Fanatic Adherence to the Truth**

**LEWY** I don't think that high school preparation has much to do with it. I think the desire to fill in the details is an ethical matter. There is a certain fanatic adherence to the truth that is necessary in mathematics; and if a person doesn't have that, he shouldn't go into mathematics, in my opinion, as a profession. In that we all share.

**MP**  *Did you know when you came to Göttingen that mathematics was what you wanted?*

**LEWY**  Yes. But I went also into physics.

**MP**  *That was a wonderful time in Göttingen for physics. Did you have any relationship to the development of quantum mechanics?*

**LEWY**  No. I was repelled by it. To my mathematical mind the things that the physicists were doing were too sloppy. In other words, they had obviously some physical intuition which I didn't have, but their mathematics was objectionable. It created an idiosyncrasy in me which prevented me from learning a number of things which I should have learned. Yes. I was convinced that the whole thing was just a lot of talk and phoniness.

**MP**  *It teaches one humility, doesn't it?*

**LEWY**  It teaches one humility. Yes. It shows, and I say this to my son very often, that different situations in science really require different types of characters, so one cannot make up one's mind what is the right way of being. This is a subject on which I have often thought. I have registered a great many observations over the years about how "wrong" attitudes or outlooks have had the most beneficial effects upon the development of the sciences, especially physics. Biases which we would completely reject, and which should have been rejected from the outset, have sometimes produced the most amazing discoveries.

**MP**  *What would be an example?*

Rowing in Germany.

**LEWY**  The prime example is the example of spectroscopy. The Balmer series, do you know that? It is the series of the lowest spectral lines of hydrogen. There was some teacher, some high school teacher, who had a tick, as one would say, for numerology—trying to explain things by connecting them with integral numbers—and he discovered that if one took the difference of the reciprocals of the squares of the integers one could somehow thereby account for the first so many lines in hydrogen—a thing which by any intelligent reasoning would have been entirely rejected. I mean, to believe that there is some merit in such an exotic thing took considerable bias. It's certainly a very unscientific attitude. Yet this discovery was of extreme importance in deciphering the spectral lines, which was eventually accomplished in quantum theory. So that's an example.

**MP**  *During your student days in Göttingen did you explore any of the other sciences?*

**LEWY**  Oh, I tried various things in addition. I would go here and there, hearing that such and such is a good, an interesting lecturer.

**Listen to the Great Man**  **MP**  *I notice that in your little Anmeldungsbuch, in which the record of the courses you attended was kept, the names of the courses are not listed, only the names of the professors.*

**LEWY**  Yes. In Europe we had the idea to go to listen to the great man more than in this country. As far as my own son is concerned, I still think that if he went to lectures even on a subject with which he is fairly familiar he might hear an aside, something that is more valuable than a whole book.

Young Dr. Lewy at twenty-three.

**MP** *You certainly heard a lot of great men. The list of names just on this one page of your Anmeldungsbuch for 1924 is impressive: Born, Courant, Noether, Franck, Ostrowski, Hilbert! And I know you also heard Herglotz and Prandtl. I think you said once that moving around in the sciences was encouraged in Göttingen.*

**LEWY** That was so. Yes.

**MP** *When did you get your Ph.D.?*

**LEWY** That was in 1926. And then I became a Privatdozent and also an assistant to Courant.

**MP** *I understand that the custom of mathematics professors' having assistants was also an innovation of Klein's. Of course, the professors in the applied sciences had always customarily had assistants.*

**LEWY** In mathematics, in my time, an assistant was often granted to a professor as a part of his contract. He'd say, "I'll accept this position provided that you give me one, two or three assistants." I think Hilbert had three assistants. One was Nordheim in physics, one was Bernays in logic, and I think there was a third one. These assistants, in my opinion, were eminently useful and some of the breadth of Hilbert's activity is explainable by his having had assistants — qualified men who could search the literature, tell him about the latest developments, and do some menial tasks. This preparation of a subject to the point where one has the facts of what has been achieved and so forth, this is such a herculean task that most of us are frightened to step outside of the subject with which we're familiar. Of course now it is even more difficult, but even at that time the amount of literature was substantial. It was eminently easier for them when they had someone to pick out the salient facts. It was thus possible to find out where the main problems were in a subject and how the things which had already been achieved could be easily presented. I myself was an assistant to Courant. I think that I learned a great deal and Courant had a lot of work, preliminary work, taken off his hands. Here in this country I have had lots of people who were called research assistants, but all that meant was that I assisted them.

**The Life of a Privatdozent**

**MP** *Were you an assistant to Courant before you got your Ph.D.?*

**LEWY** No no, after I got my Ph.D. At the same time I also then became a Privatdozent.

**MP** *As I understand, a Privatdozent was an official university lecturer although he was paid not by the university but by his students.*

**LEWY** Yes. At the same time the students who were to pay had many ways of trying to get the instruction gratis by taking examinations which were given by the dozents, whom they were supposed to pay. If the person had taken the course from me, I would give the examination. Then if he did well on it, that would enable him to take other courses from myself or from other dozents without paying.

**MP** *Were you paid directly by the students?*

**LEWY** No, they paid to the registrar. But it was a miserly little sum. Say, ten marks per semester per student. Exact equivalent at that time would have been $2.50.

**MP**  *I think I have seen a copy of the letter of recommendation which Courant wrote for you for a Rockefeller Fellowship to go and study abroad.*

**LEWY**  Does that still exist? I remember that before one got one of these fellowships, one was inspected by a member of the Board. They wanted to make sure that a person who got a fellowship would not do dishonor to the Foundation, so they wanted a personal interview. The man came and invited you to a lunch. He also wanted to see whether you had manners that were inoffensive, I guess. Yes. They were intent on keeping up a good public image.

**MP**  *According to your vita, as a Rockefeller Fellow you went first to Rome. Was there somebody special in Rome that you wanted to study with?*

**LEWY**  Well, Levi-Civita. I knew his work. I had read all his books. In applying to the Rockefeller Foundation, you had to outline who you were going to see, but you couldn't say, I want to work with him, without having asked him, you see. So it wasn't that you went to study with somebody. I continued my own work. I had my Ph.D. already, so it was not that I wanted to be given a problem to work on.

**MP**  *What was Rome like as a mathematical center, compared to what you had known in Göttingen?*

**LEWY**  Rome, even at that time, suffered from Mussolini. Science was out of favor—with the young people in particular—and that was due to Mr. Gentile, whose influence still at this time is not entirely overcome. He was a friend of another very famous Italian philosopher—Benedetto Croce. Mr. Gentile was entrusted with the ministry of education, and he introduced innovations which consisted mostly in eliminating sciences from the high school curriculum and replacing them by humanistic courses, mostly literature, philosophy, such things. This tended to give the official stamp toward more oratory and away from substance. This was noticeable even when you read the newspapers.

It was rather easy for me to meet personally many of the people, so I cannot complain from that point of view, but the general mathematical activity, as expressed in seminars, colloquia and so on, was very restricted. There were very few students. There were more professors in Rome than younger men who would actually aspire to become professors of mathematics themselves. Yes. The universities were in a fight against the fascist government. That is, it was not a declared fight, but it was a resistance, a non-acceptance of the fascist doctrines. A year after my presence there Mussolini demanded of all professors that they sign a declaration of allegiance to the fascist government.

**MP**  *A loyalty oath?*

**LEWY**  Yes. A loyalty oath. And that caused great trouble. Volterra refused to sign, but Levi-Civita was prevailed upon by his colleagues to sign; however, he signed with a declaration that he is not a fascist.

**MP**  *Vito Volterra has always interested me. It seems that he was such an impressive figure, both physically and morally. A really noble man.*

**LEWY**  Yes. He made that impression. Have I told you the story? Jacques Hadamard was giving some lectures in Rome, and then Hadamard left. And

Vito Volterra (1860–1940) refused to sign Benito Mussolini's loyalty oath.

Tullio Levi-Civita (1873–1941) was the attraction for Lewy in Rome.

Longtime friend and early collaborator, K. O. Friedrichs (1901–1982), doing mathematics in the Catskills in 1939.

afterwards came a telegram for Hadamard which Volterra opened. And it said, "Your son has been killed in the war." That was the first World War. Hadamard had just left, so Volterra looked at the train schedule, found a faster train and caught him at the border so that he could rather tell him personally about his son.

**MP**  *What a thoughtful thing to do!*

**LEWY**  The Italians have that quality of graciousness and kindness that I have found also in the Chinese.

**MP**  *Levi-Civita, too, was a really noble man, but he did not have the impressive physical presence of Volterra.*

**LEWY**  No. He was very tiny. He was also very kind. In conversation once I mentioned to him that I was interested in some book which I didn't find in the library. I mentioned it just casually. Then one morning when I got out of bed my landlady said, "There has been a gentleman here who brought you a book." I was living on the sixth floor so he had climbed all those flights of stairs to bring me the book. That was the kind of man he was.

**MP**  *Who would you say was the leading mathematician in Rome when you were there?*

**LEWY**  Oh, you couldn't say that anybody was leading. But they were all splendid men. I took the opportunity to learn a little algebraic geometry. There had been a particular emphasis on it in Italy for many decades, so there was a long tradition. There had been many outstanding men in Italian mathematics in the last century—Beltrami, Bianchi and so on. And they had had contacts with Riemann. Betti was one man who was evidently inspired also by Riemann. So there was a long tradition. I went to Enriques's class. He was a man in the Italian tradition of algebraic geometry, which was not accepted in the rest of Europe because proofs were not rigorous enough—they were quite controversial. Some of the Italians, especially Severi, were quite conscious of this. You see, they took what is generally true for a thing which is always true. For a mathematician that distinction is very important. But they made great progress in imagining what was probably correct, yes, and giving proofs that were, say, generally correct. But they did not make clear under what conditions those things were working. Enriques personified that approach. He, in his book, would give a theorem and a proof; then there would be a section—"Now there come some critical doubts." I can show you such things that he wrote.

**MP**  *Why would the idea of rigor not have penetrated in Italy when it was so strong at that time in France and Germany?*

**LEWY**  Well, as I said, Severi was quite conscious of such things—he had spent a certain amount of time in Leipzig—but Enriques was satisfied if he had some general idea of a proof.

**MP**  *Were you satisfied with the time you spent in Rome?*

**LEWY**  Oh yes! Of course I was not there only for the mathematics. Rome was a magnificent place to explore. The traffic was minimal compared to what it is now. Delightful!

The seminar of Jacques Hadamard (1865–1963) was the big event in mathematical Paris.

**Mathematics—Only for the Young?**

**MP** *How would you characterize, in a general way, the Roman mathematical situation as compared to the Göttingen situation and the Paris situation, which you were later to experience?*

**LEWY** Oh, I think that in both places, Paris and Göttingen, there was a much larger field of mathematics covered.

**MP** *Did you have the kind of situation in Italy that you had in France, where almost everybody who was anybody was trained in the capitol and then went back to the provinces for a year or two to teach until they came back permanently, in the French case, to Paris?*

**LEWY** No. I don't have that impression. Rome was more or less like other places because, you see, the system in Italy at that time did not have what we call postgraduate study separated. So while their undergraduate studies used to lead farther than they did here, there was no emphasis on the typical graduate study and research. If a student was born in, say Genoa, he went to the university in Genoa. They have a great many universities in Italy. They are in many small towns. The idea was that everyone would go to the nearest university and that the desire to change would come with more advanced learning—the desire to go to places where such was concentrated. Those students you should have seen in Rome, but you saw very few.

**MP** *Do you think that the reason for there being so many universities might be the fact that Italy was for so long politically divided?*

**LEWY** But that also should have developed diversity of enterprise, which would be good for mathematics; however, that was not the case. I think that a great many of the Italian colleagues did not have ambitions to continue their efforts after they had become installed as professors. In this country we have in places the same situation.

**MP** *I remember that when I talked to you about Courant, you indicated that you felt his work on minimal surfaces was the result of his having had to reestablish himself in mathematics when he came here from Germany.*

**LEWY** Yes. In Göttingen, as time went on, he got more and more involved in administration so that, I think, by the beginning of the thirties he was no longer actually active in mathematics. Then when he came here there was a necessity on him to establish himself in an entirely new setting. He began to work again in mathematics and did some very good work. Yes. It was a typical case of the effect of what in German was facetiously stated: *Stop when the career is closed.* Now "stop when the barrier is closed" is the sign at a railroad crossing, and *Barriere* and *Karriere* sound almost the same in German. I think that the situation referred to is rather common, and it has led to the belief that mathematics is done only by the young.

**MP** *Tell me something now about the term that you spent in Paris as a Rockefeller Fellow.*

**LEWY** Paris was much more lively in mathematics than Rome, although the thing on which the Roman faculty spent so much of its effort—this algebraic geometry—was not represented. There were very many active, productive mathematicians in Paris, so I think that Paris was comparable to Göttingen.

**MP** *That must have been a wonderful time to be there.*

**LEWY** Yes, in those days Paris was a very pleasant place. It was possible to live with any purse. In fact, I did so. In 1930 I had the Rockefeller Fellowship, which was $125 a month, which was tremendous. You couldn't use it up unless you spent it foolishly. Then later—when I went back in 1933, after Hitler came to power in Germany—I had to live on something like $30 a month, and I didn't feel as if I was living in a different world, as I would have felt in most other places.

**MP** *What interested you most mathematically in Paris?*

**LEWY** There was a special thing that was outstanding. That was Hadamard's seminar. Hadamard would have a collection of papers, a great stack, which he would have already looked over, and he would invite people to his home and there he would proceed to parcel out the papers to people to report on. Yes. Hadamard was the great attraction. He was perhaps the last mathematician who could with some justice say that he had an inkling of all fields of mathematics. That is also the reason his seminar was such a point of attraction.

**MP** *And one of the reasons he had that inkling was probably due to the seminar!*

**LEWY** Yes, yes.

**MP** *I have always been impressed by the fact that the French mathematicians of that time seem to have been much more, well, provincial—if one can call Paris provincial—than the German mathematicians. They did not travel to other countries to study. Even Picard, who was certainly something of a French chauvinist, commented that it was unfortunate that they never went abroad to study.*

**LEWY** Picard said that? That's interesting. He was very nationalistic. I remember that André Weil caused a great annoyance with Picard because he had adopted some of the theory of ideals, which was considered to be German.

**MP** *In that regard I was always very impressed that Klein urged Hilbert as a young man to go to Paris and get acquainted with Poincaré. Hurwitz did the same. He told Hilbert, "The French are very original and we must master their results before we can go on." But the French never seem to have felt that way about the German mathematicians.*

**LEWY** The French had quite a superiority complex in those days. Now, you see, we Americans have a superiority complex, perhaps because we prevailed in the second World War. I notice a great difference in the attitude of young American mathematicians between the time I came to this country, which was in 1933, and since the war. Many American mathematicians now think that their values are the right ones and should be accepted by everyone. True, mathematics is here very well developed, but still these beliefs are really due to the fact that we are more powerful politically. So it was with the French in the twenties and thirties.

**MP** *Did you, when you went to Paris at that time, feel any prejudice against you as a German?*

Henri Lebesgue (1875–1941): "Everything Lebesgue looked at seemed to be illuminated by light from another source."

A prodigy on the violin, Lewy at fifteen was a featured soloist with the Bautzen Symphony Orchestra.

LEWY    I can't say that. There were many other foreigners studying in Paris. I attended the lectures of Lebesgue at the Collège de France. It was a course on "Problems on the margin of the calculus of variations". Practically everything that he told was in some way familiar to me, but it was very interesting because everything Lebesgue looked at seemed to be illuminated by light from another source. I remember he told us a story which is illustrative. In the thirteenth century in Holland there was a professor who used to go out walking with his students. Once he said to them the following: "If you look at any simple object attentively, you will always see that there is something further that can be done with it. Take, for instance, your shoes." (At that time, of course, everyone wore shoes which were not differentiated, right and left foot.) "Your shoes are exactly the same," he pointed out to the students, "but your right foot and your left foot are congruent . . ."

MP    *That is a wonderful story.*

LEWY    Lebesgue was also like that.

MP    *Later, after Hitler came to power in Germany in 1933, you went back to both Rome and Paris.*

LEWY    Yes. I wanted to get a little distance from events in Germany. I went first to Italy with Herbert Busemann. He said I should leave Germany because I couldn't keep my mouth shut. He also eventually left, of course. So I went back to Göttingen and packed my things and went to Paris. I was offered a job at Madrid, but I was reluctant to take it because Spain at that time had just gone through a civil war, and I didn't really want to spend my life again in politically disturbed conditions. Spain, I thought, was not sufficiently confirmed in the democratic field, and that turned out unfortunately to be true.

MP    *How did it happen that you came to this country?*

LEWY    Early in July, I think, I was told by Hadamard that he had received a telegram. There had been formed in the United States a committee—the Duggan committee—which was going to pay the salary of a refugee if an American university would accommodate one, and Brown evidently was willing to have me. I never met Mr. Duggan. I understand that during the McCarthy time there were many calumnies against him and he committed suicide.

MP    *I saw a letter from you to Courant, written the next year I think, in which you said that Americans felt that they had reached the saturation point as far as refugees were concerned. At that time there must have been only about half a dozen in the country.*

LEWY    Well, of course, there was the Depression at that time. Quite a number of people in this country, who were well qualified, were looking for jobs. So one must consider the circumstances of that remark. The demand for people in mathematics and physics, of course, increased as the war approached. But at that time it was not the case. There were even people, refugees, who were well qualified who had trouble finding jobs. But it was much better than having to stay in Germany. I was very fortunate, you see. At Brown I was paid three thousand dollars, which was tremendous.

*More Mathematical People*

**MP** *You must have found the mathematical situation in this country quite different from what you had been familiar with in Europe.*

**LEWY** Generally speaking, mathematics in this country was still in a state in which it was really carried on by only a few individuals. There were men like Birkhoff, Veblen, Evans, a few men who carried on as active mathematicians while the rest of the men in the field were resting on their laurels.

**MP** *Were there really any laurels for them to rest on?*

**Mathematicians as Country Gentlemen**

**LEWY** Oh yes. Most of them had gotten the Ph.D. in Europe and often with a substantial piece of work, but due to the pleasure of living in this country or to some other reason which escapes me, they rested. For instance, Jackson—Jackson in Madison—had done a very good piece of work as a student in his Ph.D. thesis, but I don't think that he ever branched out from there. Here at Berkeley we had Mr. Noble and Mr. Haskell. Noble was a pupil of Hilbert, and Haskell was a pupil of Klein. I believe they thought that that was enough.

**MP** *That was an odd thing.*

**LEWY** Yes, but here in those days people in this country had an ideal of what a man should be, and that ideal was much closer to being a squire than to being a mathematician.

**MP** *"A scholar and a gentleman"?*

The Göttingen Orchestra in 1932; Lewy and his violin are second from the right.

**LEWY**  Yes. These people were men of quite a wide general education. They were interested in many things and mathematics was just one thing, with which they made their living and which they had been interested in, but it was not the vital part of their lives. They knew much less than we did in mathematics. On the other hand, they were more all-around people. Yes.

**Origins of "Publish or Perish"**

**MP**  *I have always thought there was a certain lack of mathematical ability in this country at that time.*

**LEWY**  Oh, no. No. Not lack of ability. But the ideal of the good life predominated. That attitude began to change about the time I came. People would talk about the large salary received by this or that person and how much work he had done. The "publish or perish" idea started about that time. Griffith Evans came to Berkeley and established it here. That was very painful for some of the older members of the department.

**MP**  *So actually the arrival of the European mathematicians in the 1930's and a changed attitude already developing here just happened to coincide?*

**Revolution in Mathematics Department**

**LEWY**  Yes. In mathematics here at Berkeley it was the result of a revolution engineered by the chemists and, I believe, also by the physicists. They were very dissatisfied with the lackadaisical attitude of the Mathematics Department. So they set up a committee that should go out and look over the situation nationwide and hire a man able to change that attitude. Of this committee no mathematician was a member and, from what I have heard, only one of the mathematicians was even asked his opinion—the others were completely ignored.

**MP**  *So they hired Griffith Evans. That was just before you came, wasn't it?*

**LEWY**  Yes. Evans was hired in 1933, I think, and came here in 1934. He hired Foster, who came here in '33, and Morrey, who came in '34, and me in '35.

**MP**  *Well, he'd been chosen to upgrade the department and he certainly did!*

The Lewys share a happy moment on their travels.

**LEWY**  It was a difficult job, but he did it with extreme discretion. No person was actually fired except one woman whose husband was in quite a substantial situation so she didn't suffer directly. On the other hand, it entailed suffering for some of the men because they were not promoted as they would have been otherwise. Several of them left. It was painful, but it was aboveboard.

There was a general desire in the country, no question, to upgrade—partially the result of the change that was taking place in medicine. The Rockefeller Board had had Abraham Flexner make a report, a discussion of the situation of American medicine versus European medicine. At first the change was put into effect in medicine, and then later it was extended to the other branches of science.

The coming of the Europeans was important, but there is no question that the improvement in quality was part of a general development which would have come about anyhow.

**MP**  *How did it happen that Brown University let you go?*

**LEWY**  A stipend from the Duggan Committee covered just two years. It was hoped that at the end of that time, the university might be interested in

Lewy had a great capacity for enjoyment.

having the person permanently. Brown University was never a very wealthy place, so it had jumped at the chance to get somebody for nothing, but when the period was over it didn't have the money to keep me. Mr. Richardson, who was in charge there and the secretary of the American Mathematical Society, wrote a number of letters for me and I got two job offers and a third "hope," which was here in California. One offer was in Louisville, Kentucky, and the other in Lincoln, Nebraska. And I—well, I followed the hope rather than the certainty.

**MP** *It appears that you did the right thing.*

**A Sleeping Bag if Necessary**

**LEWY** I felt that if I were in one of those other places, it would take me two days and a night or two nights and a day to go to see my friends in the East while to go from San Francisco wouldn't take much longer. On the other hand, I knew that San Francisco was a more cosmopolitan place. Also the West attracted me for what you might call reasons that had nothing to do with science. I had seen films of the mountains—those red mountains!— and I had seen films about Indians. Of course I had heard a great deal about California and life out here, so I was really intrigued by it. I was in kind of a romantic way attracted to the difference of the West because the East in many ways resembled Europe. I knew that the West would not, and that was to me something. And taking a chance on a job wasn't as hazardous as it might seem now. In those two years I had been at Brown I had been able to save a substantial part of my salary. I had a car, and I knew I could live on very little. I also knew that in a milder climate I could live outside. I was prepared to put a sleeping bag on the ground and live that way. But then I received a telegram—it was forwarded to me and I got it some place at the end of July—that I had a job at Berkeley—beginning July 1. That was when the contract had started. I did not begin to teach until August.

**MP** *And you have been at Berkeley essentially ever since?*

At home in most of the world.

**LEWY**   Yes. And I must say that as far as I, strictly on a personal basis, am concerned, I owe Hitler a much more interesting life than I would have had otherwise.

*October 1985 in Berkeley, California (CR).*

*HANS LEWY*   Breslau, Germany, October 20, 1904. Ph.D. 1926, Göttingen. Field: partial differential equations. Professor, UC Berkeley. Steele Prize (AMS) 1979, Wolf Prize 1985. Accademia dei Lincei, American Academy of Arts and Sciences, Göttingen Academy of Sciences, National Academy of Sciences. Books: *Developments at the Conference on Analytic Boundary Conditions*, 1950. Died August 23, 1988.

# SAUNDERS MAC LANE

One of the last Americans to study at Göttingen prior to the rise of the Nazis and the subsequent fall of that famous Mathematical Institute, Saunders Mac Lane has been a towering figure in American mathematics for over half a century. He has inspired younger people, made important contributions to algebra and logic, and written such classics as *A Survey of Modern Algebra* (with Garrett Birkhoff). He is one of only five who have served as president of both the American Mathematical Society and the Mathematical Association of America. (Others were R. H. Bing, E. R. Hedrick, E. J. McShane and R. L. Wilder.) In these roles, he created the Joint Projects Committee to bring the work of the two organizations closer together. A statesmen of science as a whole, he has been vice president of the American Philosophical Society and the National Academy of Sciences as well as one of the few mathematicians appointed by the President to the National Science Board.

□ □ □

**MP**  *I understand that your father was a Congregational minister, but from your name I assumed you would be Presbyterian.*

**MAC LANE**  Oh, that's an incorrect assumption. My father's father was a Presbyterian minister, but in the 1880's he advocated the theory of evolution. Consequently he was forced to resign from the Presbyterian church.

**MP**  *Do you come from a long line of ministers?*

**MAC LANE**  There were ministers in the background, also some farmers and various romantic characters. One served for fifty years as a minister of the Congregational Church of Norfolk, Connecticut.

**MP**  *And you were born in Connecticut?*

**MAC LANE**  Yes, in Norwich; my family then lived nearby in Taftville.

**MP**  *What was your background on your mother's side?*

**MAC LANE**  My mother—Winifred Saunders was her maiden name—came from Newport, Rhode Island. She graduated in 1905 from Mount

Holyoke College and then did some high school teaching. Later she returned to teaching: English, Latin, and mathematics.

**MP**  *Did you have brothers or sisters?*

**MAC LANE**  I had one sister, who died in infancy, and two brothers, both younger than I. One of them, Gerald, was also a mathematician active in geometric function theory. He has been at Rice and Purdue. The other brother became a school teacher and businessman.

**MP**  *I assume that you were good in mathematics in school.*

**MAC LANE**  Well, I enjoyed school and I was good at various things, including science. Initially I thought I was going to become a chemist because in the little high school that I was going to, it was not clear that any other scientific careers were open. I had read a book called *Creative Chemistry* which said that chemistry was a great field. It was only after I went to college that I shifted to mathematics.

**MP**  *Pólya told me once that of his high school mathematics teachers one was good and two were despicable. What were yours like?*

**MAC LANE**  I had a good teacher for freshman algebra. I think he was simultaneously the football coach. Then I took sophomore geometry. It was apparently thought that students couldn't learn geometry in one year so they had a second course in the junior year. The teacher in this second course didn't understand the subject and I did. I made a lot of trouble for her. In my senior year I had an expert but not particularly inspiring mathematics teacher. I did have an inspiring teacher of English, Olive Greensfelder. She got me to write a prize essay (about Lincoln) and made me editor of a (new) high school newspaper. She really took an interest.

**Undergraduate Years at Yale**

**MP**  *Then you went off to Yale.*

**MAC LANE**  I should explain that my father had died when I was in high school and my mother, my brothers, and I had gone to live with my paternal grandfather. He had been married twice, and by the first marriage had had two sons, one of whom was a very successful lawyer. So when I was a junior in high school this rather mysterious uncle, John F. MacLane, came by and looked down at me and said, "Saunders, I will send you to Yale."

**MP**  *You didn't have any say in the matter?*

**MAC LANE**  I think he added the observation that he and his brothers and his father and any number of ancestors had gone to Yale so this was the place for a Mac Lane to go. So my Uncle John sent me to Yale, cheerfully providing enough money for all the expenses. He expressed some slight interest in my going into business or into law. In fact, I had the impression that had I wished to go into law he would have sent me to the Harvard Law School. This same uncle sent something like eight or ten nephews and nieces to college.

So when I went off to Yale in the fall of 1926 I took both an honors course in chemistry and the standard freshman mathematics course. I found the chemistry rather dull. I didn't enjoy laboratory work. I had a wonderful teacher in the freshman mathematics course, an instructor working for his Ph.D., named Lester Hill. He gave me lots of encouragement and said,

Mac Lane in 1931.

"Mac Lane, why don't you take the Barge Prize examination?" They gave that examination to freshmen every year. So I took the examination, succeeded in winning the prize, and decided that maybe mathematics was a better field than chemistry.

**MP**  *The choice of a field often comes down to a teacher at some level who makes the subject exciting somehow.*

**MAC LANE**  Well, Hill made a big difference to me. He got me to take the examination and he gave me lots of encouragement. I stayed in touch with him in subequent years. But I had various other effective teachers at Yale, which was then in the process of shifting from being a school that trained people for the law and the ministry to becoming instead a great research university. After I was there for a while I figured out how to take advantage of that shift.

After taking economics in my sophomore year, I decided that my uncle ought to have a chance, so I took a course in accounting. By the end of the first month I was utterly bored. A flamboyant classmate of mine named Julian Ripley was taking honors economics, philosophy and physics at the same time, and he described how wonderful this was. So I dropped the course in accounting and signed up for honors in physics as well as in mathematics. So I majored in both mathematics and physics in my junior and senior years.

**MP**  *To quote Pólya again: he said once that he was interested in physics, philosophy and mathematics. He was not good enough for physics and too good for philosophy, so he went into mathematics. Do you think that mathematics is a lesser science than physics?*

**MAC LANE**  No.

**MP**  *Any regrets about not having gone into physics?*

**MAC LANE**  Well, it's clear that physics was at that time just at the start of enormously exciting revolutions so to have gone into physics would have been a fine and dandy thing. I have no regrets though.

**MP**  *Now, James Pierpont was among the older group in mathematics at Yale.*

**MAC LANE**  Yes, in my student days at Yale, Pierpont was the senior member of the department. He had studied in Germany, had written a good book on complex variables, and had almost discovered the Lebesgue integral. By the time I was there he was somewhat tired and not particularly inspiring. The course which he gave for sophomores was too easy. So the people who inspired me were others. There was a student of Pierpont named Wallace Wilson who complained to me that he knew more rigor than Pierpont—but he didn't know as much mathematics.

When I was a junior I went to Wilson and said, "I want you to help me read *Principia Mathematica*." And Wilson said, "Well, that's not a very good book to read. Why don't you read Hausdorff's *Mengenlehre* instead?" So I spent the junior year reading, among other things, Hausdorff's *Mengenlehre* under Wilson's guidance. This was the first serious mathematical text that I read and it made a big impression on me.

**MP**  *Did you ever get back to Russell and Whitehead?*

**MAC LANE**  Well, I bought the first volume but never quite got through it. So I didn't get around to the second and third. I think I'm not alone in that.

Then in my junior year I had another excellent teacher named Egbert Miles. He was a Ph.D. from Chicago, though not a research mathematician, but he was fascinated with teaching and given to punching the kids in his class to make them pay attention.

**MP**  *Punching them?*

**MAC LANE**  Punching them, yes. He would walk through the class and hold somebody by the shoulder and ask him a question. If the fellow didn't answer correctly, he'd give him a couple of little nudges. It's not a method that would be effective now, but he was quite a good teacher. In my junior year I took his course in advanced calculus and he quickly concluded that I didn't need to attend the course. So he said, "Why don't you read [Edwin] Wilson's *Advanced Calculus* instead? You can be the paper grader for the course." So I graded the papers at the same time I was taking the course and learned a great deal from Miles about teaching and about presenting mathematics. In fact, when Miles, who had written a book on calculus, thought he ought to write a book on advanced calculus, I spent the summer of 1930 in New Haven working with him on a draft of the proposed book, which never came to be. It seems to me in retrospect it was silly for me at that stage of my knowledge to think of writing a text on advanced calculus.

**MP**  *Does the manuscript still exist?*

**MAC LANE**  I don't know. I doubt that it was ever completed. The reason I mentioned it is that I think I learned a good deal about how to write.

**Algebra and Ore**  **MP**  *Was there anyone else at Yale who was particularly influential?*

**MAC LANE**  Yes. Pierpont, who was getting old, realized that something new had to be done, and he persuaded the Yale department to hire Øystein Ore, a Norwegian algebraist, who was knowledgeable about modern algebra in Germany. Ore was then very rapidly promoted from assistant to associate to full professor to Sterling Professor—I forget what he was when I was there, but he was young. He was giving courses, one in Galois theory and one in group theory. I am now at a loss to explain how in thunder a man could give two separate courses on two such closely related subjects. Anyhow, in my senior year I took both of these. They were delivered in a sort of offhand fashion, but there was a feeling of the excitement of what was going on then in algebra. Something new was happening. Ore said to me "Well, there is this abstract algebra that's going on in Germany—you ought to learn something about it. Get the textbook by Otto Haupt." I diligently got the text and studied the whole two volumes. It wasn't very well written, but it was sort of inspiring. It has completely disappeared from sight, of course, because in 1931 van der Waerden's famous book was published and it was infinitely superior. Nevertheless, from Ore and Haupt I learned abstract algebra. And it was exciting!

At the same time, I was taking courses in physics. I took a course in mechanics from E. W. Brown, a distinguished mathematical astronomer, once president of the AMS. He was not young, but the course was a good one, especially in his treatment of Hamiltonian mechanics. This interest has

Three Mac Lanes in 1942: Mother, Winifred Saunders Mac Lane, with Saunders (left) and his younger brother, David.

stayed with me; for example, I wrote an article in the *Monthly** on mechanics. In those days, mathematics undergraduates were supposed to study mechanics!

Also in those days theoretical physics was the center of the graduate work in physics and there was a course called Physics 100. All the first-year graduate students in physics were expected to take this and usually had a hell of a time getting through it, but as an honors undergraduate I was encouraged to take it. It was taught by a 50-year-old professor named Leigh Paige who was knowledgeable about classical theoretical physics and had made the mistake of writing a textbook on the subject. So the course was taught from his text. It was a systematic presentation of classic theoretical physics and the old quantum theory. But to the best of my knowledge there was no mention of the developments of the new quantum theory. So, as far as I can remember, in the courses that I had at Yale, it wasn't clear to me what exciting things were happening in theoretical physics.

**MP** *But algebra was exciting!*

**MAC LANE** Algebra was exciting! But I should mention something else about physics. My sophomore course was taught by a man named Jesse Beams who later became a well-known physicist, professor at the University of Virginia and a member of the National Academy of Sciences. It was a nice, interesting course. And there was an interesting laboratory with it. The laboratory assistant was another assistant professor and he got my friend Ripley and me to do some extra special experiments. The lab was exciting. And he was a man who was always smiling and cheerful. His name was Ernest Lawrence. He was then an assistant professor of physics at Yale, but that year Berkeley made him an offer and he abandoned Yale.

**MP** *Much to the benefit of Berkeley!*

**MAC LANE** Much to the benefit of Berkeley and much to my loss. I was also interested at that time in philosophy. The other teacher that I remember especially was in scientific philosophy, a man named Filmer S. C. Northrop. He later became famous for writing a book called *The Meeting of East and West*. Four years ago I got a letter from him. He was living in retirement in a hotel in Boston, and he wrote me saying that he thought that I ought to be doing such and such things to straighten out the connection between mathematics and relativity theory and the like. It so happened that I was going to Boston on other business so I arranged to call on him at his hotel. There he was, well into his eighties. He explained that he was writing a sequence of five books of which the first was in press.

**MP** *And he's still at it?*

**MAC LANE** I blush to confess I've lost track of him.

**Robert Maynard Hutchins and Chicago**

**MP** *Let's go back. You left Yale and went to Chicago for graduate study?*

**MAC LANE** There's a nice romantic story about that too. At Yale in those days football reigned supreme. And the Montclair Yale Club, in Montclair, New Jersey, which was organized by a number of rich alumni of Yale, gave a party every year to celebrate the success or to mourn the failure of the

*Hamiltonian mechanics and geometry, *Amer. Math. Monthly* 77 (1970), 570-586.

Just sailing along on his own off the coast of Maine.

football team. Somebody pointed out to them that they really ought to honor people beyond the football team so they decided to give a cup to "the man who had made his Y in life," the Y being the letter that is awarded to football, baseball, basketball, and hockey players who make the varsity. In the spring of 1929, feeling especially prosperous (this being before the famous crash), the people from Montclair decided they could do even more. They decided they would also give a cup to the man who had made his Y in scholarship. It happened that I had been a very diligent student and had got high grades. In fact, it was claimed that my grade point average was higher than that of anybody who had ever been at Yale. (Subsequently people at Yale have gotten higher grade point averages.) I showed up in Montclair to find there Robert Maynard Hutchins, who had "made his Y in life". He had just been appointed president of the University of Chicago. So there were he and I in the midst of Montclair alumni and football players, and we got to talking. Hutchins said to me, "Well, young man, what are you going to study?" "Oh," I said, "mathematics." He said, "We have a fine mathematics department in Chicago. Come out to Chicago."

**MP**  *Hutchins, recruiter for the Mathematics Department!*

**MAC LANE**  A month later in the mail I got a letter from Hutchins himself saying, "We will offer you a scholarship of $1000 a year to come and study mathematics at Chicago." I had somehow learned that there wasn't much more I could learn at Yale. I had gotten what Ore had to teach. I didn't have to think very hard. A $1000 scholarship!

In Chicago I showed up to register with my transcript and everything, scholarship in hand, so to speak, in the Bartlett Gym. There was the faculty of the Department of Mathematics beginning with Gilbert A. Bliss, the chairman, sitting there to receive the graduate students. So I went down the line. "Well, Mac Lane, were you admitted?" It turns out that I had neglected to apply for admission to graduate school at the University of Chicago.

**MP**  *But you had your scholarship.*

**MAC LANE**  Yes, but that had been arranged by Hutchins who wasn't on good terms with Bliss. But Bliss did admit me, in spite of my having on my transcript a course called Sophomore Mathematics, from Pierpont. Bliss said, "What in thunder is this course? What good is a course in sophomore mathematics?" Of course, I couldn't tell him because it wasn't a very good course anyhow.

**MP**  *Now Bliss was chair. But were any of the other grand old men of Chicago mathematics still around?*

**MAC LANE**  Chicago had had a remarkable golden age from 1892, when it was founded, until about 1910, largely due to the leadership of [Eliakim Hastings] Moore and [Oskar] Bolza, [Heinrich] Maschke, and perhaps others. They had had extraordinary graduate students: Bliss, [Leonard Eugene] Dickson, [Oswald] Veblen, [George David] Birkhoff, and others. Chicago graduate students went out and populated graduate schools everywhere—the chairman at Michigan, the chairman at Wisconsin, the chairman at Iowa, the chairman at Tulane—they all came from Chicago. And R. L. Moore at Texas came from Chicago.

**MP**  *It is an incredible story. In the West we think of Stanford as being something of an upstart but even Stanford is a year older than Chicago. It entered the scene quite late among American universities.*

**MAC LANE**  But with a bang!

**MP**  *Yes. Here was the number one mathematician at Harvard (Birkhoff), possibly the number one mathematician at Princeton (Veblen), both coming out of Chicago.*

**MAC LANE**  And the number one mathematician at Chicago, Dickson.

**MP**  *One would like to know how it was done and how that kind of thing could be repeated.*

Mac Lane in 1940.

**MAC LANE**  I have often wondered about that. In fact, I have occasionally given lectures here at Chicago on how it was at the beginning. Of course American mathematics was in a sense very primitive then. It wasn't up to the European standards, but people were excited. Dickson was the first Ph.D. at Chicago. I've looked at archives that reveal how Dickson, having gotten his Ph.D., went to Europe for a year and came back through Chicago (he was going to Texas then), and talked in the seminar about what mathematics was going on in Europe and how group theory was booming there, things of that sort.

I have a very high regard for E. H. Moore. I think a great deal of the success of Chicago was due to his early dynamic influence and interest. He was hard at work bringing modern mathematics to this bunch of untutored, cornfed kids.

**MP**  *But he did import some good people from Europe, like Bolza and Maschke.*

**MAC LANE**  He wanted to have people to support him.

**MP**  *Of course, Chicago had a lot of money at the time.*

**MAC LANE**  They had money and they had the graduate students. It was the one major graduate school where women could come and compete on an equal basis.

**Encounter with E. H. Moore**

When I was a graduate student here in 1930–31, E. H. Moore, though no longer head, was still trying to teach. What he was nominally teaching was his version of general analysis which was a more or less failed attempt to do functional analysis or Hilbert space. It didn't catch on sufficiently because he didn't publish enough, or because his publications were too tormented, too formal, or whatever. So, in addition to his course on general analysis, which was too hard for me to get into, he was running a seminar called the Hellinger integral. I signed up for it. I never did understand the Hellinger integral. But I knew somehow that Moore was a great man. But I didn't fully understand why. He said to me, "Well, Mac Lane, you had better give a talk in this seminar." He knew I was interested in foundations and he said: "There is this famous paper of Zermelo, where he proves that with the axiom of choice every set can be well ordered. Why don't you report on Zermelo's paper?" So I did. And I gave what I thought was an excellent exposition for a whole hour on Zermelo's proof that every set can be well-ordered, to Moore and his associate, [Raymond W.] Barnard, and to his Chinese students. At the end of the hour the Chinese and Barnard disappeared and Moore was there alone with me. He said, "Now, Mac Lane, that wasn't a very good lecture. You should have done so and so, and such and such. That would have been a much better presentation." My recollection is that he took about an hour to tear apart my presentation and tell me how I ought to have done it. I can no longer remember what he said to me in particular, but it was clearly with a view to getting at the heart of what was going on.

MP   *And how did you feel after that?*

MAC LANE   I think that I learned more in that one hour with Moore than in the rest of my year at the University of Chicago.

MP   *So he was a remarkable man.*

MAC LANE   On the basis of this evidence which is, I grant you, a little bit sketchy, I have the feeling that he was a remarkable teacher. And I think, in his prime, which he certainly wasn't when I knew him, he must have been a great stimulus to his students.

**Mathematics at the University of Chicago**

I didn't know Maschke, but I met Bolza once. He had left Chicago long ago and had gone back to his German professorship in Freiburg. In 1933 I dropped by to see him when I was in Germany. We went to some beer joint up on the hills above Freiburg. He blew the foam off his beer and we talked a little about Chicago.

MP   *You resisted the blandishments of the calculus of variations under Bliss and number theory under Dickson?*

MAC LANE   I took a course with Dickson in number theory. Dickson must have been nearly sixty then and a little tired. He was primarily interested at that time in the Waring problem. (If you have an integer and wish to represent it with a sum of the $k$-th powers, a certain number of them will suffice.) This problem didn't excite me. This is not a criticism of Dickson. I think Dickson was an absolutely first class mathematician, but what he was doing then didn't excite me. And analytic number theory didn't excite me. Edmund Landau was persuaded to visit the University of Chicago during that year to lecture on analytic number theory, obviously because he knew methods that were interesting to Dickson. Landau came in at the beginning of the hour, looked at our room, and said, "Oh, in Göttingen we have much better blackboards, and assistants to wash off the blackboards during the lecture." Bliss looked around the lecture room and said, "Mac Lane, get a bucket and a sponge."

**A Bucket and a Sponge**   **MP**   *So you got to follow Landau around the room washing down the blackboards.*

**MAC LANE**   That didn't improve my impression of analytic number theory. Later in Göttingen I took a course with Landau which was very precisely and elegantly presented in his particular style. He concentrated on the techniques; I was interested in why the damned thing works.

I also studied the calculus of variations, because clearly that was *the* subject at the University of Chicago. I don't think I was properly prepared, but I took this two quarter course in it. I learned about the problem of Bolza, Weierstrass conditions, fields of extremals and other things, which I haven't really thought about very much since that time.

Bliss liked to rib his class. He said that when he had gone to Paris to study, he had come into this lecture room where Hadamard, say, was about to lecture, and he had seen this man come in dressed up in fancy clothing and with a pipe. It was the flunky, who presently washed the boards and then went back and brought Hadamard in. That was the sort of respect that people in France gave their professors. "Oh," said Bliss, "in the United States nothing like that happens." Well, the students got together—I was the only one with a tuxedo—and at the next meeting of the class, appropriately attired in my tuxedo, I went around to Bliss's office, knocked on his door, and said, "Professor Bliss, your class is awaiting you."

**MP**   *He was duly impressed?*

**MAC LANE**   I'm not quite sure.

That same year Bliss lectured on the work of Morse on the calculus of variations in the large. I think this was before Morse's book was published. Bliss was aware that Morse used various results in algebraic topology, so he organized a seminar in the spring on topology, the purpose being to learn what this subject was about. In those days the only available text was a book by Oswald Veblen called *Analysis Situs* and I was told to present the essence of Betti numbers and torsion coefficients from Veblen's book. I remember distinctly laboring through the book and not understanding what in thunder the Betti numbers and torsion coefficients were about. I have looked at the book subsequently. In my view, Veblen's book doesn't really explain it very well. Well, look, it was written in 1915, at a time when algebraic topology was very new, and I think Veblen probably honestly did the best he could. It was later that Emmy Noether said that there are groups there.

**MP**   *This was your first encounter with topology?*

**MAC LANE**   My first encounter with algebraic topology. It was not a successful encounter.

**MP**   *But then it was not really a successful approach. Much of that has vanished in the meantime and been replaced, right?*

**MAC LANE**   Yes. But there was real stuff there and it would have been possible to decipher what it was really about, only I was busy writing a master's thesis, which was then required.

I also took a couple of courses in philosophy. This was at the time that Hutchins had just brought in a rather contentious figure named Mortimer Adler. He had appointed him associate professor of philosophy without consulting the Philosophy Department and half of the Department had resigned in high dudgeon. I took a course with Adler on something about logic, but I didn't learn very much. Bliss, of course, heartily disapproved of mathematics students taking philosophy. So that was Chicago.

**The Years at Göttingen**

**MP**   *You were at Chicago for one year, 1930–31, and then you moved on to Göttingen?*

**MAC LANE**   I moved on partly because I had an uncomfortable feeling about the Department. I was interested in foundations and abstract algebra. In fact, I wrote a master's thesis that was directed to those things. I tried to find axioms for systems with addition, multiplication, exponentiation, and ternary operations. I got restless to study logic. Furthermore, when I had been an undergraduate at Yale they had had a program of a junior year abroad, which was then fashionable, and I had declined a place in that program. Afterwards I had been rather unhappy that I hadn't taken that place. I had the wanderlust. I was able to get a fellowship from the Institute of International Education, so I took off for Göttingen.

**MP**   *It was still the golden age in Göttingen.*

**MAC LANE**   It was still the golden age. Göttingen is another one of these mysteries. Here was a department that was, according to present standards, small—a fifth as many professors as we have now at the University of Chicago, and a tenth as many as at Berkeley. But still in some sense it dominated world mathematics, not quite, but very close to it.

**MP**   *Hilbert was the towering figure in Göttingen.*

**MAC LANE**   He was working in foundations. I went there, of course, because Hilbert was there. I don't think I had any great knowledge of what he'd done. By the time I got there, he had retired (a couple of years before), but Hermann Weyl, Edmund Landau, Richard Courant, and Gustav Herglotz were there. The associate professors included Emmy Noether and Otto Neugebauer (I am not sure about his rank) and the Privatdozents were people like Hans Lewy and Franz Rellich.

**MP**   *Impressive. Paul Bernays was there at that point?*

**MAC LANE**   Oh, I should have mentioned Bernays; he was certainly there. Bernays was the chief active representative in mathematical logic. It was a very exciting place.

**MP**   *Who influenced you most at Göttingen?*

**MAC LANE**   Bernays, probably. Bernays and Hermann Weyl. Bernays and I both took a course of Noether's. The course was based on a paper on structure of algebras that she subsequently published. She was a rather confused and hurried-up lecturer because she was working it out as she went. I found the subject interesting, but I wasn't anxious to pursue it. The course

Proud grandfather with grandson, William Hay.

ran for two hours and there would be 50 minutes of lecture, a 20 minute intermission, and then 50 more minutes. I can recall walking up and down the corridors with Bernays during the 20 minute break, pumping him about things in logic.

**MP**  *Were there other Americans at Göttingen in mathematics?*

**How to Handle Herglotz**

**MAC LANE**  No. Well, in the first year there weren't any. In the second year Jimmy McShane came. He was brought as an assistant to Courant because Courant wanted him to translate his book on calculus into English. I took one or two seminars with Hermann Weyl, and courses with Gustav Herglotz. Herglotz was famous as the teacher of Emil Artin. He was there in a chair of applied mathematics, I think. He was a man with a vast knowledge of classical applied mathematics and classical analysis and he delivered stunningly beautiful lectures on everything under the sun: mechanics, mathematical optics, functions with positive real parts, Lie groups and goodness knows what. So I listened to Herglotz lecture on Lie groups and on geometrical optics. There are notes that were taken on his lectures on mechanics, some of which I still have, that are beautiful presentations. The man did things with great formality. He had a wonderful shock of white hair and came in to lecture with a frock coat and pique lining on his vest, in this fine lecture room. He delivered the lectures at five in the afternoon because he knew that all the assistants would then be through with their work and could come and listen. And all the senior assistants at Göttingen came. He would write down the basic facts on Lie groups in the main part of the board and then the fussy calculations he would do off on the side so that you could get the main line of the lecture but ignore the details. It was a magnificent experience. He was an extraordinarily knowledgeable and effective lecturer and a wise man. He had done some research but not very much. But these notes of his are famous. His students labored forever before he ever let them through. When I took my oral examination for the D. Phil., I had to have a major and two minors. One of the minors was in philosophy of mathematics and the other was in geometric analysis. My friends advised me how to handle Herglotz. They said he likes to talk. So this was a half hour exam in geometric analysis. It went as follows:

Herglotz: Can you tell me what the Klein *Erlanger Programm* is?

Mac Lane: Yes. It consists of considering the groups that are involved in dealing with geometry according to the group.

Herglotz: Then can you tell me how you view geometric function theory from the point of view of the *Erlanger Programm*? What would be the group?

Mac Lane: Oh, the conformal group.

There followed a half hour lecture by Herglotz on how geometric function theory fits into the Klein *Programm*. So by knowing two phrases "group theory" and "conformal transformation," I passed that part of the examination.

The other minor was in the philosophy of mathematics because that was appropriate to my thesis. That was given by a Jewish professor named Geiger who was professor of philosophy. This was in the days of the Nazis, and Jewish professors were under great pressure, so by having looked at his book on the subject I was able to get through that with no trouble at all. Bernays, who was my advisor, had disappeared because he was Jewish.

**MP** *He had been dismissed, right?*

**MAC LANE** Retired or dismissed, I forget how they explained it. So the main part of my examination was given by Hermann Weyl. Weyl had warned me ahead of time that he would examine me in differential geometry, and I had never had a course in this. I dug out some book in differential geometry and crammed. It didn't stay with me. Weyl came around to this examination with a long list of questions, and he was going to see what this irresponsible American really knew. He fired lots of questions at me, but I fired answers right back. I had had practice in examinations. The only one I got stuck on was "Please define a Hausdorff space." I forgot the separation axiom. Later I found a book of Hermann's where he forgot the separation axiom too. But I managed to answer the other questions.

**MP** *By the time you left Göttingen things must have been getting pretty bad. A number of professors had disappeared.*

**MAC LANE** Yes, Courant, Bernays, Lewy, and Noether had been dismissed, and Neugebauer didn't stay very long though he wasn't Jewish. Later, in November, 1933, Landau was driven out by a boycott. The Göttingen Mathematical Institute was simply ruined.

**MP** *Herglotz and Weyl remained.*

**MAC LANE** The story about Weyl is that in 1932 Veblen had offered him a position as professor at the Institute for Advanced Study at Princeton. Weyl had thought about it and turned it down. Then the Nazis came into power. Weyl was mindful that his wife was part Jewish and that his two sons were therefore also, according to the Nazi rules, Jewish. So after some trouble I guess he wrote Veblen, "Could I have that offer back again?" He left right after that summer semester.

Two or three days after I got my degree, I got married in the Rathaus in Göttingen, to Dorothy Jones, whom I had met in Chicago. I took a couple of my friends to a wedding dinner in the Rathaus Keller after the ceremony. Then I came back to this country and was a research assistant at Yale for a year. During that impoverished year and subsequently, Dorothy was a steady

Dorothy and Saunders Mac Lane at home in Cambridge, Massachusetts, in 1941.

*More Mathematical People*

support in my career; for example, she typed all my books and most of my papers.

**"Look, Øystein, Mac Lane has real examples!"**

Ore, who was at that time Sterling Professor, was persuaded to bring me to Yale by awarding me the Sterling Research Fellowship. He obviously wanted me to work in algebra, but I was working at the time in logic. When I went to the AMS meeting in 1933 I gave a ten-minute talk (as in those days did all young people anxious to get jobs). This ten-minute talk was on logic. I don't think the talk was of any particular consequence but at the end of the talk, Ore rose and spent ten minutes denouncing my work in logic. This did me no harm. It just served to call attention to me. Four years later, when I was an instructor at Chicago, Karl Menger set up a conference on lattice theory, which was at that time the center of algebraic interest. I had been working on other things such as field theory, but I knew some interesting lattices so I sat down and worked out a paper about some class of lattices that cropped up in fields. I went to this conference and presented a paper on a class of lattices that were not modular lattices but nevertheless had some sort of dimension function. So they were a little bizzare. After I delivered this talk, Ore got up and claimed that I was totally wrong. He thought there could not be any such lattices. In those days I worked diligently and carefully and I jolly well knew there were. My friend, Marshall Stone, who was also there, apparently got ahold of Ore and said, "Look, Øystein, Mac Lane has real examples of this, so you had better withdraw your comment." The following day Ore had the good grace to get up and say that indeed I had been right. My paper was subsequently published in the *Duke Mathematical Journal*.* I tell you all this to explain that though I owe Ore a good deal for teaching me a lot of abstract algebra, my relations with him were not always easy.

*MP   So you had to look for a job. I understand you even toyed with the idea of going to a prep school.*

**G. D. Birkhoff and Harvard**

MAC LANE   As I said, in December of 1933 I went to an AMS meeting in Cambridge and talked with George Birkhoff about a job. I also talked with Marshall Stone because he had been at Yale, though not during my period there. In fact, I rather hoped to get an appointment to the Society of Fellows at Harvard, which was then new. That was a piece of impertinence on my part. I never did get it. I also talked with Ritt at Columbia, wondering whether any of the city colleges would have some job. Not being very successful, I went up to Exeter, where there was an opening for a mathematics master. But a couple of weeks after that I got a letter from [William C.] Graustein, then chairman at Harvard, saying he would offer me an appointment as Benjamin Peirce Instructor for a year at a salary of $2,250. And I could give an advanced course. Would I accept it? This was clearly better than City College and infinitely better than going to Exeter.

*MP   The 1930s must have been the worst possible time to be looking for a position in this country. Not only was there a depression, but you were also facing the competition of all those people coming from abroad.*

*A lattice formulation for transcendence degrees and p-bases, *Duke Math. J.* 4 (1938), 455-468.

**MAC LANE** There was some contrast between the policy of Princeton and the policy of Harvard at that time. As best I understood, Veblen, who really set the style at Princeton and the Institute for Advanced Study, was greatly influential in taking care of the refugees from abroad, bringing them to this country and getting them jobs. This was magnificent that he did it. George Birkhoff at Harvard had a different policy. He felt that we also ought to pay attention to young Americans, so there were relatively few appointments of such refugees at Harvard. Instead, there they tended to appoint young Americans. It's clear that I profited from Birkhoff's policy. And it meant a great deal of difference to me that I had a two-year instructorship at Harvard. It meant an adequate salary, and a chance to give advanced courses and to talk to George Birkhoff and Marston Morse. There were some awfully good people at Harvard at that time.

*MP    By this time, what did you think of yourself as, mathematically? You could think of yourself as an algebraist, or as a foundations man, or, well, not yet a topologist, perhaps.*

**MAC LANE** Oh no, not yet. Well, when Graustein offered me the instructorship, he said that I could give a one semester graduate course. And I wrote back and said that I could give either a course in logic or a course in algebra. He wrote back, "Oh, we would love to have a course in algebra." There was then no algebraist on the Harvard faculty.

*MP    So now you were an algebraist.*

**MAC LANE** Well, I sort of became an algebraist.

*MP    Why?*

**MAC LANE** (a) Because what I had been able to do in logic was in fact not terribly surprising, though some of it might today be viewed as an attempt to do automatic proofs. There wasn't such a subject then and it wasn't clear to me that that's what I was doing. And (b), because mathematical logic was anathema to almost all mathematicians. It must have been clear to me that it would be very hard to get a good job as a mathematical logician. And indeed it was hard to get any job.

*MP    Mathematicians would probably try to push such people out into philosophy departments or something. After your Peirce Instructorship at Harvard you went to Cornell, but that was not for very long.*

**MAC LANE** I was there for a month when I got an offer from Chicago for an instructorship.

*MP    But you stayed longer than a month!*

**MAC LANE** Oh yes, I stayed for the year, but I didn't take long to accept the Chicago offer. I came in 1937 and I again worked in algebra and had very fruitful contacts with A. Adrian Albert, who was here. I saw Bliss again, but he was a little skeptical of me as always. And I saw Hutchins again. I strongly suspect that the reason I'd been brought back to Chicago was that Hutchins had said to Bliss, "Well, what about that guy, Mac Lane, who was here?"

Six months after I got to Chicago, I had an offer of an Assistant Professorship at Harvard, so I was at Harvard from 1938 to 1947.

A familiar situation.

*More Mathematical People*

Sailing mathematicians (1945): Samuel Eilenberg, David Zelinsky and Saunders Mac Lane.

**Birkhoff and Mac Lane**

MP   *In the first few years at Harvard, teaching the algebra course alternately with [Garrett] Birkhoff led to your great text* A Survey of Modern Algebra.*

MAC LANE   Yes. I had taught algebra courses at Harvard when I was an instructor, and at Cornell I taught algebra out of the book by Bôcher; at Chicago, out of a book, *Modern Higher Algebra* by Albert; and at Harvard again out of my own notes. I had taught out of most of the extant books. I knew how it should be done and so did Garrett. He had been doing the same thing. We got together and, in 1941, we published *A Survey of Modern Algebra.*

MP   *One might say you had a certain modest success with it! It must have been the standard for over 25 years.*

MAC LANE   It was the standard textbook for undergraduate courses in modern algebra. There weren't any other books that really represented the modern spirit that came from Göttingen; van der Waerden's didn't exist then in translation. Of course, the book came partly from England through Garrett, who had been influenced by Philip Hall when he worked with him at Cambridge (England). We had the good fortune to write a book on the subject at the right time.

MP   *There have been times when up-and-coming researchers would have been reluctant to write a textbook. Did you ever have any qualms?*

*For an interview of Garrett Birkhoff, see D. J. Albers and G. L. Alexanderson, *Mathematical People/Profiles and Interviews*, Birkhäuser, Boston, 1985.

**MAC LANE**   I had had this long standing interest in teaching, and I felt that it was important to have good textbooks for students. The courses on college algebra and theory of equations that were given in most universities were dull and were not the right thing. Here was a chance to do something effective so it didn't bother me at all. I didn't write a textbook in trigonometry. I remember having the impression that there were all too many textbooks in trigonometry. I thought there might well have been better textbooks in calculus. I may even have thought a little bit about that, but I didn't write a textbook in calculus.

**Eilenberg–Mac Lane**

**MP**   *Was it about this time you started your famous collaboration with Samuel Eilenberg?*

**MAC LANE**   In the spring of 1941 Michigan invited me to give a series of five or six lectures, so I talked about group extensions. This was a subject on which I had done some work and it came out of my earlier work on valuations with [O. F. G.] Schilling. I had calculated a particular group extension for $p$-adic solenoids. Eilenberg was in the audience, except at the last lecture, and made me give the last lecture to him ahead of time. Then he said, "Well, now that calculation smells like something we do in topology, in a paper of [Norman] Steenrod's." So we stayed up all night trying to figure out what the connection was and we discovered one. We wrote our first joint paper on group extensions in homology, which exploited precisely that connection. It so happened that this was a time when more sophisticated algebraic techniques were coming into algebraic topology. Sammy knew much more than I did about the topological background, but I knew about the algebraic techniques and had practice in elaborate algebraic calculations. So our talents fitted together. That's how our collaboration got started. And so it went on for fifteen major papers.

**MP**   *The time at Harvard was interrupted by the Second World War.*

In person, the famous collaborators, Eilenberg and Mac Lane.

**MAC LANE**   When the war came everybody thought that he ought to help out in the war effort. Having a couple of little children I somewhat preferred not being in the military, so there was this opportunity to work for the Applied Mathematics Group at Columbia.

**MP**   *It didn't turn you into an applied mathematician.*

**MAC LANE**   No. We were doing some immediately practical problems of calculating curves for fire control and such. It was elementary differential equations and I learned to understand more about them. But the work at Columbia was not in really profitable directions of applied mathematical research. Also it was partly administrative and I decided that I didn't especially like adminstration. I remember making a conscious decision at that time: if you want to go into business and make that your career, now is the time to do it. I didn't. I went back to Harvard, happy to go back to mathematics. Then I went to Chicago in 1947 and during the year 1947–48 I had a Guggenheim Fellowship at the ETH in Zürich.

**MP**   *To work with Hopf?*

**MAC LANE**   Yes. I spent four or five months in Zürich. The work on Eilenberg-Mac Lane spaces and cohomology of groups started from an idea of Hopf's.

**MP**   *I recall that Pólya always said that Hopf was one of the three nicest mathematicians he ever knew.*

**MAC LANE**   True. He was an exceptionally gracious and friendly person with a remarkably deep insight into what mattered.

**The Return to Chicago and the Stone Age**

**MP**   *When you came back to Chicago, there was the beginning of a new golden age, right?*

**MAC LANE**   Yes, that was another remarkable golden age.

**MP**   *I believe you have been known to refer to it as the Stone Age.*

**MAC LANE**   Well, that's another story. It goes partly back to initiatives of Hutchins. During the War, Hutchins had accepted the Manhattan Project for Chicago when other universities had declined to have it. As a result he collected Fermi and Urey and various other distinguished scientists.

**MP**   *Why had the other universities declined?*

**MAC LANE**   They were afraid of getting mixed up in it, but Hutchins had the courage to accept it. He collected these famous physicists, seized the opportunity of getting them here and created an institute to hold them. He evidently decided (or other people helped him decide) that he needed to strengthen mathematics as well, to support this physics. So he solicited Marshall Stone (whence Stone Age) as the prospective dean, perhaps, but initially he made him chairman of the Mathematics Department, which had gone downhill since the days of Moore, Maschke and Bolza. Stone built an essentially new department with the help of Adrian Albert, who was still here.

Stone did several courageous things. André Weil was at that time, clearly, the leading French mathematician of his generaton, the dynamo behind Bourbaki, but reputed to be somewhat difficult. No other leading department, Harvard, for example, had tried to hire André Weil. Stone hired him and hired Zygmund, Chern, and myself, among others. He decided that mathematics departments needed to be on a somewhat higher level, having more assistants, more support, better seminars and the like, so he made a sort of quantum jump in the style in which mathematics departments were conducted. He had the advantage of some support from the Chicago administration, though not as much as he wanted. He had the additional advantage that it was right after the war and there were all these bright kids who had been in the war and were fed up with it. They wanted to come back and do graduate work. Where would they come? There had been an effective correspondence school here at Chicago, so they had heard of Chicago. In 1947 and 1948 Stone had this tremendous collection of eager young graduate students. He had really thought about what it takes to make a department. He didn't just go at it casually; he wrote me long letters as to what he was thinking about. So with this combination of support, he made it an extraordinary golden age for Chicago. And you can see the effects on the people who came as postdocs.

MP   *When did Stone's rebuilding start?*

MAC LANE   He came in 1946. The golden Stone Age lasted until about 1960. The first defection was André Weil, who left for the Institute for Advanced Study in 1956. Then Halmos went to Michigan, Chern to Berkeley, and so on.

MP   *Who were some of those great students who came at that time?*

MAC LANE   Paul Cohen, Izzy Singer, Eli Stein, among many others. For one, John Thompson was here, a student of mine. He was a remarkable case. I had been away on leave and when I came back I was a little tired of doing homological algebra. So I gave a two-quarter course on group theory. I had the notion that group theory was a really profitable field and had been neglected recently. I was not really an expert on the subject, but I dug it out of the books and at the end of two quarters I was at the end of my knowledge of group theory. I had half a dozen students including Joe Rotman, who has subsequently written a couple of books on group theory, and John Thompson. John said to me, "Well, Professor Mac Lane, I would like to work with you." He dug up his own problems, but he came around to see me a lot. He was young. I saw pretty quickly that he was a man of extraordinary ability, but he didn't yet have full confidence in himself. We used to meet on Saturday afternoons. He would begin by saying, "Well, I have been thinking." And then he would give me an hour or two lecture about what he had been developing, and I would listen and make suggestions and give him encouragement. So it was mostly his doing, but I spent a lot of time listening to him and letting him know that I thought that what he was doing was good. Not all Ph.D. students are like that, let me assure you.

MP   *How many years later did the Feit–Thompson Theorem come along?*

MAC LANE   Four or five years later. But his thesis was already a theorem of some consequence. I have been extraordinarily fortunate in my students. My first Ph.D. (at Harvard) was Irving Kaplansky, then Thompson, and a third member of the National Academy, Robert Solovay. And there was David Eisenbud, another dandy student I've had. There were many others: Eduardo Dubuc, William Howard, Arnie Liulevicius, Roger Lyndon,

Michael Morley, Anil Nerode, and others as well.

**The Years of Administration**

MP   *Now in spite of your not liking the administrative aspect of the work at Columbia, you did return to administration by becoming chairman of the department here at Chicago in 1952.*

MAC LANE   Yes. Stone got fed up with being chairman so he resigned at the end of his second term. I was appointed chairman. I guess I thought I could do a good job of it. I'm not sure I did. It was a hard period because Hutchins had left in 1951 as president and he had been president a long time. He had not paid enough attention to the budget of the university. The effect was that it was very hard to get appointments. Though I was chairman for six years I made no new appointments and no one was granted tenure during that time. I couldn't start a new golden age; I simply managed, save for the loss of Weil, to continue it.

MP   *It's hard to preside over a new golden age when you don't have money.*

MAC LANE   At the end of that time I decided that administrative work was for the birds.

MP   *After all these years and several fields of research, are there some mathematical accomplishments that stand out in your mind?*

MAC LANE   Well, early on when I worked on field theory, I had a theorem about the constructions of fields of characteristic $p$. It got to be known as Mac Lane's Theorem. In valuation theory I proved a very nice structural theorem, and there's a lovely theorem about planar graphs that says that a graph is planar if and only if it has a suitable basis of cycles. There were some interesting papers with Schilling including one on Kummer fields. I guess that hasn't attracted much attention, but I thought it was a very nice one. And then of course there were a number with Eilenberg that had an effect. What we did had a good deal to do with the start of homological algebra. We certainly initiated the cohomology of groups and we started category theory. And the elaborate calculations of Eilenberg-Mac Lane spaces

Chairing a meeting of the Council of the National Academy of Sciences.

are still going on in some respects. So that collaboration seems to have worked out very well. Sammy is a great guy.

There are some nice papers on what are called coherence theorems which I did years ago in some Rice University studies, and then there's the paper with Max Kelly about coherence theorems for closed categories. That is connected with logic and has some very nice things in it.

**MP**  *I understand that recently you have been doing some work in the philosophy of mathematics.*

**MAC LANE**  My most recent chief activity has been writing this book on the nature of mathematics called *Mathematics: Form and Function.*

**MP**  *The day before I left California I got a flyer from the Library of Science indicating it is the selection of the month for the Library of Science.*

**MAC LANE**  I didn't know that!

**MP**  *Yes, it required a great deal of inaction on my part. It said that if I do not return the card, I will automatically receive a copy.*

**MAC LANE**  Well, I'm delighted. That has been my chief activity for the past two or three years. I guess it took me about four years to write it. The book aims to examine some of the basic parts of undergraduate and first year graduate mathematics and to see where they come from, how they fit together, what the relations are between them and what this says about the possible philosophies of mathematics. It's an attempt to revive interest in the philosophy of mathematics but based on some actual concern about what mathematics is about.

**MP**  *So you're really coming full circle.*

**MAC LANE**  I'm returning to my early interest in philosophy, yes.

**MP**  *What comes next?*

**MAC LANE**  Well I'm currently interested in a number of questions about Eilenberg-Mac Lane spaces and in following up on a paper of mine and the thesis of one of my Ph.D. students, Gerald Decker, on tensor products of complexes. And I may write some sort of a sequel to *Mathematics: Form and Function.* I'm interested in the relation between algebra and topology and the extraordinary interchange that takes place in algebraic topology—very remarkable algebraic constructions that nobody would expect, how they are forced on us for topological reasons. I would like to examine that as an exercise in the understanding of the nature of mathematics. At the moment the book exists only in a three-page outline of what might happen. It takes a while for such a thing to germinate.

**MP**  *Many years ago you visited Santa Clara. You gave a lecture, but you also sang.*

**MAC LANE**  Oh, I enjoy singing but I find that our graduate students don't sing as much as they used to. There was that wonderful song, "You can't get to heaven in a rocking chair, the Lord don't allow no rocking chairs there." There's a version of that that goes, "You can't get to heaven in a Banach space because the Lord ain't heard of any such place." From some analysts at UCLA I learned a ditty about the zeros of the zeta function. You don't know it? That's a pity. "Where are the zeros of zeta of *s*? G. Bernhard Riemann has

# SIMPLE GROUPS

*(A ditty found scrawled on an Eckhart Library Table)*
*Tune: "Sweet Betsy from Pike"*

What are the orders of all simple groups?
I speak of the honest ones, not of the loops
It seems that old Burnside the orders has guessed
Except for the cyclic ones, even the rest.

Groups made up with permutes will produce some more
For $A_n$ is simple if $n$ exceeds 4
There is Sir Mathew who came into view
Exhibiting groups of an order quite new

Still others have come on to study this thing
Of Artin and Chevalley now we shall sing
With matrices finite they made quite a list
The question is: Could there be others they've missed?

Suzuki and Ree then maintained it's the case
That these methods had not reached the end of the chase
They wrote down some matrices just four by four
That made up a simple group; why not make more?

And then came the opus of Thompson and Feit
Which shed on the problem remarkable light
A group when the order won't factor by two
Is cyclic or solvable. That's what is true.

Suzuki and Ree had caused eyebrows to raise,
But the theoreticians they just could faze.
Their groups weren't new; if you added a twist,
You could get them from old ones with a flick of the wrist.

Still some hardy souls felt a thorn in their side,
For the five groups of Mathieu all reason defied;
Not $A_n$, not twisted, and not Chevalley,
They called them sporadic and filed them away.

Are Mathieu groups creatures of Heaven or Hell?
Zvonimir Janko determined to tell.
He found out what nobody wanted to know:
The masters had missed 1 7 5 5 6 0.

The floodgates were opened, new groups were the rage,
And twelve or more sprouted to greet the new age;
By Janko, and Conway, and Fischer, and Held,
McLaughlin, Suzuki, and Higman and Sims.

You probably noticed the last lines don't rhyme.
Well, that is quite simply a sign of the time;
There's chaos, not order, among simple groups,
And maybe we'd better go back to the loops.

made a good guess. They're all on the critical line, said he, and their density's one over $2\pi \log t$." And it goes on. I concocted some stanzas of another one that goes, "What are the orders of all simple groups? I speak of the honest ones, not of the loops." I would have liked to become a poet, but I have not succeeded in doing so. I have succeeded in writing only doggerel like "What are the orders of all simple groups?"

MP    *You have had a distinguished career as a mathematician but also as a spokesman for mathematics. You are one of only five who have been president of both the American Mathematical Society and the Mathematical Association of America. And you served as Vice President of the National Academy and member of the National Science Board. Do you have any reflections on that role?*

MAC LANE    I guess I always thought it was important to have suitable mathematicians represented in national connections. We need spokesmen. When I was asked whether I would serve and give my opinions, I said yes.

MP    *Well, after this long career in mathematics, any regrets?*

MAC LANE    No. None.

*May 1987 in Chicago, Illinois (GA).*

SAUNDERS MAC LANE    Norwich, Connecticut, August 4, 1909. Ph.B. 1930, Yale; A.M. 1931, Chicago; D.Phil. 1934, Göttingen. Fields: algebra, logic. Max Mason Distinguished Service Professor, Chicago. President AMS, 1973–74; President MAA, 1951–52. Colloquium Lecturer (AMS) 1963. Chauvenet Prize (MAA) 1941, Distinguished Service Award (MAA) 1975, Proctor Prize 1979, Steele Prize (AMS) 1986. American Academy of Arts and Sciences, American Philosophical Society, Heidelberger Akademie der Wissenschaften, National Academy of Sciences, Royal Danish Academy of Sciences, Royal Society of Edinburgh. Books: (with G. Birkhoff) *Survey of Modern Algebra*, 1942; *Homology*, 1963; (with G. Birkhoff) *Algebra*, 1967; *Categories for the Working Mathematician*, 1971; *Selected Papers* (I. Kaplansky, ed.), 1979; *Eilenberg-Mac Lane Collected Works*, 1986; *Mathematics: Form and Function*, 1986.

(*Facing page*) Lecturing abroad.

# CATHLEEN S. MORAWETZ

Cathleen Morawetz, a mathematician's daughter, specializes in the applications of partial differential equations. She is the only woman who has been invited to deliver the Gibbs Lecture of the American Mathematical Society, which is traditionally on an applied subject. (She talked on "The mathematical approach to the sonic barrier.") In addition to her research and teaching, she has been director of NYU's Courant Institute, a trustee of Princeton University and a director of the NCR Corporation. She says she favors a "new plan of life" for women, according to which they would have their children in their late teens and their mothers would bring up the children.

□ □ □

**MP**  *There are very few women in mathematics, and fewer still who have done the things you have done—even fewer who have a husband of forty years and four children as well! You're really quite remarkable. We know from your* curriculum vitae *that you were born in 1923, in Toronto, the daughter of the well-known Irish mathematician, J. L. Synge.*

**MORAWETZ**  Well, I was born in 1923 and he was born in 1897, so he was only twenty-six. He was not well known then.

**MP**  *So was the position in Toronto his first?*

**MORAWETZ**  Yes. He had come to Toronto at the invitation of A. T. DeLury, the head of the Mathematics Department, who was of Irish stock and a great fan of J. M. Synge, the playwright—my father's uncle. I think my father wanted to leave Ireland at that time. He had been a student during the Easter Rebellion of 1916, and although his and my mother's sympathies were with the Nationalists [the Irish rebelling against British rule], both of their families were divided.

**MP**  *Your mother was also Irish?*

**MORAWETZ**  Yes. Also born in County Wicklow.

**MP**  *So you are one hundred per cent Irish?*

**MORAWETZ**  That's right, but I'm also Anglo-Irish because both my parents were Protestants from the south of Ireland, which is really very different from northern Ireland.

**MP**  *I am interested in the fact that you are the second of three daughters of J. L. Synge. I have read that women scientists are quite frequently second daughters. The explanation given is that a second daughter feels that she should have been a boy, so there's a tendency for her to take after the father and try to become a son in her interests. I don't know whether that is true.*

**Boy from the Word Go**   **MORAWETZ**  I was the boy in the family. I was the boy from the word *go*. But that doesn't mean that I had an especially close relationship with my father. My older sister really had a closer relationship. For instance, when we were girls and we wanted to do something he didn't want us to do, she was always delegated to negotiate with him. I would say rather that I was in competition with my father. Better not print that! [Laughs.] That was the pattern, quite different. But I was definitely the boy. In fact, it was rather funny. When I was seven and we returned to Canada from Ireland, I had had a major operation on my leg so I had my leg in a brace. It had been arranged that my father was going to look after me, and my mother was going to look after my little sister, who was just a baby. My older sister was going to look after herself. It was all very formally arranged. And the first thing my father did was to take me to have my hair cut like a boy's. This was supposedly because it was a mess and he didn't want to have to take care of it, but that's what he did. Of course that was 1930, and that was a time when people did have their hair cropped. But when the people on the ship said I was a little boy, I was very unhappy.

**MP**  *Do you mean that you were a tomboy?*

**MORAWETZ**  That's right. I wasn't very athletic, so I didn't do sports—but I was the one who played with the Meccano set. Now I do remember having a dispute with my sister about a doll, so I must have been somewhat interested in dolls, too, but in general I liked the Meccano and that sort of thing. I constructed engines and levers. And it's true I did that with my father.

**MP**  *Did your mother have any mathematical interest?*

**MORAWETZ**  She went to Trinity College and studied mathematics, but her brother persuaded her that there was no future in math for her, so she switched to history. At one point, when she was ready for secondary school, there was a competition among the Protestant girls in Ireland and she placed first. Actually she won a prize to go to the conservatory of music in London, but her mother wouldn't let her go. She went to Trinity College instead, and that's where she and my father met. After they were married—he was still in school then—she taught to support them, so she never got a degree.

**MP**  *Genetically you're really packed for mathematics!*

**MORAWETZ**  Yes. I think so.

**MP**  *When you said that you were in competition with your father, to what period of your life were you referring?*

J. L. Synge.

**MORAWETZ**   Why do I say that? Well, I just think we were in competition. It's true we had this common interest, that we liked to do these mechanical things. Later we liked to sail. We both enjoyed that very much. But there was always a wee competitiveness there.

**MP**   *Did you think you could make better levers and other mechanical things than your dad?*

**MORAWETZ**   No. Certainly not. Not at all. I should add that I was very close to my mother. I think that I had a much more intimate relationship with my mother than my sister did. My older sister, I mean. My younger sister was much younger—seven years.

**MP**   *Did you show an early interest in mathematics?*

**MORAWETZ**   Well, it was clear when I was very small that I was good at school. For example, when my older sister started school at the age of five— we began with my mother teaching us at home, but that didn't work—I made a terrible fuss. I insisted that I had to go to school too, and so my mother took me down and persuaded the principal—it was a private school—to take me. I started school at the age of three. They kept me in the first year for two years. I was very annoyed about that.

**MP**   *Three years old and in what was ordinarily first grade?*

**MORAWETZ**   I think it was called kindergarten, but you learned to read. I learned to read at the age of three.

"I'm tough."   **MP**   *You were really determined to go to school. That's a good mathematical quality—stubbornness.*

**MORAWETZ**   Yes. In fact, I had a reputation as a child for being—well, sort of stubborn.

**MP**   *Are you still stubborn?*

**MORAWETZ**   I'm tough. [Laughs.] My father said to me just the other day, "We're both tough."

**MP**   *In the article on you in* Science *a few years back, you were quoted as saying, "My father's attitude was that I had talent in mathematics but that I was not willing to work hard enough."*

**MORAWETZ**   That was later—when I was an undergraduate at Toronto. I think the earliest I remember my father telling me something mathematical was when I was beginning to study Euclidean geometry at school. At that time he also told me about cartesian geometry. I must have been twelve or thirteen.

**MP**   *And you liked cartesian geometry?*

**MORAWETZ**   Yes, I liked it, but I didn't really pursue it. We never had any formal lessons.

**MP**   *So what was it about mathematics that first captured your interest? Was it simply that you were good at it?*

**MORAWETZ**   Well, I wasn't good at arithmetic. I used to get bad marks in mental arithmetic. I found that annoying, because I didn't think it

In 1943 Cathleen (center) reported to her sister "a wonderful discussion on 'woman, career and/or married life.' Just as inconclusive as ever. But neither of us can think of a solitary case where a woman had a career and managed to have a balanced (mentally) family including an unhenpecked husband. . . . On the other hand we thought that [not having a career] produced a sort of neurosis in women like Mum and Mrs. Jones who have too much housework that they loathe and especially in the latter's case no interests when the husband isn't [at home]."

mattered. But I was a good student all around. I thought at one time in high school that I would go into history.

**MP**  *You didn't concentrate on mathematics?*

**MORAWETZ**  I concentrated on mathematics in the last year of high school—we had five years of high school in Toronto—because I had a teacher, Mr. Reynolds, who was putting us up for scholarships. These were competitive scholarships. He was a very nice man, and he ran a little class to coach about five students. Looking back, though, I realize that he ran the class for me. He taught me quite a lot. My father wasn't particularly interested in what I was doing, and I wasn't interested in discussing it with him. In fact, when we got stuck on our homework and asked him for help, he would write on a piece of paper—he always used only one side for his own work—and then the great object was to get out of his study with the piece of paper because, of course, we were so scared of him that we couldn't hear what he was telling us at the time, but we hoped that if we had the paper . . .

**MP**  *Did you go to a public high school?*

**MORAWETZ**  Yes. The high school system consisted of vocational schools and academic schools. If you wanted to go to the university, you more or less had to go to an academic school, but of the students in the academic school I would say only about ten per cent went on to the university. And, of course, nobody thought of going away to college.

**MP**  *So the scholarships you spoke about were for the University of Toronto?*

**MORAWETZ**  That's right. There was a really quite tough exam in all subjects, and after that there was a sort of mathematics problems exam, so the possibility of winning one of the scholarships was much higher if you were good in mathematics. The top ones were all won by mathematics people. I was in a very good year. The person that won the highest prize was Jim

Jenkins, who is at Washington University in St. Louis. Robert Steinberg, who's at UCLA and was just recently elected to the National Academy of Sciences, won one of the other prizes. So I was in a class with Jenkins, Steinberg and Tom Hull, who's at the University of Toronto—it was quite a group of people. I won one of the prizes too but, emotionally, I cannot forget that I cared most about the fact that there was a top prize which I didn't get. I was so disappointed that when people congratulated me—there was a whole bunch at the next level down, which were worth a lot more money—I felt like crying.

**MP**  *There are many people who come in second.*

**MORAWETZ**  It was not the coming in second. It was everyone knowing about it!

**MP**  *So is it correct that when you came to the university as an undergraduate, you did not know that you would go into mathematics?*

**Applied Mathematics— The Spirit Was Different**

**MORAWETZ**  Oh no. The way it was set up, you entered into a joint course—math, physics and chemistry. The first year you took all three, the second year you took two of the three, the third year you took one, and the fourth year you took half of the subject—in mathematics it was pure or applied mathematics. The undergraduate program in pure mathematics was very tough, and frankly I would say overloaded with courses. I was not prepared to devote myself sufficiently—it was too tough for me—so I ended up in applied mathematics, where the spirit was different.

**MP**  *What was your major called?*

**MORAWETZ**  It was called M. & P.—Math and Physics. All the Toronto people of my generation and even later know that expression. But it was much more than a major. You took nothing else.

**MP**  *You took no liberal arts courses at all?*

**MORAWETZ**  Oh well, the University of Toronto had a number of religious colleges and one that wasn't religious. The religious colleges had one hour a week for "religious knowledge." Since I was in the nonreligious college, I had one hour a week for something else. One year I took English, one year I took Oriental literature, and one year—oh, philosophy! And that's all the liberal education that I got.

**MP**  *And with your father's interest in writing!*

**"You don't *study* writing."**

**MORAWETZ**  My father's attitude, which came really from his family, was that by the time you finish high school you know how to write—that's not something you do at the university. You don't *study* writing!

**MP**  *So you graduated with a bachelor's from Toronto?*

**MORAWETZ**  Yes, but before that I had a very important interruption in my life. The second World War had broken out while I was still in high school. Toronto was, of course, a center of strong support for Britain. By the time I was in my third year of the university, half the class had gone off, including a boyfriend of mine. I wanted to do something too. So I decided to do what the boys had done, which was to join the Navy. But, you see, *they* were immediately made officers while I was told that I would have to take boot training! I was very annoyed, and my great desire to join the Navy suddenly dropped to zero. But I did want to do something, so my father got me a job at the Inspection Board of the United Kingdom and Canada, just outside Quebec City.

MP   *So you left college?*

**A Chronograph Girl**   MORAWETZ   At the end of my third year I took a year off. That was the first time I had ever been away from home. It really was a fascinating experience. And that experience came back to me recently when I saw a reference to Malcolm McPhail in the biography of Turing. McPhail was my boss. I was supposed to be a scientific assistant of some kind to him, but he had very little for me to do and I found the job very boring. I was much more interested in the life that was going on around me. So I asked for a job as what was called "a chronograph girl." This was something that I was supposed to be much too educated for, and I was, so that was a mistake; nevertheless, looking back, I realize that I was operating a very early digital computer. There were several of us. Because our work was boring, we used to play games with the machine. I realize now that standard deviations must have mattered, so the errors we produced by playing games must have been enough to throw off the results. It was disgraceful, but it wasn't really our fault. We were not properly supervised. However, it's also true that McPhail awoke my scientific interest. You see, when it rained you couldn't measure shells with this thing because it depended on an electric eye. So there was an older machine—I remember its name, a Boulangé Machine—with which you could measure velocity with a dropped rod or some such thing—and there was a scale etched on a piece of steel from which you had to read off what the speed was. Well, I discovered that the scale was wrong. It was not wrong by a great deal, but it was wrong. So I did some experiments and checked the theory and wrote a little note. That was the first time I thought, "Well, science is fun."

MP   *It hadn't really been much fun up to then?*

MORAWETZ   It had not been fun at all. I had this big scholarship, and I worried every year whether I would keep on having it. It wasn't fun. It was school. And that was terrible, because I had some great lecturers. I had Coxeter and I had Brauer and I had my father. That's, of course, another story—having your father. I also had Alexander Weinstein and Leopold Infeld. Now Infeld was not wasted on me. Infeld was a terrific lecturer. He lectured without notes, he really mostly just talked, and he rarely put anything on the blackboard. Once, though, he was talking about Green's theorem, and he wanted quite rightly to stress its importance, so at the proper moment he opened his jacket, pulled out a piece of paper, and copied from it in very large letters the formula for Green's theorem and the limiting process. I can still see it on the blackboard! I have never forgotten it.

MP   *What kind of teacher was your father?*

**"Miss Synge!"**   MORAWETZ   My father was tremendously well prepared. His lecture notes were terrific. Of course he was—basically is—a shy person, and he didn't know how to treat me in class. This is a story I often tell. He couldn't remember names, so he had the arrangement that three students would sit

*More Mathematical People*

in the front row and he would ask them the questions. Well, eventually, as you work your way through the alphabet, you come to Synge. I remember that I was in the middle, and he came to me and he looked at the name, paused, and finally said—"Miss Synge!" Of course that brought down the house. But he was always very correct. For example, every year when the faculty met to decide on honors, he absented himself if I was involved.

MP  *So after your wartime job you came back for your final year at Toronto?*

**"Competition is bad for me."**

MORAWETZ  That's right. My father was gone by then. I was no longer with that jazzy class. I was the best student now. And that's always very good for the ego. Competition is bad for me. It just throws me right down, down and out. And so I was much happier. I lived in a dorm, which was an experience I really liked. I also met Herbert Morawetz early that year. Altogether it was just a change, a wonderful change, and I really enjoyed myself.

MP  *When you then went down to MIT, were you following Herbert there?*

**Something Exotic**

MORAWETZ  No. What happened was that I wanted to do something exotic. I had found it very interesting to go and live in Quebec. It was a different culture. So I wanted to do something else exciting. I saw an ad for teachers in India, and I decided that I would go to India. And then a person I should really have mentioned long before, Cecilia Krieger, a mathematician on the faculty whom I had known from childhood, asked me what I was going to do. When I told her about India, she almost had a fit and immediately declared that if I would only apply she was sure that I could get the Junior Fellowship of the Canadian Association of University Women. So I did apply, and I did get it. The place I wanted to go was Caltech, because I had decided by then that I really didn't want to be a mathematician, I wanted to be an engineer—which was the reverse of my father, who went to college to study engineering and decided to do mathematics. So I applied to Caltech, and they wrote back that they didn't take women. And that was that. My father by that time was serving as an assimilated colonel in the American Air Force, and he was essentially incommunicado in Paris, doing ballistics tables for napalm bombs, it turned out. So I consulted Infeld, and he suggested MIT. They took me and gave me a tuition scholarship. Herbert was much relieved. He had thought that if I went to California that would be the end of us.

MP  *Tell us a little about Herbert.*

At the time of her graduation from the University of Toronto in 1945.

MORAWETZ  Herbert had come to Canada in 1939 as a refugee from Czechoslovakia. He had finished chemical engineering at Toronto the year that I went down to Quebec; he had then got a master's degree. When I met him he had his first job. He had had a terrible time getting it, you know. He had been the best student in his class, but everywhere he went he was told, "We don't hire Jews." Some people said, "We'll call you back," or something like that, but half the people at least were quite open about why they wouldn't hire him. In the end, through a friend of his father's, he got a job with the Bakelite Company in Toronto, but those people really didn't want to have him either. We had become engaged during the summer I left for MIT, and while I was gone he arranged to be transferred to Bound Brook,

New Jersey. I finished at MIT with a master's degree. Neither of us intended at that time to go on and get a Ph.D.

MP   *Was your master's in engineering?*

**The First Commuting Wife**

MORAWETZ   No. The first term I was at MIT I took a lot of electrical engineering, and I discovered two things. One was that my arithmetic was still no better than it had been, and it really mattered. The other was that I was no good at experiments. So I went back to applied math and wrote a master's thesis with Eric Reissner. By that time I was married—I got married in the middle of the MIT thing. I was the first commuting wife. Everybody thought I was crazy to commute, and everybody thought Herbert was crazy to let me.

MP   *Did you know when you married Herbert that he was a basically liberated man?*

MORAWETZ   Oh yes, he assured me that he would not interfere with my career. Did I really know? I don't know. I only believed what he said.

MP   *Did he also come from an academic family?*

MORAWETZ   No. When his father left Czechoslovakia, he was the president of the jute cartel and owned a big factory.

MP   *Did his mother have a profession?*

MORAWETZ   No, no. They were very wealthy Jewish bourgeoisie, too wealthy for the woman to have a profession. In fact, Herbert's mother had never gone to college, although she was essentially the same generation as my mother. It's not even clear that they would have sent their daughter to college in Czechoslovakia, although she like Herbert is very intellectual. She did go to college in Canada and is a writer. Even as refugees, the Morawetzes were very well off by my standards, although not by theirs. Certainly the notion that to be a good mother you have to wash the diapers was absolutely foreign to all of them. My mother-in-law, however, did have some reservations about women working outside the home.

MP   *But you wanted to work?*

MORAWETZ   Well, after I got my master's degree, I looked for a job in New Jersey. I applied to Bell Labs, and they told me that although I had a master's degree from MIT they would not let me into their general program for master's degree students. I felt that a bachelor's degree from Toronto was also worth a lot, but they didn't understand that either. I was to be pooled with the other women bachelors who could have got their degrees anywhere, you know. I was furious. I said, "I'm not interested in that!" Unfortunately I've never kept any records. It was probably on the telephone anyway. Then—it must have been at the summer meeting—no, at the Christmas meeting of the American Mathematical Society—my father met Richard Courant. Gertrude Courant had just gotten married, too, and my father and Courant were bemoaning the fact that their intellectual daughters were not going to be able to pursue their careers and so on. Now my father denies this story, but the fact is that this is what he told me at the time—Courant said, "You can't do anything for my daughter, but perhaps I can do something for yours." I was to come down and see him at NYU. So I came down, and that's

In 1946 the young Morawetzes did not see themselves as pursuing academic careers.

when I had the interview with Courant that figured in the MAA movie about him. I remember he said, "Well, I really need some reference besides your father," so I gave him the name of Alexander Weinstein, not knowing that the two men disliked each other intensely. So that's how I came to the Institute at NYU. Courant had hired me to solder connections on a machine that Harold Grad was making to solve linear equations. The job involved my commuting an hour and a quarter from New Jersey, and that was a major obstacle. The other obstacle was that Harold Grad immediately ran out and hired somebody else to do the soldering.

MP   *Because you were a woman?*

**"Can you write English?"**   MORAWETZ   He told me many years later—and I thought it was very nice of him to do so—that that was really how it was. So when I arrived there was no job for me. From time to time Courant would mumble, "Well, can you write English?" and I would say, "Yes." Finally he gave me the job of editing the Courant-Friedrichs book on shock waves.

I started at NYU in March or April. At that point I had no intention of going to graduate school. I didn't consider myself a student. But by the time September rolled around—that was '46—Courant's group had shed a lot of its military work and everybody was going back to purer mathematics. Friedrichs was planning to teach topology. That was a big thing, you know. Faculty members as well as students were going to take the course. So I decided to take it too. It was very exciting, and it was very competitive, but it was a much gentler kind of competition than what I had known before, although it's true I cried when I couldn't do the homework.

MP   *So there you were at what was not yet known as the Courant Institute, hired by Courant to solder connections but given the job of editing a book by him and Friedrichs. That was a pretty tough book. You must have exuded a certain amount of confidence.*

MORAWETZ   Oh no, I didn't at all. I was so shy that when I arrived at the Institute I would literally make a run for my office.

MP   *But you spoke English, and you came from a cultured English-speaking family.*

MORAWETZ   Yes. That was important. But there was also another thing. Courant had been having trouble with the people he'd been getting to help him with his books. Of course, there had been the mess with Herbert Robbins over *What Is Mathematics?* Then my predecessor on the shock wave book had been Jimmy Savage, and among other things Savage hadn't liked the first chapter—there hadn't been enough about entropy in it, you know. Well, my attitude was that what went into the book was what Courant and Friedrichs wanted to have in the book. If they wanted to take out all that stuff about entropy, I didn't care. I was just fixing up the English and making sure the formulas were right. And I think that was what they really wanted. The other editors had been much too eager to do another kind of editing job.

MP   *Still, it must have been a tough book to edit.*

MORAWETZ   The funny thing is that when it came out, many people said, "Well, this is nothing like his other books or their other books," but the

Richard Courant originally brought Morawetz to NYU to solder connections.

truth of the matter is that it has really held up. Just yesterday I met an engineer, a Ph.D. in aeronautical engineering, who told me that it's still the bible among engineers. I knew that it is still the bible in the theory of compressible fluid dynamics, but it was interesting to hear that it's still the bible in the engineering business. After all, it's pretty old. There are a whole lot of later books on the subject that are already totally out of date. But it's held up.

**MP** *One thing that has always surprised me is the rather casual way in which Courant took a number of women into the Institute, very much as he took you in.*

**MORAWETZ** I should say about that—Courant was wonderful to me, although he could be not so nice to me too. But I got on my feet by going there. After I had been there a year, I went in and told him that I was pregnant. He says, "Oh my god!" and he rushes off. Then he comes back and says, "You're taking your orals next week." It was his idea that if you had taken your orals, you could always come back and do your dissertation; but if you hadn't, you probably wouldn't come back. I immediately went to Donald Flanders, who I knew would understand, and said, "I can't do that. You would just be giving it to me. I couldn't stand that." So I took my orals after my daughter, Pegeen, was born.

**MP** *Just for the record, what are the years of your children's births?*

**MORAWETZ** '47, '49, '52, and '54. I got my Ph.D. in 1951.

**MP** *Can you give our readers some tips about being a mathematician and a mother?*

**MORAWETZ**   Well, I got the tips from Mildred Cohn, the wife of Henry Primakoff, a physicist who had worked at the Institute in New York. They were also on a visiting thing when we were in Cambridge, Massachusetts, in 1950–51, and we saw them fairly often. She was older than I, a very successful biochemist with several children. She obviously knew how to handle it all. She emphasized having help and the importance of paying for the help. Now, looking back, I think I should have paid more and tried to have more continuity. The best help I had was au pair people, but they stayed only a year or so. I think now that it was a little hard on the kids not to have a mother-substitute.

**MP**   *From time to time I have asked women in mathematics how they happened to choose their particular field, and my sample survey shows that most of them are in very pure fields which are clean and ladylike. But the titles of the papers here in your bibliography strike me as representing so-called "masculine" interests.*

**MORAWETZ**   Well, Mony Donsker always used to get a rise out of me by asking how come I was working in magneto hydrodynamics—that wasn't very feminine. The truth of the matter is that most women—in fact, most people—don't have the broad education that I got in Toronto. I learned a lot of physics. I took circuit theory as an undergraduate and a little bit of elasticity and optics. The applied mathematics at Toronto was very close to physics. Some of it was taught by engineers. Now it's also true that I was taking algebra with Brauer and geometry with Coxeter, and both subjects fell on deaf ears. I never got really interested in, and don't think I would be very good at, all those structure problems that occur in pure mathematics. I can still remember listening to Brauer defining fields and rings and thinking what was it all good for. On the other hand, I was very pleased when I once proved something for Friedrichs that was not applied at all!

**MP**   *Why did you do your thesis with Friedrichs rather than with Courant?*

**Not on a Platter, Please!**   **MORAWETZ**   Well, I'll tell you what comes immediately to my mind. I'm not sure though that I really think it's true. But it was because I thought it would be tougher. I constantly worried about being handed things on a platter. I felt that if I did a thesis with Courant he would just give it to me. Friedrichs wouldn't do something like that. So that was a very important thing for me. But actually what happened was this. I was between children. After I passed my orals, I went in to see Friedrichs. At that time he had stopped being interested in fluid dynamics and was tremendously involved in quantum mechanics. He put all these problems on the board and talked about various things and kept saying, "You know, you just have to be really eager and enthusiastic." And I couldn't get enthusiastic about any of them—I was back to square one. I started working on something—I've forgotten now what it was—but at the same time, you see, I was earning my stipend by working on a problem for the project that was applied—or more applied—in fluid dynamics. I had had a miscarriage after my first child and I was pregnant with my second, so I must have been a little bit in and out of it. Anyway, when I told Friedrichs that I was pregnant, the gods at the Institute arranged that my project work would be turned into my thesis. That was fine, but then after I had the child—that was John—and came back to the thesis, which involved an interesting problem in asymptotics in ordinary differential equations that Langer's theory didn't cover, I wasn't able to prove the theorem. And that, I found, was very depressing. I did some computations that partially verified the conjecture, but I was never happy with the work and never published it. Actually it was on the theory of implosions, and I did not know when I worked on the problem that an implosion was what made the atomic bomb go off. I learned that—rather Herbert told me that—when it came out in the trial of the Rosenbergs.

MP    *How did you find working with Friedrichs?*

MORAWETZ    Well, he was a little difficult at that time. He was so interested in quantum mechanics that he didn't want to think about what I was doing in fluid dynamics. Now, since I've had students of my own, I know how he felt. I had the office next to his, but I had to make an appointment if I wanted to see him. He was a very regulated person, you know.

MP    *So when did you finally get really excited about mathematics? You don't crank out papers like these [indicating her bibliography] in a state of boredom.*

MORAWETZ    Well, don't forget, juggling kids and so on has a dissipating effect on one's enthusiasm. But when I went back to MIT in 1950–51, I found the way C. C. Lin looked after me really terrific. He was organized but organized on a different pattern from Friedrichs. He would give me a problem and if I hadn't made any progress in five weeks, he would take it away and give me another one. I was at MIT a year, and after a couple of months I really latched onto something. It was again ordinary differential equations, but one of the things that helped was—you see, I hadn't been able to do the case in my thesis but these cases I could do. Also there were very interesting applied mathematical reasons for doing them. So I became quite interested. When I came back to NYU, I was again floundering. Then it was Lipman Bers who gave me a paper to read on mixed equations and—did I find a mistake in it? or make an improvement? I think it was an improvement. So then I got going on that.

MP    *That must have bolstered your self-confidence.*

**Kicking up One's Enthusiasm**    MORAWETZ    In mathematics there is frequently the problem of kicking up one's enthusiasm. Another time when I really didn't know what to work on and was struggling with a paper somebody had given me about singular ordinary differential equations with some pathological behavior, Jürgen Moser came by and said, "Ach, it's ridiculous to work on that problem." So I threw the paper away. What got me working on the wave equation, which later dominated a lot of my work, was a lecture by Joe Keller on unsolved problems. As I was sitting there, I saw that the technique I had used on mixed equations ought to have applications to Keller's problems—they were elliptic this way and hyperbolic that way—and that really worked out. I don't believe that I ever again had the feeling of absolutely floundering.

MP    *Don't you think also that for you, as for most women, the problem of having children and getting them going is not only an absorbing but a necessarily absorbing problem?*

MORAWETZ    Oh yes. Even just having the children, being pregnant and giving birth. There I was very lucky. I had an easy time. I felt better when I

The Morawetz family in front of their Greenwich Village home: Nancy, Lida, John, Pegeen, Cathleen and Herbert.

was pregnant and I did better work. And the births themselves were not a problem.

**MP** *Once you were at NYU, embedded in a pretty heady atmosphere, you certainly didn't want to be just an average NYU professor. You don't like being average.*

**MORAWETZ** That's right. Sometimes when I'm asked about my career, I say, "Look, I was such a lousy housekeeper—I was a failure at that—so I had to do a good job at something!" Sure, there was an element of that in it, you know. That's often a factor in a woman having a career. But there's one thing that you mustn't forget—that I think is very important. I came from an atmosphere where there was a sense that a woman should have a career—my mother was interested in that—but all that had somehow disappeared after the men came back from the second World War.

**MP** *That was the era of four children and a station wagon.*

**MORAWETZ** That's right. And then came the sixties when everybody suddenly rediscovered this career thing. But I had never lost track of it. That is one thing I should say. The other thing is that until the women's movement of the late sixties it really was considered very bad form for a woman to be overtly ambitious, very bad form. Everybody thought that way—my colleagues, Herbert. It was fine for me to have a career, but not actually to show my ambition. Although it was positive to say that a man was ambitious, you could never say it about a woman—except negatively. And I think of course that underneath I was always very ambitious.

**MP** *I never have had the impression, you know, that you were out after these jobs that you have got—director of the Courant Institute and so on. Whether you cultivated it consciously or subconsciously, or whether it was just your nature, you did not pose a threat to the men here.*

**MORAWETZ** I don't think that I was really "out after these jobs" or that

"Administration certainly suits me. I like it."

I posed any mathematical threat—well, I guess [laughs] that there are some of my colleagues for whom I must have posed a mathematical threat—I was looking up instead of looking down.

**MP**  *Did it seem to you an unusually long time until you became a professor?*

**MORAWETZ**  Oh yes! I was annoyed about that. It took a little longer than it should have. Of course it is also true that in a way I always worked part-time. I was paid four-fifths salary for many years. Herbert always said, "That's fraud. You work more than full-time." But I felt much better that way. No one could question, as they had at MIT, whether I was really earning what I was being paid. So that arrangement could have accounted for the delay in the appointment.

**MP**  *How did your administrative involvement at the Institute develop?*

**MORAWETZ**  It came about as a way to keep the teaching down. I used to be a very nervous and unhappy teacher, and I spent an awful lot of time preparing my lectures. If you taught in the Institute, you taught only graduate courses, so a full load was two graduate courses. I just found that a big burden. Let me see—oh, I know how it first came about. Fritz John became the director of a division, and Courant worried that Fritz didn't really want the job and it would be a burden on him, so I was made his assistant and I did the job and got in return a reduced teaching load.

**MP**  *It seems to me that women often have a way of taking care of a department. I don't mean just seeing to the coffee. They notice things.*

**MORAWETZ**  That's true. In fact, I've had young women complain that they were made the chairman of the department—it wasn't a job they really wanted—while they were still associate professors, or probably even assistant professors.

**MP**  *You seem to have thrived on administration.*

**MORAWETZ**  It certainly suits me. I like to do it.

**MP**  *What is it that you like about administration?*

**Mathematics, a Lonely Life**  **MORAWETZ**  I like the relationship with human beings. Many, many years ago one of the things that made me not want to go into mathematics was the fact that it seemed to me a very lonely life.

**MP**  *You saw this in your father?*

**MORAWETZ**  I saw it in my father, and [laughs] my children saw it in me.

**MP**  *Did you ever think seriously about leaving NYU?*

**MORAWETZ**  There wasn't any possibility of leaving. Where could I go? Most places would not have hired me. So I never gave leaving serious thought.

**MP**  *It has always seemed to me that the Courant Institute is more people-oriented than most mathematics departments.*

**MORAWETZ**  That's really true. There's no question about that.

**MP** *When was it that you started branching out into the many different organizations in which you are now so active?*

**MORAWETZ** Well, I got involved in the American Mathematical Society in the late sixties when I went to a trustees' meeting in New York to ask them to form a committee on women. I did not want the Association for Women in Mathematics to speak for all women mathematicians. I joined them later, but at that time they were terrible attackers. They even attacked Lipman Bers in the early days, and Bers was the best thing that ever happened to women in mathematics!

**MP** *They later honored him.*

**MORAWETZ** They honored him, but that was quite a bit later. They even attacked Olga Taussky. It was unbelievable. So I was on a committee for disadvantaged groups in the Math Society, and I thought there should be a separate committee for women. I was terribly afraid when I went before the Board of Trustees—or it may have been the Council. Anyway, when it came my turn to speak, I said, "There's a problem with women. You may have noticed that there are not many women mathematicians." At that point Saunders Mac Lane said, "Well, mathematics is a very difficult subject." I was not up to coping with that, but Iz Singer picked up the ball. The committee was formed and I was made chairman. That's how I got involved in the Math Society's affairs. I hardly ever even went to meetings when I was young.

**A New Plan for Women**

**MP** *What do you think are the biggest problems confronting women in mathematics today?*

**MORAWETZ** Well, as one of my colleagues has pointed out, "Mathematicians don't look very far for their wives." The result is that they're usually fellow graduate students. Women mathematicians tend to be married to men mathematicians, and so they need to find two math jobs in the same geographical area. That's very hard. Then I would say that, in spite of the fact that men are—and they really are—much more helpful and supportive these days, the burden of raising children still falls on the woman—at a time that's very important in her career—just about when she should be getting tenure. In fact, I'm about to institute a new plan of life, according to which women would have their children in their late teens and their mothers would bring them up. I don't mean the mother would give up her career, but she's already established, so she can afford to take time off to look after the children. Besides, I love being a grandmother!

**MP** *You're not particularly optimistic about change?*

**MORAWETZ** No. I'm not at all optimistic. I think there has been a big change, but I'm not sure what would really make a turnaround. Take this business of raising kids. It's very difficult. Somebody has to be in charge. So it's got to be either the mother or the father. As things are set up now, it's the mother. I see it with my daughters—they are the ones who are in charge of the children. It's very nice in a way, but it's also a handicap professionally.

**MP** *Do you think that, career-wise, women naturally operate on a different time-scale from men?*

**MORAWETZ** I think that there is something to that idea. Whether it has to do with the environment or circumstances of adolescence I don't know.

A happy but not altogether graceful landing in 1944.

J. L. Synge.

But I've rarely seen—no, I will say I have never seen an adolescent girl who's like, say, Gene Trubowitz age 19 or Samuel Weinberger age 18, whose whole lives are embedded in mathematics. They really live for that and that alone. I've never run across girls like that. But I am sure they will appear. To a large extent it is a problem of time-scale. All career patterns in science and in everything, in fact, are set up on the basis of the male. They ought to be somewhat different for women, but until there are enough women involved, that won't happen.

**MP** *What advice do you give to young women who are coming to like mathematics and to show real talent?*

**MORAWETZ** Well, there is a big difference between those who want to have a family and those who don't.

**MP** *But often you don't know you want a family until after you have had one.*

**MORAWETZ** That's very true. So you have to expect the guy to make some sacrifices, more sacrifices. That's really what it amounts to. And I think that the major sacrifice is in his standard of living. But, you see, one of the main problems is that there are so few marrying men and it's still the old thing, you know—you have to spoil them a bit to get them!

**MP** *Well, there are not too many marrying men, and among those there are probably not too many so-called liberated men.*

---

## J. L. SYNGE
### 1897–

John Lighton Synge was the youngest child of an Irish land agent whose family had held high office in the Church of England (now Church of Ireland) since the time of Henry VIII. After the "Easter Rising," he enrolled at the Irish College, learning Gaelic and "breaking out of my Protestant-Ascendancy cocoon," as he has written in a memoir for his family. Later, at Trinity, he found mechanics, combined with hydrodynamics and elasticity, "much to my taste." In his first position, at the University of Toronto, he supervised students in the "M. and P." course later pursued by his daughter Cathleen. ("Unduly heavy," it seems to him now, ". . . except for the most brilliant.") Later he headed mathemat-

ics departments at Toronto, Ohio State and Carnegie-Mellon, all with an applied bent.

In 1932 he became executor of the estate of J. C. Fields, who endowed the gold medals now awarded at every International Mathematical Congress (although he personally feels "a mathematician should work for his own satisfaction and not for awards"). Other off-beat activities have included writing stories (see "The Bright Boy and Euclid") and familiar essays and light verse as well as editing the first volume of the works of the great Irish mathematician William Rowan Hamilton.

When in 1948 the *New Yorker* noted that the refugee physicist Erwin Schroedinger was working in Dublin "of all places," Synge reminded the magazine that it was in Dublin that Hamilton had devel-

oped the mathematical theory that is at the foundation of Schroedinger's most famous work. The Dublin Institute for Advanced Study promptly sounded him out about accepting a position in Dublin himself. Initially negative, as the Dublin weather suddenly improved he was overcome "by an irrational and irresistible desire" to return to Ireland. He has lived there ever since.

Synge cites general relativity as a lifelong interest and describes himself as a geometer "regarded as a mathematician by physicists and as a physicist by mathematicians." Although mathematically he has not had so much influence on his daughter as some of her NYU colleagues, he has always been for her "a model of versatility and creativity."

**MORAWETZ**   Even if they are theoretically liberated, there is also the difficult thing for men, which is that under those circumstances they usually end up being bossed around. That's a difficult situation for anybody to be in.

**MP**   *Did any of your daughters ever show an interest in mathematics?*

**MORAWETZ**   Well, the second one, Lida, who is a psychiatrist, is definitely very gifted scientifically. Mike Artin tried to talk her into staying in mathematics, but she said that if she were to be a mathematician she would want to be a pure mathematician and she couldn't see spending her life doing anything so unuseful—furthermore, life would be too lonely. Now she sees that being a psychiatrist is a much more lonely life. I believe to some extent that she was a casualty of the anti-science attitude of the late sixties. With me my father had the attitude, well, if I wanted to do mathematics, that was fine; but he was *very disappointed* when she didn't go into mathematics.

**MP**   *I saw in the paper recently that you just collected an honorary degree from Princeton.*

**MORAWETZ**   I'm glad you brought that up because one of the things that you haven't touched on is Princeton, which was really a very important change in my life. When my youngest daughter, Nancy, was an undergraduate there, they had just gone co-ed. They had two women trustees who were both daughters and wives of Princeton graduates, and someone—I think it was McGeorge Bundy—came up with the idea that they should now look for a professional woman who had a daughter at Princeton. President Bowen called me for an interview. I had no idea why, but Herbert said, "They're going to make you a trustee." I said, "How can you ever imagine that?" But, sure enough, that's what they did. It was very interesting for me. Princeton is so very different from New York University! There is no financial struggle for modest endeavors—they have a very generous endowment. Of course they also husband their resources very carefully. That was impressive to me. Another thing that impressed me enormously was that they were so gracious, even when they disagreed. I was made vice-chairman of the curriculum committee. Then Mike Blumenthal, who was chairman, was made Secretary of the Treasury and I became chairman. The experience at Princeton led to other things. Without it I doubt if I would ever have been chosen as a director of NCR or as a trustee of the Sloan Foundation.

**MP**   *So Princeton opened up non-scientific things, all of which you enjoy?*

**Out of the Cocoon**   **MORAWETZ**   That's right, although I worry about some of them too, you know. I realize that decisions have to be made on relatively little information. I guess all administrators have that problem. I have that problem now, too. But getting out into the world was important for me because I had grown up in this cocoon at the Institute. The cocoon was nice and wonderful and fun, but it was good for me to get out.

**MP**   *Well, you've certainly done a lot of exciting things, had a lot of firsts, a lot of honors. I know that you're not inclined to line them up and rank them, but what have you felt especially proud of?*

**MORAWETZ**   I can't really answer about being *proud* of something.

**MP**   *Well, let's not use the word proud. What has given you the most pleasure?*

**MORAWETZ**  Ah, there's no excitement to beat the excitement of proving a theorem! [Laughing.] Until you find out the next day that it's wrong. It's funny that I should think of it now, but I remember when I had proved the thing about decay that Joe Keller had put up as an unsolved problem and Clifford Gardner said, "You know, there are some things that get printed. They make long and important papers. But there are other things that just simply go into textbooks." I don't know that mine made it into a textbook, but that was one of the nicest compliments I have ever had. I'll tell you, though, there is something about being a mathematician that is extremely difficult. One of my children put it this way: It's that you're on stage all the time. You can't fake or shift the subject of conversation and so on. That's very demanding of people.

**MP**  *But you like that.*

**MORAWETZ**  I guess that in a way I do, although at times it's also depressing.

**MP**  *You never wanted it on a platter. You told us that.*

**MORAWETZ**  Well, that was when I was rather puritanical about such things. Now I'd be willing to take the platter!

**MP**  *I certainly think you can be satisfied with your life.*

**MORAWETZ**  Well, I am, I really am. You know, when I was eighteen or nineteen, before I went down to Quebec, I was very depressed. I probably should have been seeing a shrink. But the fact is that as everything has gone—with all these "pleasures" of success and so on—I really never come close to feeling acutely depressed anymore. I think that maybe doing all the things I do is a protection, because many mathematicians do get depressed when they can't solve a problem they want to solve.

**Addendum by C. S. M.**  In reading this interview over, I find that I may have emphasized the need to escape from the devils of mathematics to embark on the pleasures of the real world. But it works both ways, and sometimes the devils of the real world drive one into the pleasures of studying mathematics.

*June 1986 in South San Francisco, California (DA, CR).*

*CATHLEEN SYNGE MORAWETZ*  Toronto, Ontario, Canada, May 5, 1923. B.S. 1945, Toronto; M.S. 1946, MIT; Ph.D. 1951, NYU. Field: applications of partial differential equations. Professor and former Director, Courant Institute of Mathematical Sciences, NYU. Gibbs Lecturer (AMS) 1981, Noether Lecturer (AWM) 1983. Lester R. Ford Award (MAA) 1980. American Academy of Arts and Sciences, National Academy of Sciences.

# FREDERICK MOSTELLER

Frederick Mosteller's productivity and organization are legendary. His curriculum vitae currently runs to six single-spaced pages and his bibliography to twenty-nine. He has always been fascinated with the role of chance. Subjects he has dealt with range from political polling to metastatistical treatment of medical studies to coincidence. He has been president of the American Association for the Advancement of Science, the Institute of Mathematical Statistics and the American Statistical Association. Now emeritus, he still runs two offices at Harvard and always "finds time"—although it may be at an early breakfast. He is modest about his accomplishments and sent us so many pictures of and with colleagues that a photographer had to be hired to take individual pictures of him.

□ □ □

**MP**   *It was almost forty years ago that you, Hendrik Bode, John Tukey and Charles Winsor proposed in* Science *a program for the education of what you called a scientific generalist; however, the opening sentence seems just as applicable today as it was then: "The complexities of modern science and modern society have created a need for scientific generalists, for men trained in many fields of science." Today we would add "women" as well; otherwise it's right on the mark. Was that program ever implemented?*

**MOSTELLER**   No. Every once in a while somebody writes and asks, "Did you give the course? And how did it go?" We never gave the course, so we don't know how it would have gone.

**Habits of Mind**   **MP**   *You urged that students learn the "habits of mind" of the chemist, the psychologist, the geologist and so on. According to you and the other authors, "These habits of mind and not the subject matter are what distinguish the sciences."*

**MOSTELLER**   The Battery Additive Case illustrates that point very strongly. I was told by Bill Cochran, who served on the committee to consider the effect of battery additives on the life of batteries, that the chemists

**241**

on the committee wouldn't even look at the data. They said, "There is nothing in the additives that can possibly have any effect." But statisticians said, "Well, you know, once in a while you get surprised." And indeed, in medicine, we are often surprised in what really are basically the same chemical situations. So the statisticians on the committee all looked at the data. It is true that they also concluded that there was no effect, but the point is that they looked and the chemists wouldn't.

**MP**  *The chemists had a different "habit of mind"—at least where chemicals were concerned.*

**MOSTELLER**  That's right.

**MP**  *It is also interesting that in your proposed curriculum for educating a scientific generalist, along with a great variety of science courses, you suggested a one-semester course in judging.*

**MOSTELLER**  Sometime ago I served on a special commission of the National Science Foundation which had been appointed to examine elementary and secondary mathematics education. Henry Pollak was chairman, and one thing that he very seriously proposed was a lot more emphasis on the judging of the sizes of things—because of the computer. Computers generate so many numbers that it's very difficult to know if they're right or wrong unless you have an idea in advance of what the values should be. The teachers on the commission, who had had experience with kids, also seemed to feel that teaching judging, or estimating, was very important.

**MP**  *Do you consider yourself a scientific generalist?*

**MOSTELLER**  Yes, I do.

**MP**  *How do you think it happened that you turned into one?*

"My ex-dean tells me I'm a dinosaur."

**MOSTELLER**  Well, I have always been interested in lots of things. I find it easy to get interested in what somebody else is doing. That's a big benefit if you are a consulting statistician. I think that a lot of scientists are not generalists because they are very deeply into their own problems and do not care to learn about someone else's problem except insofar as it relates to their own. Many don't want to be generalists, but I think that applied statisticians do well to begin that way. My ex-dean tells me I'm a dinosaur because there won't be statisticians like me anymore. He thinks that statisticians are going to go into specific subject-matter departments and become experts in economics or biology or whatever. He thinks that they won't jump around from one subject to another. Well, we'll see. History will answer the question.

**MP**  *The fact that you seem to be a real scientific generalist makes us curious about your own education and your early life. Your curriculum vitae tells us that you were born in 1916 in Clarksburg, West Virginia. How did a scientific generalist happen to start life in Clarksburg?*

**MOSTELLER**  My father was a glassworker at that time. Apparently that was one of the things that young men like my father did in those days. They had a good time rushing around from one factory to another all over the country. They could always get a job and make good money. Clarksburg just happened to be a place where they made glass, so my father was working there.

**MP**  *During your childhood, then, you moved around a lot?*

**MOSTELLER**  Most of the time we lived in the neighborhoods and suburbs of Pittsburgh. I did spend a year in Williamsport, Pennsylvania, and my freshman year in high school in Delaware, Ohio. Then I attended high school in Pittsburgh and went on to Carnegie Tech. I didn't leave Pittsburgh until I went to Princeton as a graduate student.

**"I just wasn't good at anything!"**

**MP**  *What were your interests in elementary school and high school?*

**MOSTELLER**  For the first four or five years in elementary school I did poorly. I had a very unhappy time. I really didn't know what was going on.

**MP**  *In what sense?*

**MOSTELLER**  Well, I wasn't good at anything the others were doing. I just wasn't good at anything! I often thought that the fact that the old lady in the first grade used to sneak up and hit me with a ruler for writing with my left hand was part of the reason for my problem. I told my mother about her, and my mother went and saw the principal. The principal called the old lady in, and they had a good discussion. The principal said, "We don't do that here," and the old lady said, "We don't do that here." Then we all parted, and she went back to hitting me with the ruler when I wrote with my left hand. It was a funny experience. I liked the old lady except for this one little thing she was doing with the ruler. So I write with my right hand. That is the only thing I do right-handed, except for using scissors.

**MP**  *Did you have a particular problem with reading?*

**MOSTELLER**  No. My mother pushed me over the top with reading. She used to read to me a lot. Then one night when she was cooking and I asked her to read some little fairy tale, she said, "You can read it—just sound it out." So I did. And she was right. After that reading went well, and I read a lot.

**MP**  *How many other children were there in the family?*

**MOSTELLER**  Just me.

**MP**  *Did your mother have a job outside the home?*

**MOSTELLER**  Before she and my father had me, she was a clerk in one of the steel mills. Then when my father became a contractor, she did the bookkeeping and the payroll and things like that for him, but at home. After she and my father were divorced—I was about twelve at the time—she did many things. Hemstitching, for instance. But then she changed to food. She was always interested in food. She took jobs that either had to do with food or with managing institutions like hotel and college dining halls. After the divorce she was always working.

**MP**  *Did she ever remarry?*

**MOSTELLER**  No.

**MP**  *Was she then your main source of support?*

**MOSTELLER**  Yes. During summers I usually worked for my father on road jobs, but otherwise he did not contribute to my upkeep or to my schooling.

Mosteller's mother, Helen Kelley Mosteller: "She was very pushy about my schooling."

**MP** *Do you recall having an increased sense of responsibility as a result of the divorce? Did you get odd jobs?*

**MOSTELLER** Odd jobs weren't easy to get, and my mother was very fussy about what I was to do. She always wanted me off the street. I didn't have many friends as a kid. I was around my mother a lot. She was very pushy about my schooling. She always worked hard with me on things like spelling and phonics. She wanted things to go well. Along about the fifth grade I suddenly picked up in school. I was good at it and enjoyed it. I didn't hate my teachers, and they didn't seem to hate me.

**MP** *What was your mother's educational background?*

**MOSTELLER** Mother was secretive about certain aspects of her life, and I was never sure whether she had had ten or eleven years of school. But it's clear to me that she didn't finish high school and that she was very disappointed not to have done so. Her father died at an early age, and she took care of the other children so that her mother could work outside the home. She was a tremendously responsible person and very bright. She had a wonderful sense of humor. She always made fun of herself and everybody else.

My father was a more serious person. As a contractor he was responsible for large enterprises. He was good at the contracting, so he went to work for a large organization as a superintendent. He would do the bidding for contracts, and then he would handle the biggest contract. Summers I worked for that organization on road jobs. My father had me doing a different job each summer.

**"Arithmetic was lots of fun."**

**MP** *You said that in the fifth grade school began to be fun. Were there any special subjects that seemed more enjoyable than others?*

Mosteller enjoys reproducing abstract geometric paintings (this one by Frank Stella) using oil crayons that his wife gave him as a present one Christmas.

MOSTELLER    I thought arithmetic was a lot of fun. We had this stunningly beautiful teacher, Miss England. She was so nice with those of us who were having trouble. She would take us off in little groups of three or four and explain the lesson all over. I think that somehow she was pretty responsible for my enjoying arithmetic. At any rate by the end of the fifth grade I was in first-class shape. I liked reading, but all the rest of English seemed a burden. I liked history and geography. All the science subjects were fun.

MP    *Was it your teachers or your mother who encouraged you to go to college?*

MOSTELLER    My mother certainly had it in mind from the start. The question of whether I would go just didn't arise. The only question was whether my father would be willing to help pay for my going. His idea was that since I was learning to do something new each summer on the road work I could soon be a superintendent or a contractor myself, so why waste time going to college. The trouble with that idea was that I didn't like the road work. I just did it.

MP    *But he had this idea of your doing different things each summer so that you would get a general picture of the work. He was something of a generalist himself, wasn't he?*

MOSTELLER    Yes. First I was helper of this, then assistant this, assistant that, then a foreman of that, and so on.

MP    *Before we get you to college, are there any special things you remember about your high school years?*

MOSTELLER    I had tremendously good teachers in high school. Every one was an absolutely outstanding person. I don't think I ever again had better teachers as a whole. There was a physicist named Deister who taught a very special kind of course. He gave fantastic lectures, just as in college, with great equipment, much of which he had made himself. And in his class if you got a low grade on the homework, you could just do it over and get a higher grade. He would not penalize you because you had done it over. The same thing with tests. This system really made the students feel that they had a chance to achieve whatever they were capable of achieving. He also taught mathematics. He was very good at it—and all the other mathematics teachers were very good. The same goes for all the English teachers. And I was terribly impressed with the Latin teacher. He was a lot of fun, and I sort of liked taking Latin from him, although I didn't care much for languages. I also took two years of German because I thought I needed to know it if I was going to college. I wasn't very good at it and didn't like it—or maybe it was the other way around. But in mathematics and physics and even in English I made excellent grades. I won a scholarship in one of those congressional merit examinations. That was rather helpful for going to college.

MP    *You went to Carnegie Tech as a freshman?*

**The Three Dice Problem**    MOSTELLER    Yes. I intended to take either physics or mathematics—not chemistry—and intended to become a high school teacher. As time went on, I became very engaged in a particular physics course. It was called Physical Measurements. I found myself very excited by that course. We kept measuring things to more and more decimal places by more and more ingenious methods. We had homework problems that were probabilistic and statistical (some least squares) in nature to go along with the general uncertainty of the measurements.

A key moment in my life occurred in one of those classes during my sophomore year. We had the question, when three dice are rolled what is the chance that the sum of the faces will be 10? The students in this course were very good, but we all got the answer largely by counting on our fingers. When we came to class, I said to the teacher, "That's all very well—we got the answer—but if we had been asked about six dice and the probability of getting 18, we would still be home counting. How do you do problems like that?" He said, "I don't know, but I know a man who probably does and I'll ask him." One day I was in the library and Professor Edwin G. Olds of the Mathematics Department came in. He shouted at me, "I hear you're interested in the three dice problem." He had a huge voice, and you know how libraries are. I was embarrassed. "Well, come and see me," he said, "and I'll show you about it." "Sure," I said. But I was saying to myself, "I'll never go!" Then he said, "What are you doing?" I showed him. "That's nothing important," he said. "Let's go now."

**The Most Marvelous Thing**

So we went to his office, and he showed me a generating function. It was the most marvelous thing I had ever seen in mathematics. It used mathematics that up to that time, in my heart of hearts, I had thought was something that mathematicians just did to create homework problems for innocent students in high school and college. I don't know where I had got ideas like that about various parts of mathematics. Anyway I was stunned when I saw how Olds used this mathematics that I hadn't believed in. He used it in such an unusually outrageous way. It was a total retranslation of the meaning of the numbers. I really thanked him. Then, as I was going out the door, he said, "Just a moment, young man." He took a book from his shelf, checked off ten problems, handed the book to me, and told me to do the problems. I said, "Yes, sir," and went home. In two weeks I brought back the answers. He looked them over, went to the next two chapters, checked off fifteen problems, and said, "Come back in two weeks."

This went on and on. Now I know that he was training me in probability, elementary statistics, finite differences, and discrete mathematics—things that wouldn't come up in the ordinary course. But we never had any conversation about whether I wanted to do the problems or why I was doing them. I was living at home and I said to my mother, "I don't understand what's going on here. I'm not taking any course, getting any grade or credit; yet I'm doing all this extra work." She said, "Well, dear, I'm sure he wouldn't have you doing it if he didn't think it was good for you in the long haul."

MP   *The problems weren't that exciting for you?*

MOSTELLER   I liked the problems all right. I just didn't know why I was doing them. He always had another book, too!

During that time—the Depression years—the government had instituted what were called NYA [National Youth Administration] projects to help students financially. Essentially you got to be an assistant to a professor. Well, when Professor Olds found out that I was making index cards for museums, he decided that I would be better off working for him. He had an enormous problem, computing the exact distribution of the rank correlation

In the early 1960's Mosteller taught statistics to millions via early morning television.

*More Mathematical People*

George B. Thomas *(top)* and Robert E. K. Rourke *(bottom)*, coauthors with Mosteller of the classic *Probability With Statistical Applications*, the textbook for Continental Classroom.

coefficient. He had written out all the possibilities for a particular sample size, and he could tell that the resulting table showing frequency distributions wasn't right. It was supposed to be symmetrical but it wasn't. So he gave me the task of checking all these papers he had stacked up to find out where the mistakes were. I would sit there with an adding machine and work away, and occasionally I would find a mistake. It seemed to me that there must be a better way of doing the job. Finally one day it came to me that there was a pattern in all those numbers: there had to be certain sums of squares that would add up just right. I began checking, and sure enough that turned out to be true. Then I was able to prove a theorem about what I had noticed—that the pattern had to occur. From then on, it was easy for me to check the problems. I was going at a great pace when he said, "What are you doing?" I said, "Well, I have this way of checking that is much better than the old way." And I showed him my theorem. He said, "I won't have you work on this anymore. Anybody can do it." So he found some new thing for me to do. In fact, after I finished my four years at Carnegie Tech, he kept me around for one more year.

MP   *So your bachelor's degree was finally in mathematics?*

MOSTELLER   Yes. I had been taking physics, but somehow—starting with the dice problem—I gradually moved out of physics and into mathematics.

MP   *Were you still thinking of becoming a high school teacher?*

MOSTELLER   Oh yes! I took courses in education. I learned that I should have a study plan, open the windows—all kinds of things like that. Actually all that helped me quite a bit later in my own teaching, partly because I learned to notice if the students were asleep.

MP   *Well, you certainly have been on the classroom stage a lot, including a nationally televised series—the Continental Classroom program. How did you happen to get involved in that?*

MOSTELLER   I had known Al Tucker when I was a student at Princeton, and I continued to see him off and on in connection with teaching matters, such as the Commission on Mathematics set up by the College Entrance Examination Board. For that commission George Thomas and Robert Rourke and I had written a book on statistics especially for secondary schools. Then we had decided to write an elementary text on probability with some statistical applications. It also happened that just at the same time I had helped the Harvard computing department on a book on binomial tables. The way I helped was to write an introduction describing a number of uses of these tables. Tucker told me that when he leafed through my introduction he decided that anybody who could do that many things with the binomial was the person to teach the course on statistics for Continental Classroom. So he recommended me. Maybe Samuel Wilks did too.

MP   *Now this television course—Continental Classroom—was it used in high schools?*

MOSTELLER   In high schools and colleges, in teachers' colleges and night schools. We even used it here at Harvard for a couple of years. The lectures were on television, but there were textbooks and assignments. We had what we called section meetings where the students could get together with an instructor, talk over their problems, have their homework graded, and maybe take quizzes.

**MP** *And the lectures on television were very early in the morning, as I recall?*

**MOSTELLER** That's right. Six o'clock! I used to get up and watch them. But we had to get up even earlier than that to make them. It was always a puzzle to me why we had to get up so early.

**MP** *Now was it a semester course?*

**MOSTELLER** Yes. I gave three lectures—Monday, Wednesday and Friday—and a colleague named Paul Clifford gave two in-between lectures which dealt with more applications and problems. We already knew each other from our work in quality control. It was a very solid course, mathematically rigorous except for a few little things. Of course we didn't have any of the fancy visuals they have on television now. It was pretty much straight lecturing, but it was considered quite successful.

**MP** *You must really enjoy teaching!*

**MOSTELLER** Yes. I worked very hard at it when I was teaching. I thought of myself as a teacher, at least in part, and I enjoyed that part. I still teach an elementary course, but today teaching is not quite so much fun for me because my administrative work takes such a toll. It's a matter of time. If you've got plenty of time to prepare, not just minimal time but time over and above that so you can produce something new for each lecture, then teaching is fun. Time is the real problem.

Mosteller today, illustrating a point.

**MP**  *I know that you have worked on early education too on several occasions, and I'd like to ask you, if you had your way, what would you do about the math training of students in elementary school and secondary school?*

**MOSTELLER**  I would try to mix in some probability and some statistics, especially data analysis, all along the way in those school systems—not to get a specific statistics course but to make sure that statistics plays a role in the mathematics and science courses as students progress. That could work out nicely, but it would take a lot of effort. You would have to get cooperation from and training for the teachers before you could do it.

**MP**  *Can we go back to Carnegie Tech for a moment? You said that Olds kept you there for a year after graduation. Why was that?*

**MOSTELLER**  All the mathematics people had the idea that I should take another year. The reason was partly that I hadn't studied what would be regarded as advanced mathematics in a university that did serious mathematics. I myself didn't know that. I had gone to Carnegie Tech because I thought it was good in mathematics. But it was an engineering school. In those days it had good mathematics for engineers but not mathematics for mathematicians. Now, of course, it is Carnegie-Mellon and a very good mathematics school.

**MP**  *So the faculty kept you there?*

**MOSTELLER**  Yes. One man gave me a tutorial in real variables. It was a whole different kind of thinking for me. A real stunner. I also taught some courses, including some night school courses. Carnegie had a very big night school program for people in local factories. Indeed even today old men walking with canes come up and tell me that they studied with me at night school when I was at Carnegie. Some of them became quite successful.

**MP**  *Was that part of Andrew Carnegie's educational philosophy?*

**MOSTELLER**  Yes. He believed in applied work along with the academic work. We took many shops during our undergraduate years. I took masonry, welding, woodworking and so on.

**MP**  *So you were well on your way to becoming a scientific generalist even then?*

**MOSTELLER**  It might be.

**MP**  *Now when the mathematics people at Carnegie Tech had you stay for an extra year, were they thinking that you would go on to a good graduate school in mathematics?*

**MOSTELLER**  Yes, although it was a surprise to me, because I was still thinking of teaching mathematics in a high school somewhere. That Christmas—it was 1938—Olds took me to the annual mathematical statistics meeting in Detroit. I remember that my mother and I had a hard time getting together enough money to pay for the trip. All the famous statisticians you can think of were there, but I believe that he took me primarily so that I could meet Sam Wilks of Princeton. He also introduced me to Harold Hotelling and others. He was trying to get me an assistantship or a fellowship somewhere. In the end I did get one at Princeton—with Wilks.

**MP**  *What kind of statistician was Olds?*

**MOSTELLER**  He was at one time the president of the Institute of Mathematical Statistics. He taught some advanced probability courses and wrote a number of papers on probabilistic or statistical problems. He also did consulting on quality control for industry. While I don't think that he had a huge number of publications, it was a good number considering the amount of teaching that he did. He was a very serious person.

**MP**  *When you went to Princeton—that must have been the fall of 1939— was there a separate department of statistics?*

**A Question for Salomon Bochner**

**MOSTELLER**  No, there wasn't. All the statistics that was done was in the Department of Mathematics. I enrolled in the Department of Mathematics. I still remember that I went to show Salomon Bochner the courses I was planning to take that first year. "Mr. Mosteller," he said, "I see that you're planning to take my course in complex variables but, as I can see from your record, you've never had a course in complex variables. Don't you think you ought to have had one?" I said, "Well, if I had already had a course in complex variables, why would I take your course?" He never even smiled. He just said, "I don't know, but all the other thirty students have already had one."

That was the only course I ever took where I learned big ideas about proofs from the teacher rather than technical details. At the beginning of the class he would tell us about the proof he was planning to give us. He'd say something like, "Now the method we're going to use for this is so and so. This is a standard method for proving all kinds of theorems, and I just want you to see what it's about and how it works." Then he'd explain everything to us in a sort of hand waving way.

**MP**  *In other words, he'd give you an overview of a particular approach?*

**MOSTELLER**  That's right. Well, I was used to somebody proving a theorem, just that theorem, to solve a particular problem, and I thought that was the way it was done, whereas the idea Bochner was communicating was that there are bundles of methods of proof and when you have these at your command you have begun to learn mathematics.

So he would give us the idea of the method of proof. Of course it was also true that it never quite worked out as it should. You see, many proofs in real and complex variables wind up with your proving that something is less than epsilon. Well, very often we'd get to the end of the hour and what was supposed to be less than epsilon turned out to be bigger than epsilon. It was not that his method wasn't right. It was just that the details of the arithmetic had slipped along the way. He would then look up at us and say, "Oh well, you can straighten it all out at home."

I left him with a great deal of affection. Al Tucker was always nice, too. I didn't get to know Solomon Lefschetz because I didn't take any course he taught. I got to know Wilks, of course, very well.

**MP**  *Tell us a little about him.*

**MOSTELLER**  Wilks was an amazingly young-looking man. I couldn't believe it when I saw him for the first time. He looked younger than I did! He was very slow speaking, always very careful not to say anything that would seem to be negative about anyone. He was a very impressive man, so thoughtful and so—so generous. I liked him a lot.

Persi Diaconis, now also a professor at Harvard, tossing dice with Mosteller, who was his thesis adviser there.

**MP**  *He was generally considered the leader, if leader there was, of American statisticians, wasn't he?*

**MOSTELLER**  At that time. Yes. I think so. More than Hotelling, because Hotelling wasn't trying to organize anything whereas Wilks understood the need for organizations, journals and so on in order to build and maintain a profession. I think Hotelling was probably very happy to let somebody else do that.

In my first two years at Princeton I saw a lot of Wilks. For my assistantship with him I did two things. One was teaching and the other was assisting with the *Annals of Mathematical Statistics*, which he edited. I edited copy, read proof, fixed up indexes, that kind of thing. Of course, sometimes I did get to read and appraise an actual paper, but that wasn't the main job. After the war started I didn't see so much of Wilks. Once I got my degree, however, I saw him often because we had the Social Science Research Council and other activities in common. He was interested in statistical applications although he published mainly theoretical papers.

**The Best Trick**  **MP**  *We have heard that you were interested in magic as well as in statistics when you were at Princeton.*

**MOSTELLER**  The interest in magic started around the second or third year at Princeton. I met a man named Frederick Williams when I was working in the Office of Public Opinion Research. Williams was interested in magic, and he showed me a trick one day. I was very enthusiastic about it, and he said, "Well, you know, we have a little magic club here." I went to a meeting of this little club, which was run by a psychology professor, Frank Taylor, who was famous for having invented what was called the peek deck. You showed the subject a deck of cards, and he would open it at random and peek at the card so the magician wouldn't see what it was, but somehow the magician would always identify the card.

**MP**  *I've experienced that trick!*

**MOSTELLER**  It's a very nice trick. At the magic club it was a rule that you had to bring a trick to each meeting, and after a while I got to thinking that

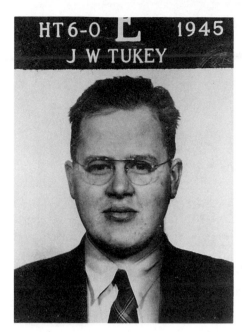

HT6-0 L 1945
J W TUKEY

This picture of John Tukey was reprinted in the *Bell Labs News* in 1985 under the heading "Can You Identify This Man?" Given as a hint was the following: "Few have had a role equal to his in shaping the information age."

it would be nice to invent a trick. Finally I did invent one. I must have five or six publications on tricks.

**MP**  *Would you tell us about one of your tricks?*

**MOSTELLER**  My best trick had to do with spelling a card. You—the subject—would think of a card and then you would spell out the name of it to yourself—A, C, E, O, F, S, P, A, D, E, S—slapping down a card for each letter. Then I would turn over the last card and that would be it—the ace of spades in this case.

**MP**  *That's a pretty nice trick, too. Did you ever do magic professionally?*

**MOSTELLER**  No. But as long as I was at Princeton, I did magic and invented tricks. After I left Princeton—that was in 1946, when I got my Ph.D.—I never did any more magic.

**MP**  *Why was that?*

**MOSTELLER**  I think the world just got a lot more serious for us. We played a lot of bridge during our last year at Princeton. That was when I was finishing my degree. We even began to get pretty good at bridge—we went to national tournaments—but I never played another serious hand of bridge after I came to Harvard.

**MP**  *You say "we"—were you married by then?*

**MOSTELLER**  Yes. Virginia Gilroy and I were married in 1941.

**MP**  *When and where did you get to know Virginia? We seem to have missed something here.*

**MOSTELLER**  I'd known Virginia from Pittsburgh. She was a freshman and I was a sophomore when I met her. It was at a tea dance. You see, we both lived in Wilkinsburg, so we had seen each other on the streetcar from time to time. She had attended the four-year secretarial school called Margaret Morrison which was the women's branch of Carnegie Tech. After she graduated she worked as a secretary at the Fine Arts Museum in Pittsburgh. She was one of Saint-Gaudens's secretaries. Not the famous sculptor Saint-Gaudens but his son, the director of the Museum. Then when we got married she got a job at Princeton as secretary to Merrill Flood, and when we moved to New York during the war she became secretary to W. Allen Wallis, who was the head of the statistical research group at Columbia. We worked in the same building in New York. I was working a few floors down with the Statistical Research Group which Princeton ran for the Applied Mathematics Panel.

**MP**  *But you didn't have your Ph.D. yet?*

**Working with Tukey**  **MOSTELLER**  No. We came back to Princeton at the end of '45 to finish my thesis. I did not see a great deal of Wilks at that time because he had been swept up into all sorts of governmental statistics things, but John Tukey was around so I would drop in and talk to him. A good deal of what I was able to do on the thesis was based on advice from John. I had a great time with him that year. We got to be close friends. We have done a lot of work together since then, mainly in the summers.

*More Mathematical People*

**MP**  *How did you happen to get a job in the Social Relations Department at Harvard?*

**MOSTELLER**  Well, Wilks was related to a lot of practical work which he never signed. He had worked a little with the psychologist Hadley Cantril, who headed the Office of Public Opinion Research at Princeton. At the beginning of my first summer, he asked me what I was going to do. When I told him I was going back to the road work, he said, "That isn't what you should be doing," and he got me a job with Cantril, who was closely connected with Gallup and Roper and Crosby, as well as Samuel Stouffer. Stouffer was in charge of a big sample survey organization that the Army had in Washington, and Cantrell sent me down there about once a week. It was Stouffer, who moved from Chicago to Harvard, who was responsible for bringing me there in 1946 as a lecturer in Social Relations. I taught statistics.

**MP**  *So you were not in the mathematics department?*

**MOSTELLER**  No, I have never had an appointment in the Mathematics Department at Harvard, although I have taught statistics for that Department as well as for the Division of Applied Sciences.

**MP**  *What exactly was Social Relations?*

**MOSTELLER**  That was a department composed of social anthropology, clinical psychology, social psychology and sociology. It was enormously popular right after World War II. It had hundreds of undergraduate and graduate students. But it was destroyed ultimately by disciplinary pressures. Now sociology and anthropology have their own departments. Psychology has returned to psychology. I still hold some appointment in psychology. My current appointments are in the Department of Statistics and the Department of Health Policy and Management in the School of Public Health. I am also Director of the Technology Assessment Group in the School of Public Health.

**MP**  *I understand that you are credited with starting the Department of Statistics at Harvard. How did that come about?*

Mosteller at his retirement party with his wife, Virginia Gilroy Mosteller, and his longtime friend and collaborator, John Tukey.

**MOSTELLER**  I tried to get a department started when Paul Buck was acting president, but he thought it was too specialized. Then when McGeorge Bundy became dean, he was interested. His undergraduate major had been mathematics, and he appointed a committee under J. H. Van Vleck (later a Nobel Prize winner), which had three charges: to consider what to do with applied mathematics, to consider what to do with statistics, and to figure out what computer we should have. After a period of something over six months, we recommended a Committee on Applied Mathematics within the Division (then) of Physics and Applied Sciences and the establishment of a Department of Statistics. The Faculty voted to establish the Department on Lincoln's Birthday 1957. Bill Cochran and John Pratt came the first year and Art Dempster, the second. Howard Aiken, who was also on that committee, figured out what computer we should get.

**MP**  *It is clear from your bibliography that, like a good scientific generalist, you have been interested in a lot of other people's problems. In fact, you seem to get interested sometimes when most other academics wouldn't. We have been told that you once had a man come into your office and announce that he had just finished tossing a die a hundred thousand times. Nobody else apparently took him very seriously, but you ended up writing a paper with him.*

**Another Dice Problem**

**MOSTELLER**  That was a man named Willard H. Longcor. He told me that there were about three things he liked to do. One was to toss dice, another was to read about the Civil War, and I forget what the third was. He felt that the dice tossing that he was doing could benefit science in some way, and he had gone around talking to various statisticians about making some use of all his work. I had always wanted to get some really good lengthy work on someone's tossing a die. I had been very interested in runs as a graduate student. A friend of mine, Alex Mood, had written his thesis on the theory of runs, and I had written on them in connection with quality control. I thought it would be nice to see what could be done—whether the actual outcome with a real person tossing real dice would match up with the theory. So Mr. Longcor bought a load of good dice from Las Vegas, and then we also bought some trashy dice, the kind that you would use in children's board games. I suggested that he have some carpet put up on the wall so that the dice would roll on the carpet, hit the wall, and bounce back. He had told me that his wife was troubled by the the noise of the dice bouncing against the wall. The carpet was a big help. He would toss the dice and keep a record. He was going to record odd and even, but I wanted him to record 1, 2, 3 versus 4, 5, 6.

**MP**  *Why was that?*

**MOSTELLER**  If there is a bias, the discrimination would show up more strongly with 1, 2, 3 versus 4, 5, 6 than with 1, 3, 5 versus 2, 4, 6. The reason is this. Dice are made by drilling holes in the sides and then backfilling. Inexpensive dice are, of course, not so carefully backfilled. So when you make a lot of holes on a side—in the case of 6, for example—and don't carefully backfill, that side will be not quite as heavy as the others so 6 will tend to come up on top more often. Well, I wanted to maximize that effect by having 1, 2, 3 versus 4, 5, 6, which gives you 6 against 18 as opposed to 9 against 12, which you get with odd versus even. But after a while

Working at home.

*More Mathematical People*

Mr. Longcor phoned me and said he just couldn't do what I wanted. He said he had made 100,000 tosses, but they were no good. He said that he was used to odd and even and he got all mixed up when he did 1, 2, 3 versus 4, 5, 6, so we would have to throw the whole 100,000 out. I thought it was very responsible of him to recognize that he wasn't doing it right and be willing to throw out all those tosses and start over. I agreed that he should do it the way he found best. We planned that he would make 20,000 tosses with one die. Then he would retire that die with the data in a separate envelope and do another 20,000 tosses with another die and so on. Finally one day we got a large crate of big manila envelopes. Each envelope had a record of 20,000 tosses and a summary showing how many runs of each kind! It was very neat recording. I couldn't believe it. There were *millions* of tosses.

The only way to check the work was by checking the runs and then comparing the results with theory. It turned out he was very accurate. I persuaded John Gilbert, who is someone with whom I've worked a lot, and a graduate student, Gudmund Iverson, to put the stuff on the computer. Then we did other, more complicated things with the data. Then we got out Alex Mood's paper on the theory of the distribution of runs. We discovered a few errors in the theory. The main formulas were correct, but the endpoints of the formulas were not quite right. We published an article with Mr. Longcor as one of the authors, summarizing the result of all his work and comparing it with the theory.

**A Man and a Die**     I regard it as an important idea. I think of it as the placebo experiment. You just have a man and a die. He's doing a random thing and recording it. In principle we have no real effect except equally likely outcomes, but the question is whether you get no effect. If you can't get no effect, then that raises questions about a lot of other things in science. We found some aberrant results that suggest that things a little unusual happen more often than the classical theory would suggest. Consequently maybe we should be a little more careful than we are when we interpret significance tests.

I think the article itself is fabulous if you look at the runs. We had good data from the Las Vegas dice and we had brand $X$ dice on the lousy side, and then we had computer results. The computer had a poor random number generator as it turns out, whereas the good Las Vegas dice were very close to perfect in comparison with the theoretical results.

Unfortunately Mr. Longcor's son-in-law got into trouble over all this. He applied for a job with the government but was told the FBI wouldn't clear him because his father-in-law was in the gambling business, which was illegal in his state. We had to go to some trouble writing to the appropriate agency and explaining our story. I suppose that it may have been hard to believe.

MP  *It's amazing that someone as tremendously busy as you would take time for a person that most statisticians would dismiss. Of course, you do have a reputation for efficient management of time. Lots of people have told us that you're the best organized person they know. What's your secret?*

MOSTELLER  One secret is having somebody doing it all at home. My wife, Virginia, does everything that has to be done except my professional work. That's a major secret! I don't understand how young people today with children and the wife working can move along at anything like the pace of someone like me when I have had this absolutely full-time support at home. Virginia doesn't just do the cooking and family tasks. She handles all our financial affairs and everything connected with our home. So that's one of my secrets. Of course, I have also been very fortunate in having had special scientific help at the office. After my second or third year at Harvard, I had a full-time mathematical assistant, Shirley Robuck. When she left, I had another, who was both a psychologist and a mathematician, Doris Entwisle. She was well organized herself. She was good not only with the actual work but also she would lean back and think about what was the matter with how we were doing everything. She got me better organized than I had been before. After she left Mrs. Cleo Youtz came, and Mrs. Youtz is just the most marvelous organizer you can think of. I have also benefited from the secretarial and administrative work of Mrs. Marjorie Olson. All these people have had an enormous impact on my total output.

I can't figure out when it was that I got organized the way I am organized now. Somewhere along the road I got this new way of doing scholarly jobs in little groups of people, and that changed the way we work.

**MP**  *Can you describe the system?*

**MOSTELLER**  Well, for example, we have a *New England Journal of Medicine* project. There are a number of research assistants and colleagues working together on that project. Sometimes they work as individuals and sometimes in a group. They take different tasks, and then we get it all together and produce a book. It takes four or five years, but the groups meet regularly every week or two. We're now working on the galley proofs of that book. Then at our National Science Foundation project we have another group of people — once in a while there is some overlap between groups but

The senior research team: Mrs. Cleo Youtz, Fred Mosteller, David Hoaglin and Marjorie Olson.

*More Mathematical People*

mostly each group is different. We're also working on a book. Students will take a chapter—it may be part of a thesis—and visiting scholars join in and say what they would like to write about. The people all report on a weekly basis to pass around memos and get criticism. We use the same system very heavily in all of these groups.

MP  *But how do you manage to keep all these people moving forward?*

**Write the Memo . . . Now!**

MOSTELLER  When I was younger, I had a lot of trouble getting students to do things, because they were always sure that they would have a better theorem or a better writeup or whatever the next week. Finally I pushed the idea of getting everybody to write the memo now and then write a better memo the following week. That's worked out well with students and with other team members. Of course, it depends a lot on having the secretarial support to get the memos out. Often I have up to five groups like that all generating articles—articles being developed with the goal of a book of some kind on some specific topic. That technique has been very successful over the last ten or fifteen years. I think that's what people talk about when they talk about my being well organized.

MP  *Much of your work is of interest to the general public. That's been a characteristic, too, hasn't it?*

MOSTELLER  A lot of that comes from being on committees. When you're on various kinds of committees, you automatically get involved in matters a more general public wants to know about.

MP  *Among many other things you have treated sex and politics, but have you ever been involved in the statistical analysis of a religious question?*

MOSTELLER  I was consulted once by a young man from the Divinity School at Harvard. He was a minister, and he found a vigorous debate going on in his congregation about whether Jesus was more oriented toward this world or toward the other world. His idea was to rate the orientation exemplified in each verse in the New Testament. I was not able to get him to do a number of things which I considered statistically appropriate, but I did persuade him not to just add his counts all up into two numbers but rather to present them book by book. That way everyone could see very substantial variations between the books of the Bible and could see why some people, looking at a particular book, would feel one way and other people, looking at another book, would feel another way.

**Coincidences**

MP  *I understand that you are currently working on a book on coincidences because you feel that since the public has a lot of interest in that subject, statisticians should address it.*

MOSTELLER  I began to collect items on coincidences. Then I got to talking to Persi Diaconis about them and we began to work together. I saw him for an hour this morning, and I hope to see him for another hour this afternoon.

MP  *Do you have a publication date in mind?*

MOSTELLER  No. It's the kind of book that has an infinite span. I don't mind going along at a very slow pace for a long time as long as the project

Lecturing on the subject of coincidence in San Francisco in 1987.

is moving. I don't get worried about finishing a book until I see that finishing it is in sight. Then I get very excited.

MP   *When we ask mathematicians whether they are able to discuss their work with their wives, more often than not they say they can't really tell them much about the subject matter. Are you able to talk about any of your work with Virginia?*

MOSTELLER   Not the mathematical part, but we often discuss time and organizational problems. It is very helpful to have somebody at a distance looking at what you're trying to do. Virginia and I talk about what we're trying to accomplish. For instance, there might be some problem like having three books going, and the question is whether we should put all our effort into just one book or continue little by little on all three. Virginia might talk with me about a strategy to accomplish the work. Very often she will have some good idea about what to do. I remember one time I finally got into the position of having just too many things going on. She counted them all up and told me that I would have to give up something. That's hard to do. But what I did was to take one of these groups and tell the people that although I would continue to read with them, I couldn't help anymore with the actual writing, they should take the book over and become the authors. That worked out fine. They just went right ahead with the same system and published the book, which was a big success.

MP   *What does a man who has such a reputation for being well organized do for recreation?*

MOSTELLER   Virginia and I work in the garden and almost kill ourselves there. It is so much fun! Then I paint with oil crayons. I used to paint in oils, but that takes so long to get started and to get cleaned up that I no longer have the time for it. Then one Christmas, Virginia bought me some oil crayons. The problem with them is that the colors don't always mix. Some do but some are treacherous. But I found that what I could do was bold and graphic work, like things by Stella, Albers and Vasarely, and I began copying some of their paintings. It is rewarding. It takes a lot of planning to find out whether the colors will work and what the sizes should be. When I finish a picture we frame it. We've got the Albers at home. It's the same Albers they made the postage stamp from, it's called "Glow." The stamp says something like "Learning Is Forever." The original is flat, but the oil crayons give the painting considerable texture. The Frank Stella, for example, looks like rivers are flowing in it. We gave our Vasarely to Yale. It contains little unit cubes in an interesting design. It is a marvelous thing because Vasarely knows how to make the same picture "pop" from one view to another as you look at it. This one has three views. Since unit cubes are so important in statistics, it seemed to me that when the Department of Statistics at Yale had their twenty-fifth anniversary, we should go down and give it to them as a present. They hung it in the department.

MP   *There is just one more question. We started our interview by talking about your growing up in Pittsburgh and your mother wanting so much for you to go on to college. Did she get a chance to see you succeed?*

MOSTELLER   Oh yes! She died about two years ago. She was aware of everything that was going on with me. She even came along when I got my honorary degree at Carnegie.

(*Facing page*) He loves to garden, but not generally in a shirt and tie.

**MP**  *So you fulfilled her wishes and then some. What about your father?*

**MOSTELLER**  He was pleased with me, too, in the end.

**MP**  *How far along did you have to get before he was pleased?*

**MOSTELLER**  I think that when I got to be a full professor at Harvard he thought that was all right.

*April 1985 in Berkeley, California (DA, CR).*

*FREDERICK MOSTELLER*  Clarksburg, West Virginia, December 24, 1916. B.S. 1938, M.S. 1939, Carnegie Institute of Technology; A.M. 1942, Ph.D. 1946, Princeton. Field: mathematics. Roger I. Lee Professor, Emeritus, Harvard. President ASA, 1967; IMS, 1974–75; AAAS, 1980; President-elect International Statistical Institute, 1989–present. Guggenheim Fellowship 1969–70, Myrdal Prize (Evaluation Research Society) 1978, Paul F. Lazarsfeld Prize (Council of Applied Social Research) 1979, Samuel S. Wilks Award 1986, R. A. Fisher Award 1987. American Academy of Arts and Sciences, American Philosophical Society, National Academy of Sciences, Royal Statistical Society. Books: *Pre-election Polls of 1948*; (with R. R. Bush) *Stochastic Models for Learning*, 1955; *Probability: A First Course*, 1961; *Probability and Statistics*, 1961; (with others) *Probability with Statistical Applications*, 1961; (with D. L. Wallace) *Inference and Disputed Authorship*, 1964; *Fifty Challenging Problems in Probability with Solutions*, 1965; (with J. N. Tanur) *Statistics: A Guide to the Unknown*, 1972; (with D. P. Moynihan) *On Equality of Educational Opportunity*, 1972; (with R. E. K. Rourke) *Sturdy Statistics: Nonparametric and Order Statistics*, 1973; (with J. W. Tukey) *Data Analysis and Regression*, 1977; (with others) *Data for Discussion*, 1982; (with others) *Understanding Robust and Exploratory Data Analysis*, 1983; (with others) *Biostatistics in Clinical Medicine*, 1983; (with S. E. Fienberg and R. E. K. Rourke) *Beginning Statistics with Data Analysis*, 1983; (with L. Moses) *Planning and Observational Studies*, 1983; (with D. L. Wallace) *Applied Bayesian and Classical Inference: The Case of the Federalist Papers*, 1984; (with others) *Exploring Data Tables, Trends and Shapes*, 1985.

# JULIA ROBINSON

Julia Robinson loved numbers from the time she was a child: "What is proved about numbers," she said, "will be a fact in any universe." As a mathematician, she specialized in that area of mathematics where logic and number meet. Her work led directly to the solution of Hilbert's tenth problem by the then nineteen-year-old Yuri Matijasevič and made her, as one Russian mathematician said, "the most famous Robinson in the USSR after Robinson Crusoe." She was the first woman mathematician to be elected to the National Academy of Sciences and the first woman president of the American Mathematical Society. Although she felt that a mathematician was best remembered by his or her mathematics, she agreed to cooperate in the following "autobiographical" sketch by her sister, Constance Reid.

□ □ □

In the normal course of events, my sister Julia Robinson would never have written the story of her life or cooperated with anyone who wanted to do so. However, with her acceptance of a public role as president of the American Mathematical Society, she found her position in regard to her personal privacy increasingly untenable. How could she object that only one woman research mathematician (Olga Taussky-Todd) was represented in the first volume of *Mathematical People* when she herself had declined to be interviewed? And what excuse could she give her sister, whom she had encouraged to write the life of David Hilbert so that students would know something about the man whose name is attached to so many concepts in their textbooks? In addition, there was increasing official pressure from the American Mathematical Society and various academies for biographical material. Finally she yielded: "Constance, you do it."

That was late in the spring of 1985 when we were bicycling at Pebble Beach. The preceding August, during the summer meeting of the American Mathematical Society at Eugene, she had learned that she had leukemia. After lengthy treatment by chemotherapy, she had finally won a remission from the disease. At Pebble Beach she said she felt as good as she ever had.

Helen Hall Bowman, mother of Julia Robinson.

I could never write about Julia without writing more intimately than she or I would wish, and it took me a while to come up with the solution of writing her "autobiography." What I wrote would then be entirely what she would want to have written about her own life. I would be writing in her spirit, not my own. She was amused by the idea and agreeable, although not completely reconciled. Then later she happened upon something by the writer Kay Boyle to the effect that the only excuse for writing one's autobiography is to give credit where credit has not been given. That seemed to her a reasonable justification, for there were people to whom she very much wanted to give credit.

Just a few weeks after we were bicycling at Pebble Beach, she learned that her hard-won remssion had ended. When I started to write, she was back in the hospital. Although she was hopeful of a second remission, she was also realistic about her chances. Every few days I read aloud to her what I had written. She listened attentively and amended or deleted as appropriate, sometimes just a word. She heard and approved all that which appears below—although she objected that my account of her life was much too long. Her own life was not. She died on July 30, 1985, at the age of sixty-five. As far as I could make it, what follows is the story of her life.

I was born in St. Louis, Missouri, on December 8, 1919, the second of two daughters born to Ralph Bowers Bowman and Helen Hall Bowman. Neither of my parents had gone to college, but both had had good secondary educations and my mother had gone to business college after graduation from high school. I learned recently from her commencement program that in high school she had elected to follow the scientific course rather than the more popular liberal arts course.

My mother died when I was two, and my father sent my sister, Constance, and me with our nurse to Arizona, where our grandmother wintered for her health. We lived twelve miles from Phoenix in the middle of the desert, very close to Camelback Mountain. Ours was a tiny community of only three or four families living under quite primitive conditions.

After my mother's death my father, who was the owner of a machine tool and equipment company, lost interest in his business. He had saved what was an enormous sum in those days and he was certain that, conservatively invested, it would provide an income sufficient to support a family. When he remarried, he closed his office and joined us in Arizona. My new mother had been Edenia Kridelbaugh before her marriage. Subsequently I shall refer to her as my mother, for I always thought of her that way.

We continued to live in Arizona for several years. One of my earliest memories is of arranging pebbles in the shadow of a giant saguaro, squinting because the sun was so bright. I think that I have always had a basic liking for the natural numbers. To me they are the one real thing. We can conceive of a chemistry that is different from ours, or a biology, but we cannot conceive of a different mathematics of numbers. What is proved about numbers will be a fact in any universe.

Ralph Bowers Bowman, father of Julia Robinson.

*More Mathematical People*

Edenia Kridelbaugh shortly before her marriage to Ralph Bowman in 1923—Julia always thought of her as her mother.

I was slow to talk and pronounced words so oddly that no one except Constance could understand me. Since people would ask me a question and look at Constance for the answer, she got into the habit of speaking for me, as she is now. My mother, who had taught kindergarten and first grade before her marriage, said that I was the stubbornest child she had ever known. I would say that my stubbornness has been to a great extent responsible for whatever success I have had in mathematics. But then it is a common trait among mathematicians.

Our family always left Arizona during the summer. Several times we went to San Diego; and in 1925, when I was five and Constance seven, my mother, who had been teaching Constance at home, insisted that my father settle some place where we could go to school. That fall we moved to Point Loma on San Diego Bay.

Except for the fort and the lighthouse, which are still there, Point Loma was at that time quite different from the expensive, overbuilt residential area that it is today. There were about fifty families scattered over the hill, not counting the military families at Fort Rosecrans or the colony of Portuguese fishermen. Like the desert, it was open to exploration and fantasy.

The elementary school that we attended was very small with several grades combined in each classroom. During our first few years both Constance and I were skipped so that later we were always among the youngest in our classes.

The most exciting event of our first years on Point Loma was the birth of our little sister, Billie, on Easter Sunday 1928. It was followed by an event which was to have a permanent effect upon my life and career.

Less than a year after Billie's birth, when I was nine years old, I came down with scarlet fever. To prevent the spread of the disease, especially to the new baby, my father took over my care. He washed all my dishes and, whenever he entered my room, put on an old duster that he had worn when we had an open touring car. The entire family was isolated and a conspicuous sign to that effect posted on the front door. When, after a month, the isolation was lifted, the family celebrated by going to see *The Ghost Speaks*. I believe it was our first "talkie."

Julia and her sister, Constance, on the Arizona desert, where they lived with their grandmother after their mother's death.

Constance and Julia greeting their father, who had come out to the desert to spend Christmas with them in 1922, the year of their mother's death.

The scarlet fever was followed by rheumatic fever, which today would be treated effectively with penicillin. My family moved from Point Loma so that I would not find myself in a class behind my old classmates when I went back to school, but I did not recover as soon as expected. Ultimately I had to spend a year in bed at the home of a practical nurse. During that year there was nothing in the world that I wanted so much as a bicycle. My father assured me that when I got well I would get one but, childlike, I interpreted this as meaning that I was not going to get well.

**Learning Patience**

I have since read that a solitary childhood or, what amounts to the same thing, a period of isolation resulting from an illness is frequently noted in the early lives of scientists. I am not sure what the significance of this finding is. Obviously I had to amuse myself for long periods of time, but I didn't do so with mathematics. I am inclined to think that what I learned during that year in bed was patience.

By the time I was well enough to go back to school, I had missed more than two years. My parents arranged to have me tutored by a retired elementary school teacher. In one year, working three mornings a week, she and I went through the state syllabuses for the fifth, sixth, seventh and eighth grades. It makes me wonder how much time must be wasted in classrooms. One day she told me that you could never carry the square root of 2 to a point where the decimal began to repeat. She knew that this fact had been proved, although she did not know how. I didn't see how anyone could prove such a thing, and I went home and utilized my newly acquired skills at extracting square root to check it but finally, late in the afternoon, gave up.

**An Almost Kafka-like Experience**

In the fall of 1932, a few months before the election of Franklin Roosevelt, I entered the ninth grade at Theodore Roosevelt Junior High School. For me it was an almost Kafka-like experience. I was a beginner in a game that everyone else in my class had been playing for two years. I made many stupid and embarrassing mistakes and ate lunch in a corner as quickly as I could so that no one would notice that I was alone. Finally a girl named Virginia Bell invited me to eat with her and her friends. She became my best and only friend as long as I remained in San Diego. A few years ago, when I returned for a colloquium lecture there, I visited her and found that although much had happened to us both in the interim we were still just as congenial as we had been during our school days.

At Roosevelt I was introduced to algebra by a woman mathematics teacher. Before graduation she made a valiant effort to explain to the class that sometimes the best students in math could not get math honors because they had not received grades at their previous school.

**The Only Girl in Math and Physics**

The mathematics course at San Diego High School was standard for that time: plane geometry in the tenth grade, advanced algebra in the eleventh, and trigonometry and solid geometry in the twelfth. There were two women mathematics teachers, and I took classes from both of them. After plane geometry (which fulfilled the University of California's entrance requirement), I was the only girl still taking mathematics. I was also the only girl in physics. I was very shy, so it may sound strange for me to say that entering a roomful of boys did not disconcert me. Unlike many shy people I have never given much thought to what other people think about me. I believe this attitude is a legacy from my parents. My father conveyed it by example, but my mother frequently articulated it to us. Naturally I was interested in some of the boys in my math classes, but they didn't pay any attention to me except when they had a question about the homework. None of them ever seemed to be bothered by the fact that a girl was getting the best grades.

My high school mathematics teachers were all well qualified to teach the subject at that level. There were, however, no enrichment programs in the high schools in the 1930's, no math days at the local college, no well publicized competitions. None of my teachers encouraged me to do more advanced work. Of course I did try a few of the usual things, like trisecting the angle. Once—and this is just about the only piece of personal direction that I recall—one of my teachers, it may have been the head of the department, who was my counselor, advised me that now that I had learned to solve math problems I should learn to be neat.

On the back of this picture of Julia her father noted: "It doesn't do her justice."

We had all been given an intelligence test—I think it was the Otis—while we were still in junior high school. Constance had done very well on it but I, being a slower reader and unaccustomed to taking tests, had done poorly. She found out later, when she was herself a teacher at the high school, that my I.Q. was recorded as 98, two points below average. The result was that even after we were in college, Constance, who took her classes lightly while devoting herself to the school paper, was being called into the office to find out why she wasn't doing better while I was being called in to find out why I was able to perform "above ability."

My friend Virginia Bell was an art major—she later became an art teacher and supervisor in the San Diego City Schools—and, encouraged by her and by the fact that one semester of art or music was a requirement, I took an art course in which I learned something about perspective and among other things drew an impressively realistic baseball. I was a great baseball fan, keeping box scores at games and spending my allowance on the *Sporting News*. In spite of my complete lack of musical ability or appreciation, I had a crush on the Metropolitan Opera's baritone, Lawrence Tibbett, who starred in several movies at that time. When he gave a concert in San Diego, my mother got tickets for us and my father, an inveterate photographer, took a picture for me of the billboard advertising the concert. I learned from my father how to shoot both a rifle and a pistol and once wrote a paper on barrel rifling for physics. I mention these things only to show that I was not absorbed entirely in mathematics.

In retrospect, I see my high school years as very relaxed compared to those of young people today. There was no pressure to get into a "good" college, and my parents were seemingly unconcerned by the fact that on occasion I was in an English class that was not college preparatory. They were concerned, though, that I had only one friend and didn't seem to know how to make any others.

Of course, since we were still in the middle of the Depression, I was always conscious of economic pressures. My father's savings were being eroded more rapidly than any of us dreamed. He listened every noon to the stock market report, and his mood for the next twenty-four hours depended on whether the market had gone up or down. We never went without anything essential, but we had no such luxuries as trips during summer vacations. I remember that our next door neighbor, a civil engineer, lost his job and began to make jigsaw puzzles, which along with Monopoly had become a national fad.

**"My father told her not to worry."**

When I graduated from high school, I received awards in mathematics and the other sciences I had taken as well as the Bausch and Lomb medal for all-around excellence in science. My selection for this last was not approved by some of the science teachers because I had never taken chemistry, a subject that to this day I know nothing about. After the award assembly my mother expressed some concern about what the future could hold for such a girl, but my father told her not to worry—I would marry a professor. My graduation present was a beautiful and expensive slide rule, which I christened "Slippy."

It had always been taken for granted that Constance and I would go to college. That meant the local state college (now San Diego State University). State, as it was called, had been until quite recently a teachers' college and, before that, a normal school. Very few of my high school classmates went away to college after graduation, but a number attended State for two years and then transferred to Berkeley or UCLA. Those who remained took some education courses and got one of the several teaching credentials that were

BOWMAN, JULIA H.

S atisfied when horseback riding
D estined to go to State College
H ails from Roosevelt Junior High School
S pecializes in mathematics

Julia Bowman in the yearbook of the Class of 1936 at San Diego High School.

*More Mathematical People*

offered. My mother had always inculcated in us the idea that a girl should equip herself to earn a living. She placed an especially high value on a teaching credential because it qualified the holder to do a very specific thing for which she would be paid.

At State there were only a few Ph.D.'s on the faculty. Neither of the two mathematics professors had a doctorate. There were no women teaching mathematics but I remember women, with doctorates, teaching biology and psychology.

Naturally I elected to major in mathematics. The lower division majors followed the usual sequence of courses in analytic geometry and calculus. There were thirty-five or forty math students, most of them planning to be engineers. There were also girls who were going to be teachers. At that time I had no idea that such a thing as a mathematician (as opposed to a math teacher) existed.

By the beginning of my sophomore year all the savings that my father had so confidently expected to support his retirement had been wiped out. He took his own life that September, leaving only an insurance policy on which he had borrowed to the limit and an unimproved lot on Point Loma. We moved to a modest apartment and received some regular financial help from our aunt, Lucille Hall, an elementary school teacher in St. Louis. In spite of our straitened circumstances, Constance and I continued in college. Tuition at that time was $12 a semester.

In the upper division at State the number of math students dropped precipitously, those who were going to be engineers having transferred to other colleges. Two, and only two, upper division mathematics courses were offered each semester. All the math majors had to take them. In a way this was a good system because we focused on those two in a way we wouldn't have if there had been a larger number of courses offered. In my junior year I took advanced calculus, which completed the calculus cycle although it wasn't so advanced as Math 104 (real analysis) at Berkeley. I also took a course in algebra that was the equivalent of Math 8, a lower division course at Berkeley. There was something called Modern Geometry, which was really very old-fashioned (nothing non-Euclidean). The History of Mathematics was also offered. It was probably in that class that I read E. T. Bell's *Men of Mathematics*, which had just been published.

**An Influential Book**  Mathematics was by far my favorite subject, but I hardly knew what the subject was. The only idea of real mathematics that I had came from *Men of Mathematics*. In it I got my first glimpse of a mathematician per se. I cannot overemphasize the importance of such books about mathematics in the intellectual life of a student like myself completely out of contact with research mathematicians. I learned many interesting things from Bell's book. I was especially excited by some of the theorems of number theory—he was a number theorist himself—and I used to recount these to Constance at night after we went to bed. She soon found that if she wasn't ready to go to sleep she could keep me awake by asking questions about mathematics.

Neither Constance nor I was interested in teaching elementary school or qualified to get one of the special credentials offered in art, music or physical education. We settled reluctantly on the very limited junior high school credential. I took some of the required education courses and found them boring. Also, when Constance graduated, I learned that a junior high school credential did not guarantee a teaching job. It was not highly regarded by school superintendents, who could get teachers with the more comprehensive general secondary credential for the same salary. To obtain such a credential, however, you had to take a post-graduate year on one of the campuses of the University of California.

When, six months after graduation, Constance still had no job, my mother, with great courage and faith in the future, dug into the family's small savings and sent her to Berkeley. Happily the gamble paid off. Even before Constance had finished the course work for the new credential, she was hired as an English/Journalism teacher and faculty adviser of the school paper at San Diego High School.

I now conceived an absolute passion to go away to school, too—whether to Berkeley or UCLA, I was not particular—any place where there was a real department of mathematics. A young Ph.D. in astronomy from Berkeley, Clifford E. Smith, had joined the faculty at State; and although I don't remember his encouraging me to go away, he did give me a glimpse of something beyond Mr. Livingston and Mr. Gleason. I am sure he found the students at State quite a change from the politically conscious students at Berkeley. One morning he announced that we were excused from turning in our homework because he knew that we had been up late the night before listening to the radio. We looked bewilderedly at one another, none of us aware that Chamberlain and Hitler had just come to an agreement in Munich that would still, almost fifty years later, symbolize appeasement and dishonor.

### A Fortuitous Arrival

After Constance had her job and could help with my expenses, I told the math professors at State that I wanted to go somewhere else the following year. Mr. Livingston, the head of the department, tried to dissuade me. The college was planning to inaugurate an honors program, and I was obviously the only mathematics student whom he could propose. Mr. Gleason, however, said that I should go and that I should go to Berkeley rather than to UCLA.

I arrived at Berkeley most fortuitously as far as mathematics was concerned, although of course I did not realize it then. At the beginning of the 1930's the other science departments had persuaded President Sproul to bring in someone of recognized achievement to head the mathematics department and upgrade it. The mathematician who had been chosen was Griffith C. Evans. He had almost immediately hired Alfred Foster, Charles Morrey and Hans Lewy. The year before I arrived he had brought Jerzy Neyman from England.

My mother expected me to get a general secondary credential, just as Constance had; but the adviser for math majors planning to go into teaching discouraged me. I never understood why, but Constance tells me that although there were a number of women teaching mathematics in junior and senior high schools, as I have indicated, there was a definite drive (affirmative action?) to bring more men into secondary education and it was thought this could be done most easily in the sciences.

I took five courses in mathematics that first year at Berkeley, including a course in number theory taught by Raphael M. Robinson. The fact that Raphael was teaching number theory was a stroke of luck—for us. Evans had hired Dick Lehmer as the department's number theory specialist, but Dick had had to fulfill a year's commitment to Lehigh before he could come to Berkeley and Raphael had been assigned to teach number theory in his

Raphael M. Robinson, now Professor Emeritus at Berkeley, in a thoughtful mood.

place. In the second semester there were only four students—I was again the only girl—and Raphael began to ask me to go on walks with him.

Although I had lost some credits by transferring, I was still able to get my A.B. in a year. I applied for jobs with various companies in San Francisco, but they were not interested in my mathematical training—they asked if I could type. (A few years later, after we were in the war, they suddenly did become interested.) I applied to Evans for a teaching assistantship, but he was trying to bring students from other universities to Berkeley. He told me that the only possible position for me was at Oregon State. Since it was an undergraduate department and I would not be able to go on with my studies, he advised me not to take it. Neyman, hearing of my plight, quickly arranged for me to get some of the money that had been allotted for Betty Scott, his half-time lab assistant. As I remember, she wanted a little more time for her studies anyway—she was an astronomy major then, now of course a long-time professor of statistics at Berkeley—so she took two-thirds of the half and I took the other one-third. I remember that Neyman asked me how much I needed to live on. I said $32 a month and he got me $35.

## The Ugly Duckling

I was very happy, really blissfully happy, at Berkeley. In San Diego there had been no one at all like me. If, as Bruno Bettelheim has said, everyone has his or her own fairy story, mine is the story of the ugly duckling. Suddenly, at Berkeley, I found that I was really a swan. There were lots of people, students as well as faculty members, just as excited as I was about mathematics. I was elected to the honorary mathematics fraternity, and there was quite a bit of departmental social activity in which I was included. Then there was Raphael.

During our increasingly frequent walks, he told me about various interesting things in mathematics. He is, in my opinion, a very good teacher. He thoroughly understands a large part of mathematics, both classical and modern, and has it so well organized in his mind that he is able to explain it with exceptional clarity. On one of our early walks, he introduced me to Gödel's results. I was very impressed and excited by the fact that things about numbers could be proved by symbolic logic. Without question what had the greatest mathematical impact on me at Berkeley was the one-to-one teaching that I received from Raphael.

## Neyman to the Rescue

Although I had done well in mathematics, my mother was concerned about my getting a real job and earning some real money. Earlier, I had taken a civil service examination for a job as a junior statistician; now I was offered a job as a night clerk in Washington D.C. at $1200 a year. My mother thought that I should accept it, but Raphael had other ideas. At his insistence I came back to Berkeley for a second graduate year and, this time, received a teaching assistantship. I wanted to teach calculus, but Neyman asked Evans for me and so I taught statistics (which I found very messy, not beautiful and clear and true like number theory). At the end of the semester, a few weeks after the Japanese attacked Pearl Harbor, Raphael and I were married.

Mina Rees has observed that it is hard to name a woman mathematician who isn't married to a man mathematician. I think what she says was very true in her generation and also in mine, although no longer true. I doubt that I would have become a mathematician if it hadn't been for Raphael. He taught me and has continued to teach me, has encouraged me, and has supported me in many ways, including financially. Through his position as a professor at Berkeley, he has provided me with access to professional facilities and society. Although he is a much better and much broader mathematician than I, his research is not so generally appreciated, since he has pursued his own interests rather than current fashions or flashy problems. He keeps up with modern developments even now in his seventies, working through the recent proof of the Bieberbach conjecture, for example; but he has always been a rather old-fashioned mathematician—as he says, he has liked to work on "neglected problems." I feel that his work is very interesting and should be much better known, and I am planning to take it as the subject of my Presidential Address at the AMS meeting in New Orleans this winter.

## A Kind of Academic Limbo

When we were married, there was a rule at Berkeley that members of the same family could not teach in the same department. Since I already had a one-year contract as a teaching assistant, this rule did not immediately apply to me. I didn't really like teaching statistics, especially since Neyman, convinced that American students were woefully ignorant of statistical theory, had conceived the idea of using both lecture and lab periods for lectures and making the students do the lab work on their own time. I wrote and asked Evans if I could teach mathematics instead. He did not respond, but Neyman heard about my letter and became very angry. He stopped using me as a T.A. and left me in a kind of limbo for the rest of the academic year, doing absolutely nothing for the money I was regularly being paid. He did not hold a grudge, however. During the war he employed me in the stat lab, and my first paper came out of the stat lab work. Actually I did not want to publish it because someone else had already proved the same thing, although in a different way, but Neyman insisted. (He always encouraged students to publish before they got their degrees.) For many years I avoided him because I found it almost impossible to say no to him, but I understand that when I was proposed for membership in the National Academy of Sciences he was one of my most enthusiastic and energetic supporters.

Because of the nepotism rule I could not teach in the mathematics department the next year, but this fact did not particularly concern me. Now that I was married, I expected and very much wanted to have a family. Raphael and I bought a house and, although I continued to audit math courses, I was really more interested in shopping for furniture. When I finally learned that I was pregnant, I was delighted—and very disappointed when a few months later I lost the baby. Shortly afterwards, visiting in San Diego, I contracted viral pneumonia. My mother called a doctor. His first question after he examined me was, "How long have you had heart trouble?" It was true that I had always puffed, especially climbing the stairs to the math classes on the third floor of Wheeler Hall (only professors were permitted to use the elevator in those days); but no one, including my obstetrician, had ever shown more than a cursory interest in the condition of my heart. I believe the doctor in San Diego had had rheumatic fever himself and was thus more familiar with the resulting buildup of scar tissue in the mitral valve. He advised me that under no circumstances should I become pregnant again and told my mother privately that I would probably be dead by forty, since by that time my heart would have broken down completely.

For a long time I was deeply depressed by the fact that we could not have children. Finally Raphael reminded me that there was still mathematics. He had written a paper about simplifying definitions of primitive recursive

*More Mathematical People*

functions, and he suggested that I do the same thing for general recursive functions. I worked very hard on the problem during the year 1946–47, when we were at Princeton, and published my results the following year. I cannot honestly say that the mathematical problem eliminated the emotional problem, but it did help to take my mind off it some of the time. When we came back to Berkeley, I began to work toward a Ph.D. with Alfred Tarski.

Tarski, a Pole, had been caught in the United States as a visiting lecturer at Harvard when Germany invaded Poland in 1939. Unbelievable as it now seems, a permanent position had not been found for him between 1939 and 1942 when Evans brought him to Berkeley. Like Neyman, Tarski was a tremendous addition to our department. In my opinion, and that of many other people, he ranks with Gödel as a logician.

Previously, in the summer of 1943, I had audited a seminar given by Tarski on Gödel's results. In the seminar he had read us a letter from Mostowski, who had been his only Polish Ph.D. Mostowski wanted to know whether it was possible to define addition in terms of successor and multiplication. I played around with the problem and in a couple of days came up with a very complicated definition. It is still rather surprising to me that I was able to do this, considering the low probability of a mathematician's going directly to a definition. Tarski was immensely pleased and made some remark to the effect that my work was so original that it would do for a thesis. In writing up my result, however, I kept generalizing and simplifying it until it became essentially trivial. I knew without Tarski's telling me that it wasn't enough for a thesis. Later he suggested a problem about relation algebra. I never really got anywhere with it or maybe just didn't work very hard, since I wasn't particularly interested in it.

Tarski had great respect for Raphael and often talked with him about problems. One day at lunch at the Men's Faculty Club (in those days women were not allowed in the main dining room at lunch), he mentioned the question whether one could give a first order definition of the integers in the field of rationals. This was not meant as a suggestion for a thesis topic for me but when Raphael came home, he told me about it. I found it interesting, and I just began to work on it without saying anything to Tarski. I think that a great deal of the difficulty that students have in producing a thesis goes back to the fact that they are not really interested in the problem that they are given, just as I was not interested in Tarski's problem about relation algebra. I consider myself very lucky to have come so early upon a field and a problem that excited me.

Julia Robinson's thesis adviser, Alfred Tarski (1902–1983), who founded the Group in Logic and Methodology of Science at Berkeley.

### Tarski Was Delighted

In my thesis, "Definability and decision problems in arithmetic," I showed that the notion of an integer can be defined arithmetically in terms of the notion of a rational number and the operations of addition and multiplication on rationals. Thus the arithmetic of rationals is adequate for the formulation of all problems of elementary number theory. Since the solution of the decision problem was already known to be negative for elementary number theory, it followed from my results that the solution of the decision problem is negative for the theory of rationals. When I took my work to Tarski, he was delighted. It was then that he told me that he had been concerned that the other thing had become so simple (although it is still included in my thesis).

Tarski had always recognized that the decision problem for the theory of arbitrary fields would be undecidable if the integers could be defined in the field of rationals. That was why he had been interested in the problem in the first place. So he added a section to my thesis pointing out that undecidability for arbitrary fields follows from my work. I always gave him the credit for that result, since he was the one who recognized it; but he always gave me the credit, since he had not been able to establish it himself. Later somebody produced a simpler and more direct proof for a different field, but I don't believe that anyone has improved on my work on definability in the rational field.

Tarski was a very inspiring teacher. He had a way of setting results into a framework so that they all fit nicely together, and he was always full of problems—he just bubbled over with problems. There are teachers whose lectures are so well organized that they convey the impression that mathematics is absolutely finished. Tarski's lectures were equally well organized but, because of the problems, you knew that there were still things that even you could do which would make for progress. Often, of course, he had problems that he didn't give to students because he thought they were too hard, and sometimes he was mistaken about what was an easy problem. Bob Vaught once went to him, terribly depressed because he felt that he hadn't been able to accomplish anything in mathematics. He asked for an easy problem that he was sure to be able to solve, and Tarski gave him this problem—it's still unsolved! Fortunately Bob went on with mathematics anyway.

In 1948, the same year that I got my Ph.D., I began to work on the tenth problem on Hilbert's famous list: to find an effective method for determining if a given diophantine equation is solvable in integers. This problem has occupied the largest portion of my professional career. Again it was Tarski, talking to Raphael, who started me off. He had noticed that the numbers that are not powers of 2 can be existentially defined as the solution of a diophantine equation. One simply has to show that the number contains an odd factor; for example, $z$ is not a power of 2 if and only if there exist integers $x$ and $y$ such that $z = (2x + 3)y$. He wondered whether, possibly using induction, one could prove that the powers of 2 cannot be put in the form of a solution of a diophantine equation.

**"I like to work on that kind of problem."**

Again Raphael mentioned the problem to me when he came home. I am sure that Tarski was thinking about the Tenth Problem, but I wasn't—in the beginning. Probably if I had been, I would never have tackled it. I was just thinking about that specific problem. It was a problem that was not of particular interest in itself; however, it appealed to me. I like to work on that type of problem. Usually in mathematics you have an equation and you want to find a solution. Here you were given a solution and you had to find the equation. I liked that. I would have worked on the problem very hard without the connection to the Tenth Problem, but soon it became clear to me that that was where it came from. I haven't worked on very many problems, and the ones that I have worked on have been problems that I find interesting even when I recognize that they would not be so interesting to other people. That is partly because I've never been held to getting results and to publishing or perishing. As Raphael says, the problem of overproduction of mathematics would be solved if we just changed the *or* to *and*.

I wasn't able to show that the powers of 2 cannot be expressed as the solution of a diophantine equation. In fact, I became discouraged right away, because proving something by induction over polynomials, as Tarski had suggested, is very difficult. Instead I started to work in the other direction, trying to prove that powers of 2, like non-powers of 2, could be so expressed. When I couldn't do that either, I turned to related problems of existential definability. The relevance of my efforts to Hilbert's problem is clear from the fact that a set of natural numbers is existentially definable if and only if it is the set of values of a parameter for which a certain diophantine equation is solvable. The main result in my paper, "Existential definability in arithmetic," was the proof that the relation $x = y^z$ is existentially definable in terms of any relation of roughly exponential growth.

**A "Prize" Problem but No Prize**

Raphael had a sabbatical coming up in 1949–50. Since I had had virtually no teaching experience, I wanted to teach at UCLA that year. As it turned out, however, I spent the year doing research at the Rand Corporation in Santa Monica. Oliver Gross was there, and he was interested in George Brown's fictitious play problem, which had been proposed as a means of computing a strategy for zero-sum games. The idea was that you set up two fictitious players. The first player makes a random choice of moves, and then the second player does the best thing against what the first player has done. Then the second player takes the average of the two strategies—in other words, weights the probabilities equally—and does the best thing. Then the first player weights the choices of the second player and so on. The question was whether, if this procedure were continued indefinitely, it would converge to a solution of the game. A number of people at Rand had tried to prove that it would. Von Neumann had even looked at the problem. And Rand was offering a $200 prize for its solution. In my paper, "An iterative method of solving a game," I showed that the procedure did indeed converge, but I didn't get the prize, because I was a Rand employee. I was once told by David Gale that he considered the theorem in that paper the most important theorem in elementary game theory; but I cannot judge, since I never again did anything in game theory.

Even while employed at Rand, I continued to think about problems of existential definability relevant to Hilbert's tenth problem. Since there are many classical diophantine equations with one parameter for which no effective method of determining the solvability for an arbitrary value of the parameter is known, it seemed very unlikely that a decision procedure could be found. But a negative answer would be an answer, too.

In 1950, at the first post-war International Congress at Harvard, Martin Davis, who had just completed his thesis under Emil Post, presented a ten-minute paper on his theorem about reducing recursive enumerable sets to a particular form, and I presented a ten-minute paper on my work on existential definability. That was the first time I had met Martin. I remember that he said he didn't see how my work could help to solve Hilbert's problem, since it was just a series of examples. I said, well, I did what I could.

During the 1950's, in another field, I experienced a failure that still embarrasses me. (I think our failures should be included along with our successes.) There was a lot of money available for mathematical research at that time, and Hans Lewy got me into some work on hydrodynamics that was being done at Stanford under Al Bowker. It was not my field, and I shouldn't have taken it on, but I did. Although I worked very hard, I was able to prove absolutely nothing. When the year was up, I resigned without even turning in a report. I had nothing to report. Bowker later became Chancellor here at Berkeley, and I could hardly bring myself to look him in the face.

After I escaped from hydrodynamics, I read an article about Adlai Stevenson, then the governor of Illinois, which interested me very much. I became even more interested after he was nominated for president and promised in his acceptance speech "to talk sense to the American people." (This was in the middle of the McCarthy era.) Although I did not entirely abandon mathematics, I spent a lot of time on politics in the next half dozen years. I was even county manager for Alan Cranston's first political campaign.

**"They were more polite to me."** And I continued to struggle with the Tenth Problem. In 1961 Martin Davis, Hilary Putnam and I published a joint paper, "The undecidability of exponential diophantine equations," which used ideas from the papers Martin and I had presented at the International Congress along with various new results. The paper discusses what is sometimes referred to as the Robinson hypothesis (or, as Martin calls it, "J.R.") to the effect that there is some diophantine relation that grows faster than a polynomial but not too terribly fast—less than some function that could be expressed in exponentials. If so, then by my earlier result, we would be able to define exponentiation. It would follow from the definition that exponential diophantine equations would be equivalent to diophantine equations and that, therefore, the solution to Hilbert's tenth problem would be negative. At the time many people told Martin that this approach was misguided, to say the least. They were more polite to me.

By the time the joint paper was published, my heart had broken down, just as the doctor in San Diego had predicted; and I had to have surgery to clear out the mitral valve. One month after the operation I bought my first bicycle. It has been followed by half a dozen increasingly better bikes and many cycling trips in this country and in Holland. Raphael sometimes complains that while other men's wives buy fur coats and diamond bracelets, his wife buys bicycles.

**A Birthday Wish** Throughout the 1960's, while publishing a few papers on other things, I kept working on the Tenth Problem, but I was getting rather discouraged. For a while I ceased to believe in the Robinson hypothesis, although Raphael insisted that it was true but just too difficult to prove. I even worked in the opposite direction, trying to show that there was a positive solution to Hilbert's problem, but I never published any of that work. It was the custom in our family to have a get-together for each family member's birthday. When it came time for me to blow out the candles on my cake, I always wished, year after year, that the Tenth Problem would be solved—not that I would solve it, but just that it would be solved. I felt that I couldn't bear to die without knowing the answer.

Finally—on February 15, 1970—Martin telephoned me from New York to say that John Cocke had just returned from Moscow with the report that a 22-year-old mathematician in Leningrad had proved that the relation $n = F_{2m}$, where $F_{2m}$ is a Fibonacci number, is diophantine. This was all that we needed. It followed that the solution to Hilbert's tenth problem is negative—a general method for determining whether a given diophantine equation has a solution in integers does not exist.

(*Facing page*) On one of the many outings she was able to enjoy after heart surgery in 1961.

Martin did not know the name of the mathematician or the method he had used. I was so excited by the news that I wanted to call Leningrad right away to find out if it were really true. Raphael and other people here said no, hold on—the world had gone for seventy years without knowing the solution to the Tenth Problem, surely I could wait a few more weeks! I wasn't so sure. Fortunately I didn't have to wait that long. Three days later John McCarthy called from Stanford to say that in Novosibirsk he had heard a talk by Ceitin on the proof, which was the work of a mathematician named Yuri Matijasevič. John had taken notes on Ceitin's talk. While he was doing so, he had felt that he understood the proof, but by the time he got back to Stanford he found that he couldn't make much sense of his notes. He offered to send them to me if I wanted to see them. Of course I wanted to, very much.

### The Next Best Thing

When I received the notes, I sent a copy to Martin even before I went over them myself. He told me later that he was always glad that I had let him go through them on his own. It was the next best thing to solving the problem himself.

It was quite immediately clear what Matijasevič had done. By using the Fibonacci numbers, a series that had been known to mathematicians since the beginning of the thirteenth century, he had been able to construct a function that met the requirements of the Robinson hypothesis. There was nothing in his proof that would not be included in a course in elementary number theory!

Just one week after I had first heard the news from Martin, I was able to write to Matijasevič:

". . . now I know it is true, it is beautiful, it is wonderful.

"If you really are 22 [he was], I am especially pleased to think that when I first made the conjecture you were a baby and I just had to wait for you to grow up!"

That year when I went to blow out the candles on my cake, I stopped in mid-breath, suddenly realizing that the wish I had made for so many years had actually come true.

I have been told that some people think that I was blind not to see the solution myself when I was so close to it. On the other hand, no one else saw it either. There are lots of things, just lying on the beach as it were, that we don't see until someone else picks one of them up. Then we all see that one.

In 1971 Raphael and I visited Leningrad and became acquainted with Matijasevič and with his wife, Nina, a physicist. At that time, in connection with the solution of Hilbert's problem and the role played in it by the Robinson hypothesis, Linnik told me that I was the second most famous Robinson in the Soviet Union, the first being Robinson Crusoe. Yuri and I have since written two papers together and, after the 1974 De Kalb symposium on the Hilbert problems, Martin, Yuri and I collaborated on a paper, "Positive aspects of a negative solution."

I have written so incompletely and non-technically about my more than twenty years of work on the Tenth Problem because Martin, who contributed as much as I to its ultimate solution, has published several excellent papers telling the whole story. These include both a popular account in *Scientific American* and a technical one in the *American Mathematical Monthly*.

Yuri Matijasevič at the time he was working on his solution of Hilbert's tenth problem.

*More Mathematical People*

The three whose work resulted in the solution of Hilbert's tenth problem, together for the first time: Martin Davis, Julia Robinson and Yuri Matijasevič.

When any one of Hilbert's problems is solved or even just some progress made toward a solution, everybody who has had any part in the work gets a great deal of attention. In 1975, for instance, I became the first woman mathematician to be elected to the National Academy of Sciences although there are other women mathematicians who in my opinion are more deserving of the honor.

**Professor Robinson's Wife**

When the University press office received the news, someone there called the mathematics department to find out just who Julia Robinson was. "Why, that's Professor Robinson's wife." "Well," replied the caller, "Professor Robinson's wife has just been elected to the National Academy of Sciences." Up to that time I had not been an official member of the University's mathematics faculty, although from time to time I had taught a class at the request of the department chairman. In fairness to the University, I should explain that because of my health, even after the heart operation, I would not have been able to carry a full-time teaching load. As soon as I was elected to the Academy, however, the University offered me a full professorship with the duty of teaching one-fourth time—which I accepted.

In 1982 I was nominated for the presidency of the American Mathematical Society. I realized that I had been chosen because I was a woman and because I had the seal of approval, as it were, of the National Academy. After discussion with Raphael, who thought I should decline and save my energy for mathematics, and other members of my family, who differed with him, I decided that as a woman and a mathematician I had no alternative but to accept. I have always tried to do everything I could to encourage talented women to become research mathematicians. I found my service as president of the Society taxing but very, very satisfying.

Other honors, including election to the American Academy of Arts and Sciences, an honorary degree from Smith College, and a generous grant from the MacArthur Foundation, have come with disconcerting speed. Even more general notice has been taken of me. *Vogue* and the *Village Voice* have inquired after my opinions, and the *Ladies' Home Journal* has included me in a list of the one hundred most outstanding women in America.

All this attention has been gratifying but also embarrassing. What I really am is a mathematician. Rather than being remembered as the first woman this or that, I would prefer to be remembered, as a mathematician should, simply for the theorems I have proved and the problems I have solved.

*JULIA BOWMAN ROBINSON*   St. Louis, Missouri, December 8, 1919. A.B. 1940, M.A. 1941, Ph.D. 1948, UC Berkeley. Field: logic. Professor of Mathematics, UC Berkeley. President AMS, 1983–84. Colloquium Lecturer (AMS) !980; Noether Lecturer (AWM) 1982. MacArthur Prize Fellowship 1982. American Academy of Arts and Sciences, National Academy of Sciences. Died July 30, 1985.

# MARY ELLEN RUDIN

Mary Ellen Rudin is now the first occupant of a chair endowed in honor of the pioneering English mathematician Grace Chisholm Young, and one of the most respected workers in set theoretic topology, but for many years she had "no real job" in academia—and liked it that way, she says. She has a bibliography of some seventy research papers and says she likes best to do mathematics surrounded by her family, in the living room of her "very open" Frank Lloyd Wright house. She believes she might have followed any of a number of other interests if the legendary R. L. Moore had not signed her up for mathematics during freshman registration at the University of Texas: "I am a mathematician because R. L. Moore made me a mathematician."

□ □ □

**MP**  *Tell us something about Hillsboro, Texas, where you were born.*

**RUDIN**  I don't know anything about Hillsboro, Texas. I lived there only two weeks. My father was a civil engineer. He worked for the State Highway Department so home would change as the projects that he was working on changed. He was building something in Hillsboro. He was there for a brief period of time and probably stayed an extra week or two, maybe an extra six months, because I was about to be born; but as soon as I was born, we moved on to the next project in a different town.

**MP**  *You mentioned something to us earlier about growing up in primitive conditions. Were you were actually living where he was working—in construction camps?*

**RUDIN**  No. We always lived in towns near where he was working. When I said primitive conditions, I was referring to the fact that when I was about six he was sent to a little town in southwest Texas called Leakey—spelled just like the name of the anthropologist, and actually it is his family for whom the town is named. It is in the hills of southwest Texas. It is about 3000 feet high in the canyon formed by the Frio river with mountains on all sides. In those days you entered the town by going fifty miles up a dirt road—you had to ford the river seven times to get there. It was the county seat, but to get to the other town in the county, which was over a mountain, you had to go back out the fifty miles and take a different road up a different canyon. My father was there to build a new road, but the Depression hit and the State Highway Department never completed the road while we lived there.

**MP** *So was your father out of a job?*

**RUDIN** No. He bought land for the road, he surveyed for the road, he made plans for the road, but they never got the money to *build* the road. He stayed there for a long time. I had almost all my growing up in this little town in southwest Texas. It was a real mountain community. Many kids came to school on horseback. We had a well and an electric pump, which gave us running water, but most people didn't have running water or any of the things that you think of as being perfectly standard. Yet it was wonderful. There were miles of wild country and beautiful trees along the river. Everywhere there was a beautiful view.

**MP** *What did your mother think about living there?*

**RUDIN** She was a little shocked at first, I think, but she learned to enjoy it.

**MP** *Where had she come from?*

**RUDIN** She had come from a town in the foothills of the Allegheny mountains, which she thought of as the center of culture and education. Both my grandmothers grew up in this same town, and they both went to college there.

**MP** *Both grandmothers?*

**RUDIN** Yes. The town was Winchester, Tennessee, and there was a college there for women which had been founded just at the close of the Civil War.

**MP** *What was the name of it?*

**RUDIN** It was, let me see—Mary Sharp College. It was a real college for women. They had art and music and things like that, but they also had philosophy and mathematics and so on. It was quite unusual at that time and in that part of the world to have a college for women that wasn't just a finishing school. My paternal grandmother, who was born in 1852, attended this college and was very good at mathematics. She was proud of that. My other grandmother was not so particularly good at mathematics. At least she didn't brag about it later in life.

**MP** *Did your grandmothers teach after they graduated?*

**RUDIN** No. They both married quite young and both had families—one had eight children and the other had six. But they valued education tremendously and always talked about their own educations. They educated their daughters as well as their sons and saw to it that all their children had some kind of advanced education. By the time my mother came along, this same little town had a coeducational school called Winchester Normal, and she attended that. Then she went to Peabody in Nashville, which was a teachers' college, and took some courses at Vanderbilt, too.

**MP** *What was your mother's maiden name?*

Baby Mary Ellen Estill.

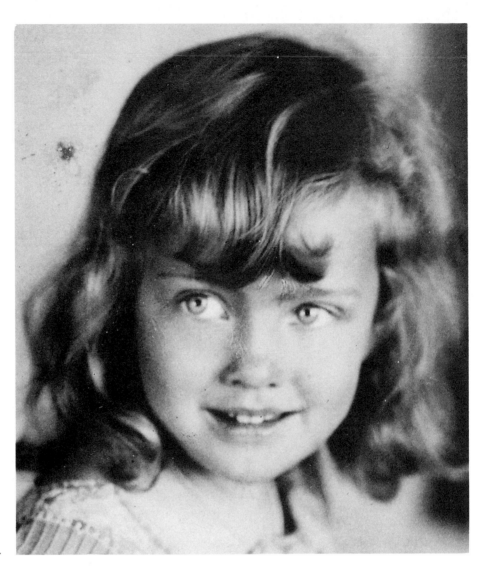

She remembers liking all subjects as a child.

**RUDIN** Irene Shook. It's Dutch, but I don't think it was spelled that way when it was Dutch. My father was Joe Jefferson Estill. The name is French, but it wasn't spelled that way when it was French either. They were both descended from people who came to the United States long before it was the United States; that is, in the early 1700's. They came over the mountains from Virginia and settled in the valleys of Tennessee. My father's family were mostly lawyers and doctors, but the story is that they made at least part of their living playing cards. My mother's people were farmers primarily.

**An Only Child of Two**     **MP** *Were you an only child?*

**RUDIN** Yes. No. I was an only child of two. I am ten years older than my brother so I was raised in a way as an only child. When I left home, he was ready to enter first grade. I love him dearly—we are very close friends—but he's more like a nephew or a son than a brother.

**MP** *Tell us about the schooling you received in Leakey.*

**RUDIN** It was a very simple community. Nobody had any money at all. We were rich because we had a regular salary coming in. But the principal object that existed in the town was the school, and it was a very good school. I was definitely not the best student in my class. There were five of us who graduated, and there was one girl who was much smarter than I. There was another very bright kid. I was maybe third out of five. I went to the university thinking that I would make C's but I made A's without any trouble.

MP  *How do you account for the fact that the school was so good in such a little town?*

RUDIN  Many of the teachers were the children of ranchers who lived there, and they had come back home to teach. The number of jobs available in the world at that time was limited. I suspect that they would have had other opportunities in another time and place. But the community valued education.

MP  *It would be interesting to track the children from that community over time to see if the education really has paid off.*

**Lots of Time to Think**

RUDIN  Elton Lacey, who is chairman of the math department at Texas A. & M., also grew up in that same little community. We had a very good school, and there were some very bright kids. We also had a lot of time to develop games. We had few toys. There was no movie house in town. We listened to things on the radio. That was our only contact with the outside world. But our games were very elaborate and purely in the imagination. I think actually that that is something that contributes to making a mathematician—having some time to think and being in the habit of imagining all sorts of complicated things. We thought of wherever we were as some wonderful land. And this is my house and this tree is a castle and that's where you whatever, depending on whether we were wanting to be Hollywood stars or whether we were wanting to be in antiquity. The number of books we had to read was fairly limited. The school library consisted of a cabinet about this big. We had more books at home than there were in the school library. All my friends read the books in our house, too. Although I came from a group of people who were educated and who valued education tremendously, I grew up in very primitive, simple surroundings where I had lots of time just to think. But there was never any question about the fact that I would go to the university and that I would do something with my education. My mother had been a teacher before she married. She expected that I should earn my living and that what I did should be an interesting thing to do.

MP  *What interested you most in school at that time?*

RUDIN  I enjoyed school, but it isn't clear to me that I was interested in one particular thing or that one thing interested me more than the others. I liked school as much for my friends and for talking with my friends about the ideas we found there as for school itself. I certainly didn't like school to the exclusion of play.

MP  *You sound like a normal kid. Third down in a class of five.*

RUDIN  That's exactly how it was.

MP  *How did you happen to go to the University of Texas?*

RUDIN  Well, my father had gone there. He considered it a first class place.

There was always time for a fishing trip since there was no movie house in town.

*More Mathematical People*

**MP**  *When you set off for the university, did you have in mind a special subject that you wanted to study?*

**R. L. Moore**

**RUDIN**  Oh, absolutely not! My father went along with me because he had an old girlfriend who taught English there and he wanted to talk to her about what I should take. They both felt that I should take just a perfectly general liberal arts course, partly to find out what I was interested in and partly because they both believed very strongly—and my mother certainly felt that way too—that one should be educated in the sense of having a broad education. So on the appropriate morning I went to the gymnasium to register for the things they had decided on. There was a mass of people, but there were very few people at the mathematics table so I was sent over there. The man who was sitting at the table was an old white-haired gentleman. He and I discussed all kinds of things for a long time. I now know the kinds of things that he must have asked me. There would have been lots of sentences with *if* and *then*. I used *if* and *then* correctly. I also used *and* and *or* correctly from a mathematician's standpoint. At the end of our conversation he signed me up for the courses that I had written on my little slip of paper. When I went to my math class the next day, I found that the professor was R. L. Moore—the same man who had talked to me at the registration table.

**MP**  *You met him literally on your first day on campus?*

**RUDIN**  On literally my first day on campus I met R. L. Moore. And *literally* on my first day I *was selected* by him.

**MP**  *How large was the university at that time?*

**RUDIN**  Eleven thousand students.

**MP**  *That's still rather large for him to be sitting there in the gym and evaluating individual freshmen.*

**RUDIN**  He always did that. He was looking for students.

In Leakey, Texas: "We had more books at home than there were in the school library."

**MP**  *Well, he got you.*

**RUDIN**  Yes. There was no one else in that first math class who was at all bright so far as I could tell. It was a trig class. The next semester I took analytic geometry, and R. L. Moore taught it. The next semester I took calculus, and R. L. Moore taught it. It never occurred to me that that was really peculiar. I was not very smart! But I was fully aware that in some way he was teaching for my benefit. He would call on other people first and let them fall on their faces. Then he would have me solve the problem for them. I was always the last person he would call on.

**MP**  *Did this involve going up to the board?*

**RUDIN**  Yes. Everything was set up on the basis of proving theorems from axioms. It never occurred to me that there was any other kind of mathematics. At the end of the calculus course, for instance, I'm not sure I knew that the derivative of $\sin x$ was $\cos x$. But I could prove all sorts of theorems about continuity and differentiability and so on!

**MP**  *In other words, you were getting an introductory analysis course.*

The legendary R. L. Moore (1882–1974)—pictured shortly before he registered Mary Ellen for his calculus course.

RUDIN   Exactly. And it was a first-rate course in introductory analysis. But it wasn't until I taught calculus myself that I learned all those formulas. Now I find it really incredible!

MP   *So, after Moore lassoed you, you immediately zeroed in on math?*

RUDIN   Oh no! I found the whole university just fascinating. There was that rare books library that had everything in the world in it, and I loved to go there. I loved the history courses. I loved the English courses. I enjoyed physics very much. I took a lot of philosophy. Even in my senior year I took courses all over the map—almost as much philosophy as mathematics, almost as much history as mathematics, almost as much English as mathematics, almost as much Spanish as mathematics. I was equally good, as far as I could tell, in all these subjects. Even though I was having this special coaching—you might say—in math, it was still just one of many things I was taking. When I was a senior, I went to the vocational guidance office and said, "I have just taken a broad general course, and now I feel I should be specializing in something. I clearly need some advice." They gave me a whole battery of tests. Afterwards they said, "You're kidding! You don't know you're good in mathematics?" I said, "I know I'm good in mathematics, but I can do other things too. I don't want to teach high school." Which is really all it occurred to me that one could do with mathematics. They said, "Just relax. They'll invite you to stay and go to graduate school." And indeed within a week (I almost suspected that they had called the math department) I was offered an instructorship. So I stayed and went to graduate school. I am sure Moore would have caught me anyway. He knew exactly what he was going to do with me. He just hadn't told me yet.

MP   *Did you have any mathematics teachers besides Moore?*

RUDIN   Well, yes, but not until my senior year. Then I had a course in algebra from somebody else and a course in differential equations from somebody else.

MP   *So you had a course from Moore every semester?*

**"I'm a child of Moore."**

RUDIN   Every single semester during my entire career at the University of Texas. I'm a mathematician because Moore caught me and demanded that I become a mathematician. He schooled me and pushed me at just the right rate. He always looked for people who had not been influenced by other mathematical experiences, and he caught me before I had been subjected to influence of any kind. I was pure, unadulterated. He almost never got anybody like that.

MP   *You* are *a child of Moore.*

RUDIN   I'm a child of Moore. I was always conscious of being maneuvered by him. I hated being maneuvered. But part of his technique of teaching was to build your ability to withstand pressure from outside—pressure to give up mathematical research, pressure to change mathematical fields, pressure to achieve non-mathematical goals. So he maneuvered you in order to build your ego. He built your confidence that you could do *anything*. No matter what mathematical problem you were faced with, you could do it. I have that total confidence to this day. You give me the definitions, and I'll solve the problem. I'm a problem solver, primarily a counterexample discoverer. Part

*More Mathematical People*

of that is a Moore thing, too. That is, he didn't always give us correct the-orems, at least half of his statements were false. So we had to think about them as a research mathematician might. I still have this feeling that if a problem can be stated in a simple form that I can really understand, then I should be able to solve it even if doing so involves building some complicated structure. Of course, I have had some failures. You can guess how often.

**MP**  *But you've never failed in confidence?*

**RUDIN**  No, having failed 5,000 times doesn't seem to make me any less confident. At least I don't feel bound by any serious constraints or doubts about my ability.

**MP**  *Tell us a little more about your graduate school experience.*

**RUDIN**  I had entered the university in 1941. That was the beginning of the war for the United States, and all Moore's students went off to war except Bing, who had an old injury which didn't allow him to go. Because of the speeded up wartime schedule, I had just three years as an undergraduate, but graduate school for me was fantastic. I started in December 1944, and by September 1945 the war was over and the men were back. So I started with R. D. Anderson, R. H. Bing, Ed Moise—let's see, who have I left out? Ed Burgess was there, too. There were five of us.

**MP**  *That's quite a collection!*

**"I was the killer."**  **RUDIN**  We were a fantastic class. Each of us could eat the others up. Moore did this to you. He somehow built up your ego and your competitive-ness. He was tremendously successful in that, partly because he selected peo-ple who naturally had those qualities he valued. He immediately separated Moise and Bing, who were further along than the rest of us. But still we were really together, and we have all been very close to each other for our entire careers. That is, we were a team. We were a team against Moore and we were a team against each other, but at the same time we were a team for each other. It was a very close family type of relationship. Actually in our group there was another, a sixth, whom we killed off right away. He was a very smart guy—I think he went into computer science eventually—but he wasn't strong enough to compete with the rest of us. Moore always began with him and then let one of us show him how to solve the problem correctly. And, boy, did this work badly for him! It builds your ego to be able to do a prob-lem when someone else can't, but it destroys that person's ego. I never liked that feature of Moore's classes. Yet I participated in it. Very often in the undergraduate classes. I mean, I was the killer. He used me that way, and I was conscious of being used that way.

**MP**  *You were Moore's only woman student?*

**RUDIN**  Moore had several women students after me, and he had had two women students previously. The first, Anna Mullikin, wrote a fantastic the-sis at Pennsylvania and then immediately went off to China as a missionary. The next was Harlan Miller. She later taught at Texas Women's College and was very influential as a teacher and an administrator, but she never did any research mathematics after her thesis. He was tremendously disappointed in both of these women.

**MP**  *How did Moore conduct a graduate class?*

RUDIN    He didn't lecture about mathematics at all. He put definitions on the board and gave us theorems to prove. Most of the time we didn't have the theorem proved that was supposed to be proved that day, and so we discussed whatever. We discussed life. And while we were doing that, he worked on us in various ways. He obviously worked on me—now that I think about it many years later—to make *very* sure that I would continue to do research after I got my degree. He viewed his two earlier women students as failures, and he didn't hesitate to tell me about them in great detail so I would realize that he didn't want to have another failure with a woman.

MP    *He must have had some male failures, too.*

RUDIN    Oh, he had plenty of male failures. There's no question.

MP    *You were saying that you would talk about things other than mathematics in class. What sort of things?*

RUDIN    Moore would come in and stand at the board and sort of start the conversation. "Miss Estill, do you have anything to report today?" "Mr. Anderson, what do you have to say?" There were maybe three people in the class, always a small group.

MP    *So if nobody had anything to report?*

RUDIN    Then we would start discussing something—it could be politics or anything. Ed Burgess, for instance, remembers the following incident, which I don't remember at all. We were discussing locking doors. I said that I would never lock the door to my house unless my husband insisted. Ed says that Moore literally pounced on that, saying, "Husband! But, Miss Estill, I thought that you were going to be a mathematician." Moore intended to elicit a response from me; but although he may have had his doubts, I never saw any contradiction in being both a housewife and a mathematician—of the two I was more driven to be a housewife. Now I don't remember this particular incident, but I do remember that locking doors was a subject that we often discussed.

MP    *Was there much interaction among the Moore students outside the classroom?*

RUDIN    Very little. We went our own ways and did our own things.

MP    *Were there any social things with Moore and his wife?*

RUDIN    Once in a blue moon there would be something social, but Mrs. Moore didn't do social things very easily and maybe he didn't either. Actually there weren't a lot of social things in mathematics at the University of Texas in those days.

MP    *Tell us about your thesis.*

RUDIN    It was one of Moore's many unsolved problems. His technique was to feed all kinds of problems to us. He gave us lists of statements. Some were true, some were false, some he knew were true, some he knew were false, some were fairly easy to prove or disprove, others very hard. There would be all kinds of unsolved and solved problems in the same batch, and there was no way of distinguishing between them. We worked on whatever we jolly well pleased. I solved one of the unsolved problems. Actually I found a counterexample to a well-known conjecture. The technique I used is now called "Building a Pixley-Roy Space". Two mathematicians named Pixley and Roy tried to read my thesis, which was written in Moore's old-fashioned language and was not terribly well written besides, and gave a beautiful simplified description of the technique. At the time I wrote my thesis, I had never in my life seen a single mathematics paper!

MP   *You had never read* any *mathematics papers?*

**On Not Reading Mathematics Papers**

RUDIN   I told you that I was pure and unadulterated. I only knew the mathematics that Moore fed me. The mathematical language that he used was his own. I didn't know the standard definition of *compact*; I didn't know the correct definition of *limit point*. I didn't know how mathematical words were used at all. Instead of *open set*, for instance, he used *region*. His language was completely different from the language of the mathematical literature. I didn't know any other language.

MP   *He told his students—at least so I have heard—"I don't want you going to the library and reading papers."*

RUDIN   I don't remember ever being told that I shouldn't read mathematical papers, but I was never tempted. It's true, however, that he sometimes encouraged people to go out into the hall so that they would not hear a proof. I would not do such a thing. If somebody proved something first, he proved it first, and I would listen to it.

MP   *Why do you think Moore did that?*

RUDIN   He wanted to build your independence—whether the other person's proof was right or wrong. Of course if it was wrong, he'd be delighted to have you there because then you could discover that it was wrong.

MP   *How would he know a proof was wrong in advance?*

RUDIN   First of all, he did have some inner sense. Second, he tried to get students to have the attitude that they didn't want to listen to someone else's proof. I rebelled against that, but there were people who did go out. I think that none of our group ever went out. That wasn't our style. But when you read about Moore, you will read that he tried to get people to do that.

MP   *He never referred in class to other people's work?*

RUDIN   Never, never, never.

MP   *You grew up in a strange world.*

RUDIN   In a strange, unreal world. Completely. I still dislike reading mathematical papers, and I learn any other way I possibly can. My first two or three papers were all written in Moore's old-fashioned language.

MP   *How did you feel about your mathematical education later?*

**"I felt cheated."**

RUDIN   I really resented it, I admit. I felt cheated because, although I had a Ph.D., I had never really been to graduate school. I hadn't learned any of the things that people ordinarily learn when they go to graduate school. I didn't know any algebra, literally none. I didn't know any topology. I didn't know any analysis—I didn't even know what an analytic function was. I had had my confidence built, and my confidence was plenty strong. But when my students get their Ph.D.'s, they know everything I can get them to learn about what's been done. Of course, they're not always so confident as I was.

**MP** *Reading other people's work is a great way to destroy one's confidence.*

**RUDIN** Maybe it is. At least that was Moore's opinion.

**MP** *Weren't there any departmental requirements at Texas? Any qualifying exams for the doctorate?*

**RUDIN** He *was* the department. I took exams in philosophy, which was my graduate minor, but I never took an exam in mathematics in my life. Moore students were good in direct proportion to how fast they learned after they got out. I still feel seriously deprived by the shortage of the things I learned. I resent that, I guess, but at the same time I'm conscious of how much—well, I wouldn't have been a mathematician at all if it hadn't been for R. L. Moore.

**MP** *How about finding a position after you got your Ph.D.?*

**RUDIN** Getting a position was just like going to graduate school. I never applied for one. Moore simply told me that I'd be going to Duke the next year. He and J. M. Thomas, who was a professor at Duke, had been on a train trip together. Duke had a women's college which was sort of pressuring them to hire a woman mathematician. So Moore told Thomas, "I've got the very best, and I'll ship her to you next September."

**MP** *What feelings toward Moore, as a person, did you develop over time?*

The young instructor conducts a class on her favorite subject.

*More Mathematical People*

"I never applied for a job in my life."

RUDIN   Oh, I had very warm, enthusiastic feelings for him, although I also had very negative feelings. I was conscious of both levels. I was aware that he was bigoted—he was—but I also was aware that he played the role of a bigot sometimes in order to get our reactions, maybe even to keep us from being bigots. I'm never sure to what extent that was true. Moise, for instance, was a Jew. Moore always claimed that Jews were inferior. I was a woman. He always pointed out that his women students were inferior. Moise and I both loved him dearly, and we knew that he supported us fantastically and did not think that we were inferior—in fact, he thought that we were super special. On the other hand, he wanted us to be very confident of ourselves in what he undoubtedly viewed as a somewhat disadvantaged position. Now then, did he play the role of a bigot to elicit a response? I have no idea.

MP   *His talking about his former women failures probably made you say to yourself, "I'm not going to be one of those!"*

RUDIN   I can't say that I really ever identified with them. Something else Moore built into all of us was our responsibility to be part of the mathematical community—to take part in the American Mathematical Society, very strongly, and to take part in the Mathematical Association of America even though it was not a research organization. He believed in going to meetings of professional organizations and participating in the meetings. That's something that all of us have done more than our share of. Moore was president of the American Association for the Advancement of Science; and Moore, Whyburn, Wilder and Bing were all presidents of the AMS as well as colloquium lecturers for the AMS and members of the National Academy of Sciences. Moore, Wilder, Bing, Moise, Young and Anderson were MAA presidents. All of us have served on endless committees for these organization.

MP   *What about editing responsibilities?*

RUDIN   He believed very strongly in doing that, too.

MP   *Even though he never read?*

RUDIN   Oh yes, he considered publication absolutely vital. We should publish and be very involved, even if we shouldn't read too much about what other people were doing.

MP   *But he sent you off to Duke never having read anything?*

RUDIN   Right.

MP   *And Duke was where you met Walter Rudin. Will you tell us a little about Walter, too?*

RUDIN   Walter had grown up in Vienna. He was part of an old Austrian Jewish family. His great-grandfather, who was a philanthropist, had been knighted by Franz Josef. However, when the Germans came into Austria in 1938, the Austrians rejected their Jews, and Walter now totally rejects his Austrian background. His parents managed to send Walter and his sister to school in Switzerland. It was maybe six months before they themselves could leave Austria. They left without a thing except the clothes on their backs. They showed up in Switzerland thinking that they would live there forever,

Just married—Walter and Mary Ellen Rudin in 1953.

but it very soon became clear that that was not a possibility. So they moved on to France where they again expected to live forever. But then the French became very frightened about having so many German-speaking refugees in the country so they put Walter and his father in internment camps in different parts of France. Walter volunteered for the working corps in the French army. He was nineteen, I guess, and he was in the French army for about two weeks before the Germans came in. He was told by the French that he could just walk away. He got to England and spent the war years there. After the war he came to visit in this country, where his parents had managed to come. He went down to Duke to see his sister, who was in graduate school—she's a chemist—and while he was there he talked to the people in the math department. He had never gone to college, but he persuaded them that maybe he could be a junior. Four years later he had a Ph.D. in mathematics. So we were both fresh young Ph.D.'s. We went together, but we didn't—I think there were times during that year when I was interested in marrying Walter and there were times when he was interested in marrying me, but it was never at the same time. We were both just starting out in life.

**MP** *When did you and Walter get married?*

**RUDIN**   We got married in '53. Walter was going to Rochester that year, and jobs were very scarce. During the time at Duke I had worked on problems related to Souslin's conjecture and had constructed a lot of weird connected sets in the plane, one of which disproved a conjecture of Wilder's, so I was beginning to be reasonably well known. Wilder arranged for me to go to the University of Michigan. You see, he had applied for a grant for me. I hadn't applied, he had applied.

**MP**   *So it was an extension of the Moore method by a Moore student?*

**A Built-in Family**

**RUDIN**   Well, when Wilder wired that he had the money for me, I wired back, "I'm sorry but I'm getting married and going to Rochester." And Wilder arranged for the grant to be transferred from Michigan to Rochester! I always had this built-in family that really took care of me. For instance, I gave colloquia at Virginia, where Whyburn was. It never occurred to me that it was slightly difficult to be a woman mathematician.

**MP**   *But when you married, there was absolutely no guarantee that you would have anything to do at Rochester.*

**RUDIN**   No, but it absolutely never occurred to me to worry. I was married.

**MP**   *Did you and Walter ever discuss the question of your career?*

**RUDIN**   No. Of course not. I didn't know any couple that did. I didn't even think of mathematics as a career. The University of Rochester hadn't known I was coming with Walter, but they immediately gave me a calculus class to teach. So I taught. I had a private office. I didn't really have a position, but— oh well, I was a temporary part-time something. And that's the kind of job I have had almost all my life until 1971, when I became a full professor. I have had non-jobs wherever we happened to be. I loved my non-jobs. I always had all the goodies that go with being a mathematician. I had graduate students, I had seminars, I had colleagues who loved me. I never had committees. I never had a trigonometry class. I was always just asked, "Is there something you'd like to teach this semester?" And I would say, "I think I'll teach a graduate course in . . ." or maybe "I think I'll take this semester off." I often had grant money. It didn't make that much difference in my life though, since Walter always had a good job. But I was a mathematician, and I always thought of myself as a mathematician.

**MP**   *And a mother.*

**RUDIN**   Oh yes. We had two babies in the first two years. So I was very busy and very happy as a mother and certainly expected to be a mother and wanted to be a mother very much. At first, at Rochester and later at Yale, I had great responsibilities at home because I had friends rather than hired people helping me with my children. When we moved to Madison, however, I happened on an absolutely fantastic woman named Lila Hilgendorf. She had been the wife of a farmer and had had six children. She was wonderful with children.

**MP**   *By this time you had your four?*

**RUDIN**   There were still just two; but from the beginning, after we moved to Madison, she came regularly to my house. She cared for the children and

The Rudins on their honeymoon.

did some housecleaning. When I would walk into the house, she would walk out; and when I had to go, she was there. We had that relationship until she died this year. She was absolutely the best mother I ever saw, and my children just adored her. One thing that she did for me was absolutely fantastic. The first weekend after my retarded child was born, she said, "Oh, I just have to have him for the weekend!" And he went to her house for the weekend for the rest of her life. Actually he lived at her house the last several years. So when people ask me how it is, in my position, to have four children, I have to say that when you've got Lila, it's easy. I am afraid that few women will ever have such an easy, non-pressured career as mine.

MP  *You were, nevertheless, cranking out papers at quite a rate.*

RUDIN  Oh yes. Terrific. But I didn't have to prove to anybody that I was a mathematician, and I didn't have to do all the grungy things that you have to do in order to have a career as a mathematician. The pressure was entirely from within. I did lots of mathematics, but I did it because I wanted to do it and enjoyed doing it, not because it would further my career. Then, when the time came that I was relatively free, it all of a sudden became possible for me to become a professor. I was instantly made a professor. I mean, the guilt feelings in the math department were such that nobody even asked me if I wanted to be a professor. I was simply presented with this full professorship. My first reaction was to say no, but Walter persuaded me that I should say yes. He said, "It's insurance I can't buy you. Why don't you just ask for half-time?" So I had a full professorship halftime until I discovered that I was building no retirement. They multiply by half three times: half the number of hours, half the amount of salary, and half the years of service.

**MP**  *An eighth.*

**RUDIN**  Precisely. The children were grown by then so I decided to teach fulltime, but I'd really like to go back to halftime. Teaching takes a lot of time, and even though I enjoy it and have had some wonderful graduate students, I think a halftime career is just great.

**MP**  *Especially when you have a husband.*

**RUDIN**  It's a function of having somebody to earn a living for you.

**MP**  *You say that you enjoy teaching and you have had some great students. Do you use the Moore method of teaching?*

**"I don't believe in the Moore Method."**
**RUDIN**  No. Not at all. I guess I don't believe in it. Also I have not got the patience.

**MP**  *What is your way of teaching?*

**RUDIN**  Oh, I'm a perfectly straightforward, enthusiastic lecturer.

**MP**  *You bubble.*

**RUDIN**  I bubble, and I get students enthusiastic. I'm able to explain things. I'm a good lecturer, I think. I've never tried to use the Moore method—I guess because I got burned by having been a student under it. Bing, however, always used the Moore method. And there are other Moore students and students of Moore students, and so on, who have used it and used it very effectively—combining it with teaching students to read. Nobody ever does it Moore's way. Fortunately. I do try, however, to give students interesting problems to work on.

**MP**  *How do you find interesting problems?*

**RUDIN**  Oh it's easy. There are a lot of interesting problems around.

**MP**  *When you give a student a problem, have you more or less worked it out in your head?*

**RUDIN**  Sometimes.

**MP**  *Pólya told us that he never gave a student a dissertation problem unless he knew that it could be done. We pressed him. Did that mean that he had done it himself? He said, well, yes.*

**RUDIN**  Effectively. Yes. Of course, I have had students who don't need any assistance of that kind. That's the kind of student that a teacher loves to have. They teach you all kinds of things. You don't teach them. But you also have students who need a particular problem, and you try to give it to them. My technique is not so much to have solved the problem completely as to have in mind two or three things that I think can be done and to have done enough thinking about them to see that they are not too difficult. I try to give my students two or three things to work on. I believe in working on several things at once, even though I find it difficult to do that myself. I really like to concentrate on one thing. That's one of my worst flaws as a mathematician.

**MP**  *Incidentally, how do you actually do mathematics?*

RUDIN    I lie on the sofa in the living room with my pencil and paper and think and draw little pictures and try this thing and that thing. I'm interested in how ideas fit together. Actually I'm very geometric in my thinking. I'm not good at numbers at all. Although I do like combinatorics, I'm not really interested in numbers. Walter says that I think one number is just like any other number.

MP    *So you do mathematics lying on the couch in the living room of your Frank Lloyd Wright house?*

**"The house lends itself perfectly to my mathematics."**

RUDIN    Yes. It's a very easy house to work in. It has a living room two stories high, and everything else sort of opens onto that. It actually suits the way I've always handled the household. I have never minded doing mathematics lying on the sofa in the middle of the living room with the children climbing all over me. I like to know, even when I am working on mathematics, what is going on. I like to be in the center of things, so the house lends itself perfectly to my mathematics.

MP    *What about Walter and his mathematics?*

RUDIN    He likes more privacy. We have a study that is quite private, and that is Walter's study. My study is in the middle of the living room—in the middle of our one-room house.

MP    *Then in effect you have no study?*

RUDIN    No. Never have had a study. Never have had any interest in having one.

MP    *I remember reading that Harriet Beecher Stowe wrote her books on her knee in her kitchen with all her children around her.*

The Rudin children: Charlie, Catherine, Eleanor and Robert.

Grace Chisholm Young

**RUDIN** I like that situation. I feel more comfortable and confident when I'm in the middle of things, and to do mathematics you have to feel comfortable and confident.

**MP** *It's interesting that you now occupy a professorial chair honoring the English mathematician Grace Chisholm Young. She was a woman with six children, I believe. Do you happen to know if she operated the same way?*

**RUDIN** I think she must have, basically. Let me get you some things about her from her son, L. C. Young, who is in Madison. You will love them. There's a letter written to her by her husband, who was the mathematician W. H. Young, saying, "Mine the glory now and the knowledge. Yours the knowledge only. But later, when all the loaves and fishes are in, you will get your glory." Something like that.

**MP** *A woman mathematician needs a very special man for a husband.*

**RUDIN** Right. Right. Right.

**MP** *You mentioned earlier that during your college years your social friends were not mathematicians. Now who are your friends?*

**RUDIN** They're more mathematicians now, and the reason is that mathematics in Madison is a very large thing. It includes all kinds of people so it's easier for Walter and me to know mathematicians than to know anyone else. We have very close mathematical friends.

---

# GRACE CHISHOLM YOUNG
## 1868–1944

Grace Young was a "super woman" before the term was invented. In 1889, having initially studied to be a pianist, she entered Girton, the first college in England dedicated to a university education for women, and began to study mathematics. Five years later, under the direction of Felix Klein in Göttingen, she became the first woman to pass the normal examination in Prussia for the doctor's degree. The following year she married her Girton mathematics tutor, W. H. Young, and inspired him—at the age of forty—to obtain a Göttingen degree as well.

The Youngs settled in Switzerland, where she raised their six children and pursued interests in music, languages, biology, education and writing as well as mathematics. She also completed the course (although she did not take the final examination) for a medical degree. Her husband "commuted" to support the family, fulfilling professional obligations at universities as farflung as Aberystwith and Calcutta, all the while sending home mathematical ideas for his wife to study and develop.

"I hope that you enjoy this working for me," he wrote. ". . . I feel partly as if I were teaching you, and setting you problems which I could not quite do myself but could enable you to . . . . The fact is that our papers ought to be published under our joint names, but if this were done neither of us would get the benefit. . . ."

Their mathematical collaboration (220 papers and articles and several books) was indeed so close that future historians of the science have treated it as a joint bibliography. Among his contributions to mathematics are his discovery (independent of Lebesgue) of the Lebesgue integral and his work on Fourier series and cluster sets. Her most important independent work is a group of papers in which she studied derivatives of real functions.

During the second World War, after the fall of France, the Youngs were inadvertently separated. They both died before the end of the war, and so never saw each other again.

*We are grateful to the mathematician Sylvia Wiegand for this information about her grandparents' life and work.*

---

**MP**  *Your mathematical family.*

**RUDIN**  Yes. We have both had lots of graduate students so now we have students and students of students. We're as close to our grandchildren—mathematical grandchildren—as we are to our students. Then we've both had very strong mathematical families behind us. I've described the Moore family to you. And Walter also has worked with a special group of mathematicians in France and Sweden and the U.S. It includes a whole group from the University of Chicago who were students of Zygmund's. This group has been a very strong mathematical family for Walter. We recently went to Yugoslavia for a month, and every place we went we were tremendously welcomed and tremendously taken care of by members of our mathematical families who are there.

**MP**  *What vocations have your children followed?*

**RUDIN**  Our oldest daughter is a linguist. She is an expert on syntax, Bulgarian syntax in particular, but she knows many other languages—south Slavic languages are her specialty. She's married to an anthropologist. Our second daughter is an engineer. She got an undergraduate degree in physics. She works for 3M in Minneapolis and is married to a computer scientist and engineer. Our youngest son is going to be a biochemist and an M.D. He's still in school. And our retarded son is the janitor for the local pizza parlor. Walter says he's our greatest success. He's living way beyond his intelligence while the others are just living up to theirs! I claim that all these kids have inherited the family talent. They're all mathematicians of a sort.

**MP**  *Wait a minute now. . . .*

The Rudin home, designed by Frank Lloyd Wright, has 150 windows.

*More Mathematical People*

RUDIN   How does mathematical talent show itself? It's in pattern recognition. And the linguist daughter, the engineering daughter, the geneticist—it's obvious with them. But even our retarded son has a tremendous amount of this ability. He doesn't have very good judgment, but he has certain specialized talents which seem to me to be very much of the pattern recognition type. He loves history. He can tell you what happened on certain dates. He doesn't know what the facts mean, but he likes to fit them together. He also knows the bus system in Madison absolutely perfectly. If you want to go from anywhere to anywhere at a certain time, he can tell you when the bus will come and where it will go.

MP   *Tell us, when you are at a party with a lot of people who are not mathematicians, and people ask what you do, what do you say?*

RUDIN   I say, "I'm a mathematician."

MP   *And then?*

RUDIN   And then they tell me that mathematics was their worst subject and they need me to help them balance their checkbooks. The same thing they would tell a male mathematician.

MP   *If they ask what kind of mathematics you do, what do you tell them?*

RUDIN   When people ask something like that, I always try to answer them. Not very successfully I'm afraid. I say that there are lots of problems in mathematics that are interesting but have not been solved, and every time you solve one you think up a new one. Mathematics, therefore, is something that expands rather than contracts. And I tell them that these questions are interesting just because you've followed a line of reasoning up to a certain point and the next natural thing to ask is what you're looking at. But that's really not explaining to them what kinds of things might be interesting to me. Sometimes that's pretty hard to explain—even to another mathematician.

MP   *Why do you think that there are not more women in mathematics?*

**Women Mathematicians and Stamina**

RUDIN   Well, it isn't clear to me. I recently talked to some high school students on "What is mathematics?" and, among other things, I talked about that very question. Mathematics is obviously something that women should be able to do very well. It's very intuitive. You don't need a lot of machinery, and you don't need a lot of physical strength. You just need stamina, and women often have a great deal of stamina. So why do not more women become mathematicians? These were high school kids, and I gave them the statistics. When they start out as first graders, the girls are actually a little ahead of the boys because they read better. We know that this is genetic, and we don't worry about it. At the end of elementary school, the girls say that they don't do mathematics very well and the boys say that they do, even though there's evidence to the contrary. At that point girls and boys are approximately the same except for their attitude toward the subject. But then when they get to high school, things change. At Wisconsin we send out to the high school students in the state some really wonderful problems that the math department has worked very hard to develop. These are problems that don't require special knowledge—they just require talent and hard work. We send them around to the high schools in the state and tell the students if they are willing to look at these problems and send us their solutions, we'll grade them and we'll start communicating directly with them, giving them more problems.

MP    *So you're developing a talent bank?*

RUDIN    That's right. It's called the Talent Search. It was started by Grace Chisholm Young's son. But the point of my story is that we almost never get any high school girls to respond. They won't do the hard problems. They're doing their homework better than the boys at that point. But why won't they look at the hard problems?

MP    *Do you have any ideas?*

RUDIN    I really don't. It must be something. There are people at Johns Hopkins who say that it's genetic. Maybe it is, but I really don't believe it. I think that for some reason, probably sociological, girls are refusing to look—they just simply won't *try* something that they view as a hard problem in mathematics. But boys for some reason are willing and eager to look at the hard problems. We'll get forty kids from the state to come to the university at the end of the year, and we're very lucky if there are two girls among them. Now at the university some girls do begin to get really interested in mathematics, and by the time they get to graduate school some are very good—actually a fairly substantial group of them. They seem to recover later, but it's very weird at the high school level.

MP    *You've said that doing mathematics is different for women today than it was for you. Probably not as good?*

**Washing Socks or Doing Mathematics**

RUDIN    Oh, I don't know that it's not as good. In fact, I think that maybe it's better for the following reason. If you do something professionally, it's harder for you to quit. You stay with it in hard times. The young women today are much more professional. We were amateurs. We were enthusiastic amateurs, but we were amateurs. I'm of the housewives' generation. We did what we did because we loved it. And some of us were lucky. For us things worked out, and we did very well. Some were not so lucky, and they just dropped out along the way. But the young women mathematicians today are thinking in terms of a career from the beginning. It's true that they want a fulltime job. They want to do all the research in the world. They want to have a husband and children. They want to have a home. We wanted everything too—in spades—but the one thing we didn't demand, in fact it never occurred to us, was a career. The fact that they are thinking in terms of a career means that when it's a question of washing the socks or doing mathematics, they will often do mathematics. I think it was easier to quit doing mathematics in our day.

MP    *But you didn't quit.*

RUDIN    No. I had the enthusiasm to do it. Julia Robinson certainly didn't quit. But there were those who did. I think we're getting a lot better young women mathematicians now than in my day.

MP    *Certainly a lot more.*

RUDIN   I think that if you get a lot more you'll get more that are better. I think that's happening. And that's really very satisfying to me. I see it coming.

*July 1986 in Oakland, California (DA, CR).*

MARY ELLEN RUDIN   Hillsboro, Texas, December 7, 1924. B.A. 1944, Ph.D. 1949, Texas. Field: set-theoretic topology. Grace Chisholm Young Professor of Mathematics, Wisconsin at Madison. Hedrick Lecturer (MAA) 1979, Noether Lecturer (AWM) 1984.

# STEVE SMALE

Steve Smale makes news as well as mathematics. In the nineteen sixties he was known as an anti-war activist who, with Jerry Rubin, organized national "Days of Protest" against the Vietnam War and held a press conference, critical of U.S. policy in Vietnam, on the steps of Moscow University. Today he is familiar to the general public for his mathematical work through James Gleick's best-selling *Chaos*. He has worked successfully in a number of mathematical fields and says he is "not loyal" to any field or even to mathematics itself. He avoids getting into a rut by changing fields and activities. The latter include taking photographs, collecting museum-quality crystals, and making an ocean passage to the Marquessas in his 43-foot ketch with a two-mathematician crew.

□ □ □

**MP**  *I see that you were born in Flint, Michigan. Did you grow up there?*

**SMALE**  No. When I was five, we moved to the country. I went to a one-room schoolhouse all through elementary school.

**MP**  *Was your father a farmer?*

**SMALE**  We lived on a farm—near Flint—but he worked in an automobile factory. The farm was ten acres. Small. So it wasn't really a farm. We could have a vegetable garden though. The school was pretty interesting. It had one teacher who taught all nine grades, five classes to each grade, and who did all the janitorial work, cooking school lunches, the library work and all that. She had never finished college, but she had a lot of energy.

I think it was a good education I had, although on the technical side the teacher was not very sophisticated. There was quite of bit of interchange between the grades. I did more helping out of students, maybe, than I would have in a regular elementary school. It had its good features, I think. That's why I tend to be a little bit "anti" these big urban schools which are very systematic and professionalized. The kids don't get such a good education. In a technical sense you could not say that what I got was a good education, but in a fuller sense it was good. There were only thirty students at the school, but these students somehow succeeded well in the county-wide test at the end of the eighth grade. There were about a thousand students taking it. I came in first. My father was pretty proud of that. My sister did well, too, when she took the test.

**MP**  *What do you regard as the good elements of the education you got in that one-room school?*

**Armchair Revolutionary**

**SMALE**  Independence was created. I was interested a little bit in mathematics, and I could go to the encyclopedia and see how they solved little linear systems. But there was also the home. My father was quite a figure in the home. My father didn't finish college, but he had gone to college. He was an armchair revolutionary.

**MP**  *I guess it was that period, the period of the American workingman.*

**SMALE**  He wasn't really a workingman in that sense. He was a white-collar worker. He worked in a ceramics laboratory of AC Sparkplug. He wasn't even union. And he wasn't an activist like me. Actually I had my first political row in high school. The chapter on evolution in the biology textbook was omitted. Evolution just wasn't taught in the high school, and I tried to get a petition to have it taught. I am not sure I succeeded in getting even one other person to sign the petition.

**MP**  *What grade were you in?*

**SMALE**  That was probably the tenth or eleventh grade. Maybe '45 or '46. I was born in 1930. I wasn't ahead of my class or anything. I was just normal.

**MP**  *But were you good in math?*

Growing up in Michigan: Judith, 4, and Steve, 6, helping a farmhand.

*More Mathematical People*

**Mathematics Not First Love**

SMALE    I think I was pretty good. But in high school I was interested more in chemistry. A friend and I organized a little partnership to manufacture rare organic chemicals. It was sort of a joke in some ways. We were looking through the *Chemical Engineering News*—an engineering-chemical journal where firms were advertising for a pound of various rare chemicals. Sometimes we would write a letter saying that we could manufacture them, but we didn't have stationery and we never got a good response. We weren't mature enough. I had a laboratory. I still lived in the country, so we had a chicken house. (My father had gone into the egg business for a while.) It was a big place, and the loft was converted into a chemical laboratory.

MP    *So your parents were very encouraging of your interests?*

SMALE    Pretty much. They didn't have much money though. It was very modest.

MP    *I can imagine a lot of parents being not so keen on having their son out in the laboratory, maybe blowing up the place.*

SMALE    In fact, I did blow up a bottle of something right near my sister.

MP    *Do you have any other memories of that period? Teachers from that period who really stand out?*

SMALE    Well, I can remember at least three or four teachers. None of them exactly heroic, but they were all rather positive teachers.

MP    *So in high school there was no particular indication that mathematics was going to be a prominent feature in your life?*

SMALE    Oh no. No, no. I did pretty well in math but O.K. in other subjects too. I came in second or third in my high school class of one hundred as far as grades went.

MP    *Were there other things you did in high school?*

The small boy has the look of the man.

SMALE    Chess. I started with my father, and then I joined a chess club. I played in the National Junior Tournaments. I would come in—at the beginning—toward the bottom, but at the end I was coming in maybe in the top third. Eventually, a few years later, I played in the National Open. I ended up fiftieth out of 130 or so.

MP    *Did you have other special interests during that period?*

**A Great Book**

SMALE    I went to an astronomy convention a couple of hundred miles away, amateur astronomy. I had a telescope which my father built for me. You know, it was pretty small-time. I played with amateur radios for a while. Eventually I built a radio receiver that was just earphones and a crystal. Very, very minimal kinds of things. Then my father helped me build the aerial, super aerial, which would allow the radio receiver to be made from practically nothing. Mostly though I was interested in chemistry. I remember reading *Organic Chemistry* by James Conant, which I thought was a great book.

MP    *What does your sister do?*

SMALE    She taught for some time in ghetto schools in the Detroit area. She now has a day care center in Ann Arbor which she started. She works in her house. It's still very small. She's doing O.K.

**MP**  *How about your mother? What role did she play in your upbringing?*

**SMALE**  Probably lots. It's hard to say exactly.

**MP**  *Mothers keep the place together while the others are blowing up the chicken coop!*

**SMALE**  Right.

**MP**  *So, summarizing, would you say that you were a reasonably outstanding student in high school?*

**SMALE**  Real small-time kind of stuff.

**MP**  *No one ever said you were a child prodigy?*

**SMALE**  No. I had a teacher who was not sure that I should go to Ann Arbor. The competition was pretty heavy—you know, people coming from city high schools. It was a mixed picture at the time. I think that going to Ann Arbor was a big jump.

**MP**  *Did your going away to college put a financial burden on your family?*

**SMALE**  Not really. My parents didn't have to pay for my education. My grandfather—my mother's father, who had been a Latin teacher—had left me a thousand or two thousand dollars. I think that covered it pretty much. Also I had a tuition scholarship for the four years.

**MP**  *When did you leave chemistry for mathematics?*

**SMALE**  I left chemistry for physics. I was a physics major in my first three years in college.

**MP**  *Then when did mathematics come in?*

**SMALE**  Actually I was doing pretty badly in physics. Eventually, in my senior year, I failed a course. As I say, I was a B student in college. I may have got an A or two. I thought I could hardly fail mathematics.

**MP**  *So it wasn't a question of special attraction?*

**SMALE**  Well, you know, it was mixed. I liked mathematics somewhat, and I did pretty well, off and on. Mathematics was, you know, A's and B's usually.

**MP**  *But by the time you graduated, you were really interested in mathematics?*

**SMALE**  Oh no. Not much. I was playing a lot of chess and I played Go, a lot of Go. But, well, I applied to graduate school. I had taken a couple of graduate courses in math as an undergraduate and not done altogether badly.

**MP**  *Were you thinking about an academic career?*

**SMALE**  Vaguely. Yeah, vaguely. An academic career in mathematics was somewhat natural for people who were math majors and who were doing as well as I was—which was fairly well. I had good spots and weaknesses.

**MP**  *I am still trying to find out at what point you actually took off in mathematics.*

A high school graduate, and already an activist.

**SMALE**  Well, certainly the first year of graduate school was poor. I was warned by Theodore Hildebrandt, the chairman of the department, that unless my mathematics grades improved I would be kicked out of the graduate program. At that time I was very active in politics in college. Very, very active. It was a question of avoiding the draft that kept me studying in college at all.

**MP**  *You were opposing the Korean War?*

**SMALE**  Oh yes. I was a Communist at the time.

**MP**  *Were you a member of the Party?*

**SMALE**  I was a member of the Party, right.

**MP**  *How did you happen to join the Communist Party?*

**SMALE**  Well, I had been very heavily involved in left-wing politics. I came from that kind of Marxist tradition. My father was more of a revolutionary than I was, but he was not active.

**MP**  *Did your mother have any leanings in that direction?*

**SMALE**  She tended to go along with my father, I guess.

**MP**  *Politics was not a woman's business?*

**SMALE**  Exactly. But, you know, I was really active in these political things. I had gone to Eastern Europe maybe as a junior in college. I was in East Berlin for a "Youth Festival." It must have been 1951 or something like that. I was active in a peace group. When I came back, I organized a "Society for Peaceful Alternatives" on campus. I was also very active with the Young Progressives. Then I was also organizing a chess club. So I was put on probation during my senior year.

**MP**  *Because of your political activities, or for academic reasons?*

**SMALE**  For political activities. Not for academic reasons. I was always at the B level as an undergraduate. There was never a question of flunking out.

**MP**  *But those political activities must have taken enough time that it was hard to keep mathematics going.*

**SMALE**  Well, I didn't keep it going too well. The mathematics was a little lackadaisical. Sometimes in an easy course I would do very, very well. Sometimes in hard courses I would just drop out, as in some graduate courses which I was taking as an undergraduate. But there were some good signs in that period. And then I did better after the first year of graduate school.

**MP**  *After the warning?*

**SMALE**  Yeah.

**MP**  *You had to choose?*

**SMALE**  Yeah, I did. Eventually I became quite anti-communist. As far as I am concerned, I found communism not very effective. I am not a Communist today. The Communist Party—at first I just became inactive, and then I dropped out.

**MP**  *Do you think that was because the mathematics got to be just a lot more interesting?*

**SMALE**   Partly that. Also I met Clara—Clara Davis—during the fall of 1954. That was my third graduate year. She was the first girl I'd had a long-term relationship with. She was the student in charge at a co-op. She's a very stable person.

**MP**   *Sort of an anchor?*

**SMALE**   Right. We got married at the beginning of 1955.

**MP**   *So you hadn't known each other too long.*

**SMALE**   A couple of months.

**MP**   *Was there some point, though, when things in mathematics just got to be a lot more interesting for you?*

**SMALE**   That's right. There was this warning by the chairman of the department. Then I started becoming a lot more serious about mathematics. That was starting my second year of graduate school in the fall of 1953. Actually already I had spent some of that summer trying to read topology.

**MP**   *Was that the thing that caught you?*

**SMALE**   Well, I won't say that. You were required to pass a German test for the Ph.D., and I did seriously take a look at the book by Alexandroff and Hopf on topology, which was in German. And then Raoul Bott was teaching this course—it was a year course in topology. That was very important to me. So I was beginning to spend a lot more time with mathematics.

**MP**   *Did topology have a particular attraction for you?*

**SMALE**   No, I think it was just there.

**MP**   *It was just there?*

**SMALE**   Right. Topology was just becoming very fashionable, and Bott was a topologist. So that's why I think that topology was just there.

**MP**   *You think that you could have become something else, some different kind of mathematician, quite easily?*

**"I'm not loyal to my subject."**   **SMALE**   Oh yeah, sure, that's right. I did quit topology in the summer of 1961—just six years later. I just quit completely. I did these things in topology which probably got me the Fields Medal. Then, well, I just left the subject. You see, it's a complex phenomenon, my relationship to topology. You know, I'm not so loyal to mathematics as most mathematicians are.

**MP**   *You're not loyal to mathematics?*

**SMALE**   No, no, no. In many ways I'm different from most people. I'm not loyal to my subject. That's why I can go into economics, for example. I can become a professor of economics, and when the economics department and the mathematics department have a fight, I don't take sides. In general, I don't feel loyalty to a subject. If I go to a football game, I don't take sides either.

**MP**   *I guess loyalty is the wrong word.*

**SMALE**   No, loyalty is a good word. But in some sense I am not forgiven by a lot of people in topology, right?

Smale met Clara Davis, now Mrs. Smale, at the University of Michigan.

**MP**  *You really feel that?*

**SMALE**  Yeah. Definitely.

**MP**  *Topologists feel that you abandoned them?*

**Betrayed Topology**  **SMALE**  That's right. That's a very common feeling. People told me that I had betrayed topology, and people are worried today that I may be betraying dynamical systems. I did make a very clean break with topology in '61. I just said that I thought the questions connected with dynamical systems were more interesting. That's the most clean break in mathematics I've made. Certain topologists felt—some topologists, at least, and probably many—that I wasn't a topologist anymore and that I was sort of, you know, dismissible. I understand that, because by leaving the field I sort of implied that maybe it wasn't so interesting. You know, people took it that way.

**MP**  *How would you describe dynamical systems to a layman?*

**SMALE**  In dynamical systems you are studying the passage of states in time, such as physical states or states in the laboratory or states idealized in mathematics—how they develop in time.

**MP**  *In a human sense, how did you become interested in that particular subject?*

**SMALE**  In a human sense? Well, I don't know. Even back when I was a topologist, I got involved with some questions in dynamical systems. I've written an article about how it happened. You can read it. The person whom I knew who tried to get me involved in that subject was especially Mauricio Peixoto in Brazil. The development of dynamical systems became prominent earlier in Brazil than elsewhere. That's why I go there a lot.

**MP**  *It seems that much of the time you have just become interested in what somebody else is doing.*

### Doing What's Important to Science

**SMALE**  I'd say that in the last twenty years I've put a lot of thought into what I want to do, so I don't still get pushed by circumstances so much. I was pushed more by circumstances in the early years. Now these years—well, I really try to assess what I can do well that's important to science. I have spent quite a bit of time just making an assessment of where I should put my energies.

**MP**  *How do you do that? What are your criteria?*

**SMALE**  It's probably from people I know and from what I read. I try to get some kind of a global perspective about science, and a world perspective about the mathematics which I do know and which I can use—where my strength lies. You know, I think computer science is some kind of revolution, a kind of revolution in mathematics which is different from what a lot of mathematicians see—a different kind of revolution.

**MP**  *What is it to you?*

### Algorithms and Foundations

**SMALE**  Oh, I think it's the emphasis on algorithms which will have an effect on the foundations of mathematics. For me it's related to that, but the main questions are just, you know, *alive*.

**MP**  *I don't quite understand what you are referring to when you say that the emphasis on algorithms will have an effect on the foundations of mathematics.*

**SMALE**  I don't know if I understand exactly myself. You know that traditionally algorithms have been very much related to logic and the foundations. As a subject they fit into what is called recursive function theory, at least some kind of general understanding of algorithms does. It's different with particular algorithms. But when you speak of general algorithms, or of all the algorithms for solving a problem, then you're getting closer to questions involving the foundations of mathematics. It's through recursive function theory. This is a little vague, I'm sure, but my feeling is that algorithms and computer science itself are still a little farther than they should be from, you know, the main stream of mathematics. I'd like to see them closer. And not so much based in logic but based in continuous mathematics, in the calculus and analysis. Actually if that happened, it could have some feedback in foundations, making the foundations of mathematics more continuous rather than discrete. These are just things I think about without having too clear ideas about them. It is certainly a little vague in my mind. You can say that looking at numerical analysis from a topological perspective or the systematic study of algorithms has been my perspective the last years, and that's what I'm involved in now.

**MP**  *What you did in '61—namely, to put topology aside and take up dynamical systems—that was quite a courageous thing to do, because you* *were doing very well in topology. And a lot of people would say, "Gee, that is very, very risky, Professor Smale, because what makes you think that you will be able to do as well in another field?"*

**SMALE**   Well, by then I had written a paper or two in dynamical systems and had some results.

**MP**   *You mean you had a place to jump?*

**SMALE**   Yeah. That was part of it. I also had a kind of—well, I think that there was some truth in the statement that the main problems in topology I'd solved. Dimensions 3 and 4 were left open, but somehow they seemed to me important but exceptional cases. You know, the structure of manifolds of dimensions greater than 4 was in principle mainly reduced to homotopy algebra type of questions. That was really my feeling at the time. Of course, dimensions 3 and 4 are huge subjects in their own right. But that's the way I am.

**MP**   *They were not the subjects that you wanted to spend your time on?*

**SMALE**   Right. It was more interesting to me to go on to other things. I think I wrote and said that the problems of the discrete dynamical system in the 2-sphere were ever so much more exciting and mysterious than anything left in topology. That was my feeling. And there was a lot of truth in that.

**Autobiographical Writing**

**MP**   *It's interesting that you seem to like autobiographical writing. You have mentioned the article on how you got involved with dynamical systems, and we've read the article you wrote about your controversial press conference at the International Congress in Moscow in 1966. Is it true that you have started to write your autobiography?*

**SMALE**   I have half of it here if you want to see it. Actually I wouldn't call it an autobiography. It's only the political part of my life.

**MP**   *What motivated you to start writing?*

**SMALE**   I got a Miller Fellowship, which gave me a whole year off. I don't teach that much anyway, you know—I feel my time is my own. But I thought it would be interesting to write about the experience at the congress in Moscow and other things in that period. People are always asking me about things then. There are a lot of stories that I want to develop. I was actually central to the early Vietnam protests.

**MP**   *But now have you given up the autobiographical project?*

**SMALE**   Only temporarily. I had that one essay published in the *Mathematical Intelligencer*. There are about six chapters more. But it is hard for me to do very much writing. It's hard for me to do more than one thing at a time.

**MP**   *Do you feel that in writing autobiographically you have got a new perspective on your life?*

**SMALE**   I don't think in those categories.

**MP**   *But you do think it's a story worth telling?*

**SMALE**  Yeah. It's personal, you know. My personal involvement in those exciting days. Sometimes I write things out. I do like to take some time to shift—it's refreshing to do a lot of shifting—from mathematics or science or other activities. For instance, when I went into photography—I wanted to be able to take pictures of our crystal collection—I got a few cameras and spent six months learning to take pictures. You can get into a rut if you are always doing the same thing.

**MP**  *You did dynamical systems for quite a while. Then you got into economics. In the citation you wrote for Gerard Debreu, when he won the Nobel Prize in economics, you mention that Debreu came down to your office to ask you some mathematical questions related to his subject. I don't know whether you had met him prior to that . . . .*

**SMALE**  No. I had never met him.

**MP**  *That was when your interest in mathematical economics started?*

**SMALE**  That's for sure. It was like my situation in dynamical systems. I got into that a little before '60, and it was '61 I think when I finished my last paper in topology. Then I threw myself into dynamical systems completely. In '63 I went over to the calculus of variations and infinite dimensional manifolds and sort of unified those subjects. That interest lasted for three years. My last year at Columbia I taught a course in that, and I got really involved. Then in 1966 I came back to dynamical systems. That was probably the biggest time in dynamical systems for me. There was a lot of growth. Especially around my students. During that period, 1966 to 1969, that's when I had most of my best students. And then around 1969, 1970 I tried going into several other things. A little bit here and there. A paper on electrical circuits which is a basic chapter in my book with Moe Hirsch. Then I gave the Colloquium Lectures for the American Math Society around 1970. They were on applications of global analysis. Then I gave four talks—one in biology and one in economics—I think that was after I met Debreu, yeah, it was—and then one on electrical circuits and one on mechanics. Really there was a period there when I was just groping around a little bit. I was doing some things in different areas of classical mechanics. That's when I got to know Debreu, and a year or two later maybe is when I got serious about economic questions. And for a few years I spent most of my time in economics.

**MP**  *Then economics is not a current interest?*

**SMALE**  Well, actually, a little bit. Because I see Debreu a lot. But the last few years I have started drifting away. To related questions. Now it's computer science and algorithms. But, you know, it's not like my leaving topology. It's a more gentle transition from economics toward computer science.

**MP**  *Do you think that in recent years you have consciously given up political activism in order to concentrate more on mathematics?*

**SMALE**  I still see myself sometimes as a little active. I'm not anti-activism. I went to Germany in 1983. Did I give you a copy of the speech I gave in Germany? The one on the arms race? Isn't that what you'd call activism?

**MP**  *Definitely. Although it's not quite like being on the barricades with Jerry Rubin!*

Gerard Debreu, a Nobelist in economics, who stimulated Smale's interest in that subject.

Passport photo in June 1954 when he went to an international student congress in East Berlin.

**SMALE**   I haven't talked to Jerry for a few years. Actually, just before I went on sabbatical—that was a year and a half ago—*Life* wanted to take a picture of Jerry and me on the tracks for the troop-train demonstration. But I was leaving for Paris, and he couldn't get away in time. Moe Hirsch substituted for me, and he and Jerry were taken on the troop-train tracks. Of course, Moe, too, was involved in the Vietnam Day Committee and all that.

**MP**   *How did it happen that your own feeling about communism changed?*

**SMALE**   Oh, that's been a gradual process. It goes all the way back to Ann Arbor. And, you know, at first it was more—you might say more moral. Already in Ann Arbor, things were upsetting to me. I was upset at the things that happened in Hungary. That was '56. So I became more anti-communist. I was really anti-communist during the Vietnam War—but I was just more anti-American. Then Afghanistan. Also during my visits to Russia—1961 and 1966—I learned more. I became more sophisticated, I think. I feel, at least I say to myself, that the system is pretty destructive. Pure socialism, you know. I feel that one has to have a kind of mixture, some kind of free-market economy and government control of production mediating each other. The Soviet Union is so extreme, so pressurized, that there's no decentralization of the economy. Then it has this great number of destructive effects. So it's kind of evolved with me. Now I call myself an anti-communist. That doesn't mean I'm right-wing, although I may be right-wing on some issues.

**MP**   *On what issues?*

**SMALE**   Social Security, for instance. The younger generation is paying for the older generation now, and people my age or younger—people who will become sixty-five or seventy in the future—won't have anywhere near the standard of living of older people today. When everybody else's income gets cut by inflation, Social Security doesn't. So I tend to agree with the more conservative senators who say we've got to stop raising Social Security all the time.

I'm still, and have been most consistently throughout my whole life, against the military. Not completely, you know, but I do feel that we must de-emphasize military solutions of problems. So I know with that I am on the left-wing. My reactions are sometimes more radical than those of most liberals. I'm just conservative part of the time.

**Changing Feelings about Communism**

**MP**   *Do you think your involvement with economics has contributed to the change in your feelings about communism?*

**SMALE**   I think it has helped me to get a better perspective. I've read a lot of papers, and I think I now have some understanding of the conflicts between capitalism and socialism. Probably the best solution is to have some kind of balance between the two. This is the position I've evolved to.

**MP**   *I'm very impressed by the fact that at fifty-five, when you could be relaxing a bit more, you're going very, very strong in mathematics.*

**SMALE**   Fifty-five isn't that old.

**MP**   *You've given us some insights about how you keep going. Your interests are diverse. New things attract your attention.*

*Steve Smale*                                                                                    **315**

**SMALE**    Yeah, that's how I avoid getting in a rut. However, you know, you lose more than you gain by doing that. I don't have a niche. Other mathematicians have a niche. If I'd stayed in topology, I'd have a niche.

**MP**    *A definite niche.*

**SMALE**    So I don't have that, and I also don't keep a kind of continual following. I've been working on this kind of complexity theory for a few years, but in some sense it's not an existing subject at all, you know. And in this situation, you don't have the existing people and it's not so easy sometimes. You have to start from scratch. My seminars are really not too big. If I'd stayed in one field, I'd have much bigger seminars and much more influence. So it's a little mixed. But I do avoid getting into a rut.

**MP**    *We talked just briefly earlier, but that was before we turned on the recorder, about "talking about mathematics" to members of your family—your children and your wife. I see that you have two children. How old are they, and what subjects of interest have they pursued?*

**SMALE**    They're twenty-eight and twenty-six. They're both in their last year of graduate school at Berkeley, finishing their theses. My son's in mathematics and my daughter's in biological psychology.

**MP**    *What area of mathematics is your son in?*

**SMALE**    Partial differential equations and geometry.

**MP**    *Was it apparent at an early age that he was going to take up mathematics?*

**SMALE**    Well, in high school he failed algebra twice.

**MP**    *Twice!*

**SMALE**    Twice. At that time I did not think he would be a mathematician.

**MP**    *Your children have observed your rather active involvement in politics, which must have set you apart from the parents of many of their friends.*

**SMALE**    Sure. We talked about politics a lot. You know they tend to be more left-wing than I do. I think that my son's pretty wise politically. He discusses at a very sophisticated level what goes on in the country. My daughter is not quite so political. But she and I get in big arguments sometimes.

**MP**    *It sounds as if they both turned out fairly well for you.*

**SMALE**    Yeah. Only I'm not sure how their theses are going to wind up. You know, it's not easy writing a thesis these days.*

**MP**    *Your wife said that she had some idea what you actually do. Do you feel that you've been able to tell her about your mathematics?*

**SMALE**    Not the technical side of the mathematics. But she knows the kind of mathematics I do and sees the way I work.

**MP**    *How do you work?*

---

*MP NOTE: Since then, both Nat and Laura have received their doctorates. Nat has a National Science Foundation post-doc at Stanford. Laura also has an NSF post-doc and is in Africa, studying hyenas in the Masai Mara.

Smale's son, Nat, is a mathematician. When Nat was flunking math in high school, Smale says, "I didn't think he would be a mathematician."

**SMALE**  Naturally.

**MP**  *You don't have a schedule?*

**SMALE**  No.

**MP**  *You don't get up at 5 a.m.?*

**SMALE**  I do get up at 5 a.m. Yeah, since I got back from Brazil, I've been getting up at 5 a.m.

**MP**  *Do you work on mathematics then?*

**SMALE**  It's not usually mathematics. It's organizing the day. You know. there are a lot of things that have to be done around the house. And a sailboat is—well, it takes a lot of time. It's a big boat. Also administration. I'm co-chairman of that MSRI program on complexity theory, and it takes a lot of time. And I'm colloquium chairman for the department. I teach halftime and have for a long time. I'm teaching only one course, but it's a course that takes a lot of thought. This is a very busy time for me. It's good. I like it. Our mineral collection takes a lot of time, too—organizing it and doing things connected with it. There are lots of aspects to that. And so I get up at five. I get sleepy by nine or ten. We are usually in bed by ten.

**Sailing**  **MP**  *You mentioned at lunch that you were planning a long ocean passage in your boat in a couple of years. What kind of boat is it?*

**SMALE**  It's a a 43-foot ketch. It has three private staterooms, a living room, galley. It weighs sixteen tons—it's built for cruising.

**MP**  *When did you get it?*

**SMALE**  A year or so ago. For the preceding two years, I owned a 30-foot Catalina. That was when I really learned to sail, in the Catalina.

**MP**  *So you bought this bigger boat pretty much with this plan in mind of making an ocean passage?*

**SMALE**   Not exactly. But I had in mind the ideal boat that I wanted, that would be safe and comfortable, something I could take into the ocean, so that I would never feel that I wanted a third boat. When I bought the first boat, I thought it was temporary—that if I liked it, then I would buy another boat. The second boat was to be the final boat.

**MP**   *Back to mathematics—would you tell us how you think about mathematics? I've got the paper you wrote for the* Monthly *back in '69 entitled "What is global analysis?" And there are several pictures in it. Are you a geometrical sort?*

**SMALE**   Tendencies, yes. Tendencies toward being geometrical, but I don't think—well, some people even attack me for not being geometrical enough. You know, I'm not absolute about anything, and I like to think broadly. Algebra, I think that's my weakest subject, but at least I'm not afraid of algebra. I'm quite willing to deal with algebra if necessary.

**MP**   *But when you're starting to think about a problem in a new area, are your images geometrical?*

**SMALE**   Depends. Not necessarily. I think a lot of things I'm doing now, more formal power series, algebra of power series and things like that, are not geometrical. I do work geometrically sometimes. I guess I don't feel too much into one thing. That gives me advantages and disadvantages. I don't want to be too much in a niche.

**MP**   *When you have a mathematical problem—say there's a problem right now that interests you, do you sit down and think about it?*

**SMALE**   Sometimes I do. Sure. But it's not that I have to get away from everything and just be by myself. I might think about it for half an hour before dinner or after dinner. I think I'm able to do more by combining things—like my course, which I combine with my research. I'll probably prepare my next lecture at the same time as I try to prove my next theorem. It

Smale perfected his photographic skills so that he could take pictures of his museum-quality crystal collection. This one, of Brazilian quartz, was part of a crystal calendar he and his wife published in 1981.

*More Mathematical People*

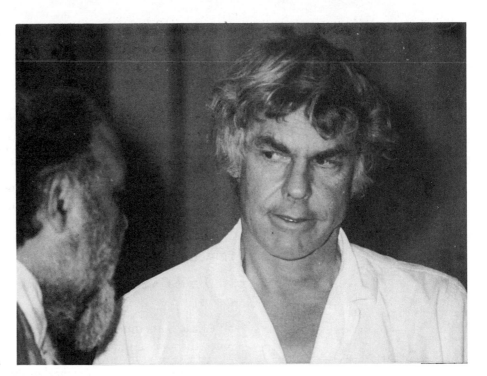

In serious conversation.

saves a lot of time. But it's heavy. Three hours a week is like giving three seminar talks a week. But it's good because it keeps me trying to prove new theorems.

**MP**  *Do you completely put out of your mind your past work and interests — like topology?*

**SMALE**  Well, no. In some sense I try to figure out, you know, a topologist's perspective toward these other subjects, or a global perspective toward what's called numerical analysis. When you consider the class of algorithms, you are dealing with something more global than just what numerical analysts have been dealing with traditionally. They have been looking at things more in the limit. So when I take a kind of topological point of view I take in a lot of these things. More of what you call global. Yes, in some sense that does give a different way of looking at numerical analysis.

**MP**  *A different point of view certainly.*

**SMALE**  Right. So in some sense I'm into numerical analysis these days. But, you know, when you consider it from the point of view of computer science, you ought to know the cost of a process and not just the limiting cost. So that combines it with — almost puts a geometrical flavor into numerical analysis by looking at it from the computer science point of view. It is a little paradoxical because one thinks of computer science as the farthest thing in the world from geometry and topology. But when you try to combine numerical analysis and computer science it forces a topological point of view.

**Crystals**  **MP**  *To change the subject for a moment, you have quite a collection of minerals here, some of which you have been nice enough to show us, and I want to ask about their appeal for you. Your wife mentioned that she was the one who really had the interest to begin with.*

**SMALE**   Right. She was very interested, but not in the sense that she would actually go out and get them, you know. Then at some point my father gave me a mineral. In 1968.

**MP**   *Back to Dad again!*

**SMALE**   At about the same time, three of these coffee table books came out with beautiful pictures of minerals. So about that time I realized that maybe one could compete with museums. Then pretty quickly, even in the first month or two after I had picked up some minerals, I was driving all over the state to every mineral shop and trying to buy minerals. I was pretty naive, but I put a huge amount of energy into it.

**MP**   *It hit you hard?*

**SMALE**   Right.

**MP**   *Is that the way you hit new subjects in general? You just really go after them?*

**SMALE**   Sometimes I do that. Yeah. I put a huge amount of energy into it. Since then we've put most of our income into minerals.

**MP**   *Do you think the original motivation was the beauty?*

**Beauty Integrated with Rarity**

**SMALE**   Beauty having to do with a kind of competitiveness, too. If you can get some mineral that no museum or collector has, there's something—that makes it more beautiful. Beauty is very integrated with rarity. You know, it's all right if somebody who doesn't know much about it thinks it's beautiful, but if there are thousands of the same, then it'll never win any beauty test. Beauty is connected so much with innovation and priority.

**MP**   *And how about beauty in mathematics?*

**SMALE**   Yeah, it has to be something special to make it beautiful. If it's just ordinary, it's not beautiful.

**MP**   *Well, you've worked in many areas now and accomplished a lot. When you look back—and I realize that there are still things to come—of the things you've done so far, are there any that please you more than the others, whether it's in mathematics or not?*

**SMALE**   Oh, there's always a kind of rating. I'm not sure what is more important. Dynamical systems and topology probably.

**MP**   *But you don't look back with a certain personal fondness on any particular work?*

**SMALE**   Oh, I wouldn't deny that! But I don't think in exactly those terms. Three years ago I went back and taught a course in differential topology, the first time in twenty years, so I taught about my old theorems, you know. Then the next year I taught the dynamical systems course. Making the break I did with topology—I wouldn't do that again.

**MP**   *More mellow in general?*

**SMALE**   Yeah. Today I wouldn't suddenly break with my past the way I did in '61. It was really a big jump. I won't say I regret it, but I wouldn't do that kind of thing today.

Smale learned to sail in the *Red Emma*, which he named himself, but he took the *Stardust*, a 43-foot ketch so named when he bought it, on his ocean passage to the Marquessas.

**MP**  *Didn't you say in some of the things we have read here that at one time you consciously decided that you could not devote so much time to activism—that mathematics was the thing?*

**SMALE**  Well, I didn't say definitely. I thought that sometimes I could take off from mathematics for a few months and do something else. Even in late years. You know, write this autobiography. That took—how many years ago has it been? Six years. But I had to take off from mathematics. I can't do two things at once. At least not very well. Maybe sailing a little bit. But collecting minerals, I did take off from mathematics to do that. The same with photography—I just stopped doing mathematics. Because it takes a lot of energy for me to start something new very seriously.

**MP**  *Do you feel that you come back to mathematics more refreshed?*

**SMALE**  Perhaps. Sometimes if I don't get anywhere and I'm not going strong, I'll leave a subject and come back to it a year later, and sometimes then I'll make good progress.

**MP**  *When do you think you function best? When do the ideas really flow and jell?*

**A List Maker**  **SMALE**  I enjoy the beaches and hiking. If mathematics is there, so much the better. I tend to be pretty casual about my work. I like to work, you know, in the most comfortable position. I do make lists, however. Yeah, I'm a list-maker. I'm very organized. I maybe spend too much time organizing my life. Like what things I should put priorities on. I'm casual but organized. I even sometimes make lists of foods that we should emphasize, you know, the healthiest foods. I have so many pages of lists that it would blow your mind. I remember with the boat I had about eight pages, single spaced, double column—a list of things I had to pay attention to. Then I refine my lists. I refine them continually. I like to cross off something that is really done. Usually it's half done. Then it's a revised item on the list.

**MP**  *I'd like to talk a little bit about your teaching. I've heard you lecture three times, and every lecture has been really good.*

**SMALE**  Pretty casual though.

**MP**  *Well, relaxed. But they were really well organized. You had clearly thought about them, or you knew the subject so darn well that you didn't have to.*

**SMALE**  Usually, in recent years, I don't spend much time preparing a lecture—just a few minutes.

**MP**  *A few minutes!*

**SMALE**  Yeah, but it's usually something I'm working on. That's why I'm a good speaker. I speak on things that I really know very well, things I've been working out. So to prepare I just have to put things together. If I gave a lecture on something I didn't know, then I would have to spend a month working on it, but I don't put myself in that situation. And, you know, my lectures are always a little rough on the edges. I don't write anything out in advance. I don't use notes and I don't use those—what do you call them?—overhead projectors. It seems to make it easier that way. If I forget some-

Steve and his father, Laurence Smale.

thing, I just leave it out. I never put in such detailed proofs that if I forget something it matters. So then it's easy because I don't have to depend on those things.

**MP** *People usually don't want to see all the details of a proof; they just want to feel that they understand.*

**SMALE** That's just the point. I don't feel I can spend too much time preparing a lecture—even for my class. I combine my preparation with my research. I'll work on a problem for a while, and while I'm thinking about it I'll go to my class. I try to be sensible and organize things, you know, in

## LIKE FATHER

Since Laurence and Helen Smale also live in Berkeley, we had the rare opportunity to meet the parents of one of our subjects. The Smales are a forthright, independent and active pair. This year the ninety-year-old Mr. Smale celebrated his birthday, as he has every year since moving to the Bay Area, by walking across the city of San Francisco, a distance of 7.5 miles, "as a way of checking on how I am doing."

Asked about his own early activism, he said that he first began to question his strict Methodist up-bringing after reading Emerson's essays. He enrolled at Carnegie Tech, planning to become a mining engineer, but joined the Navy when the United States entered World

War I. Seven years later, having wandered over the world and spent enough time in a mine and at the Michigan College of Mines to know that he had mistaken his vocation, he enrolled at Albion College in Flint, Michigan. Within days he had published the first issue of the *Maelstrom*, "the official organ of the Maelstrom Society," of which he was the only member. He hoped that before the next issue he would be joined by "a youthful host of poets, philosophers, artists, disciples of free love, . . . budding anarchists, communists, nihilists, atheists, agnostics, pacifists, citizens-of-the-world, and any others of the anti-Philistine persuasion attending Albion College, if such there be." But thirty minutes after the *Maelstrom* appeared, he was

expelled and also arrested, charged with selling and distributing obscene literature.

Since he was not "the long-haired anarchist . . . weakling 'red' type that is referred to as the 'parlor bolsheviki'," mysterious "others" were suspected by newspapers as far away as the *Detroit Free Press*. The English was too correct and "the quotations . . . not from the books that anyone who is pursuing a technical education would read."

Mr. Smale, however, says that the project was entirely his own. He had had hopes of being hired by a newspaper but got instead a job as an assistant in the ceramics laboratory of AC Sparkplug, where the future Mrs. Smale was working as a secretary, and never returned to the academic world.

the right order—direct and concise; but the actual preparation of a lecture per se—not much time. Next semester I am going to be teaching freshman calculus.

**MP**  *Are you looking forward to that?*

**SMALE**  Oh, a little mixed. I haven't taught it for ten years or so. I used to enjoy it when I did. One thing that makes it worse is that it's for non-math people, so they won't be very well motivated. I like to have students who jump up and yell at me. That's one thing that makes it easier for me. And it happens in a lot of my classes, my lectures, too. People say things and ask questions a lot. I do make mistakes, because I don't prepare too well. If I make a mistake, people get up and yell at me. That's O. K. if there are not too many. If I make very many mistakes, then it gets worse. I don't deliberately make mistakes, but my level of preparation is such—even the big calculus sections will ask a lot of questions.

**MP**  *You're less likely to be making mistakes there, though.*

**SMALE**  Yeah, but you can make mistakes.

**MP**  *Having heard about your early education in a one-room country school, I am wondering how you feel about a program like the Russian one where the brightest students in math from all over the Soviet Union are put together in special schools.*

**SMALE**  I feel O. K. about it. I think it's good to have strong peers. If you're trying to make everybody the same, then I think it's probably a little destructive.

**MP**  *But your own experience seems to have been different.*

**SMALE**  Oh, I wouldn't say that. When I was a freshman in college, I was in a special class. And the math classes in high school were probably selective.

**MP**  *But from your description, although you were good in math in high school, you weren't considered a math prodigy, were you?*

**SMALE**  No.

**MP**  *So such a program might well have missed you. Apparently it wouldn't have made any difference.*

*October 1985 in Berkeley, California (DA, CR).*

*STEPHEN SMALE*   Flint, Michigan, July 15, 1930. B.S. 1952, M.S. 1953, Ph.D. 1956, Michigan. Fields: topology, dynamical systems, economics, numerical analysis. Professor of Mathematics, UC Berkeley. Plenary Lecturer (ICM Moscow) 1966, Colloquium Lecturer (AMS) 1972, Plenary Lecturer (ICM Berkeley) 1986, von Neumann Lecturer (SIAM) 1989. Veblen Prize (AMS) 1966, Fields Medal (IMU) 1966, Chauvenet Prize (MAA) 1988. American Academy of Arts and Sciences, National Academy of Sciences. Books: (with Morris W. Hirsch) *Differential Equations, Dynamical Systems, and Linear Algebra,* 1974; *The Mathematics of Time: Essays on Dynamical Systems, Economic Processes, and Related Topics,* 1980.

# WILLIAM P. THURSTON

Bill Thurston is probably the only mathematician to be featured in a lead story on the front page of the *Wall Street Journal*. His work in topology reminds a fellow mathematician of Mozart's in music. The only senior faculty member at Princeton with an office on the third floor, otherwise occupied mainly by graduate students, he is now trying to teach a computer to draw the way a mathematician does. He attributes some other mathematicians' lack of interest in computers to "mathematical immaturity." Thurston is also well known for his active opposition to the support of mathematical research by military funding. We need, he says, "to convince the academic community that money is not necessarily good for it if it is bad for society."

□ □ □

**MP**  *We have a feeling from some of the things we have read that you became a mathematician very early in life. So let's start at the very beginning. When and where were you born?*

**THURSTON**  I was born in Washington D.C. on October 30, 1946. We lived in Washington for four years, and then we spent a year in Holland. I went to kindergarten in Amsterdam. It was an interesting experience for me, and it affected my development. I'll tell you about that later. Then we moved to suburban Maryland, where I grew up.

**MP**  *How did your family happen to go to Holland?*

**THURSTON**  At that time my father was an aeronautical engineer at the Naval Ordnance Laboratory. He had something like a sabbatical and went back to school in Holland for a *doctorandus*, a kind of doctorate without a thesis. Later he worked for the Air Force Office of Scientific Research, awarding grants.

**MP**  *This is jumping ahead, but I am wondering if your interest in the pure aspects of mathematics has been a kind of revolt against your father's very applied work?*

**Mathematics after Dinner**

THURSTON   Oh no, I don't think so. I got a lot of my geometric approach from him, and excitement about mathematics too. Sometimes after dinner we would get off on some topic. Here's one example. My brother asked how you would find the area of a triangle in terms of its sides, so we all sat down and spent a lot of time deriving Heron's formula. My father had heard of it, but we reconstructed it for ourselves. There were lots of things like that. My father had a good geometric sense although he didn't have any real training in pure mathematics. When I was in high school, I remember, he was fascinated by the fact that some mathematician had told him about primes of the form $4n+1$. We played with them, trying to figure out whether it was true that they could always be written as the sum of two squares and, if so, why it was true. We tried to work it out. Without number theory it was not something we were going to be able to do. But my father enjoyed working on the problem. It was very mysterious to him. He came up with the idea of using complex numbers. He also tried to understand quadratic residues. The proof actually involves factorization with complex numbers, so he was making progress. He also had a sense of mathematics being associated with practical things. I guess I have that same sense. I kind of take it for granted.

MP   *You take it so for granted that you never mention it.*

**"All mathematics is applicable."**

THURSTON   For instance, I enjoy talking with Tony Jameson, who is writing codes to be used in designing airplanes. To do that, he has to triangulate the exterior of the plane. Some of the ideas I have are related to that. You don't necessarily think about airplanes and Riemannian manifolds together, but I think that doing so clarifies insights. It's the same mathematics, whether it's applied or not. It's just important to think of a problem in a general context. I really think all mathematics is applicable.

MP   *Did your mother also have an interest in mathematics?*

THURSTON   Not really. But she taught me to use the abacus, and that's one of the things that I remember enjoying when I was little. I was just so amazed that ten of these beads made one of these, and ten of these—you could get up to really huge numbers.

MP   *Did she have a profession?*

THURSTON   No. She was at home all the time. There were four of us children to take care of.

MP   *But before she married?*

THURSTON   She went to college and majored in Latin. She was a teacher for a year before she got married. She taught grades 7-12 English in a rural school. She was interested in literature and language, so we talked about words and etymology. She was most influential for mathematics in the early years, but she continued to have influence.

MP   *You said earlier that you would tell us how the year in Holland was important for your development.*

THURSTON   Yes. I went to kindergarten in Holland. Parts of the public schools were in a way adaptations of the Montessori system. I enjoyed kindergarten there—at least in memory after I got back to the States—because of the fact that the kids could pick their own activities. And there were many

Three-year-old Billy Thurston deep in thought.

Thurston spent his kindergarten year at a Montessori school in Amsterdam.

interesting activities going on in the classroom all the time. I liked that way of working on my own.

**MP** *Which activities interested you?*

**THURSTON** I don't remember very well the specific things. Mainly it was the atmosphere that impressed me. And the teachers, who cared about individuals. Of course, I got special treatment because I didn't come in speaking Dutch. The teachers all spoke good English. At the end of the year I could understand Dutch and speak it, but I resisted actually using it.

**MP** *Why was that?*

**THURSTON** I was somehow hung up about it.

**MP** *When you came back from Holland and entered school in Maryland, how did you find that?*

**THURSTON** I had a hard time for a while. I hated all the drills in arithmetic. And then there was a phase problem. I had been in kindergarten, but when I came back I was in the middle of first grade, so I had to have some tutoring in reading.

**MP** *Were there any special programs for the "gifted"?*

**THURSTON** No. It was standard. I was pretty disenchanted with the whole educational system. That is something I thought about as a child. I didn't like going to school very much. Things gradually got better though. I didn't hate high school, and I did well eventually in advanced placement classes. What I didn't like was the pace of school. If I became interested in a subject, biology or mathematics, I found it unpleasant to have to put everything aside after an hour and go on to something else.

**MP** *You would have liked to pursue it?*

**THURSTON** I would have liked to pursue it when it interested me.

**MP** *Did you read any books in high school, any books about mathematics, that aroused your interest?*

**THURSTON** I don't remember any as being really influential. What I do remember is Martin Gardner's column in *Scientific American*. It is too bad that it is no longer around.

**MP** *What things interested you other than mathematics?*

**THURSTON** I enjoyed English for a while. I enjoy lots of things, to tell you the truth, but I'm not as talented in some things. I can imagine having become many different types of people.

**MP** *Tell us a little bit about your siblings. What kinds of things have they done?*

**THURSTON** I have an older brother, Bob, roughly three years ahead of me, and a sister, Jean, roughly three years younger. Then I also have another brother, George. He was born when I was ten. My older brother teaches the fifth and sixth grades in Washington. My sister is a budget analyst for the Metro System in Seattle. She really enjoys that type of thing, finding ways of doing things more efficiently. My younger brother has just finished his Ph.D. in biophysics at MIT. He is working as a post-doc.

**MP**  *Were there any mathematicians in your family? Uncles? Aunts?*

**THURSTON**  No. My grandfather was a teacher and later the superintendent of a small school district in Ohio. He talked about teaching quite a bit. I think he enjoyed it.

**MP**  *The reason I asked that question is that something I have read indicated that you wanted to be a mathematician at a very early age. I think that at such an age I didn't even know that mathematicians existed.*

**THURSTON**  I don't think I did either. I was interested at an early age in mathematics but not in what you might call "official mathematics." In about the seventh grade I got the idea that some work I did in school could be used as a thesis if I were to get a Ph.D.

**MP**  *When you say "something I did in school," are you referring to your discovery in connection with zigzag paths on a rectangular grid?*

**THURSTON**  Yes. I was thirteen at the time so I didn't have much of an idea what it would be like to be a mathematician. It was hard for me to imagine original mathematics, thinking of something that no one else had thought of before. Then I had a funny experience in about the eighth grade when one of my teachers said that there was a great need for Ph.D.'s in mathematics because there were only a couple of them — something like that. That teacher gave me a completely strange impression of mathematics and mathematicians! As I remember, at that time I imagined becoming an inventor or a scientist, but in rather vague terms. When I went to college in 1964, I thought I might become a biologist.

**MP**  *Where did you go to college?*

**THURSTON**  I went to New College, which is now part of the University of South Florida. My future wife, Rachel Findley, who was from Chicago, and I were two per cent of the first class. That's where we met.

**MP**  *How did it happen that you chose to go to a college that had just started?*

**THURSTON**  Well, I went through a lot of college catalogues. Most of them listed lots of requirements that made them sound pretty much like the system we had just had in high school. I really didn't like that. So I was much taken with the initial propaganda from New College.

**MP**  *And how do you feel that it worked out?*

**THURSTON**  I think it worked out very well for me. And I think it worked out well for a lot of other people. But it definitely depended on the idea that everyone is responsible for his own education. It was easy for people to drift. The school was very turbulent at first.

**MP**  *Can you expand a bit on how it was turbulent?*

**A Freshman at Lido Beach**  **THURSTON**  Well, the dorms weren't ready when we arrived, so they put us up in a fancy hotel out on the Lido Beach. The college itself was set up in one of the Ringling mansions in Sarasota. We were bused in and bused out. They were building fancy dorms designed by I. M. Pei, but after three months the dorms were still not finished. The tourist season had begun and they couldn't afford to keep us in a hotel any longer, so they hastily converted

*More Mathematical People*

No need to pass the watermelon: Bob, Jean and Bill Thurston in 1953.

the science lab, which was finished, into a dormitory for the girls and the stable into a dormitory for the boys. We were very densely packed! Actually I took to camping out most of the time under a sheet of plastic. Other times I made a deal with a security guard. If I could hide someplace in the library where he couldn't find me, I could stay. I found many weird places to hide. Then in the middle of the year at a faculty meeting the president announced that he didn't know where the next paychecks would come from. A lot of the faculty started looking for other jobs. About half resigned after the first year, including most of the science faculty. The next year there was a new bunch of people and a new president. But there was still a lot of uncertainty.

MP   *This was in the mid-sixties?*

THURSTON   Sixty-four to '67. It was a three-year program at the time.

MP   *Was the college started by some wealthy patrons?*

THURSTON   It was Sarasota millionaires. At first it was going to be a Sarasota college, but then they developed higher aspirations and advertised to National Merit finalists and semi-finalists. I was a finalist. The first year students came from all over the United States. Only two were from Florida.

MP   *It isn't so common for millionaires to go for something so innovative.*

THURSTON   There are all kinds of millionaires. Some of them used to hang around with the students.

MP   *How long did you stick with biology?*

THURSTON   That idea didn't work out very well. That's one of the things about a small college—the opportunities are mixed. There were not many teachers in biology, so if I didn't hit it off with one teacher there were not many others to choose from. But then too I was interested in many different things. I studied psychology and philosophy, for instance. We didn't have grades, but we did have written evaluations. And I kept getting the message that my true talents didn't lie in subject X but in mathematics.

MP   *Were there any good mathematicians on the faculty?*

A high school senior in 1963.

**"If I didn't produce a baby, I would be flunked."**

THURSTON   They were not research mathematicians, but they were good teachers. A lot of my education consisted of reading books. I would get advice from the teachers about what books to read. Going to classes was not much fun.

MP   *By the time you graduated in 1967, you must have decided on mathematics.*

THURSTON   I thought I might be interested in topology or logic at that point. I had read Steve Kleene's book on logic—I had been guided into reading it as an independent study project—and I had been fascinated by what he said about Brouwer and the intuitionists. So I wrote a senior thesis in mathematics on intuitionist topology.

The summer after graduation I got married, and my wife and I both started as Ph.D. students in mathematics at Berkeley. I chose the logician Alfred Tarski as my initial adviser. I went to see him and told him I was interested in intuitionism. He told me that at Berkeley I should just forget intuitionism!

MP   *How did you find Berkeley otherwise?*

THURSTON   It was a little bit of a shock. It was more like high school. The beginning graduate classes were regimented. There were not many questions. The teacher often just wrote things on the board, and everyone took notes. I had never taken notes until then.

MP   *Did you find that your New College experience had prepared you well academically?*

THURSTON   I had no trouble with the work at Berkeley, but it took a while before I talked with many people on the faculty. I was not very aggressive in seeking them out. At New College the faculty were very available.

MP   *You were at Berkeley during a period of great political upheaval on campus.*

THURSTON   Yes, there was also that. For instance, I was active in organizing the mathematics graduate students during the Cambodian invasion. There were also other factors. One was the draft during the Vietnam war. When I went to Berkeley as a graduate student, I applied for C.O. status instead of asking for a student deferment. For the first two years I was there I was going to a draft counselor and working on applications for C.O. status and thinking a lot about those issues. I spent a lot of time in the summer after my first year of graduate school working in the San Francisco jails. This was the O.R. [Own Recognizance] bail bond project. For me it was to be a warmup for doing alternative service as a Conscientious Objector.

MP   *Did you have any religious basis for asking for Conscientious Objector status?*

THURSTON   I had been attending Quaker meetings and my wife and I had had a Quaker wedding, but I didn't have the kind of beliefs that the draft board thought I should have, although I was and still am a pacifist. They asked me a lot of questions. Finally they came straight out and asked, "Do you believe in God?" I gave them some kind of metaphysical answer that didn't satisfy them. So they finally turned down my appeal. My wife and I decided to start having children. We wanted to have children anyway, but

*More Mathematical People*

Bill and Rachel Findley Thurston with Dylan, their firstborn, at Berkeley in 1972.

that is what precipitated it. Our first child was born about the beginning of my second year at Berkeley. In fact, he was born the day I took my generals. Those were the qualifying oral exams. At that time they were scheduled on Saturday, but there were so many people that they had to be scheduled for two consecutive Saturdays. The morning of the day I was scheduled, which was the first Saturday, Rachel was sure she was going to have the baby, so I called up Hans Lewy, who was in charge of all the generals, and asked if he would give me a postponement. He wouldn't. He said that if I didn't show up at the exam and if I didn't produce a baby, I would be flunked. I didn't have the guts to take the chance. So I drove Rachel to the hospital, then drove back for the exams. I called the hospital every hour. Then after the exams I went back to the hospital. She had the baby forty-five minutes later.

**MP** *Who was the chairman of your committee?*

**THURSTON** Donald Sarason, who was my graduate course adviser. He was very sympathetic.

I had got an induction notice, probably in the summer of 1969, but after the baby was born I got a fatherhood deferment. I think I would have refused induction. It would have been a lottery then, depending upon the judge I would have got. I had friends who had refused induction and had been assigned to alternative service. But of course there had also been the case of David Harris [former Stanford student body president], who was jailed when he wouldn't accept induction. I just wasn't ready to go and fight in Vietnam.

**MP** *Did you ever consider going to Canada?*

**THURSTON** I wasn't enthusiastic about Canada.

**MP** *Even with fatherhood and the draft, you were definitely into mathematics?*

**THURSTON**  I was really into mathematics. I talked a lot with other graduate students but not much with faculty until the last two years. During the five years that I was there, we had a lot of really great students.

**MP**  *How did you happen to settle on topology?*

**THURSTON**  Actually I'm not sure that I'm really a topologist. I was interested in dynamical systems at Berkeley, so I began talking to the group around Steve Smale. It was a nice cohesive group talking about a lot of interesting questions. Then I started working with Moe Hirsch. He was accessible and interesting to talk to. I'm not at all sure how it all happened.

**MP**  *How do you think of yourself mathematically as of now?*

**Mathematical Elbow Room**

**THURSTON**  I guess I'm a topologist, but there's a lot of topology that I don't know. I think of myself as learning the outskirts of mathematics. I think mathematics is a vast territory. The outskirts of mathematics are the outskirts of mathematical civilization. There are certain subjects that people learn about and gather together. Then there is a sort of inevitable development in those fields. You get to the point where a certain theorem is bound to be proved, independent of any particular individual, because it is just in the path of development. I enjoy trying to find mathematical topics that people haven't thought to think about. Then I work there. I like elbow room.

**MP**  *Yet from things you have written and said it seems that you have a strong sense of mathematics as an entity.*

**THURSTON**  Yes, I do.

**MP**  *The popular articles about you imply that there are a lot of ramifications of your work in cosmology and such. Is that of interest to you, or is that just something that people have stuck onto your mathematics?*

**THURSTON**  I don't think too much should be made of the connection. It's a way of explaining things to someone who hasn't thought about what topology might be. We can describe what it would be like to live in a three-dimensional manifold. Many people find that exciting. I think a number of people at an early age find themselves faced with a paradox when they think about the universe. I remember that as a child I was really worried. Did the universe go on forever? I couldn't believe it could be infinite. So if it didn't go on forever and ever, where was the end? I couldn't imagine a wall there, because what would be on the other side? So now there's this idea that it's a curved space. That frees people from the paradox, and they like that. But I don't think the cosmological connection is the most important thing in my work. It's useful for explaining to non-mathematicians what topology is about, communicating with people in general but not particularly with mathematicians.

**MP**  *Then you don't think of yourself as a cosmologist?*

**THURSTON**  No, I definitely do not.

**MP**  *Would you feel better if it turned out that something you did had a practical value?*

**THURSTON**  Yes. I like to see mathematics related to the real world.

Mathematicians jokingly define a topologist as someone who doesn't know the difference between a doughnut and a coffee cup. Pictured, Bill's coffee cup.

**MP**  *The impression given in the article about you which appeared on the front page of the* Wall Street Journal, *"Princeton's Thurston Thinks about Imaginary Shapes, Ignores Possible Uses," implied that you didn't.*

**THURSTON**  That was the headline writer's interpretation. I was trying to communicate to the reporter the idea that basic research in mathematics is detached from reality in its motivation.

**MP**  *We all know that non-euclidean geometry and matrix algebra, which were pursued for their pure intrinsic mathematical interest, turned out many years later to be the mathematics that physicists needed in relativity and quantum mechanics. Perhaps mathematicians should try to come up with still more examples of pure mathematics that has much later turned out to have applications. That would help to explain to people that mathematicians don't have to worry when they're doing mathematics about the uses for what they are doing.*

**THURSTON**  That's a good point. I myself think that progress in basic mathematics will eventually have its effect, in unpredictable ways, on applications. So it's important, at least much of the time, to keep from being tied down too much to a particular application. It's important to see the mathematics and then, after you understand the mathematics, to try to fit it into a particular application. The patterns are often hidden when you have too many specific images floating around. There's really no difference when you think about basic research—what topological spaces are and the patterns involved—and what might come up in a very practical situation, if you can free yourself from the specifics that get in the way of seeing what's really going on.

Actually the concept of number is a good illustration of the importance of pure mathematics. The trouble is that people think they are already familiar with numbers—1, 2, 3, for example. It's hard for them to back off and see what really abstract notions they actually are. We use them for very diverse things. We use them to count. We use them to measure. It would be silly to have an arithmetic course in counting people, where you learn that 3 people plus 5 people is 8 people. And another arithmetic course in measuring distances—3 kilometers plus 5 kilometers is 8 kilometers. In some contexts you have fractions and so on, but you don't have half a person or negative people. So there are really very different contexts in which numbers are used. They're a basic instance of abstract mathematics that everyone uses.

### Thinking Is Easier Than Writing

**MP**  *I have been intrigued by your statement, made in regard to not publishing some discovery, that it's just easier to think things than to write them down.*

**THURSTON**  It's very time-consuming to write things down.

**MP**  *So you don't worry about not getting things written up?*

**THURSTON**  I worry a lot. I try to avoid thinking about new subjects. But I still get behind. It's too easy to be distracted. There are too many interruptions.

**MP**  *You apparently do a lot of things connected with mathematics besides doing mathematics. Today, in a snowstorm, you've come up to New York* *from Princeton to talk to us. You spent most of Sunday in New York at the airport at a meeting of the Science Policy Committee. You have been active with a group of mathematicians concerned about the increased military funding for mathematics. In fact, I saw that you were the author of a long letter on that subject in a recent issue of the* Notices of the American Mathematical Society. *I was very interested in your conclusion to that letter, which I have here:*

> There is great power in truth and sincerity. The mathematics community has tremendous reserves of human potential energy. If we are lean and hungry, we are likely to use our energy. If we are honest, it is likely to be effective . . . .. Let us tell the NSF, tell the Congress, and tell the public what mathematics is really about."

*How do you think that can be done?*

**THURSTON**  I think there are many opportunities, if we're ready to take them. One thing that is very important is the education of children. I think that in the long run that's where the effort should be focused. There's a tremendous amount of waste in mathematical education. I think there are a lot more people who would really enjoy mathematics, who would get a lot out of it and find it useful, if they had not been really turned off to it by the way it's taught. In the elementary schools in Princeton that my kids have attended, there is an annual event called Science Day. They bring in scientists from the community, and we spend a day going around from class to class talking about things. I have enjoyed doing that quite a bit.

**MP**  *What have you talked about?*

**THURSTON**  I have done different things every year for ten years or so; for example, topology, symmetry, binary counting on fingers . . . . I find that kids are really ready to pick up mathematics in the way that I myself think about it. Of course, it's toned down.

**MP**  *Can you be a little bit more specific about the way you think about mathematics?*

**THURSTON**  That's a tough question. It might be nice to give an example. At one time I went into a class of kids and made lots of equilateral triangles. We made a tetrahedron by putting three triangles at each vertex. Then I asked what happens if you put four triangles, and they constructed an octahedron. Then with five triangles at each vertex they constructed an icosahedron. But with six triangles they found that the construction just lies flat. And then I asked about seven triangles at each vertex. They pieced it together and they got these hyperbolic tesselations in four-space. They loved that. The kids did. But the teacher really felt ill at ease. She didn't know what was happening.

**MP**  *Teachers are afraid of making mistakes.*

**THURSTON**  Yes. I have also observed from all the teacher contacts I have had—and I guess our kids have had some pretty good teachers—that elementary school teachers tend to be enthusiastic about reading and writing but are just not enthusiastic about mathematics.

**MP**  *Has your wife continued to pursue her interest in mathematics?*

The Boy Scout packs for an outing.

THURSTON   No. She found out pretty soon it was not her thing. She was a computer programmer for several years. She then settled into something that she thinks is really her field—nuclear disarmament. Right now she has a project she's running. The thrust of it is to arrange for groups of citizens to talk to decision makers in the military in an atmosphere of discussion, not one of confrontation or demonstration or demand.

MP   *I would like to go back to the conclusion to your letter in the* Notices, *where you wrote that mathematicians should tell the public in general what mathematics is about. In a sense it seems that mathematics has let go of the things by which it could most easily explain itself to the public, such as computer science and statistics.*

THURSTON   I think there has been a trend lately for mathematicians to become involved in more practical kinds of things like computer science, mathematical systems, applied mathematics. I'm not sure why mathematicians let go of statistics and computer science.

MP   *Partly it's just sheer size.*

THURSTON   Partly size, but partly also that mathematicians enjoy being in the ivory tower.

MP   *Would you enlarge on the last half of that statement?*

**Mathematicians and Ivory Towers**

THURSTON   I think that most mathematicians love mathematics for mathematics' sake. They really do like the feeling of being in an ivory tower. For the most part they are not motivated by applications. But I believe that, whatever their personal motivation is for doing mathematics, in most cases the mathematics they generate will ultimately have significant applications. The important thing is to do the mathematics. But, of course, it's important to have people thinking about applications too.

MP   *You did come off as awfully "ivory tower" in that* Wall Street Journal *story:*

> "There are mathematicians, and then there's the rest of the world, and not much interaction between the two," says Mr. Thurston, content with that arrangement. That much of his best work may never find a real-world application—especially since he doesn't bother to tell industry about it—misses the point, he says.
> "I don't do it for the bottom line," Mr. Thurston explains. "The inner force that drives mathematicians isn't to look for applications; it's to understand the structure and inner beauty of mathematics."

THURSTON   I was really trying to explain to the reporter the long range impact of mathematics.

MP   *He certainly didn't pick up on it.*

THURSTON   No, he didn't. He was very uneasy with mathematics. I did teach him about Pascal's triangle and a few other things of that type. I was just trying to be honest about what mathematicians feel, not necessarily what they should feel. I guess I was trying to communicate to him that mathematics is fun and interesting.

MP   *It does seem that applications do follow, all in the fullness of time.*

**THURSTON**  Sometimes the time is too full. Personally I like to see lots of relations between lots of different things. I really enjoy the kind of integration you can have when you take very particular nitty-gritty questions and tie them together in very abstract theories.

**MP**  *Unlike you, many mathematicians often give up even trying to explain mathematics. On the other hand, reporters often come to them, not only with ignorance, but also with hostility.*

**THURSTON**  It's partly a question of just getting more coverage in the media. There's such a vacuum in what people know about mathematics. I see that as part of the problem. If the public could just know more about what mathematics is and what's going on . . . .

**MP**  *It has always seemed to me that mathematicians should try to get on top of their subject and tell people about it without actually trying to explain it. After all, they can't really explain it.*

**One Hundred Mathematical Words**

**THURSTON**  I think that one helpful thing would be just getting some mathematical words accepted by the public. The precise meaning is not so important. It would be good to be able to use them when you are talking to people without always having to explain. When physicists talk about physics, they use a lot of words that people have heard (and feel familiar with) but don't really know the meaning of. For instance, the names of all these particles. The same is true in biology. There are a lot of undefined words that are vaguely explained from time to time. People who really care to know find out what they mean from the explanation. Other people just take them as atoms, as it were. So I think that's what needs to be done in mathematics. For instance, if *topology* were a more common word, it wouldn't be necessary to go back and explain it every time the topic came up. If you use an unfamiliar word, people expect an explanation. So it's a cumulative process. I don't mean to be too precise about explaining what the words mean.

**MP**  *It seems that most mathematicians have real qualms of conscience when they say something that isn't precisely correct with all the hypotheses present. A few don't worry so much about it, especially if their reputation is such that people know they know.*

**THURSTON**  Right.

**MP**  *We might start thinking—which hundred words about mathematics would we like to see in common circulation?*

**THURSTON**  They don't need to be defined. People either know them or they don't. The point is that they don't worry about them when they hear them.

**MP**  *Because they're used to hearing them.*

**THURSTON**  You could have a bunch of mathematicians brainstorm.

**MP**  *Just like the St. John's list of the one hundred best books, we could have the Princeton list of one hundred mathematical words that should be in general circulation.*

**THURSTON**  I'll ask around the Common Room.

The Thurstons were married in a Quaker ceremony and the marriage certificate, signed by the wedding guests, hangs in their Princeton home.

**MP**  *Why not begin right now? What ten words, just off the top of your head, would you like to see in general circulation?*

**THURSTON**  How about these? *Manifold. Fundamental group. Homology.*

**MP**  *You would include* topology, *too, wouldn't you?*

**THURSTON**  *Topology,* and the distinction between *topology* and *topography.* Yes. And somehow we should work in *geometry,* although most people tend to think that they know what it is. Let's put it in. That makes five, I think. O.K. Then *homotopy. Homotopy* and *isotopy.*

**MP**  *Now you're getting tough.*

**THURSTON**  Tough? No, those are easy. Those are concepts people can understand. *Homeomorphism. Simply connected. Transformation.* They should also have an idea of what is meant by an *ordinary* n-*dimensional space.*

**MP**  *It does seem to me, from some of the words you suggest, that the work that you do is not all that accessible once you get past describing topology as rubber sheet geometry.*

**THURSTON**  That's true of most mathematics. Very little is easily accessible. But I think a lot more of it can be explained so that a lot more people understand it. On the level we're talking about. I like to try to make mathematics easy, not to make it hard. I think there is a tendency among mathematicians to try to make it hard. I try to combat that when I see people wrap up their mathematics in formal fancy theories that make it less accessible.

**Does Vision Distract from Seeing?**

**MP**  *You yourself have a reputation for having an almost supernatural ability to visualize mathematical things. The question came up the other day whether there was any mathematician who has been blind from birth. I think you said someplace that you thought it would be easier for a blind person to do the kind of visualizing you do.*

**THURSTON**  Did I say easier?

**MP**  *Do you actually know of any mathematician who has been blind from birth?*

**THURSTON**  Yes. Bernard Morin at Strasbourg. He is a topologist, a very good one. Has he been blind from birth? I'm not sure. But he told me that he enjoys reading my papers because I explain things geometrically enough for him to understand without having to see the figures. He creates images in his mind.

**MP**  *Is he the mathematician who figured out how to turn the sphere inside out in a concrete way?*

**THURSTON**  Yes. It's something most people have a great deal of trouble visualizing. In fact, I think that vision is somehow distracting to the spatial sense, because we have a spatial sense that is more than just vision. People associate it with vision, but it's not the same. If I close my eyes and imagine what this room is like, I will have a sense in my mind that there's a table here and something here and there. It will be a sense of the room which doesn't have much to do with perspective. It's hard—that is, it takes a lot of training—to go from a spatial image to a picture on paper. So these things

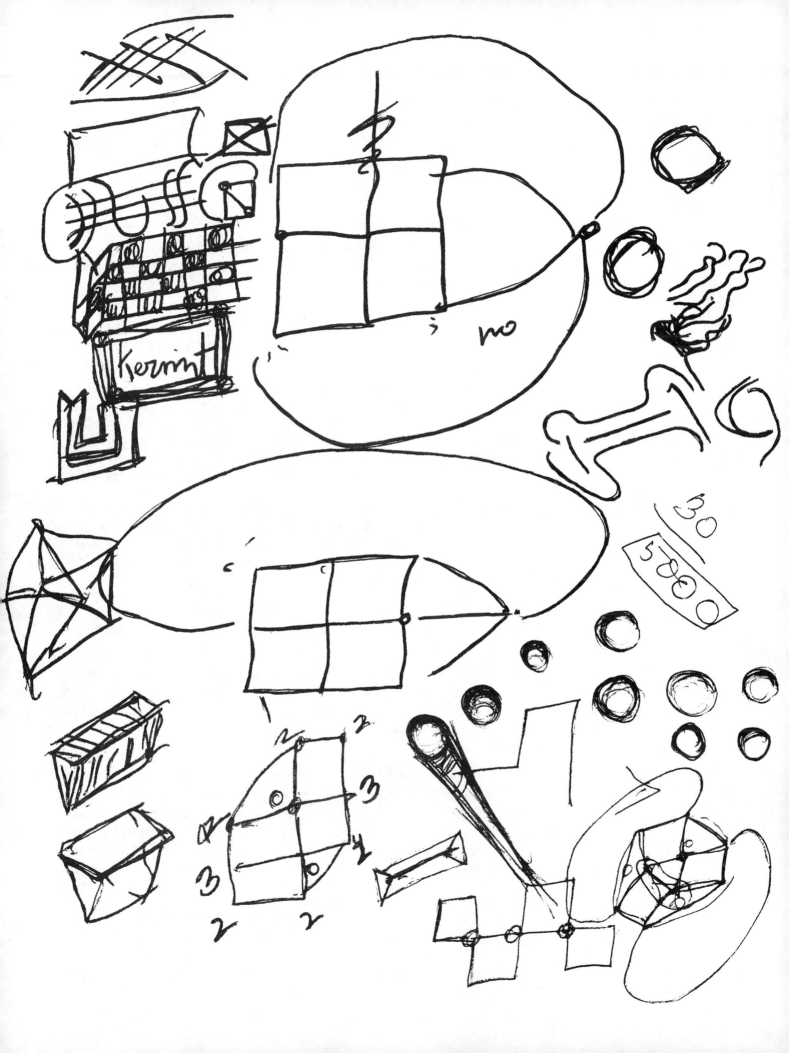

are not necessarily stored in our minds in a visual sort of way. We translate what we see into a sense of space. If you think of it, you realize that if you imagine a table with four chairs around it, it doesn't matter whether you can see the seats of the chairs. You just know that they are there. It's kinesthetic as well as visual. Sometimes pictures can get in the way. Sometimes one can evoke better pictures in one's head just by words. The spatial image is important, but it's what's in the head that counts.

**MP** *And yet you have recently become quite interested in computer graphics.*

**THURSTON** Yes. I've been working with several people here and at Bell Labs. One of the projects we've worked on is how to have an efficient way to sketch a picture. A lot of very fancy computer graphics pictures are done by essentially trying to mimic the physical model of how light is reflected into the eye. It is a very computation-intensive approach. But in a way it's also very simple and unintelligent. You construct a mathematical model of your object and what you think is the imaginary light source. You take a whole bunch of light rays, and you trace where they go. They arrive at the eye. That gives a little bit of color to it. You often take shortcuts. For example, often people ignore shadows but sometimes they put them in. On the other hand, a topologist, when he gives a talk, goes to the blackboard and if he wants a picture of a torus, he just makes three curves. People know what it means. It's a nice effect. So we are working on trying to do that with a computer. Well, it's not quite the same process as that of a topologist because he doesn't care exactly what the shape of the torus is. He just wants something that is a torus. So on the computer we're using exact shapes but figuring out good algorithms to do these simple line drawings rather than the fully shaded drawings. That's one of our projects.

Another project we've been working on is making movies illustrating the immersion theorem. Actually it's a computer program. You draw a curve on one screen with a mouse and it will deform into a circle automatically. It's pretty neat. The plan is to do a sphere next. Steve Smale proved in particular that you can turn a sphere inside out through immergence. We have a piece of this film completed, a preliminary version. It's working out well.

**MP** *What audience do you have in mind for it?*

**THURSTON** Well, it's not exactly to the state that we are completely sure of the audience. It would be nice if we could make it understandable to high school mathematics students, but it would also be useful to show professional mathematicians. Most of them have never heard of the immersion theorem.

**MP** *Maybe you should state the theorem here.*

**THURSTON** It's that the space of immersions of a manifold in another manifold is homotopically equivalent to the space of bundle injections from the tangent space of the first manifold to the tangent bundle of the second.

We've also been writing a program to illustrate the geodesic flow on the space of polyhedra. You can think of starting with a potato and watching it evolve with the geodesic flow. So far our program works with the octahedron. We expect it to work much more generally.

It takes a lot of time to write the computer programs, and it takes a lot of expensive equipment. We're shorthanded and we haven't had easy access to the equipment.

(*Facing page*) A child or a mathematician? A leaf from one of Thurston's many scratch pads.

I spend quite a bit of time with computer graphics. This is an example, I think, of a practical thing that, when you start analyzing it, is just beautiful mathematics. It's very helpful to know about algorithms and mathematical ways of thinking about abstract rather than concrete things when you are working with computers.

**MP**  *Do you actually use computer graphics in your regular work, or is this just a side interest?*

**THURSTON**  Actually I became interested in computer graphics because it seemed very difficult and time-consuming to try to produce pictures for things I wrote. I guess that is one of the things that has slowed me down. I always try to put pictures in my papers.

**MP**  *You had quite a few in the article you and Jeffrey Weeks did for* Scientific American.

**THURSTON**  There I had a nice situation. Good commercial artists can start with a rough picture and produce a finished version. I can draw a picture that looks convincing—that is, it will give you the information—but it won't look finished. For that you have to hire a professional illustrator. I guess I imagined that with computer graphics I could generate some of those figures myself.

**MP**  *Have you been disappointed?*

**THURSTON**  It's harder than I thought.

**MP**  *This summer, at the International Congress in Berkeley, the three Fields Medalists were asked at a press conference if they used computers in their work. Each one of them—Donaldson, Faltings and Freedman—said no, he didn't use computers. Then Leslie Valiant, who had just won the information science award, volunteered that he didn't use computers in his work either!*

**THURSTON**  Well, that's not the whole story about Fields Medalists and computers. This year the Illinois Science Lectures were on mathematics. I was invited along with Smale, Milnor and Mumford—all of us were Fields Medalists—and it turned out that every one of us used computers quite a bit! So maybe it's really a case with the new Medalists of immaturity.

**MP**  *But their saying that they didn't use computers in their work not only pleased the newspaper reporters but also pleased mathematicians. I think it reassured them that they are not being replaced by computers.*

**THURSTON**  I think mathematicians could do a little catching up on that subject. Part of the reason they don't use computers is lack of money.

**MP**  *Part of it could also be their discomfort with the fact that the four-color theorem, which they couldn't prove, was proved by using a computer. They're still not sure it is really a proof.*

**THURSTON**  Why do we try to prove things anyway? I think because we want to understand them. We also want a sense of certainty. Mathematics is a very deep field. Its results are stacked very high, and they depend on each other a lot. You build a tower of blocks but if one block is a bit wobbly, you can't build the tower very high before it will fall over. So I think mathematicians are concerned about rigor, which gives us certainty. That's one reason

Alfred Tarski (1902–1983), leader of the Berkeley logicians, told Thurston to forget about Brouwer and intuitionism at Berkeley.

The Thurston "boys" out for a spin on Einstein Drive at the Institute for Advanced Study: Nathaniel, Bill and Dylan.

that we concentrate so much more on proof than do other scientists. But I also think proofs are so that we can understand. I guess I like explanations rather than step-by-step rigorous demonstrations. It seems to me that that is the source of the dissatisfaction with the proof of the four-color problem. We don't have a humanly comprehensible explanation of why every map can be colored with four colors. Maybe there's no explanation. But we would like to know.

**MP** *Maybe there's no explanation?*

**THURSTON** I don't think we have any guarantee that every phenomenon can be explained or proved.

**MP** *Even in mathematics?*

**THURSTON** In fact, we have formal theorems such as Gödel's that it is impossible, don't we? But that's hard—the question is how it ties in with the philosophy of mathematics. Is it really different? I'm referring to the fact that people use these various things that have been proved in logic to try to make conclusions about mathematics. Some mathematicians then begin to take a sort of solipsistic attitude and say that we can make mathematics up, however we like. It's not determined. I guess I believe in a sort of mathematical reality, but it's a reality that we can't hope to understand completely. It's hard to justify mathematical reality solely on the basis of formal reasoning.

**"I could have been a logician."**

**MP** *Do you think that you could have been a logician if you hadn't been turned away by Tarski when you came to Berkeley?*

**THURSTON** I could have been a logician. I was also very interested in topology, though. I found it fascinating.

**MP** *What made it so fascinating to you?*

**THURSTON** I think that I was first attracted by the imagery that comes with topology. I liked the geometric imagery and the idea of being able to see something about spaces of various dimensions. With topology I saw that you could really give a rigorous mathematical definition of what it means to be connected, or simply connected, to have a hole in something. All these things that seemed before to be purely qualitative or to be vague concepts—these had rigorous definitions.

**MP**  *But that same thing could have been done, perhaps, in algebraic geometry or something else.*

**THURSTON**  Possibly. But I never learned algebraic geometry. I guess that I have always been fascinated by the way mathematical problems—and other problems, too—can be formulated in a geometric way. And some things have solutions that become very transparent if you formulate them in a geometric way.

**MP**  *You mentioned just a few moments ago that money has a lot to do with mathematicians' not having more to do with computers. I know that you have been trying to get funding for your work with computers, but you have refused to accept military funding.*

**THURSTON**  Right. Over the last several years I have ended up wasting a whole lot of time in computer administration, the sort of thing that in another department would be done by a technician or some staff person. I have become the staff person for computing in our mathematics department.

**MP**  *How has that happened?*

**THURSTON**  It has happened, I guess, because I have been the main person in the Mathematics Department who is using computers. Well, at least the initial person. There's now an applied mathematics section as well. In that section they use computers quite a bit. But it's been very time-consuming for me, and it's not clear that the benefit is worth it when I have to spend all this time personally just maintaining the computer, let alone programming it. Programming is one of the most discouraging things. The rate of translation of ideas into working programs can be very slow, so you tend to lower your sights quite a bit. On the other hand, a lot of these things could be done pretty efficiently by programmers. So if there were money to hire staff to maintain computer systems and programmers to write interesting programs and to be informed about what is available—there is this huge amount of technical stuff, you know—then I think mathematicians would find computers much more useful. The payoff would be quicker. One wouldn't have the sense of being stuck in the muck.

**MP**  *Is the problem unique to mathematics?*

**THURSTON**  Yes, I think so. It's partly a historical phenomenon. In the laboratory sciences graduate students and post-docs do a lot of nitty-gritty work. But that kind of thing hasn't been necessary in mathematics, so it's hard to establish a system where graduate students have to start spending a couple of years programming for a professor.

**Money and the Academic Community**

**MP**  *But now, in the present climate, getting funding for mathematics which is not military is almost impossible, isn't it?*

**THURSTON**  It's not quite so dire as that. Available funding is about sixty per cent civilian. And I don't think it's a problem just for mathematics. It's a problem for all science and engineering. Maybe it has only a long-term solution, but I think of it as solvable. There are two important things that need to be done. One is to convince the Congress of the importance of basic research and of the educational system. These are worthwhile goals in themselves. The other thing that needs to be done is to convince the academic community that money is not necessarily good for it if it is bad for society. I believe very firmly in that.

*February 1987 in New York, New York (GA, CR).*

WILLIAM P. THURSTON    Washington, D.C., October 30, 1946. B.A. 1967, New College; Ph.D. 1972, UC Berkeley. Field: topology. Professor of Mathematics, Princeton. Veblen Prize (AMS) 1976, Waterman Prize (NSF) 1979, Fields Medal (IMU) 1982. Hedrick Lecturer (MAA) 1987; Colloquium Lecturer (AMS) 1989. American Academy of Arts and Sciences, National Academy of Sciences.

# ROBIN WILSON

Robin Wilson is on the faculty of the Open University in Oxford, an educational innovation originally proposed by his father, Harold Wilson, the English prime minister (1964–70, 1974–76). He also comes regularly to America to teach a concentrated course in some branch of mathematics at Colorado College. He has other ties with the U.S., having taken his Ph.D. at the University of Pennsylvania. Wilson's interests extend far beyond graph theory and combinatorics, subjects on which he has authored or coauthored thirteen books. He also writes on Gilbert and Sullivan (four more books), plays the recorder and sings with a number of choirs, reviews musical performances for the *Oxford Mail*, and edits a regular column in the *Mathematical Intelligencer* on mathematical postage stamps.

□ □ □

**MP**  *Tell us first about your early years.*

**WILSON**  I was born in 1943, during World War II, in London. In fact, I'm officially a Cockney, since I was born "within the sound of Bow Bells." Later, because my father taught there during the war, I was the youngest person to live in University College, Oxford. Apparently my nappies [diapers] used to be strung out on a line across the front quadrangle! I would sometimes yell and scream and throw myself flat on my face outside the front entrance of the college. I don't do that anymore.

When I was four my family moved to London and we lived in Hampstead Garden Suburb for many years. Most of my formative years were in Golders Green, in North West London. I went to a girls' school for the first few years! It was just across the road, very convenient. Boys were allowed until the age of eight: after that they were considered unsafe.

From the very beginning I liked school—a lot of fun. And right from the very beginning, I certainly enjoyed mathematics.

**Brick Walls and Multiplication**  **MP**  *Can you recall what made it interesting? Was it easy?*

**WILSON**  It was certainly easy, but I think I always had a fascination for numbers. There were various influences. On my mother's side my uncle was

**345**

a professor of electrical engineering. My father's father was an industrial chemist. He could multiply any two numbers up to a thousand in his head. Every birthday I would receive a letter saying, "Dear Robin, Happy Birthday. Next year is 1957 and the square of that is such and such, and the cube of that is such and such." When he drove along in a car, he would factorize every car number coming along. [License plates in England have three-digit numbers.] He once actually drove into a brick wall while multiplying out car numbers in his head.

Later on when my father became Prime Minister my grandfather was interviewed by a young press man. As soon as the press man walked in, my grandfather said, "What's your phone number?" And he said something like "2523." "Oh, the square of that is such and such." And this poor man was so flabbergasted, that the interview went completely to pot. When I was a teenager, I used to sing in our church choir and the sermons used to go on a bit, so I used to do things like multiply the numbers on the hymn board, or square all the numbers up to a hundred. I wasn't at all good at it, really. But I enjoyed playing with numbers and puzzles.

**MP**  *Did your father have any such interests?*

**WILSON**  My father was interested to some extent, yes, and he knew a certain amount of mathematics. He was later a fellow of the Royal Statistical Society.

Young Robin.

*More Mathematical People*

Robin helps his father, an economist and a fellow of the Royal Statistical Society, with some calculations.

**MP**  *But his training was in economics?*

**WILSON**  Yes. He went to Oxford as a historian, but while there he changed to the politics, philosophy and economics course. In fact, I believe he did the best paper on economic theory between the two wars. He was an undergraduate at Jesus College, which was where I later taught. Then he was a don at University College and did some teaching at New College. But he was also working with [William Henry] Beveridge, the distinguished economist. He went into Parliament in 1945 as soon as the war was over, one of the new boys in Clement Attlee's government. He later said he left academic life to go into politics because he couldn't stand all the backbiting and all the jealousy! In fact, in 1947, at the age of thirty-one, he became the youngest cabinet minister of the century.

**MP**  *What else were you doing at this time?*

**WILSON**  I enjoyed my school work and was very involved with school. I tended to be either very good or very bad at my work. If I enjoyed something, I worked hard at it and got near the top of the class. If I didn't enjoy it, I tended not to bother and I was often at the bottom. I went to University College School in Hampstead. It was a day school and a very liberal-minded one. We had quite a rigorous training I now realize. I took up Latin at nine and Greek at ten. And by the time I took O-levels [a nation-wide examination] at fourteen, I had been pushed ahead a year. By that time I had done five years of Latin and four years of Greek, but only two years of French. To make way for Greek, I had to drop history and geography at the age of twelve. It was really quite an unusual education.

But I always enjoyed mathematics. I particularly enjoyed algebra. I really took to that immediately, but I never found geometry easy. I enjoyed music too. I played the recorder. I never shone at it at the time, but later on I became quite good. At the age of eleven, we were doing all sorts of things. The music master took us through the tonic sol fa scale and we had to sing a song in terms of do re mi—we sang it three or four times as a class. Then he handed out music paper and said, "Right, we're going to go through it once more, and I want you to write it down in E major." So we first had to put in the key signature and the time signature and then write it out. Some people found that very difficult but I enjoyed it.

Anyway, at fourteen I specialized after taking O-levels. Normally in England you specialize at sixteen. Originally I had wanted to be a classics don. At the age of eleven I decided I wanted to teach, but at that time it was Latin and Greek. I loved the technical side of learning those languages, but my father pointed out to me, "Look, as you go on there's going to be more literature and you're not a literary sort of person—but you've always loved mathematics." The trouble with going into mathematics was that I had to do physics and chemistry. I was not good at them, and I hated practical science. But I did it so that I could carry on doing mathematics.

**Appendicitis Led to Mathematics**

When I was thirteen, on holiday with my family in the Isles of Scilly off the coast of Cornwall, I needed an emergency operation for appendicitis. I read two books in hospital. One was Jerome K. Jerome's *Three Men in a Boat*, and the other was Lancelot Hogben's *Mathematics for the Million*. I just loved Hogben. Some of it I couldn't understand, but much of it I did. I remember coming across the idea of dividing one polynomial by another. I knew how to multiply them together, but I had never divided them before. So every time my father came to visit me in hospital he brought some more polynomials that he'd multiplied out. I also remember being turned on by Northrop's *Riddles in Mathematics* and the proofs that the square root of two is irrational and that there are infinitely many primes. I surprised the nurses by announcing, the day before I came out of hospital, that I was 5000 days old!

**MP**  *It sounds as if your father was really supportive of your early interests.*

**WILSON**  Yes, both my parents were very good in that. Also they never tried to push me in a particular direction politically, or as far as religion was concerned. I went to Sunday school, but they never tried to impose their views on me. Basically, their view was that whatever I wanted to do was fine. If I wanted to serve in a shop, that was fine, as long as I was doing what I enjoyed. They never got worried by my school reports, even though my teachers often felt I was not applying myself as much as I should. It is certainly true that I worked best under pressure, and still do.

**MP**  *Oxford must have applied some pressure if you took a first class Honours degree.*

**WILSON**  Yes, it did. But before that, I had lots of exams at school. At sixteen I took A-levels [a higher nation-wide exam] in mathematics, physics, and chemistry, and was told that if I passed chemistry I could then drop it and just do pure math, applied math, and physics. So I did. I was actually near the bottom of the form in chemistry, although I now realize that I quite enjoyed organic chemistry because that ties in somewhat with graph theory—basically problems in chemistry are often related to enumeration

Young Wilson disguised as a Native American.

problems and trees. Surprisingly it was Tom Lehrer who helped me with chemistry.

**MP** *Tom Lehrer?*

**WILSON** Yes. About six months before my A-levels, I heard Tom Lehrer's record of "The Elements." For some reason, my chemistry improved enormously from then on! I listened to that song over and over again, and I got through the exam.

**Free Biscuits**    **MP** *Did the fact that it was set to Gilbert and Sullivan have any influence?*

**WILSON** It could well have done. My interest in Gilbert and Sullivan — and my first opportunity to see their operas — began at the age of eight. I got hooked by the age of about twelve. I was very involved with G & S when I was at school.

I was also in the school choral society. We were given free chocolate biscuits if we went along, and that's what first got me there. The result was that choral singing has always been one of my great loves — even without the chocolate biscuits! By the time I left school I had sung Mendelssohn's *Elijah* twice, Handel's *Messiah*, Mozart's *Requiem*, and Bach's *B minor Mass*. I have never had a good solo voice, so I've always been in the chorus, and I have sung regularly ever since I was twelve.

**MP** *Were these musical interests present as early as your interest in mathematics?*

**WILSON** Not really, no. I suppose they were in me to some extent, but I didn't actively get interested until I was about eleven. I didn't have any music at home, except the music that I created for myself. My parents weren't active musicians. It's something that obviously was there but took longer to develop.

**MP** *Your children are also very musical?*

**WILSON** Yes. They were singing harmony at the age of seven, just making it up as they went along, and they learned to read music at that age. If you learn at that age it's easy; later it's very difficult.

**MP** *You have a younger brother. What does he do?*

**WILSON** He's a mathematics teacher — actually a natural scientist who drifted towards mathematics. He and I are very different. I am a pure mathematician who has occasionally drifted towards the applied, but he comes from the opposite direction. Basically we're a family of teachers. My father's mother was a teacher. My mother's brother was a teacher. My mother's father was a Congregational minister, which also involved teaching. So there was a lot of teaching on both sides of the family. Later I married a teacher whose parents are both teachers and whose brother is a teacher.

**All Bloody Facts and No**    **MP** *Do your children want to be teachers?*
**Bloody Vision**

**WILSON** Well, I did ask them at the age of two what they wanted to be: one said, "I want to be a nurse" and the other said, "I want to be a burglar"!

When I was about sixteen or seventeen, Aneurin Bevan [the great politician who founded the British health service in the Attlee government] asked my father what I was going to be when I grew up. My father said, "Well, it

*Robin Wilson*

**349**

looks as though he's going to be a mathematician." Bevan replied, "Just like his father, all bloody facts, no bloody vision!"

**MP**  *How did you find life at Oxford?*

**WILSON**  I loved it. The great thing about Oxford is that there's always so much going on. I just spent all my time concentrating on the particular things I enjoyed, like mathematics and music. In mathematics I was very involved with the Invariant Society.

**MP**  *The Invariant Society?*

**WILSON**  Yes, the undergraduate mathematical society. The reason it was called the Invariant Society is that it was set up in the 1930s by some mathematicians who couldn't think what to call it, so they said, "Let's get a textbook down, open it to an arbitrary page, and choose the first word which is usable." The first word was "invariant."

**MP**  *How did you get involved in the musical life at Oxford?*

**WILSON**  I was involved from the beginning, mainly with the college choir. I also played the recorder quite a bit at that time and gave a lot of recorder concerts.

In my second year in Oxford I became secretary of the Balliol College Musical Society, which has been going since 1885. Many distinguished performers have appeared there, like Joachim (for whom Brahms wrote the violin concerto), Solomon, Rubinstein, Yehudi Menuhin, and others. I was responsible for looking after the performers on the day that they came to give their concerts. So that was really quite exciting. And I went to various recorder courses. Edgar Hunt was one of the people in the Carl Dolmetsch school, which got recorders established in England. It was in a course that

Joy and Robin Wilson with their newborn twins, Jennifer and Catherine.

he organized in France that I met Joy, who later became my wife—she's a better recorder player than I am. Her father was a music teacher, so she had piano lessons, violin lessons, recorder lessons, and she played in a family consort.

MP  *Why did you decide to study in the U.S.?*

**"Where's Philadelphia?"**    WILSON    I was all set to do graduate work in Oxford and had lined up a supervisor to work with on infinite group theory. Then suddenly on the notice board in Balliol Lodge there appeared a letter that changed my life! Three distinguished Philadelphians had been Rhodes Scholars at Oxford. They had loved their time there, so they had endowed a scholarship for British students for a year at the University of Pennsylvania. I hardly knew where Philadelphia was, although I had been to the States by that time. My father did a lecture tour there in 1962 and I came with him. We had a marvelous time. I went to a press conference given by President Kennedy, and I met U Thant at the United Nations. I also met Eleanor Roosevelt, Arthur Schlesinger, Averill Harriman, Hubert Humphrey, and many others.

MP  *What was your father's political role at that time?*

WILSON    He was not then leader of the Labour Party—he was the shadow Foreign Secretary.

But back to Philadelphia. They were looking for people likely to do well in their final examinations, who also had interests outside their academic study. I think it was the music that got the scholarship for me as much as anything. I said I wanted to go and hear the Philadelphia Orchestra. So I went to the States initially for one year. What happened, in fact, was that the University of Pennsylvania got me doing some teaching. All graduate students taught for a year before they could get a doctorate. I loved the teaching—it was mainly calculus, in classes of about thirty. And they said, "We'd like you to stay and we'll give you a teaching fellowship." It was a very difficult decision for me to make. I was by that time courting Joy by airmail. It took me a month eventually to decide to stay.

So I had another year at Penn. During that time I met number theory for the first time. I'd always been fascinated with number theory, but I didn't know much about it. While at Penn I went to some lectures by Emil Grosswald. I really got excited and started working with him, just "learning the trade" in number theory. When he went on sabbatical the next year, he recommended that I look at the bigger institutions. I wrote to various people, including N. C. Ankeny at MIT, who was working on sieve methods and had written a major paper on them in 1966. Ultimately I went to MIT for a year on a research fellowship from Penn. I don't think the people who paid knew that the check was being sent to me at MIT, although the members of the Penn Mathematics Department were in on all this, because they realized that it would be the best thing for me. I wrote my thesis in a year with Ankeny, on the large sieve in algebraic number fields. The large sieve hadn't been generalized to algebraic number fields at that stage, and that was what I was working on.

MP  *What did your family think about your staying in the United States for a Ph.D.?*

**WILSON**    My father thought I should come back to England. By returning to England I would be known to people; there's a problem if you get "out of the system"—you're just a name applying from afar. He was very conscious of that. But I decided to stay in the U.S. There was quite a "brain drain" at that stage from Britain to the United States, and the British had instituted a sort of "reverse-the-brain-drain-grant" to encourage British academics to go back to England. I got one of these, which enabled me to live anywhere I wanted in Britain while I got myself re-established. I chose Cambridge, which was then the best place in the world for number theory. I got married as soon as I returned to England in 1968.

What happened in the meantime was a remark that Patrick Gallagher of Columbia University made to me that changed my life. When I was in New York, working with him on number theory, he said, "Have you come across the work of Gian-Carlo Rota at MIT? He has been extending number-theoretic functions, such as the Möbius function, to partially ordered sets and lattices." I was quite fascinated by this idea. So I went to Gian-Carlo's lectures as soon as I got back to MIT. It so happened that he was giving a course in combinatorics, and in his very first lecture he talked about the Möbius function. I was hooked! I quickly got excited by combinatorics and decided to switch over to that as soon as my number theory thesis was finished. So when I got back to England I spent a year learning combinatorics and basic graph theory. But I was still interested in number theory, as I still am.

**A Classic Year at Cambridge**

It was a classic year for Cambridge. It was the year that Alan Baker solved the two problems that led to his Fields Medal. John Conway had just discovered the Conway groups. It was also Harold Davenport's last year. Davenport was exceedingly kind to me. I had written a paper based on my thesis. In trying to understand it, he decided to rewrite it in a better style. He got only halfway through, because he died shortly afterwards. (Nothing to do with the paper, I hope!) But I learned a lot about mathematical writing by comparing what I had written with the way he had improved it.

**MP**    *Was there any combinatorics at Cambridge?*

**WILSON**    There was some. I went to some graph theory lectures by Hallard Croft. Béla Bollobás had been in Cambridge the previous year, but he spent a year in Oxford the year that I was in Cambridge. Then when I went to Oxford he went back to Cambridge, so we didn't overlap. But there were a few combinatorial lectures. Dominic Welsh came to Cambridge and gave an absolutely wonderful lecture on matroids. I was already interested in matroids, because Rota had done work along those lines in his book on combinatorial geometries. But I found that I preferred Welsh's axiomatic approach—essentially [Hassler] Whitney's original approach in his 1935 paper on matroids. I hadn't really studied that way of doing it before. I got very interested in matroids, and later on I wrote a survey on them for the *Monthly*, which won the Lester R. Ford Award given by the MAA.

I spent a lot of time that year trying to get a job, and eventually I got a three-year lectureship at Jesus College, Oxford. They had just introduced combinatorics into the undergraduate syllabus, but when Welsh went on sabbatical there was no one to teach it. So I was the first person to lecture on combinatorics at the undergraduate level at Oxford. I was also involved with tutorial teaching on a wide range of topics: linear algebra, group theory, combinatorial mathematics, Lebesgue integration, complex analysis, real analysis, spectral theory, and probability.

**MP** *Wasn't it also about this time that your* Introduction to Graph Theory *was born?*

**WILSON** Yes. While I was teaching that introductory course on combinatorics, I realized that there was no graph theory book at the appropriate level. In fact, just at that time, Frank Harary's classic text on the subject appeared. It was an important advance in graph theory, but it was too detailed and high-powered for what I needed in Oxford. So I wrote up some notes for the Oxford Mathematical Institute—I wrote them in just six weeks. How I did it I just don't know, but those notes formed the foundation for the book. I hadn't realized what was involved in expanding them into book form but soon found out! Two years later the book was complete and it came out just as I finished teaching at Oxford. Since then it has done extremely well. It has come out in three editions and six languages.

**MP** *At that time it was slightly offbeat to be writing a book on that subject.*

**WILSON** Yes, it was. Oliver and Boyd had done a series of undergraduate texts that were very inexpensive. I saw them as the right format for the book. So I wrote to the editor of the series, Iain Adamson. He was very keen on the idea, and he said "yes." Then he checked with the other editors, and they said "yes." Then for safety's sake they decided to send the manuscript to a couple of referees, who I later found were distinguished combinatorialists, and they said "no." But by that time the editors had already informed me that they wanted to go ahead.

**MP** *Why did they say no?*

**"Saving" a Book**  **WILSON** They didn't like my approach and the way some of it was written. But, in fact, some of their comments were very valid, and very helpful. I took note of most of them and revised the manuscript. I think their comments improved the book a lot. I had to go to Edinburgh to "save" the book, and I remember a tense lunch where I had to argue for it. I don't know how many copies it's sold, probably about 35,000 by now. The amazing thing is that there are now many books on graph theory that are far better than *Introduction to Graph Theory*, but none at that size and price. After seventeen years it still seems to hold its own, although the subject has changed a lot since then. Many writers on graph theory let their enthusiasm carry them away and end up by writing books which are too long and too expensive. This is still *the* inexpensive one. In its second and third editions it's been improved a lot, but it's not the way I would write a book on graph theory now. In fact I have been preparing another book on graph theory. It's based on the Open University course on combinatorics, and it takes a very different point of view.

**MP** *I like your quotations in* Introduction to Graph Theory—*things like "Go forth, my little book, pursue thy way. Go forth and please the gentle and the good." There are several lovely quotations like that at the beginning of each chapter. And I liked the way you concluded by saying, "Finally I should like to express my thanks to my former students, but for whom this book would have been completed a year earlier, to Mr. William Shakespeare and others for their apt and witty comments at the beginning of each chapter, and* *to my wife Joy for many things which have nothing to do with graph theory."*

**WILSON**   And the one on planarity says, "Flattery will get you nowhere." When Clive Kilmister first reviewed the book in the *Times Higher Education Supplement*, he gave the book a rave review but ended up, "The author annoys a little with his choice of quotations at the beginning of each chapter."

I think I was influenced in writing the preface by Peter Freyd's book on category theory, where there are several "funnies" at the beginning of the book.

**All Out for the OU**   **MP**   *How did the Open University start?*

**WILSON**   I wasn't involved at the beginning but I was very sympathetic, not least because it was one of my father's inventions. In fact, he claims that it was the most worthwhile thing that he did. He got Jennie Lee, the Minister for the Arts, to do all the detailed work, but he was the one who had the idea and pushed it through against opposition from absolutely everybody— opposition from the Treasury and opposition from the academic establishment. When he made the opening speech about it in Glasgow in 1963, only one paper reported that speech. It was a real battle to get it through. In fact, there was a lot of doubt about its future when the Labour government lost power in 1970. The Conservatives' Chancellor of the Exchequer thought it was a lot of nonsense. But then he died suddenly. The decision was turned over to the then Minister of Education, a certain Margaret Thatcher, who let it go for a year to see how it worked out.

**MP**   *How did you get involved?*

**WILSON**   In the first summer of the Open University, in 1971, many university academics got involved as Summer School tutors, and these Summer Schools were so successful that the future of the University was assured. That's how I got involved—as a Summer School tutor. I went in basically sympathetic and I came out wildly enthusiastic.

The Open University is, of course, a university for adults who never had the opportunity to get a degree, or who want to get more training in a

The Open University, occupying a seventy-acre campus in Buckinghamshire, is the center of a nationwide network of thirteen regional offices and two hundred and fifty study centers that serve some hundred thousand people each year.

particular subject. Many of them have not done any mathematics for twenty or thirty years, and then they take one of our courses. After six months of OU work—consisting of reading correspondence material, listening to audio cassettes or working with a home experiment kit, watching TV programs and attending local tutorial classes when they can—they go to Summer School for a week where they have direct contact with an instructor. I remember some of the students sitting in a bar, talking animatedly about the linear algebra and calculus they'd been learning. Their enthusiasm was amazing. In fact, the second year I taught in Summer School, I was talking to two Yorkshiremen in their early forties. They worked in a paint factory and had done no previous mathematics. When I met them, they had been studying for only eighteen months with the Open University, but they were already doing Euclidean spaces, normal forms of matrices, least squares approximation, and many other things that were studied by students in Oxford, and they were understanding them at least as well.

The reason for this success is, I believe, twofold. The Open University has always gone to a lot of trouble to produce teaching material that is as good and clear as possible. But the main reason it works well is because we have such very highly motivated students. Most of the time they're working on their own, yet they are determined to get through. It's the hardest way of getting a degree. In fact, I just found the idea so exciting that I decided that I would go all out for a job at the Open University when my three-year position at Oxford was finished.

**MP**  *What precisely do you do at the OU?*

**WILSON**  Perhaps the best way of illustrating it is to talk about the course team on combinatorics that I was leading. I had always wanted to put on a course on combinatorics. It happened that some of the people in the Design discipline of the Technology faculty had also thought about putting on a course on combinatorics as related to design, so we got together. It was some time before we were talking the same language, but by the end of the day we had a course team with about a dozen mathematicians and technologists. The idea was to write a course on combinatorics which anyone could study as long as he or she had some training in mathematics or science or technology. They needed to have done a basic mathematics course, and they also needed to have had extra experience in one of those different areas. The resulting course, "Graphs, Networks and Design," consists of about 1500 pages of printed text, several audio-cassettes, and sixteen 25-minute television programs which go out on the national BBC network.

**Following the Chancellor of the Exchequer**

There's a nice little story about that. The Chancellor of the Exchequer, Sir Geoffrey Howe, was giving his budget speech one year, outlining his plans for the economy. The very next program was one from our course, called "What Is Combinatorics?" A lot of people who went to make a cup of coffee after the budget programme came back and found themselves watching combinatorics. I hope they noticed the difference. Many people came up to me the next day and said, "I saw your combinatorics program on television."

So I spend a lot of time writing correspondence and broadcast material. It's quite difficult at first. You're writing in a team. You send what you've done around to the rest of the course team and it comes back covered with red ink. And then you have to take all those comments on board. But if you've got a course team that works well, it's a wonderful experience and you learn a lot from your colleagues. What you do has to be thought out very carefully in advance. It's not just deciding the previous night what you're going to say in a lecture, or even deciding what you're going to do while you're in the lecture. For each television program the detailed planning starts at least three months beforehand. And the final script has to be sorted out in time to commission models, graphics and computer animations. Our BBC producers need to be thoroughly familiar with the subject so that they can translate the academic's views into what is televisual. They are very professional and all mathematics graduates.

**MP**  *So you feel you can actually teach mathematics with television.*

**WILSON**  You cannot teach *only* with television, because it's very ephemeral. What you can do is to put the right visual picture into people's minds, and you can reinforce something they've previously met. You can display complicated three-dimensional models. And you can use animations to display non-static material. For our combinatorics course, the theoretical material in the printed texts contained networks with up to about ten vertices. But most of the networks that arise in real life have hundreds or thousands of vertices, and we presented these large networks on television. We had a case study on the design of gas pipeline networks in Louisiana, based on a *Scientific American* article. And we went to various factories that use critical path analysis. Professor [Jacobus H.] van Lint did a lovely program on the Mariner 9 space probe: how do you design a code to get messages back to earth from Mars when the strength of the signal is no stronger than a car brake light? Most of the TV programs had a strong practical flavor. One of them was filmed on location in Holland. The Dutch had used a standard algorithm of Christofides and Viola to solve a problem of where you locate fire stations so that you can get to anywhere in the city in the minimum amount of time. The program was filmed largely in Rotterdam, where they had actually applied this algorithm. The theoretical part of it was filmed with Christofides in London.

**MP**  *Do you also teach some courses for Oxford?*

**WILSON**  I do a little bit of part-time teaching for one of the Oxford colleges, about three hours a week. This is actually encouraged by the OU Mathematics Faculty. We claim to produce some of the best educational material, so it's obviously essential to get out and do some face-to-face teaching. It's also why I come to Colorado College for two months every year.

**MP**  *How did that start?*

**WILSON**  There has been quite a two-way link between the Open University Mathematics Department and the University of Denver. Two mathematicians from Denver, Bill Dorn and Mike Martin, had spent extensive periods of time at the Open University. In return, I was the fourth person from the OU to visit Denver. While I was there I found that there was a local Rocky Mountain Section meeting of the MAA in Colorado Springs, so I thought I'd offer to talk about the OU combinatorics course. The organizer wrote me a very nice letter saying, "We'd love for you to talk. In fact there's someone here, John Watkins, who is teaching a course using your graph theory book and would like to meet you." John Watkins and I got on really well. The end result was that I was invited to Colorado College for a whole semester in 1982. I now go for two four-week blocks each year.

**How to Locate Fire Stations**

At the BBC, presenting a lesson for an Open University course, "Introduction to Pure Mathematics."

Wilson, right, with his coauthor, Lowell Beinecke.

**MP** *Since your* Introduction to Graph Theory, *you have had fifteen books come out on a range of subjects.*

**WILSON** I tend to have all sorts of ideas for books. I get enthusiastic and they take me over. But there are other ways I get involved. Norman Biggs wanted to write a history of graph theory where one teaches the subject by presenting edited versions of the original papers. He was looking for people to help him, and both Keith Lloyd and I were interested. We spent a very happy couple of years working on that.

**MP** *How did you get interested in edge colorings?*

**WILSON** My interest in edge colorings arose out of a single sentence in Harary's book to the effect that if you have a graph with maximum degree Δ, then the number of colors you need to color the edges so that adjacent edges are differently colored must be either Δ or Δ + 1 but, as Harary pointed out, it is not known which graphs need Δ and which need Δ + 1. I found that a very interesting problem. At a conference in Maine in 1971 I met Lowell Beineke for the first time and we wrote a short paper on that. It was not a profound paper, but it sparked things off, giving rise to a whole range of papers and to a book on edge colorings I wrote with my former Ph.D. student, Stanley Fiorini.

But more and more my papers have tended to be expository. I don't regard it as a lesser activity. All of us in the world of mathematics have the same aim, and that is to extend our subject. The top researchers produce a lot of wonderful results and are advancing mathematics all the time, but you also need people to explain mathematics in a clear way. I'm not in competition with Fields Medalists.

**Mathematics and Music**

**MP** *Three of your last five books have been on music, and you've become a music critic for the* Oxford Mail. *Is the balance going to tip, with less mathematics and more music?*

**WILSON** That's not likely, because I have a very heavy writing load at the Open University. However, I have always been very involved with music on many different levels. For example, as a recorder player I played a Vivaldi recorder concerto recently with the leading baroque orchestra in Philadelphia. It was a tremendous ordeal.

I've also been a great Gilbert and Sullivan enthusiast since my early teenage years. The D'Oyly Carte Opera Company performed Gilbert and Sullivan operas from the 1870s until 1982. On the night they closed I thought there must be some way of keeping up interest in the company. I had the idea of doing a pictorial history of the D'Oyly Carte with archival photographs from the earliest times right up to the closure of the company. I collaborated with the former general manager of the company, and Dame Bridget D'Oyly Carte put lots of material at our disposal. We ended up with a very attractive book which I look back on with great pleasure. It's a coffee table book that sold well on both sides of the Atlantic. I'm happy to report that the D'Oyly Carte has recently started up again, with great success.

One of my forthcoming projects is to do a pictorial history of mathematics with the same format. I've always felt that there are very few mathematics books that appeal to a general reader. Mathematics is very intimidating to many people. John Fauvel, a colleague of mine at the Open University, is a specialist in the history of mathematics, with a lot of

A sampling of Wilson's book jackets.

experience in writing history of mathematics for a general audience. We are intending to cover mathematics in its widest sense, with spreads on Egyptian papyri, Arabian astrolabes, and mathematics in art, as well as the mathematics of Newton, Hamilton, and so on.

Another mathematician who's keen on music is Alan Borthwick, whom I met at an Open University summer school. He was one of my OU tutors, a mathematician by day and a professional tenor by night. We have compiled three books of Sullivan's ballads—not songs from the Gilbert and Sullivan operas, but some of his drawing room songs, which are very attractive and had been out of print for fifty years.

As far as being music critic for the local paper is concerned, that started off because of my interest in baroque music, choral music and in light opera. I was asked to review by the *Oxford Mail*, which has about seven music reviewers. So I started reviewing performances of baroque music—with my singing and recorder playing, I have had much experience with that—and Gilbert and Sullivan. That's expanded quite a bit, and I now also review orchestral concerts, grand opera and musicals. Most of the choral works I review I have actually sung in, so I know what they're like from the inside. Sometimes I review well-known performers, the Vienna Choir Boys, for example, or the Kings College, Cambridge, Choir, and sometimes I review an amateur choral or operatic society. It has given me some wonderful musical experiences and expanded my musical horizons.

**MP** *I have seen a picture of you with Eugene Ormandy. How did you happen to meet him?*

**WILSON** I was in Philadelphia while my father was in office, so the press was pestering me for an interview. I was asked why I had come to Philadelphia, and I mentioned that I was looking forward to hearing the Philadelphia Orchestra. I was misquoted as saying the main reason that I was in Philadelphia was to hear the Philadelphia Orchestra. The next thing I knew,

*More Mathematical People*

I had a delightful letter from Eugene Ormandy offering me free tickets in his wife's box whenever I wanted to go. I went twelve times the first year and got to know Eugene and Gretel very well. They were very, very kind to me and introduced me to many major figures such as Aaron Copland, Leopold Stokowski, Yehudi Menuhin and Montserrat Caballé. As you can imagine, that was tremendously exciting. I still visit Gretel Ormandy whenever I'm in Philadelphia.

**MP** *You have travelled in both mathematical and musical circles. Is there a connection between mathematics and music?*

**WILSON** There are certainly many mathematicians who are involved with music. You don't have to be mathematical to be involved with music, but I think there certainly is a link, for various reasons. One is that they are both creative arts. When you're sitting with a bit of paper creating mathematics, it is very like sitting with a sheet of music paper creating music. Both have rules which you must follow. They are also both languages. A page of mathematics and a page of music are both meaningless unless you happen to know what the various symbols mean and how they relate to each other and you understand the rules that they satisfy. But there's obviously a difference, in the sense that a piece of mathematics is superseded by a better, or more general, bit of mathematics, whereas Mozart was not superseded by Beethoven. You still enjoy listening to Mozart.

**MP** *But you can't hear mathematics.*

**WILSON** You can experience it in the same way as you experience music. If you've got the training, you can experience music just by reading the page. I know musicians who prefer to read music rather than hear it, because if they are following a score then the composer is speaking to them directly

---

## DINNER WITH ALISTAIR COOKE

I twice had dinner at the White House. Once was in 1966, when I was studying in Philadelphia and my father was visiting Washington. We were greeted by President Johnson and Lady Bird. I remember being struck by how incredibly tall he was, and how really kind—a very gracious host. It was quite a nervewracking but wonderful experience. The second occasion was in 1975 when I was in Washington to give a talk to the MAA and receive the Lester R. Ford Award. That happened to coincide with another visit of my father to Washington, so I was invited to din-ner with President and Mrs. Ford. It was a wonderful evening and a chance to meet Hubert Humphrey again, for whom I always had the very highest regard. I also met Henry Kissinger, but I couldn't talk to him because I had a mouth full of caviar and I was afraid that if I spoke I might disgrace myself! At the meal I found myself sitting next to Alistair Cooke, who was very charming, and absolutely fascinating to listen to. The very next Sunday when I was back in England I turned on his "Letter from America" on the radio. He started off by saying, "I went to a very boring dinner at the White House. There was no one interesting to talk to." That amused me a lot.

Wilson lives in Oxford, England, most of the year, but here we find him in Oxford, Colorado.

and they get the perfect performance, whereas if they hear a performance by an orchestra, it won't be perfect. I don't agree with that attitude, but it certainly exists.

**MP**  *What do you mean by "experiencing" mathematics in the same way?*

**WILSON**  We are all aware of the fact that we can look at a proof and find it very elegant or beautiful. It turns us on in some sort of way, but it's usually something that a mathematician will understand and no one else will. In his *Mathematician's Apology*, Hardy presented a couple of proofs that mathematicians find beautiful—proofs like Euclid's that there are infinitely many primes and the proof that the square root of two is irrational. Although Hardy tried very hard, I suspect that most non-mathematicians really would not appreciate them. You've got to know what you're talking about, and obviously the more mathematics you know the more you can understand what is behind it. It's like music. If you hear a piece of music you can understand it on many different levels. It may have a nice tune. If you know how the piece is constructed, and how the harmony and counterpoint work, you can appreciate it on a deeper level. It's also like painting. You can look at paintings that are just nice views. If you know something about painting, about the circumstances under which the painting was constructed, or about the principles of painting (for example, the use of the golden section), then you can appreciate it on a deeper level. Beethoven and Bartok both made extensive use of the golden section in their compositions. If you know about things like this you can appreciate their music on a deeper level. This is the great thing about arts such as mathematics and music and painting. They can all be appreciated at different levels.

**MP**  *A lot of people would say that mathematics is very difficult to appreciate at the same aesthetic level as when you hear a tune and say, "Gee, that's a pretty tune."*

**WILSON**  No, that's not true. A lot of people appreciate the beauty of mathematics, even though they don't think they're doing mathematics—for example, if they do puzzles in newspapers. A lot of magazine puzzles are basically mathematical. Many people don't think of them as that—they just enjoy the logic of solving the puzzle. Those who play chess—and this is the point Hardy was making—are basically indulging in a mathematical exercise, whether they're solving chess problems or just playing for the fun of it. There are a large number of games—chess, Go, even tic-tac-toe—which involve mathematical thinking. Many people wouldn't call it mathematics, but that's essentially what it is. Chess is really just a part of combinatorics.

**Days at No. 10**

**MP**  *Let's go back for a moment. What was it like living at No. 10 Downing Street? You were at Balliol when your father first moved in there. Right?*

**WILSON**  Yes. The reason I chose Balliol was because it was one of the colleges that my father had absolutely no connection with at all. I was very sensitive at the time about the connection. I didn't suffer as badly as my brother, who was still in high school while my father was in power. I was over here in the U.S. most of the time, so I escaped. I was determined to get my doctorate and to establish my own career. At least I was not following the same career that he was.

Now the connection doesn't bother me at all. My father has been out of office for thirteen years. But his position did result in some great experiences for me.

I remember some wonderful parties at No. 10. Probably the finest of them was for the astronauts Armstrong, Aldrin and Collins. They were on a world tour after their great success. We had a party with a lot of stars of stage and screen. My father liked to make these parties as unstuffy as possible by inviting such people. He also invited a group of schoolchildren from a local comprehensive school on the grounds that space travel would be a part of their future. The children were the only ones allowed to get the astronauts' autographs. He also invited a Member of Parliament to this party, the sole reason being that his name was Eric Moonman!

When my father resigned in 1976, there was a special dinner that he arranged for the Queen and Prince Philip at No. 10. It was marvelous to be able to go to that. But possibly the most exciting occasion of all was in 1969 at the Commonwealth Prime Ministers' Conference. There were three dinners at Chequers, and it was a great opportunity to meet leaders like Pierre Trudeau, Lee Kwan Yew, Archbishop Makarios and Kenneth Kaunda. Chequers is the Elizabethan home that the Prime Minister can use at any time. My twin daughters were christened in the long gallery of Chequers, and they had their first birthday party there.

Playing the crumhorn with Collegium Musicum, Colorado College's early music group.

**MP**  *How were you treated in America when your father was in power? Wilson is a common name. Did people think you were just another Wilson?*

**WILSON**  I had the advantage of having a common name and of being in university circles. Also I was not the direct equivalent of the President's son; that equivalent is Prince Charles. In the university, once the initial reaction had worn off, I was just treated like any other student. I remember Harold Davenport, who I suspect was not a great supporter of my father, saying, "All I'm interested in is his mathematics." That was the general attitude in universities. If I did well in mathematics, then they would respect me, and if I didn't, they wouldn't.

**MP**  *You've certainly seen a lot of the political life through your father, yet you yourself have never been personally involved in politics.*

**WILSON**  That's true. It's quite interesting, actually, that there are other politicians' children who have chosen to get away from "real life" and to immerse themselves in pure mathematics. For example, the son of Lee Kwan Yew, the Prime Minister of Singapore, was a pure mathematician. In fact, Béla Bollobás in Cambridge apparently described him as one of the finest

students he had ever had. The son of Mendès France is a well-known topologist. Whether it's a reaction against politics or what, there certainly have been a number of politicians' children who have got involved in pure mathematics.

**MP**  *What's the single biggest reason that you are not interested in the political life?*

**WILSON**  Well, there is really no reason why I should be. I come from a family of teachers and mathematics teaching has always been in me. The reason I do mathematics is that it's always what I've enjoyed most of all, and I've wanted to teach ever since I was eleven years old.

*May 1988 in Santa Clara, California (DA, GA).*

*ROBIN WILSON*  London, England, December 5, 1943. B.A. 1965, M.A. 1969, Oxford; M.A. 1966, Ph.D. 1968, Pennsylvania. Fields: graph theory, combinatorics, history of mathematics, number theory. Senior Lecturer in Mathematics, Open University. Books: *Introduction to Graph Theory*, 1972; (with N. L. Biggs and E. K. Lloyd) *Graph Theory 1736–1936*, 1976; (with S. Fiorini) *Edge Colourings of Graphs*, 1977; (with L. W. Beineke) *Selected Topics in Graph Theory 1, 2, and 3*, 1978, 1982, 1988; *Graph Theory and Combinatorics*, 1978; (with L. W. Beinecke) *Applications of Graph Theory*, 1979; *Applications of Combinatorics*, 1981; (with F. Lloyd) *Gilbert & Sullivan: The D'Oyly Carte Years*, 1984; (with F. Holroyd) *Geometrical Combinatorics*, 1984; (with A. Borthwick) *Arthur Sullivan Songs, Books I, II, III*, 1986, 1987, 1988; (with others) *Let Newton Be!*, 1988; (with J. J. Watkins) *Graphs: An Introductory Approach*, 1990; (with R. Nelson) *Graph Colourings*, 1990.

(*Facing page*) The Wilson family in 1952: Harold and Gladys Baldwin Wilson with Robin (left) and his younger brother, Giles.

# INDEX